P9-AQR-733

TECHNICAL COLLEGE OF THE LOWCOUNTRY
LEARNING RESOURCES CENTER
POST OFFICE BOX 1288
BEAUFORT, SOUTH CAROLINA 29901-1288

The Music of
What Happens

TECHNICAL COLLEGE OF THE LOWCOUNTRY
LEARNING RESOURCES CENTER
POST OFFICE BOX 1288
BEAUFORT, SOUTH CAROLINA 29901-1288

There are the mud-flowers of dialect
And the immortelles of perfect pitch
And that moment when the bird sings very close
To the music of what happens.

Seamus Heaney, "Song"

The Music of What Happens

Poems, Poets, Critics

HELEN VENDLER

TECHNICAL COLLEGE OF THE LOWCOUNTRY
LEARNING RESOURCES CENTER
POST OFFICE BOX 1288
BEAUFORT, SOUTH CAROLINA 29901-1288

Harvard University Press
Cambridge, Massachusetts
London, England   1988

TECHNICAL COLLEGE OF THE LOWCOUNTRY
LEARNING RESOURCES CENTER
POST OFFICE BOX 1288   025360
BEAUFORT, SOUTH CAROLINA 29901-1288

27.44

Copyright © 1988 by the President and Fellows of Harvard College
All rights reserved
Printed in the United States of America
10 9 8 7 6 5 4 3 2 1

This book is printed on acid-free paper, and its binding materials
have been chosen for strength and durability.

Library of Congress Cataloging-in-Publication Data

Vendler, Helen Hennessy.
   The music of what happens.

   Includes index.
   1. American poetry — 20th century — History and
criticism. 2. English poetry — 20th century — History
and criticism. 3. Poetry. I. Title.
PS325.V46 1988   811'.5'09   87-21240
ISBN 0-674-59152-6 (alk. paper)

5-15-90

For Marian Connor

... I wondered how it could utter joyous leaves standing
    there alone without its friend near, for I know
    I could not.

Walt Whitman

Contents

IV   Recent Writing

Acknowledgments

In collecting these essays, I felt again the generosity of all those who, one way or another, sponsored them and saw them into print. I am especially grateful to William Shawn, until recently the editor of the *New Yorker*; to Robert Silvers, editor of the *New York Review of Books*; and to Leon Wieseltier, literary editor of the *New Republic*. I thank them for their hospitality, courtesy, and editing intelligence. I regret deeply that Howard Moss, who first welcomed me to the *New Yorker*, should not have lived to receive my thanks for his encouragement and friendship.

During the time some of these pieces were written, I enjoyed a sabbatical leave from Harvard, a Harvard research subsidy, an NEH Senior Fellowship, an ACLS travel grant, and a Rockefeller Foundation residency at Bellagio. These grants were not awarded for the work collected here, but this work benefited from the support and leisure they provided. I thank my referees, who enabled me to have such grants.

My colleagues at Boston University and at Harvard have offered me that conversation and friendship without which no writing can be carried on.

This volume is dedicated to a lifelong friend as inadequate homage to her quick mind, her gift for laughter, and her tender heart.

The Music of
What Happens

Introduction

Most of these essays on critics and poets were written in the last ten years, while criticism was struggling through one of its periodic generational changes. In a 1986 essay in *Raritan*, W. J. T. Mitchell, who edits *Critical Inquiry*, called the present tendency in criticism "a shift in emphasis from *meaning* to *value*," explaining meaning-centered criticisms as those interested in "interpretations," and value-centered criticisms as those "focussing on the problems of belief, interest, power, and ideology." As master-terms of criticism, *meaning* and *value* (in Mitchell's sense) may seem important to others: to me they seem marginal. The criticism of art should not be chiefly a matter either of interpretation(s) or of discussion of ideology. Of course, criticism may, along the way, make an interpretation or unveil or counter an ideology; but these activities (of paraphrase and polemic) are not criticism of the art work as art work, but as statement. "Art works," said Adorno in his *Aesthetic Theory*, "say something that differs in kind from what words say" (1970; English version, 1984, 263).

Paraphrase, interpretation (in the usual sense), and ideological polemic are legitimate preliminary activities putting the art work back into the general stream of statements uttered by a culture. All of these statements (from advertising to sermons) can be examined for their rhetorics of persuasion and their ideological self-contradiction or coherence, but such examinations bracket the question of aesthetic success. It is impossible, of course, to name a single set of defining characteristics that will discriminate an aesthetic object from one that does not exert aesthetic power, but that is no reason to deny the existence of aesthetic power and aesthetic response. Though aesthetic response is culturally conditioned, and tastes differ even among those within a single culture, nevertheless the phenomenon of aesthetic response always remains selective. Nobody finds everything beautiful. And no other category ("the rhetorically complex," "the philosophically interesting," "the overdetermined," "the well structured" and so on) can be usefully substituted for the category "the aesthetic."

It is natural that people under new cultural imperatives should be impelled to fasten new interpretations (from the reasonable to the fantastic) onto aesthetic objects from the past. But criticism cannot stop there. The critic may well begin, "Look at it this way for a change," but the sentence must continue, "and now don't you see it as more intelligibly beautiful and moving?" That is, if the interpretation does not reveal some hitherto occluded aspect of the aesthetic power of the art work, it is useless as art criticism (though it may be useful as cultural history or sociology or psychology or religion). There is a parallel with musical performance: all sorts of "interpretations" of a sonata are possible, and their number is theoretically infinite; but unless the interpretation accurately reveals a newly perceived coherence of structure, or a newly exposed line of development, or new harmonic interest, it can make no cognitive or emotional claim to replace an older interpretation; and the musical listener, having heard something merely eccentric or ingenious, will depart dissatisfied.

The aim of a properly aesthetic criticism, then, is not primarily to reveal the *meaning* of an art work or disclose (or argue for or against) the ideological *values* of an art work. The aim of an aesthetic criticism is to *describe* the art work in such a way that it cannot be confused with any other art work (not an easy task), and to *infer* from its elements the aesthetic that might generate this unique configuration. (Ideological criticism is not interested in the uniqueness of the work of art, wishing always to conflate it with other works sharing its values.) Aesthetic criticism begins with the effort to understand the individual work (aided by whatever historical, philosophical, or psychological competence is necessary for that understanding); it is deeply inductive, and goes from the single work to the decade of work, from the decade of work to the lifetime of work, from the lifetime of work to the interrelation with the work of other artists.

What does it mean to describe an art work so that another viewer, reader, or listener will recognize this as a just aesthetic description? It will not do to name each note in a piece of music in sequence, or make an inventory of all the objects pictured and the colors used in a painting, or describe the topic and meter of a poem. Aesthetic description aims at something finer and more analytic than any of these grosser methods. The first rule of thumb is that no significant component can be left out of consideration. A critic must notice not only (to use Seamus Heaney's words from which I take my title) "what happens," but also "the music of what happens," and must perceive the pertinence of both "the mud-flowers of dialect / And the immortelles of perfect pitch." And the second rule of thumb is that the significant components are known as such by interacting with each other in a way that seems coherent, not haphazard.

Critics with an interpretative or ideological *a priori* (by contrast to critics with an aesthetic *a priori*) seem, to someone who knows a poem well, bent on leaving out whatever in a poem is not to their purposes, or on distorting, in the service of argument, what they do find to describe. I have argued in one of these essays against such a reading (a Freudian one by Lionel Trilling) of Wordsworth's Immortality Ode. Both ideological and hermeneutic (or interpretation-centered) critics want to place the literary art work principally within the sphere of history and philosophy, while an aesthetic critic would rather place it in the mimetic, expressive, and constructivist sphere of the fine arts — theater, painting, music, sculpture, dance — where it may more properly belong (as I have argued here in an essay on Geoffrey Hartman).

Critics who see interpretation as their *raison d'être* fundamentally regard the art work as an allegory: somewhere under the surface (as in a biblical parable) there lies a hidden meaning which it is the critic's responsibility (as it was the exegete's duty) to reveal. Such an ultimate disregard for "surface" in favor of a presumed "depth" goes absurdly counter to the primary sensuous claim of every work of art, the claim made precisely by its "surface" (these words, these notes, and no others). An interpretation of meaning or a disclosure of value should be not an endpoint but a means of returning to the mingled freedom and necessity of the words-as-arranged-on-the-page. Form, after all, is nothing but content-as-arranged. Content disarranged (as in paraphrase) leaves form behind, usually unnoticed. And a scrutiny that notices chiefly rhetorical figures and their predictable self-undoing leaves out the larger conduct of the art work — its play with genre, intertextuality, etymology, tonality, levels of aesthetic function.

It goes without saying that there are discursive elements (topics, plot) and ideological elements (belief, interest, position-taking) in every work of art. Art must say something and must care about what it says; and every artist uses "ideas" (as well as images, phonemes, echoes, textural contrast, feelings, myths, and so on) as part of the raw material of composition. The artist uses ideas, that is, as functional parts (rather than as ideological determinants) of the work. "A poem," says Khlebnikov, "is related to flight, in the shortest time possible its language must cover the greatest distance in images and thoughts." ("On Poetry," c. 1920, from *The King of Time*, 1985, 153). In the long run, topicality of statement and situational *engagement* are the first things in an art work to fall to the ravages of time. Every artist feels this with a pang. As the culture ideologically supporting a work decays, the work becomes "merely" (merely!) beautiful. "The Museum Shop Catalogue" by John N. Morris shows the process in action:

> The past is perfectly darling —
> These pretty things that come along with us!
> Mary and Siva house without oppugnancy . . .
>
> Everything here has been imported
> Over some frontier. At last
> It is all a kind of art entirely.
>
> And really they *are* just lovely,
> Perfectly lovely, these things.
> In vain do I deplore . . .
>
> Mary and Siva
> Accompany our lives.
> Although a loneliness persists.
> They are only beautiful now.
>
> (*Poetry* 144, August 1984, 262–263)

That the work of art had something to say and *that* there was an urgency in saying it, remain evident both in its propositions and in its rhetoric; but who except believing Christians could now read George Herbert with delight if truth of doctrine and ideological relevance were the chief basis of aesthetic response?

"With delight" is a necessary phrase for an aesthetic criticism. One can presumably discuss both the *meaning* and the *value* (in Mitchell's sense) of a work in which one has taken no delight whatever (and the signs of aesthetic interest are notably absent from criticism centered on either *meaning* or *value*). But one cannot write properly, or even meaningfully, on an art work to which one has not responded aesthetically. The art work "falls into shape" only when it is perceived as an art work (not when it is read as a rearrangeable set of propositions, tropes, attitudes, or beliefs).

These remarks will seem truisms to those who are naturalized within aesthetic response, a response different, both in its cognitive and in its "delighted" aspects, from the response we give to material that is primarily expository or hortatory. The twentieth-century critic most faithful to art's two sides — its originating propositions and beliefs and its necessary subordination of these to intrinsic efforts of form — is Theodor Adorno, whose own aesthetic base in music made him see the folly of a criticism confining itself simply to *meaning* or *value,* alone or together. In his tireless reiteration of the truth that art, unlike other mimetic or expressive or discursive activities, obeys a law of form, which it is the critic's duty to infer and articulate from its embodiment, he struggled to enunciate a theory of social value for art, a theory which does not rest on the ideological content of the art work. (In this, he partly followed Benjamin, who saw advances in technique as the intrinsic social value of art.) "The more aware technical and aesthetic analyses become of the importance of *tour de force* in art," says Adorno, "the more fertile will they be" (*Aesthetic Theory,* 265).

Because the first thing that is usually remarked when a new work appears is its propositional meaning and its ideological values, it is all the more necessary that an aesthetic criticism should give it its due as *tour de force.* An aesthetic criticism will investigate *how* and *why* the art work is as it is, using its propositions and values as a bridge to its individual manner, its texture, its temperament, the experience and knowledge it makes possible, and its relation to other art works. Each new cultural idea of the beautiful has to be critically defined — whether it be a new musical chromaticism, or analytic cubism, or a new populism in language, or a new indeterminacy of closure.

The critic of new objects works in the dark. In Stanley Cavell's words,

> [The critic] is part detective, part lawyer, part judge, in a country
> in which crimes and deeds of glory look alike, and in which the

public not only, therefore, confuses one with the other, but does not know that one or the other has been committed: not because the news has not got out, but because what counts as one or the other cannot be defined until it happens; and when it has happened there is no sure way he can get the news out; and no way at all without risking something like a crime or glory of his own.   (*Must We Mean What We Say?*, 1976, 191)

Samuel Johnson, in his "Prologue" for David Garrick, said it earlier:

> Hard is his lot, that here by fortune plac'd
> Must watch the wild vicissitudes of taste;
> With ev'ry meteor of caprice must play,
> And chase the new-blown bubbles of the day.

Chasing our new-blown poetic and critical bubbles — some of them very beautiful — is of necessity the work of many diverse voices. I offer these essays in aesthetic criticism as the reports of one voice — confident in its attachment to poetry, but conscious that the art of poetry is far larger than any single description of its powers.

I

On Criticism

1

The Function of Criticism

Like all other perennial human activities, criticism exists because it gives pleasure to those who perform it. And, like historical and philosophical writing, it also seems to give pleasure to people who, though they do not themselves write it, like to read it. If one function of criticism is to give pleasure to its critic-producers and its reader-consumers (including the artists who create the art it comments on), then to speak of the function of criticism means to look at the nature and range of such pleasures, and how they can be defended.

But there is, other than pleasure, another function of criticism, anciently regarded as the nobler one: to explain some complex state of affairs — whether the relation of parts in an aesthetic whole, or the development of an artist, or the nature of creation in a given historical period. This older conception of criticism has been unsettled lately by a considerable skepticism. Geoffrey Hartman and Harold Bloom, refusing to group criticism with other forms of discursive writing, claim it as a creative product, indistinguishable in its aim, means, and end from novels, poems, or plays. As Bloom recently put it, "I behold no differences, in kind or in degree, between the language of poetry and the language of criticism." Bloom adds, as a corollary, that he denies (with Richard Rorty) "that there is or should be any common vocabulary in terms of which critics can argue with one another." In short, criticism for Bloom is expressive, not expository; creative, not discursive; and unamenable to the debates appropriate to the sciences or the humanities.

I want to take up some of these issues here; but since I am a critic incorrigibly unhappy without a text to dwell on, I will use as my guide through this topic some texts by poets and critics who have

9

themselves reflected on criticism and its relation both to art and to life.

My first text comes from John Ashbery's "Litany." Just as every dog has his day, the poet suggests that critics too have their day, an ephemeral one. Every act of criticism is confined to a specific moment by the act of creation on which it is parasitic; as Ashbery puts it, criticism goes to a first night, writes its critique, and becomes itself "music of the second night":

> We know how the criticism must be done
> On a specific day of the week. Too much matters
> About this day. Another day, and the criticism is thrown
>   down
> Like trash into a dim, dusty courtyard.
> It will be built again. That's all the point
> There is to it.

Criticism is like civilization; in Yeats's words, "All things fall and are built again," and our pleasure in the building, rather than any immortality in the product, is our motive. The Ashbery poem reaches its most original point in its central Escher-like architectural fantasy, in which pleasure in the art work and criticism of it are at once cohabitors and competitors:

> They are constructing pleasure simultaneously
> In an adjacent chamber
> That occupies the same cube of space as the critic's study.
> For this to be pleasure, it must also be called criticism.

The mutual competing-for-space engaged in by pleasure and criticism appears in Ashbery's certainty that the chamber where pleasure is constructed occupies the same cube of space as the critic's study; and yet Ashbery allows for the successive nature of the two activities (in which criticism follows upon pleasure) by describing the chambers as adjacent ones. Ashbery is here formulating more explicitly the relation between pleasure and criticism which Keats implied in the "Ode on a Grecian Urn," where the spectator cannot be, at one and the same time, lost in empathetic pleasure and critically mindful of the Urn as an art work in marble. Artists are glad to have created an empathetic pleasure in the spectator; but insofar as the critical act subsequently holds aloof from the aesthetic illusion (of representation, of verisimilitude, of emotion in act) it sets the artist's teeth on edge.

To the artist, "too much conceiving" (to use Milton's words) seems a dangerous state. Milton may have intended only praise when he wrote, as a reader, his sonnet in memory of Shakespeare; but he recognizes that the double critical act of reading Shakespeare and thinking about him turns the reader himself to stone, as he becomes no longer himself but a mausoleum for the spirit of Shakespeare. The reader's own imagination is suppressed by Shakespeare's usurping power:

> Then thou our fancy of itself bereaving,
> Dost make us marble with too much conceiving;
> And so sepulchred in such pomp dost lie,
> That kings for such a tomb would wish to die.

It is this quelling and Gorgon-like power of art that is known to the artist and critic alike. The critic's wish to quell and master arises, when it does, directly as a reaction to the quelling he has himself undergone, described here by Milton and enacted by Keats's speaker as the Urn overmasters him. Each time Keats, as spectator, is quelled by the power of the Urn, he reasserts himself, as critic, by recalling the limits of the Urn's medium — speechless, it cannot declare its own legend; immobile, it cannot allow its trees to shed their leaves; confined, it cannot send inhabitants back to the little town. In this ode Keats is critic as well as beholder, and the ode, itself a work of criticism on a putatively real art work, asserts itself in the Bloomian manner as a rivalrous countercreation, motivated of course by pleasure (the Urn can express a flowery tale more sweetly than our rhyme) but also by a competitive intent.

It is odd to see terms of pleasure and rivalry come to the fore in remarks on criticism, when for so long the terms in which criticism was discussed were the acquisition of knowledge and a secular evangelism in the dissemination of learning. The Arnoldian notion of criticism as making known the best that has been thought or said has now come under attack. One attack says that the criterion of "the best" conceals a political agenda aiming at an elitist canon-formation. The second attack says that "making known" implies a coercive homiletic intent, rather than a disinterested inquiry or a free play of the mind. Canon-formation, while acknowledged as psychologically inevitable, is seen as anything but innocent; and the Arnoldian tone of moral instruction and high seriousness is found repellent both by those who prefer to see criticism as neutrally explanatory and by those who see it as exuberantly self-expressive.

Oddly enough, the act of criticism has been exempt, on the whole, from delicate psychological investigation. Crude explanations for its existence are not wanting, and they possess the usual quantum of crude truth: criticism is said to spring from the envy felt by the artist manqué, or from the contentious passion of the hostile scholar, or from the moral severity of the secretly complicit Puritan. More recently, Bloom has proposed that the love of poetry is another variant of the love of power, that we read (and presumably write) "to usurp an illusion of identification or possession; something we can call ourselves or even our own . . . The critic too becomes a demiurge."

It is hard, given this Freudian delight in unmasking, to suggest motives for criticism other than the discreditable (if entirely human) ones of envy, competition, defensive reaction-formation, power-seeking, and spiritual parricide. These motives, when successfully enacted, are all powerful sources of pleasure; and no doubt there is criticism that has been occasioned by them, and which bears traces — in the rancor, spite, or triumph of its style — of its origins.

But just as there may be many motives for entering a single profession — medicine, for instance — so too there are many motives for the writing of criticism, and I want to suggest that it is chiefly by its style that we know the motives and the aims of a given piece of criticism. We can shed light on the function of criticism by thinking about some of the styles in which it is done. If a change of style, as Wallace Stevens said, is a change of subject, then the criticism which uses a coercive style is different — has a different subject — from the criticism which uses a diffident style, and both will be different from the criticism which is sadistic, or fantastic, or soberly taxonomic.

The single most interesting thing about criticism, in fact, is the number of styles it has found it possible to voice itself in. The motives and intentions implied by a style like Dr. Johnson's are not the motives and intentions implied by a style like Henry James's. The differences are not to be attributed to the passage of time; they are much more the result of temperament, and of the critic's convictions about the social function of criticism (as we can see by comparing contemporaries like R. P. Blackmur and Randall Jarrell, to mention only the dead). It is invidious to ascribe, as Bloom seems to do, a single set of motives to all writers engaging in the single genre that we call criticism. Each critic attaches himself differently to literature; each sends out different signals to his readers; and we may read both the attachment and the signals in the literary style of the author. In this way, Frank Kermode "reads" Susan Sontag's style as an index to her motives, which he takes to be a passionate defense of certain intellectual heroes: "Sontag uses the word 'avidity' with noticeable frequency. . . ; and the renunciation of avidity, the ceasing to admire it in others whom one desires to emulate, is, given the cultural role she has assumed, all too difficult." Later, Kermode speaks of Sontag's own "avidity for ideas and detail," of the "heat and rush of her prose," of her "avid deference." Her style is very different from his own — the cool, pleasant, understated style of the *causerie*. These antithetical positions imply a difference in the conception of criticism.

At most, we can find a family resemblance between examples of criticism. There is not, nor can there be, something that can be called (as Bloom calls it) "the language" of criticism, which he professes to be unable to distinguish from "the language" of poetry — as if either genre had ever been thought of as having a single language. Poetry cannot be satisfactorily defined as an art that uses language in a special way; on the contrary, it has always been known that any attempt to define it by its language is bound to fail. If poets use metaphor, so do historians and philosophers; if poetry is concise, so are proverbs and maxims; if poetry rhymes, so does doggerel. Whatever distinguishes poetry from other forms of literature, including the writing we call criticism, it is not any special use of language. Nor can we any longer, living as we do in the age of the prose poem, define poetry by an unjustified right margin.

The critics who profess to see no difference between literature and criticism chiefly rest their case on two easily remarked similarities between the two genres — they are both impassioned and they both use "literary language." Ruskin on Turner is surely impassioned, and as surely full of rhetoric and figure; he has certainly, in writing his criticism, written a literary essay. However, we do recognize a difference, not in the use of language, but in the inner organization of parts, between the openly fictive genres (drama, novel, and poetry) and the apparently nonfictive genres (homily, criticism, the philosophical essay). It is probably an error to attempt any single definition of this difference, but the fictive genres, which we usually refer to by the word "creation" (a word we rarely use of the nonfictive genres) seem, broadly speaking, to face not only outward but inward. Fictive genres are at least in part centripetal; nonfictive ones are more likely to be linear. By some such structural principle, and not by any remarks about language, we recurrently distinguish the essay from the poem — just as we distinguish the James of the Prefaces from the James of the novels.

James, in fact, can tell us a good deal about what it is to be a critic. The more discreditable motives attributed to critics can scarcely be attributed to the James who writes critical prefaces to his own novels; he is not envious of himself, or eager to usurp his own place, or defensively ready to damn his author, or hasty to commit covert parricide. But he writes criticism of wonderful interest, curiously tracking, with a detective's instinct and a historian's passion for accuracy, the feats of his own imagination at its self-imposed task, the way his imagination outwitted the resistance of the work. James's language in the Prefaces is recognizably Jamesian; but who does not feel the difference in structure between the patient linearity of the Prefaces and the convergent centripetal gravitation of the novels? We feel of course the secondary nature of the Prefaces; though James asserts himself there with perfect serenity, the priority of the art work is taken for granted even in the desire to create a different sort of artwork in the essay.

Bloom, to come to his essential argument, speaks vehemently for an interested criticism, the criticism that artists write, where they defend, directly or indirectly, their own creative practice. One question that might be raised is whether such a criticism can be written by critics who are not themselves novelists, poets, painters, or composers. And there are of course blindnesses in the criticism written by artists. It is invigorating because it rises from passion and ego, and it is best when it is most sympathetic — when James writes on Hawthorne, or Hopkins on Barnes, or Blackmur on Stevens. It is at its most suspect when it springs from hostility or defensiveness — when James writes on Whitman, or when Woolf writes on Bennett. The interested criticism of an artist and criticism with an ideological intent are not far apart in motive, but artist-criticism is more interesting because artists are one of a kind, while ideological critics come in herds.

It seems to be thought today either that there can be no such thing as a disinterested criticism, since all discourse is said to be covertly ideological; or that disinterested criticism, since it is dispassionate, must be unimpassioned. A criticism professing disinterestedness is called naive; how can it be unaware, it is asked, of the subjectivity and selectivity of its own observation?

This objection seems to me itself naive. No scrutiny can exist without an angle of vision. Looking at a single poem, one critic is describing the lyric structure, another the influence of Shelley, and another the use of archetypes; but this does not make their observations "subjective" in the sense of unreliable. An enormous number of valid remarks can be made about any art work, and perfectly reliable connections can be made between these observations and others. Critics making observations can have a common language of debate; more rhapsodic critics, who use the text chiefly as a base from which to depart, cannot, and do not want to, have such a common language. Both kinds of critics are nontrivial: the first kind are the scientists of literature, the second the rhapsodes of literature; the first invite discursive reply, the second repel it by their style, but invite it by their energy. Probably society needs both sorts of critics; and it is clear that these two extremes of criticism are provoked by two quite different sorts of pleasure in the object.

Roland Barthes — who is both scientist and rhapsode of literature — suggests, in *The Pleasure of the Text,* that the different sorts of critics are psychoanalytically determined — that fetishists are drawn to the singling out of "quotations, formulae, turns of phrase," that obsessives become "linguists, semioticians, philologists: all those for whom language returns," and that those with paranoid inclinations want to consume or produce "stories developed like arguments, constructions posited like games, like secret constraints." Each of us may recognize favorite critics somewhere in this new mythology of humors; and Barthes, who himself thought of becoming a psychoanalyst, speaks of course from curiosity about his own motives.

In his insistence on pleasure as the motive for all writing, including the writing of criticism, Barthes reminds us of the error of analyses which emphasize the writer only as a person alienated, deprived, and dispossessed: "These analyses forget . . . (since they are hermeneutics based on the exclusive search for the signified) the formidable underside of writing: bliss." For Barthes, the critic is the voyeur, taking his pleasure in watching literature; and readers of criticism, if they fall into Barthes's model, will read as voyeurs of the critic's pleasure

TECHNICAL COLLEGE OF THE LOWCOUNTRY
LEARNING RESOURCES CENTER
POST OFFICE BOX 1288   025360
BEAUFORT, SOUTH CAROLINA 29901-1288

in literature, thus creating "the doubled, the trebled, the infinite perversity of the critic and of his reader." The dutiful style of any criticism which forgets the bliss of seeing and writing derives from a Puritan style of self-righteous cultural prescriptiveness which treats knowledge as anything but "delicious." Barthes is amusing and grim on the French deploring of the "national disgrace" (as they call it) of general illiteracy: "Now this national disgrace is never deplored except from a humanistic point of view, as though by ignoring books the French were merely forgoing some moral good, some noble value. It would be better to write the grim, stupid, tragic history of all the pleasures which societies object to or renounce: there is an obscurantism of pleasure."

Ashbery and Barthes concur on the intimate connection between art, pleasure, and criticism. The criticism described by Barthes sets itself fiercely against the criticism which originated in biblical hermeneutics, where the motive of the critic is to interpret a sacred text written or inspired by God. When Deity is the author, that author does not write for the happiness of writing. Duty rather than pleasure must therefore be the critic's impetus also, in such a model. And not the text's power to incorporate, and confer, bliss, but rather its power to incorporate, and impose, sacred truth, is its claim to attention.

These two models are radically incompatible. The Barthian model, centering on bliss, refuses to dispense with the signifier; the biblical model, centering on "truth," finds its true repose in the signified. Though the second, hermeneutical, model could not finally avoid form-criticism, it regards attention to the form chiefly as a means to a higher end. It is from the hermeneutical model, with its persistent allegorizing tendency, that the vulgar notion of there being a "hidden meaning" in literature has arisen. The secular critic stays his eye on the surface; the religious critic chooses to pass through the surface in search of divine meaning. Both sorts of critics are always with us, though under different names. The two critical schools will always remain distrustful of each other, each finding the value of the work of art by a method repellent to the other.

It remains true that the tension between the two schools reminds us of the double nature of the work of art. The hermeneutical critics — who look for meaning, import, philosophy, social truth — remind us of the links between literature and its social and philosophical milieu; the explorers of the bliss of writing remind us of the links between literature and the other expressive arts — music, painting, and sculpture.

I said earlier that I would take up the writer's hostility to criticism. It comes, of course, from being unappreciated or misunderstood; and the history of criticism is full of such mistreatment of writers. But it is also true that the poet is often opaque to himself, and senses in his bafflement an obscure need for the critic, a dependency only sporadically acknowledged which by reaction-formation is itself a hidden cause of the barrier between the poet and the critic. Speaking for all poets, John Ashbery, mildly reproachful and yet needy in the instinctive motions of his art, proffers in "Litany" the idea of a perpetual "new criticism," one acknowledging its own ontological dependency on the artists:

> First of all, the new
> Criticism should take into account that it is we
> Who made it, and therefore
> Not be too eager to criticize us: we
> Could do that for ourselves, and have done so.

Ashbery objects to criticism's taking itself for object: for him, criticism is only the outer rind of poetic thinking:

> Nor
> Should it take itself as a fitting subject
> For critical analysis, since it knows
> Itself only through us, and us
> Only through being part of ourselves, the bark
> Of the tree of our intellect.

Ashbery's final image in "Litany" is one of criticism and poetry engaged in a symbiosis so complete that it becomes an identity, even if a perplexed and perpetually frustrating one:

> The new
> Criticism . . . is us: to inflect
> It is to count our own ribs, as though Narcissus
> Were born blind, and still daily
> Haunts the mantled pool, and does not know why.

The obscure but intensely narcissistic and pleasure-filled relation of artists to their own work is fulfilled only when they see the work made intellectually accessible; and the obsessive relation of the critic to that authorial work ensures the production of criticism. The broader public desire for critical mediation of the forgotten, or the new, or even the received objects of cultural veneration also ensures the continual production of writing about writing. If there is anything both Ashbery and Barthes suggest to us, it is that the same chamber holds pleasure and criticism in an inseparable cohabitation. The culture at any given moment may not notice either its contemporary poets or its critics; nevertheless they tirelessly embody and interpret culture, living like spies in the territory of what Barthes calls the *Doxa,* the received opinions of the petrified past. Ashbery's remark to the poet is true of the critic too:

> One can live
> In the land like a spy without ever
> Trespassing on the moral, forgotten frontier,
> In the psalms of the invisible chorus
> There is a germ of you that lives like a coal
> Amid the hostile indifference of the land
> That merely forgets you. Your hand
> Is at the heart of its weavings and nestlings.
> You are its guarantee.

Behind Ashbery's words — "You are its guarantee" — we hear Shelley's claim that the poets are the unacknowledged legislators of the race; in the invisible chorus we hear an echo of Stevens's secondary choirs; in the hand at the heart of the weavings and nestlings of culture we approach something like Seamus Heaney's conviction of the maternal incubation-powers of the poet, bearing meanings like new-laid eggs to the back doors of houses. In all of these functions the poet is abetted by the critic — at least in those moments when the critics take in the guarantee, hear the invisible chorus, and look for the eggs in the nest.

Ideally, the critic is something other than the scholar. Ideally, he is the artist himself in a moment of dispassionate inquiry; at second best, he is the artist *manqué.* "Everyone can easily understand," said

Baudelaire in his 1855 essay on the Exposition Universelle, "that if the men whose task it is to express the beautiful were to conform to the rules of narrow-minded professors, beauty itself would disappear from the earth . . . In the multiple productions of art there is something always new which will forever escape the rules and the analyses of the school!" The critic who is an artist *manqué* will himself be looking for the beautiful bizarre, not the beautiful familiar — or, at the very least, looking for both. The beautiful new is always bizarre: in Wordsworth's more sedate formulation, the artist must create the taste by which he is enjoyed. The bizarre new is what Barthes calls "the writerly" — to the critic as well as to the writer who conceived it, it gives that shock of pleasure which Barthes calls, borrowing the word from Baudelaire, *jouissance*. It is caused, says Baudelaire, by astonishment: "Astonishment, which is one of the great delights (*jouissances*) caused by art and literature, comes from this very variety of types and sensations." The temperaments which seek astonishment are not the temperaments that seek the comfort of the received forms of the past; and so the critic in his *jouissance* finds himself poised uneasily between the artists, who thrive on the new, and the scholars, who are uneasy before it. He has a foot in both camps and is wholly at ease in neither; among artists he senses himself the artist *manqué,* among scholars he feels light-minded.

An ideal criticism would bring speculative thought, life experience, and anterior texts equally to bear on the written work, but no critic's mind can move in these three directions at once. Finally, each critic must choose a single predilection. What Marianne Moore says of poetry and what it provokes in the reader seems true: "[Poetry] must be a distinct distillation of personal experience / that interests me impersonally." The impersonality of the interest provoked is what makes the poem available to criticism: "It compels analysis," as Moore says, "and does not disappear under admiration." Analysis is, so to speak, admiration methodized. But there are two problems inherent in a criticism which regards art as a distillation of personal experience compelling admiration and analysis. The first is that criticism may dwell on the experience — either its biographical origin or its putative universality — to the exclusion of the art which has distilled the experience; or that it will lose itself in admiration and take on the slightly defensive tone of the insecure and evangelistic advocate. "Philosophic criticism," on the other hand, by its very distance from the immediate conditions of life from which the poem arose, and from its speculative rather than admiring tone, avoids these dangers, while of course encountering other dangers peculiar to itself — a tendency to forget the art and gusto of the text in favor of its thought or milieu — or a worse tendency to make itself more important than the text occasioning it.

The origin of criticism is twofold, and both origins bear on the social function of criticism. The first, ignoble, origin is the pleasure of refutation: criticism is the revenge of the student who once, perforce, sat silent while things that seemed untrue were said unrebuked, and poets who loomed large in the mind were ignored in the classroom. In this sense, every generation of young critics refurbishes lapsed reputations and corrects the misperceptions of the generation that taught them. The social function of the aggressive component in criticism is to restore the neglected and discover the new. But the second origin of criticism is the truer one. The pleasure here lies in discovering the laws of being of a work of literature. This pleasure of poetics is not different from the pleasure of the scientist who advances, at first timidly and then with increasing confidence, a hypothesis that makes order out of the rubble of data. The rubble seems to arise and arrange itself into a form as soon as it is looked at from the right angle. That is one way of putting it. Sometimes in literature it is not so much that the rubble of diction arranges itself into a form; rather, what was previously heard as cacophony is now heard as song. It is hard to explain how this happens; it resembles listening to an alien music until its sequences and its intervals begin to seem natural. The music does not so much assume a form as teach itself to us as an intelligible new language, until, like Siegfried, we can understand the speech of birds. The enlargement in being able to hear a new voice, or see a new law of being, seemed to Keats like discovering a planet or an ocean, a revelation comparable to the ecstatic moments known by astronomers or explorers. If discovering Neptune or the Pacific Ocean has a social function, so does discovering (to the public gaze) the poetry of a new poet; or new aspects to the poetry of an old poet. Texts are part of reality, and are as available to exploration as any other terrain.

Wallace Stevens called all the efforts to describe mental objects "description without place." They are, he said, "integrations of the past," and he thought that such efforts to map mental configurations were as important as our maps of the geographical reality surrounding us:

It matters, because everything we say
Of the past is description without place, a cast
Of the imagination, made in sound.

No art work describes itself. Only by repeated casts of the critical imagination is the world around us, including the world of literature, finally described and thereby made known, familiar, and integral.

2

Looking for Poetry in America

What is there to say about a poem? about poetry? about a national poetry? about a poetry and the culture from which it issues? These questions animate three recent books: Dave Smith's *Local Assays,* Robert Hass's *Twentieth-Century Pleasures,* and Robert von Hallberg's *American Poetry and Culture, 1945–1980,* all published in 1985. These volumes perhaps answer, rather than face, the hard questions that must underlie any critical remarks. We have no well-developed literary theory of lyric poetry, chiefly because Aristotle codified his poetics in the light of epic and dramatic poetry. The hard questions might be said to be: Is there anything at all useful that can be said about a lyric poem? If so, in what terms? Are the terms determined by the poem, by its own culture, by our culture, or by transcultural philosophic universals? Can a poem be taken as a sign of its culture and, if so, how? How does a critic or a culture arrive at canonical preferences? Is the poem as linguistic sign different from the poem as cultural token, and if so, how? Can the word "poetry" as a collective noun have any intelligible meaning? Is meaning confined within national and historical borders (allowing one to speak intelligibly of "English poetry" or "Greek poetry," but not of "poetry")? Is "poetry" mimetic, a representation of an external world? If so, is it mimetic through its images, or through its internal structures, or in some other way? Is all poetry necessarily narrative, even the briefest lyric?

Every act of practical criticism, as the theorists remind us, assumes positions silently taken on these questions. Someone who often makes a pronouncement about "poetry" — as the poet Dave Smith does — assumes a universal notion to which the word must refer. Someone who entitles chapters "Tourists," "Politics," and "Pop Culture" —

as Robert von Hallberg does — assumes that a cultural and social mimesis can be found in poetry. Someone who groups essays on Lowell and Creeley with essays on Tranströmer and Milosz — as Robert Hass, also a poet, does — claims the right to describe poetry written in languages he does not read.

In these books, arguments about basic premises — Is "poetry" a possible object of thought? Is it legitimate to read poems as sources of, or reflections of, cultural practice? To what extent can one "understand" a poem one reads in translation? — are not put forth. There are practical arguments justifying the omission. Two of these books — those by Hass and Smith — are largely collections of reviews or occasional essays directed at the general reader; the third, von Hallberg's, hopes to cover a fair amount of cultural and historical territory. Yet in each case one would have liked some consideration of first principles, some account of stumbling blocks, some justification of the road taken. And one would like to be sure that some of the theoretical questions had been silently put, and satisfactorily answered, before the writing of the essay was undertaken.

Robert Hass, for instance, writes about Milosz (whom he has translated with the help of a native speaker of Polish and of Milosz himself) as though Milosz were writing in English, and as though all it took to understand Milosz were a knowledge of Polish history. Of course Hass wishes to keep his eye on Milosz's long and full career, not to "distract" us with ways and means of translation. But precisely in this eliding of the linguistic and cultural difficulties of Milosz's work — which Hass is better placed to appreciate than the rest of us — something valuable vanishes from the essay. Nor is a joke on the subject of one's own linguistic ignorance a way out of the difficulty. Writing on a (translated) poem by Tranströmer, Hass speaks of looking "across the page, with edified ignorance, at the Swedish." "Edified ignorance," as a phrase, is full of charm, not least the charm of honesty; but charm is not a secure base for criticism. Hass continues, on Tranströmer, in what seems to me a self-contradictory statement: "This is the way I come at *Baltics* which I like to read. I can't know how good a poem it is because I know it only in Samuel Charters' translation, but it is very interesting to me. Tranströmer is one of the most remarkable European poets of his generation." Surely this is not satisfactory. Did Keats know how good Homer was in Chapman's translation? If so, how? How does Hass know that Tranströmer is a remarkable European poet if he cannot know how good the poem is? Does he like to read it because "it is very interesting to me" or is it very interesting to him because "I like to read" it? The reader yearns for something more hard-headed here: a sense of questions asked, by the author, of himself, before he set pen to paper.

In Smith's book, the questions posed and answered before the writing began would have had to be of a different order. Smith tends to press on us large declarative sentences: "Poetry is a dialect of the language we speak, possessed of metaphorical density, coded with resonant meaning, engaging us with narrative's pleasures, enhancing and sustaining our pleasure with enlarged awareness. In comparison to ordinary uses of language, this dialect is characterized by efficient discipline: of sharper imagery, focused symbols, connotative power, deployed rhythmic suggestion." If this is all equally true of the novels of Dickens or Proust or the criticism of Carlyle (as it is), then what is the reason to predicate it only of "poetry"? The prior question might have been asked: Is there anything that can be said of "poetry" that is *not* true of Proust or Dickens or Carlyle, and if so, what? In his wish to praise "poetry," Smith is, here and elsewhere, really praising all imaginative writing, all poesis; but he could have made the extent of his claim clear — or restricted the claim to what is peculiar to lyric.

Robert von Hallberg — to take another example — writes, speaking of the work of James Merrill, "For Merrill, energy, invention, and ornamentation — not signification — are what make poetry." But he does not suggest how signification can ever be said, in speaking of poetry, to be something different from those very qualities of energy, invention, and ornamentation. Nor does he explain where signification could be said to lie, if not in the invention of energetic words which, with their musical and figural ornamentation, correspond to the state of mind in question. Von Hallberg offers, as an example of Merrill's tendency to periphrasis, two lines "describing a ski lift." The two lines seem to him a leisurely self-indulgence: "Economy be damned: Merrill takes time to have fun." The two lines in question are:

> Prey swooped up, the iron love seat shudders
> Onward into its acrophilic trance.

Now these two lines are not "describing a ski lift"; they describe one's feelings in committing oneself to that ski lift, a different matter entirely. One feels like Ganymede scooped up in Jovian iron talons; the seat, made for two, resembles those porch gliders or love seats made just big enough for courting; the seat (with no visible machinery in it) lurches upward as though it had a reverse psychosis to acrophobia; one feels abducted, a forced participant in its mad love of heights. "I feel I have been swooped up by a bird of prey, clapped into an Iron Maiden 'love seat,' and made an unwilling partner in a *folie à deux*" is what this passage, very *economically*, "signifies." The "invention" and "energy" and "ornament" *are* its means of signification, and what it describes is a brief moment of panicky inner sensation, not a ski lift. Whether lyric "signifying" is properly the mimesis of a thing (a ski lift) or a state of mind (here, comic panic) is a question that one wants von Hallberg to have faced, if only to make his argument more persuasive.

I am only too painfully aware that exactly these reproaches could be uttered — have been uttered — about my own essays on poetry. And I do know the impossibility of a return to first principles before each sentence one commits to paper. However, we have all recently been put on notice, by the salutary sternness of literary theory, that our terms are likely to be interrogated, and that we might first interrogate them ourselves. And though nobody likes to be reminded of this obligation, I take the reviewer's — and fellow practitioner's — privilege to make the reminder, as much to myself as to the writers under review. Poetic language is itself so finely discriminating that it must impose a practice of discrimination and nuance on its critics as well.

The conduct of any critical argument is evinced as much by its tone as by its premises, as Matthew Arnold knew when he criticized the prevailing tones — evangelistic, assertive, homiletic, denunciatory, hortatory — of the English criticism of his day. He thought it entirely too "Hebraic," and urged a "smiling Hellenistic lightness" (James Merrill's words) on English public discourse. Arnold's own flexibility and sardonic wit can be said to stand for the Hellenic form of argument, over against Carlyle's Hebraism. Eliot's criticism — the most powerful of the twentieth century in English — descended more directly from Arnold than from Carlyle or Ruskin, and it set the "cool" analytic tone of the New Criticism, which aimed at the casual sophistication of the French *causerie* without ever quite attaining it.

It is improbable that any of these three European models — the Hebraic, the Hellenic, the *causerie* — could survive unchanged in the

United States in this last quarter of the twentieth century. They were in fact challenged by the lively, intimate comedy and pathos of Randall Jarrell's reviews, so absorbing his reader into the joint enterprise of appreciating poetry that they seemed a letter from a friend. But Jarrell's wit and sureness of taste could not become repeatable; he established no school. The Hebraic model has been of use to Marxist and feminist criticism in their earlier stages, but both have rapidly become increasingly academic, theoretical, and speculative. The gracious lightness of the Hellenistic model has been more visible in the writing of foreigners — Frank Kermode and Roland Barthes come to mind — than in the work of American-born critics. The *causerie* repels the earnest American mind by its relaxation of manner. When we interrogate these three books, we find the Hebraic tone still with us, but wearing its rue with an American difference.

In the work of the two poets, Hass and Smith, a determined effort toward the colloquial (by contrast to the discursive or written model) keeps asserting itself. Academic writing may seem to the poet too enslaved to the head, too unconscious of the body, too much that of the scribe, too little that of the bard, manifesting too strongly the formal written character, too little the genial social utterance. Both Hass and Smith want to rehabilitate the personal essay. Hass's essay "Images," after quotations from Blake and Eliot and Basho, continues: "My wife in the lamplight is rubbing lotion into her skin and examining mosquito bites. That morning we had been lying on warm granite beside a lake the melting snow fed and her breasts are a little sunburned." Two pages later we are back to Chekhov, Williams, Cézanne, Blake, Wordsworth, Machado, and Milosz. A few pages later: "I am a man approaching middle age in the American century, which means I've had it easy, and I have three children, somewhere near the average, and I've just come home from summer vacation in an unreliable car. This is the *selva oscura*." Moments of such bathos mark the difficulties of the tone Hass has chosen. This kind of writing, while wanting to be social, informal, and seductive, is in fact so stylized — in its intimacy to total strangers — as to be unsettling. Or perhaps this is only the Californian manner, and we will all be doing it in a few years. All critics feel some confidence that the course of their sensual life has reverberations in their intellectual life (and vice versa), but it is not certain that interpolated narratives of the one belong in the testimony of the other.

When Hass writes plain criticism (as in his admirable expositions,

for the commmon reader, of the work of both Rilke and Milosz), he
is interesting, learned, and deft, though sometimes, to my taste,
sentimental. He is too fond of coercive words: *terrible, painful, won-
derful, terrifying, agonizing, mysterious, shocking, raw, seductive.*
Such words not only say "Admire with me"; they are shopworn. I
know, from experience, Hass's difficulty here; one wants not only to
describe a great writer like Rilke but also to praise him, to draw
attention to his qualities in terms the general reader will recognize
as praise. Poets feel so keenly that academic teachers dilute the
intensity and volatility of poetry that they press ever harder, in their
own writing about poetry, to insist on the passional investment that
art calls for from its readers.

Dave Smith shares this insistence of tone, especially in urging on
us, in two essays, the power of Robert Penn Warren's poetry: "What
terror now not to know what had been certain reality, to have to
conjecture 'perhaps' and to relive the old contingencies, the old hope
of continuity — and what courage to make this choice! . . . For even
if the promise of reality will be only the scalding of flesh and the
not-knowing, passion is all. Passion is feeling; man is feeling; poetry
is feeling. In his self-interrogation Warren rejects his earlier *Tempest*
tone and, like Lear, calls on the crack of winds." The tone heard
here — a very American one — is that of the lay sermon, in which
the spiritual instruction of a pupil is undertaken by a spiritual initiate.
What is odd, in both Hass and Smith, is that this celebratory, initia-
tory, and hortatory tone coexists, as I have said, with remarks from
the sensual life of every day. Smith's essay on Richard Hugo begins:
"I had been rereading Richard Hugo's poems during the 1979 World
Series in which the all but trounced Pittsburgh Pirates made a stun-
ning and memorable comeback to win going away. I remarked to a
friend watching that last televised game that Hugo was the George
Raft of poetry. I meant to imply that Hugo was a player of tough-
guy roles. My friend, without blinking, said that Hugo was instead
closer to the manager of the Pirates, or would be if he chewed. We
were, I think, both right." A paragraph later, the tone has changed
to the academic: "Reading Richard Hugo's *Selected Poems* one dis-
covers a poet of unusual continuity in vision and execution. There
are the benchmarks of change and of some evolution, but he does
not show the radical alterations of style or thought which mark his
contemporaries." A few pages later, we are listening to a lay sermon:
"[Hugo's] poems depend upon his own hard self-accusations: he

drinks too much, he wastes himself, he lacks courage, he is fat, ugly, uneducated, unsophisticated, inferior, an orphan. Who among us isn't all that? Who isn't a wrong thing in a right place? And who doesn't carry imagination's dream of getting right, that particular fervor of our national mission?"

What is implied by such changes of tone cohabiting in a single essay is a refusal to take a single position or to accept a single form for critical writing. Is an essay on poetry an anecdotal conversation between friends, or a critical description, or an exhortation to a higher self-scrutiny? Does it descend from the familiar letter, from the gloss on the sacred text, or from the sermon? The control of tone in Samuel Johnson, in Arnold, in Eliot, even in Jarrell, means that they were surer of their authority of position and of the homogeneity of their putative audience. Critical practice in America nowadays suggests that the critics are not sure of themselves or of the audience they address.

This uncertainty about where one stands is visible even in the third book under discussion here, a book written by a university critic for an academic audience. Unlike the books by Hass and Smith, it is not composed of occasional essays directed by the expectations of a particular journal or by the presumption of a general audience. Nonetheless, von Hallberg too mixes the formal with the vulgar: "On occasion Merrill can be snotty, often when he deals with people he considers, if only for the sake of a poem, his inferiors." Or he can move into the homiletic tone of spiritual instruction: "Pinsky writes with confidence that not every perception needs to be rendered striking in order to count as poetry; the importance of much of life rests on its being understood in common with others, live as well as dead. That too is richness, though it is bare of braveries." Usually, however, von Hallberg maintains an academic distance. When that distance becomes jarring, one begins, reading him, to sympathize with the poets and with their wish to break down that distance. Here, for instance, is "Hell," a war sonnet by Lowell:

> "Nth Circle of Dante — and in the dirt-roofed cave,
> each family had marked off its yard of space;
> no light except for coal fires laid in buckets,
> no draft of air except the reek, no water,
> no hole to hide the excrement. I walked,
> afraid of stumbling on the helpless bodies,

afraid of going in circles. I lost the Fascist
or German deserters I was hunting . . . screaming
vecchi, women, children, coughing and cursing.
Then hit my foot on someone and reached out
to keep from falling or hurting anyone;
and what I touched was not the filthy floor:
a woman's hand returning my worried grasp,
her finger tracing my lifeline on my palm."

And here is von Hallberg's comment: "The poem moves nicely toward its emblematic conclusion (Lowell rather liked to close poems with tableaux . . .)." One may find, as I do, that this comment moves rather too quickly outside the poem it addresses; it recoils, one could even say, from the inner shape of startled contrast in the poem — the stumble, the expectation of the filthy floor, the surprise of the human hand. The poem, considered from the inside, ends not with a "tableau" or an "emblem," nor is it "moving nicely" toward a conclusion. Rather, it ends with a moment of surprise, gratitude, steadiness, conveyed in the three quiet verbs "touched," "returning," and "tracing," after the powerful kinetic verbs "hit," "reached out," "falling," "hurting." It is the tendency of the academic critic to stand aloof and say, "Nice conclusion; emblematic tableau." Von Hallberg continues, of the ending, "Its point is perfectly clear. Human mortality is the thing that can keep us from hitting absolute bottom." It is this too rapid moving on to "points" and propositional summings-up that sets poets' teeth on edge, and makes them stress instead the dynamic inner movement of the poem.

These examples are sufficient to show how baffling it is to attempt to write well about poetry. Not only can one offend by a too rapid movement to précis; there are other perils. One's critical language is always in danger of being usurped by, or contaminated by, the metaphoric and passional language of the poet in question; and the more original and powerful the poet, the greater the likelihood of such contamination. Critics of Warren begin to sound grand and visionary, of Hugo, tough and hard-bitten, of Rilke, yearning and delicate, of Stevens (as I know from my own prose), Francophone and rhapsodic. The alternative, of course, may be to sound remote and external to the poetry.

But a greater problem for those of us writing commentary on poetry is the American compulsion to "communicate," intensified by our profession as teachers. The wish to reach out to audiences rapidly becomes a tendency to write down to them. We assume that readers need paraphrases of works written (after all) in their own language, and that they require a rehearsal of elementary moral attitudes. None of us, I fear, escapes such tendencies. But it is worthwhile occasionally to remind oneself that one's writing exists first of all as a way of explaining things to oneself, and not to others. All of us — including the three writers under discussion — become most interesting when we address a question genuinely unanswered when we sit down to write.

There are such questions in each of these books, since each contains an implicit argument about contemporary American poetry. Each of these critics is answering for himself the question "Which recent poets have moved me, or assuaged me, or enlightened me in powerful ways?" There is some overlapping of the answers, and some difference in the perspectives; but these critics (all of them near the age of forty) are essentially defining and defending their own youthful attachments of twenty years ago. These are all really books about the Sixties.

Dave Smith, himself a southern writer, argues for the importance of Robert Penn Warren and James Dickey, as well as for James Wright, Richard Hugo, and Philip Levine. These are all "masculine" poets (though in different ways) and they are perhaps less attractive to women (I speak for myself here) than to men. Penn Warren writes in large elemental terms, with a cosmic sense of the degree to which nature and man are pitted against each other and yet constrained to a symbiosis; he reaches for the grandest of words, the most transcendental of symbols, the most ambitious claims of moral vision (even when that vision is despairing or occluded). His poems open themselves out into long, loose-limbed sequences, ranging far in space and time. Smith loves this large reach in Warren, and writes generously about it, for example in a passage on a poem about migrating geese:

All bodies of the world's body are husks, vehicles, containers, for that current which may pass through even small wires. Energy is life. Warren is recalling the totemic and hieratic images that for fifty years have served toward defining the condition of joy: hawk, owl, beasts, lovers, landscapes of crag and sublime contrast . . . It is not, therefore, surprising that even in this ferociously eschatological reexamination of everything, Warren would return to [the migrating] geese, to his feeling for that image of what was moving in the blind darkness. He had felt his passion was mirrored in the unchosen and lyrical yearning of the geese.

As usual, Smith's emphasis — here as in his other essays — is on the poet's repertory of images. Smith is far less likely to examine the poet's words as such — yet this is where an adverse criticism of the poets he admires would begin. Warren's image of the migrating geese in the poem "Heart of Autumn" may in itself be a moving one; but can the same be said of Warren's language about it? In watching the geese, Warren says, he feels himself transformed:

> I stand, my face lifted now skyward,
> Hearing the high beat, my arms outstretched in the tingling
> Process of transformation, and soon tough legs,
>
> With folded feet, trail in the sounding vacuum of passage,
> And my heart is impacted with a fierce impulse
> To unwordable utterance —
> Toward sunset, at a great height.

A reader might well be put off by the tough legs with folded feet, by the awkwardness of syntactic difference between the apparently parallel arms, and legs, by the phrase "my heart is impacted with," by the unpleasing changes of rhythm, and by the nineteenth-century "sublimity" in the words about inexpressibility at the close. A poem can of course survive such difficulties, and perhaps Warren's poem does. But I would like to see greater recognition of the questionable nature both of Warren's language and of his large moral assertions. (Smith quotes approvingly, "Passion / Is all. Even / The sleaziest.") A criticism that loves imagery is likely to slight both phrasing and syntax.

Smith is more willing to concede problems in Philip Levine's writing. His praise reveals some of the qualities he values in a poet, as he says of Levine: "Though he takes on the largest subjects of death, love, courage, manhood, loyalty, etc., he brings the mysteries of experience down into the ordinarily inarticulate events and objects of daily life. His speaker and subject is the abused and disabused spirit of the common yet singular self. He risks the maudlin, the sentimental, the banal, and worse [in order to be] 'A man alone, ignorant / strong, holding the burning moments / for all they're worth.'" In poets like Levine and Hugo, a rough confrontation with the ordinary, in order to make it articulate, stirs Smith's admiration. His fine essay on Hugo — the best, to my mind, in the book — sums up in a quick and excellent portrait sketch the way in which the life of one male writer might speak to that of another:

> Fatherless and abandoned by his teenage mother, Hugo was raised by elderly, severe grandparents in White Center, Washington, then a semi-rural, poor suburb of Seattle. Enforced churchgoing left him feeling he owed something, spiritually dunned all his life. Shy, awkward, and isolated, he believed himself not only the cause of his ill fortunes but also unregenerately weak, worthless, and ever "a wrong thing in a right place." He grew up admiring local toughs for their violent courage. He extended this admiration later to sardonic movie stars, detective heroes, and British Royal Air Force flyers, who seemed to have a stylish, right manhood. He feared, hated, and coveted girls, and compensated by making himself a skilled baseball player, fisherman, and dreamer. His tutelary spirits appeared early and never abandoned him — waters, sky, hills, ocean, fish, birds, and drunks. All meant unimpeachable and continuous acceptance, private dignity, and sweet, if unrecognized, belonging.

In a passage such as this, Smith's narrative talent and gift for description carry the reader into Hugo's sensibility with consummate ease. James Wright's poetry of the depressed Ohio working class moves Smith to another form of identification; and he can say of Dickey's "wandering hero" that though he is "engaged in motorcycling, hunting, flying, climbing mountains, or making love," nonetheless he is "like most Southern writers, divided in his loyalties to the self as macho realist and the self as intellectual."

It is clear that these were the poets on whom Smith depended in the Sixties and Seventies for spiritual kinship and sustenance. He can read other poets with appreciation — there are commendations here of Sylvia Plath and May Swenson, for instance — but those are admirations from a distance. The question, "How can a man act and yet think, plunge into nature and yet live in the mind?" is the most urgent one for Smith and for the poets he most warmly recommends to our attention; this question generates his canon.

Robert von Hallberg's central question has to do with what he calls "culture poetry" — a poetry that speaks from, of, and to the center of its own culture, rather than from an adversary position. Von Hallberg argues against the view which supposes that the poet must always be an outlaw, speaking from the margins of society to a coterie of other marginal listeners, occupying himself with esoteric or hermetic concerns. Von Hallberg wants to prove that there have been, between 1945 and 1980, many American poets who shared the general experience of other American citizens, and wrote about those central experiences in an accessible language embodying centrist positions, political and cultural. This is an interesting and fresh argument, and von Hallberg makes a persuasive case for it, up to a point.

Von Hallberg is writing a sociology of literature in the Fifties, Sixties, and Seventies while leaving out the chief protest movement of that era, the Beats. Of course he excludes them a priori, since his intention is to write about poets taking positions at the center of things and writing of widely shared experiences. But his chapters nonetheless cry for the inclusion of the Beats, whose positions may now seem more central than they did at the time. A chapter on "Tourism" that leaves out Ginsberg's poems of Europe and India, a chapter on "Pop Culture" that leaves out the Beats' original incorporation of pop culture, a chapter on "Politics" that leaves out the Beats — these are impoverished chapters, finally.

Because the topics of von Hallberg's book are so interesting, one wants to see them fully treated; and a full treatment of tourism, politics, and pop culture in poetry between 1945 and 1980 would be good to have. However, von Hallberg wants to exclude "outlaw" poetry, and so the Beats must go. But what dictates that Ammons be excluded, and Ed Dorn included? One must simply take von Hallberg's canon as the grouping of poets who have meant most to him — Turner Cassity, Ed Dorn, John Hollander, Anthony Hecht, Robert Lowell, James Merrill, Charles Gullans, Robert Creeley, Robert Pinsky, James McMichael — a selection that has the virtue of originality and new combinations. Lowell and Merrill are rather uneasily accommodated in the argument, since von Hallberg slights Merrill's poems of sensuality (not a centrist experience?) and Lowell's poems of domesticity and divorce in favor of Merrill's poems about tourism and Lowell's about politics (the topics under which they are treated). Von Hallberg — with tastes resembling those of Yvor Winters for the rational and the metrical — in effect compiles a selective anthology of contemporary poetry to show that various common American activities — going abroad, engaging in political action, participating in pop culture, living in suburbs — have entered American poems. (Von Hallberg argues as well — perhaps truly, but I think unconvincingly — that systems analysis too has entered American poetry, notably in the work of Robert Creeley.)

Von Hallberg raises, by the topics he chooses, the question of what lyric poetry ought to be doing about social questions. He tends to praise poets (Charles Olson, for instance) for a "commitment to didactic, discursive poetry" and to suggest that social structures and positions are ripe material for poetry: "As a subject for poets, the recent history of intellectuals is rich, complex, and central to the national culture. Moreover, most of the audience for poetry comes from this class, which makes the analysis and representation of the subject all the more compelling." Though von Hallberg is right in fearing that poetry can thin itself out to insignificance when it forgets the social and public life, I think his notion of social responsibility in poetry is too narrow. He laments: "From the end of World War II until the early 1960s American poets had *little to say about* the differences between the intelligentsia and the working classes . . . Poets seldom *spoke of* the one corner of the class structure that concerned them most directly" [italics added]. "To have something to say about" and "to speak of" — von Hallberg's verbs — suggest that the only way poetry can include political and social realities is to make statements about them. This is the criterion used by Allen Tate when he remarked that Keats's ode "To Autumn" was a beautiful piece of style but had *little to say*. (Geoffrey Hartman has shown that it has everything to say about social change in the way it alters the structure of the Greek cult hymn and attitudes of worship.) It may be that discursive "speaking of" is not lyric's way of embodying social realities. "In truth," said Yeats, "we have no gift to set a statesman right" — but he did not mean by that, as his work shows, that one could not embody political and cultural realities in verse. Von Hallberg limits the means of lyric when he wants from it discussions of the class structure or differentiations between the intelligentsia and the working classes.

The great work of reinscribing social and political content in lyric has to be done anew in each generation. Tennyson's "Idylls" and Browning's monologues did it for the Victorians; for us, it was done by the great modernists. But because the modernists often embraced cultural positions that the larger American public did not ratify, that public, von Hallberg believes, began to think that poets (such as Pound and Eliot) were always on "the other side." And because modern poetry was difficult (his argument continues), the public gave up on the reading of poetry altogether. Now, the mere sight of lines of poetry frightens average readers, who need, in his view, to be reassured that there is a great deal of contemporary poetry that they could both read and ratify. Hence his book.

It's an argument to which one may accede with some reservations. The reasons why the general public does not read poetry are probably neither political ("Read those outlaws? those fascists? never!") nor psychological ("I could never figure out that difficult stuff"). Rather, the reasons for the marginal status of lyric poetry tend, I would guess, to be largely historical and institutional. Poetry is not systematically and intensively taught in America as it is in Europe; since most world poetry does not reflect American history or culture, it has been thought irrelevant to our nation. Each European nation cherishes its poetry (and the classical poetry born on the same soil from which it grew) as part of the deposit of patriotism, and therefore institutionalizes it in the schools. There are no such reasons for America to institutionalize Virgil or Milton. A critic's demonstration that poetry is really about your life and mine and can be understood without difficulty cannot institutionalize poetry in America if a large social commitment to it as a patriotic value does not exist.

That large social and educational commitment may eventually be made here, at least to American poetry (it is probably too much to hope that it will be made to classical and European and English poetry). And von Hallberg's reminder that American poetry embodies a great deal of American cultural history, as it has been experienced by large numbers of Americans, will help perhaps to create that commitment. Dave Smith and his chosen canon of poets remind us, too, that the Depression, industrialization, worker migration, and so on also appear in the contemporary lyric. It is useful to be told — especially in the moment of private lyric — that a poet can aim at the whole of political and social reality. Von Hallberg's chief example of such a poet is Robert Lowell. Yet von Hallberg is uneasy with Lowell, for reasons not explicit, but which may be deduced from the ways in which Lowell does not fit von Hallberg's demands: "It is proper . . . to ask of the very best political poets . . . that they offer guidance on particular political issues, that they be of abiding help in the determination of political policy (that we ask of political poetry at least as much as we do of political prose) . . . If we ask of political poetry only that it be surprising, opinionated, extreme, we would sell poetry short because along with such a notion goes the belief that prose, not poetry, bears the greatest intelligence and utility in regard to our collective public life." Although Lowell certainly believed in the political witness of poetry, he did not use his poetry to give advice on public policy. In fact, he referred to his letter to the President attempting to give such advice as "my manic statement." Lowell's poetry narrates his own political actions and fears; it is autobiographical rather than homiletic. Even the most powerful poets (Milton, Wordsworth) have turned to prose when they wanted to address political affairs directly. The symbolic nature of poetry, and the discursive and explanatory nature of prose, obtrude themselves here, and von Hallberg should perhaps have explored the generic differences that press a poet who wants to enter political discourse toward the use of prose.

Von Hallberg is far more comfortable when he writes about the poetry of his contemporaries Robert Pinsky, James McMichael, and Frank Bidart — all of them with connections to California. These poets lie well inside his central wish — that American lyric should reflect the surrounding American culture. All of them are explicit and discursive poets, without prejudice toward the common life, about which they all write with unforced sympathy (von Hallberg accurately perceives a patronizing of the common life in some other poets purporting to treat it). Von Hallberg has high praise for Pinsky's *An Explanation of America* ("one of the markers by which the literary history of this period will be known") and for McMichael's *Four Good Things* ("I can imagine no greater justification of the line of culture poetry during the last four decades than that it led to a book of such range of feeling and delicate intelligence"). This praise, however, avoids engaging the question of flatness of language in such poetry: "Pinsky writes with confidence that not every perception needs to be rendered striking in order to count as poetry; the importance of much of life rests on its being understood in common with others, live as well as dead."

This passage, it seems to me, confuses two things — the nameable experiences we all share (love, grief, and so on), and a believable rendering of those (very intangible) experiences in language. To clothe common perceptions in striking language, not to enunciate striking perceptions, is the function of poetry. Every perception, without exception, does indeed, in poetry, need to be rendered strikingly; it does not need to be rendered striking. All poetic language is language strenuously composed beyond the requirements of information, and therefore striking, perhaps most striking when most apparently "transparent."

One of the most provocative of von Hallberg's chapters takes up explicitly the question that the two other books under discussion here take up implicitly — the question of the poetic canon. Von Hallberg believes that critics consciously set canons (the books that should be read, or studied in school, or anthologized) in order to establish standards of judgment for an audience, and that they thereby cooperate in an ultimately political objective: "Canonists worry about what will enable a community of readers to distinguish first- from second-rate thought and expression. A national canon stands as proof that such distinctions can be made so as to command assent; that the nation asks from its writers support for its policies, at the very least its educational policies; that one national objective is to preserve, by education, a hold on the past and a claim on the future." I don't think that most of these assertions hold water. In the issue of *Critical Inquiry* (of which von Hallberg is an editor) devoted to the question of the literary canon, Hugh Kenner established, briefly and clearly, what to me seems the truth of the matter — that canons are not made by governments, anthologists, publishers, editors, or professors, but by writers. The canon, in any language, is composed of the writers that other writers admire, and have admired for generations. The acclamations of governments, the civic pieties of anthologists, the hyperboles of marketing, the devotion of dons, have never kept a writer alive for three or four hundred years. It is because Virgil admired Homer, and Milton Virgil, and Keats Milton, and Stevens Keats, that those writers turn up in classrooms and anthologies. And writers admire writers not because of their topics (Blake and Keats thought Milton quite mistaken in his attitudes) but because of their writing. And writers admire writing not because it keeps up some schoolmasterly "standard" but because it is "simple, sensuous, and passionate" (as Milton said) — strenuous, imaginative, vivid, new. The canon is always in motion (as Eliot reminded us, and as formalists have always known) because new structures are always being added to it by subsequent writers, thereby reshaping the possibilities of writing and of taste; but the evolving canon is not the creation of critics, but of poets.

As for the nation asking from its writers support for its policies, at the very least its educational policies, it is hard to imagine any free modern nation either making such a request or obtaining such support (dictatorships are another matter). No writer of any substance would support what passes, in most modern nations, for elementary and secondary education in the humanities — rote learning, indifference to the mother tongue, and a complete absence of genuinely subversive, fanciful, imaginative, or critical thought. Von Hallberg genuinely wishes — as who does not — that America could export a coherent high culture along with its pop culture. And perhaps in time that may happen. But it is not so easy to have a canon here as in a comparatively tiny and homogeneous European country. The very diversity of taste in these three books suggests that we have, for the contemporary scene, an Yvor Winters canon, a southern male canon, and a Californian canon. One could easily add a women's canon, an East Coast canon, a black canon, a Naropa canon of Buddhist writing, and so on.

Robert Hass's Californian canon is a polyglot one. Like von Hallberg (they were both trained at Stanford), he admires Wright, Creeley, McMichael, and Lowell, but he adds Tranströmer, Brodsky, Milosz, and Rilke, judging them to be normal possessions for the younger American poet. As indeed they are, along with Neruda, Amichai, Vallejo, Zbigniew Herbert, Trakl — the list could be extended almost indefinitely. The contemporary American poet-critic is far more likely to read across — in world poetry of the nineteenth and twentieth centuries — than to read back in English verse. (A well-known poet and teacher of creative writing remarked to me, unashamed, that he had never read George Herbert.)

Most of the aspiring young poets in creative writing classes know no poetry by heart. It looks as if the classical and English canon may be slipping out of our grasp, to be replaced by a modern canon of unrhymed and translated pieces. This will surely not stop the mighty workings of the imagination, and Hass's book demonstrates how powerfully Milosz and Rilke have entered his ways of thinking about poetry. And yet what can substitute, in a poet, for a hoard of poems in the mother tongue, known so intimately that they become nature, not art? (Of course it is even better if the poet has three or four mother tongues, as Milton did.) In this way, Pope was nature, not art, to Byron; and Tennyson to Eliot; and Shakespeare to Browning. Can Rilke in translation be nature in the same way to Hass?

The anxieties revealed by these books center on the use of poetry and the claims that may be made for poetry. The ritual and liturgical uses of poetry have so far vanished that it seems unlikely that they will reappear.

None of the three writers dares claim only an aesthetic value for poetry. Von Hallberg wants a directly civic value, Smith and Hass want an ethical value, all three want a strongly mimetic value and a strongly communicative value. These are of course questions not to be settled in a review, but I myself think aesthetic value, properly understood, quite enough to claim for a poem. No matter how apparently mimetic it may look, a poem is an analogous not a mimetic imitation, algebraic and not photographic, allegorical and not historical. What it represents, ultimately, is its author's sensibility and temperament, rather than the "outside world" — but of course that sensibility and temperament have been shaped by the historical possibilities of the author's era. Thus, in representing a sensibility, the poem does represent a particular historical moment. The poem ingests, it is true, the outside world (which it uses for its images, its symbols, and its language), but it does so, as Marvell said, in order to color everything with the mind's color, reducing to zero ("anni-hilating," said Marvell) the entire creation into its own mentality:

> The mind, that ocean where each kind
> Doth straight its own resemblance find;
> Yet it creates, transcending these,
> Far other worlds and other seas,
> Annihilating all that's made
> To a green thought in a green shade.

Even the civic, even the ethical, take on, in the achieved poem, that suffusing green — and so become not the civic or the ethical but "Wordsworth's sensibility in an ethical moment" or "Lowell's sensibility musing on civic virtue" — another of the protean "fire-born moods" of the mind (Yeats), another waving of the various light in the mind's plumes (Marvell), another unique snowflake (Merrill), "another bodiless for the body's slough" (Stevens). Naturally, all kinds of ethical and civic topics turn up in poetry, as do trees and flowers and ladies' eyes; but they are all material for the transformation into green. Once they are "greened," they enter into the dynamic system of relations within the poem, and their allegiance is reordered in that magnetic field, which extends outward to the entire *oeuvre* of the poet, and thence to culture itself. The referentiality of language in a poem is more inward than outward, even when the topic of the poem is a civic or ethical or mimetic one.

This does not mean that a poem has no subject but itself or language; on the contrary, a poem may very well be about one's mother, or the march on Washington, or the Warsaw ghetto. But it is about such things as they figure in the psychic and linguistic economies of a particular temperament and body of work; and those economies are taxing, subtle, and complicated systems to describe. No short essay can do them justice; not even many books (when a great poet is in question) can do them justice.

Because language is the medium of poetry, and language cannot, when used according to any of the possible rules of its coding, *not* communicate, there is, it seems to me, no need to worry about poetry's "communicating" itself. All poems grow easier with time, even *The Waste Land*. And there is no need to worry about "universality" or speaking for everyone. "The true poem has a single human voice . . . yet it is also the echoing voice of all men and women," according to Smith. This is to claim too much: "It is the vice of distinctiveness," said Hopkins, "to become queer." Perhaps all good poems are in this sense very odd, in order to be distinctive, to serve a restricted group of readers (as perhaps Smith's own "masculine" poets do) in order to represent the very distinctions upon which experience and language depend.

In trying to speak for "all men and women" the poet risks losing selfhood altogether. The United States is probably one of the less coherent nations of the world, and poets rightly feel uncertain about their canon, their audience, and their culture. Eight thousand years from now, when American culture is as old as European culture now is, our descendants may find themselves in possession of a consolidated and homogeneous culture. For the moment, we have to be patient with our own diversity, and even rejoice in it.

All three of these books contain ambitious and successful essays inviting the reader to appreciate the poetry that the author admires. I think especially of Smith on Hugo and Wright, of von Hallberg on Pinsky and McMichael, of Hass on Milosz and Rilke. The two books by poets both contain personal essays as well, among which Hass's reflection on images and Smith's fragment of autobiography ("An Honest Tub") help to define the poetic vocation as they experience it. All three books are uneven and uneasy as they protest too much, in terms not well defined, the value of poetry. Their very uneasiness seems to me a sign that criticism assuming an authoritarian and impersonal voice (which may conceal, as we know, many private anxieties and a personal program) is being challenged in a revealing, awkward, and morally hortatory American style, confiding and hectoring at once. It sets all the old questions of commentary up for investigation once more, and that is surely what each generation of critics is born to do.

3

Critical Models:
On Geoffrey Hartman

We like to feel, in America, that we have lost that insularity which used to be a subject equally of jokes and of laments. With the world's books in our libraries, the world's art in our museums, the world's music in our concert halls, and, supremely, with so much of twentieth-century art and literature our native product, we tend to think that the days when we had to be apologetic about our culture are over and gone. It comes, consequently, as something of a shock to have our insularity sharply, if suavely, taken to task by Geoffrey Hartman, whose polemic *Criticism in the Wilderness: The Study of Literature Today* (1982) has aims grander than its title might imply. It does speak about criticism and about the study of literature (and its more specialized reaches will be debated among professionals), but its cumulative force makes it a passionate essay on American culture by a foreigner (Hartman is German-born, and teaches comparative literature at Yale) who, though long naturalized, still looks on us from the vantage point of a different country of origin and, most crucially, from a different mother tongue. Prejudice and predilection alike play a part in Hartman's picture of his adopted country, and his sinuous arguments double back on themselves so rapidly, so ironically, and so ingeniously that it is sometimes hard to say whether he is arguing against what he loves or in favor of what he doubts. Nonetheless, his larger drift is clear, and, briefly, it runs as follows.

America is a child of England, in its thinking and in its education in the humanities. (Hartman does not take up the sciences or the arts.) It is, in consequence, markedly impoverished in its capacity for thinking religiously, philosophically, or critically; the empiricism and positivism of the English philosophical tradition have governed our American intellectual procedures and styles, and divorced our critical thought from living connection with the largest questions of metaphysics, private ethics, and social responsibility. T. S. Eliot set an American cultural style, derived from Matthew Arnold, in which criticism was reduced to a humble service function — that of explaining and judging the work of art; art was primary, criticism secondary. Hartman quotes Eliot, in "The Function of Criticism," explaining that although art itself, in its creative thought, is a criticism of life, and artists are in that sense critics, the critic has nothing creative in him: "You cannot fuse creation with criticism as you can fuse criticism with creation." Though Hartman does not say so outright, he implies that this subservience of critic to artist is oddly American, and may spring from our old, abashed sense of European creative sovereignty. In Europe, his argument goes, critic and artist were in the past more likely to be one and the same person; vernacular literature was not until rather recently a university subject, and the person writing an essay on a piece of art was likely himself to be what Eliot called "a practitioner" of that art — a poet or a novelist, or even a painter or a musician. An essay was simply one manifestation of the self as creator, and creative work another. The man of letters (to confine the case to literature) wrote in many different forms — some speculative, some critical, some creative; some public, some intimate; some formal, some informal. The man of letters felt able to write about issues other than literary ones; he read as naturally in historical or philosophical or legal or religious texts as he did in epic or pastoral. Milton is one of Hartman's examples of this ample reach; Pound appears as a writer who had the right notion of scope but went "bad in a good cause" — that of relating the realm of art to politics.

In Hartman's myth of decline, this freedom of discourse has been abandoned by university critics; instead of being widely informed and broadly read, speaking in the public forum on matters of general concern and bringing the ethical and aesthetic perceptions gained from their reading into social discourse, they have timidly drawn in their horns, turned inward, and generated ever narrower critical writing. Into this breach, in Hartman's myth of salvation, come the revisionist critics, bringing good news from Germany and France, in the shape of philosophical criticism informed by religious, social, and structural thinking, and placing art and letters once again in a wider and deeper context. Those who resist them are clinging to an outmoded English model of "sublimated chatter" — a donnish discourse of civilized conversation, a restricted or accommodated style fearful of the more speculative extravagances of the mind — and a "pastoral" model of criticism, which is based on the needs of the immature flock of students rather than on the "theological" demands of sophisticated interpretation.

If this were only a description of a literary-critical quarrel, it would be of limited interest. But Hartman's argument, though conducted on a literary-critical base, is really an argument against American taste in culture and American educational practice — and is probably sounder in its broader cultural attack than in its more theoretical plea for a different sort of critical act. Hartman's most intense question is, in fact, not only a literary one; it is equally a philosophic or religious or psychological one — the old question, What have we done with the gods? For Hartman, this question can be asked: How is the part of our imagination that used to occupy itself (to put it crudely) with thinking up gods now occupying itself? What replaces, in literature, the sacred? What, if anything, has replaced the binding authority of a sacred book? And if interpretation used to be the attempt to discover what the divine Word meant, what parallels can we find between that older activity and the interpretation of texts as we now engage in it? Finally, the activity of commenting and speculating on texts used to be justified by the sacredness of the text and the ultimate concerns of religion; can we now seriously justify this activity at all?

These are not new questions, religiously or philosophically speaking, but they have not been invoked in the Anglo-American critical world until recently. (The poets, of course, have thought of little else, but the critics who raised the point abandoned it, in Hartman's view, too quickly and too easily, with references to "the poetry of religion" or "emotive language.") Hartman sets himself squarely against the aesthetic and social line of literary study (from New Criticism through Leavis and Frye), which has governed the past several decades in the English-speaking world. And he also sets himself emphatically (though tacitly) against those who would place the study of literature within a wholly secularized study of linguistic signs, who see commentary as a form of decoding rather than as a form of hermeneutics, the interpretation of sacred texts.

Our American pragmatism and delight in evidence make us suspicious of the hermeneutical model, which discovers under or within the text at hand another, "truer" text, or what the original text "really" means (as the Song of Solomon, for example, though it appears to be a love poem, was found by allegorizing exegetes to be a text concerning the love of God for the soul). This model, by which a text recedes into more and more analogies of itself, is dear to the speculative and playful and historical mind of Hartman, who sees the allegorizing tendency of the human intellect, as it is displayed in history, to be irrepressible; it becomes the basis for "philosophical" criticism. By contrast, the prevailing mode of rhetorical and grammatical commentary, embodied in what Hartman calls for convenience "practical" criticism, seems to him, for all his ritual politeness, a poor thing, absurdly reductive of both the mind and the text. He calls the conflict of practical with philosophical criticism "a real war, which has lasted for more than fifty years and has intensified in the last decade."

Hartman writes as a teacher of American university students who have not grown up in that architectural and civic context which surrounds Europeans and reminds them that art always issues from a historical, religious, and philosophical ground. It is no use, Hartman argues, giving our students a piece of literature and asking them to "read" it; they haven't the cultural equipment to read it. The "close reading" of the text becomes ludicrous when the student has no idea of the view of man, nature, God, and history underlying it. Hartman, in his pity for our cultural nakedness, therefore proposes a program that would reinstate the literary text in a continuum of other texts, exposing the student (and, in the case of graduate students, the prospective teachers of the next generation also) "not only to literature narrowly conceived but also to important texts in philosophy, history, religion, anthropology, and so forth." This is disarming; who could object? But Hartman's next sentences betray the oddity of his intellectual position: "If we [departments of literature] give special attention to fiction and poetry it is because they are insufficiently examined elsewhere, and not because they are privileged. In exchange we must hope that other departments of knowledge will augment their interest in fiction and poetry, and in interpretive methods developed by us."

Like all utopias, this view of historians and philosophers teaching poems and novels while teachers of literature expound texts in philosophy and history has an ingenuous appeal, the more so since this sort of cross-fertilization is already, to some extent, taking place. And as Hartman stands before us wreathed in the names that, in small print, wander across his book jacket (Carlyle, Eliot, Bloom, Benjamin, Arnold, Frye, Burke, de Man, Derrida, Freud, Empson, Gadamer, Auerbach, Leavis, Iser, Lévi-Strauss, Lukács, Coleridge, Richards, Nietzsche, Heidegger, Brooks, Bourne, Ricoeur, Adorno, Ransom, Pater, Blackmur) he is himself a representative of the plenitude of intellectual possession for which he speaks. He predicts that though we once dissociated literature from "thought-systems of a religious, political, or conceptual kind," we are now "returning to a larger and darker view of art as mental charm, war, and purgation," and that his program follows a logical result of this intellectual advance.

But is this true? Has there ever been a critic — even one in the Anglo-American tradition of practical criticism — who did not regard art as "mental charm, war, and purgation"? Two different questions are at stake here: what art *is* (in the experience of the artist or the audience), and how it is best talked about (by the commentator), whether as experience or as artifact. And must the answer be a matter of mutually exclusive alternatives? Surely it can be suggested that a philosophical and poetic mind like Hartman's will prefer one approach, an ethical mind like Leavis's another, a scientific mind like Richards's another, a synoptic mind like Frye's another. And yet Hartman's claim is not so easily dismissible, because he attacks us, and our educational system, on another ground. We have provided our students, he says, with a criticism (and consequently with a range of thought) originating out of only one "text-milieu": "Every literary theory is based on the experience of a limited canon or generalizes strongly from a particular text-milieu. To take the metaphysical poets as one's base or touchstone, and to extend their 'poetics' toward modern poetry and then all poetry, will produce a very different result from working from Cervantes toward Pynchon, or from Hölderlin toward Heidegger." In too placidly restricting ourselves in this country to a limited canon of reference, we limit the ways we think — and here Hartman touches a nerve, and we feel the justice of the accusation. The terrible poverty that our writers have felt — the poverty that, as Wallace Stevens puts it, amounts to our owning a bare gray jar in the wilderness of Tennessee instead of a Grecian Urn in the British Museum — is still with us, a conceptual as well as a monumental or architectural poverty. It is linked to our uneasily coexisting New World arrogance and New World humility; it produces our naïveté.

If we possessed an ampler range of thought (and Hartman wants to import into our culture the Frankfurt School and the Hegelian philosophical tradition as well as a broad canon of European literature), our discourse would be deeper, fuller, and freer — and our society, as a result, deeper, fuller, and freer, too. Hartman envisages ambitious essays, written by a new breed of commentator, that would be in themselves literature; "interesting prose," "severe intellectual poems," he calls these essays, thinking of Pater, Valéry, Ortega, and Freud as models.

Like all manifestos, this one reflects its author — his own canon (German and French rather than, say, Russian or Greek in spirit), his own practice (the speculative essay), his own concerns (interpretation rather than explication, the sacred rather than the secular, idealism rather than empiricism), his own origins (European), his own poetics (Romantic rather than neoclassical), his own stylistic preferences (for the decorated, the whimsical, the deliberately exaggerated rather than for the "accommodated," the conversational, the decorous), his labor "to stay within [the negative or indeterminate] as long as is necessary" rather than to come to a firm, demonstrative end of argument. But it is Hartman's very one-sidedness that gives his book its force. To our assertive American wish for fact and certainty, he recommends a subtler and more dialectical play of mind; for our Anglo-American formation, he urges a forcible dose of modern European thought; against our post-Enlightenment skepticism, he proposes a rethinking of the origins and function of the sacred: "If what remains of religion is its poetry, what remains of poetry is its heterodox theology, or mythmaking. As all poetry and indeed all writing . . . is scrutinized by the critical and secularizing spirit, more evidence of archaic or sacred residues comes to light . . . The sacred has so inscribed itself in language that while it must be interpreted, it cannot be removed." To this Hartman adds, in the most disputable of all his remarks, that "one might speculate that what we call the sacred is simply that which must be interpreted or reinterpreted." This statement, by its deep nostalgia, begs the whole question of the difference between art and religion: to Hartman, it seems that "representation is the only Presence we have."

Hartman is fundamentally as unhappy with the language of French linguistic criticism and that of Russian Formalism as he is with the language of the Anglo-American literary tradition. His book amounts to a plea for a cohort that will read what he has read, be enabled by what has enabled him, profit from what he has profited from, see the importance of the sacred as he sees it. The plea is made reasonable, and even compelling, by the exquisite, original, and profound essays on literature that Hartman has written over the past thirty years (*The Unmediated Vision, Wordsworth's Poetry, Beyond Formalism,* and *The Fate of Reading*). And yet we can imagine another plea, equally addressed to the cultural poverty of our students, equally a call for reform in the curriculum. The maker of this plea would come wreathed not in the names of the company that includes Hegel, Freud, and Benjamin but in the names of musicians, painters, sculptors, and architects — names from that milieu in which literature is perhaps more at home than it is with philosophy, social thought, and religion. In that milieu of the arts, literature appears, over against the sacred, as an element quintessentially profane — embodying, as Yeats said, impulses diametrically opposed to the cultic, communal, ritualized impulses served by religion. In such a model of instruction, the critic is an interpreter not as the exegete of a sacred text is an interpreter but, rather, as a pianist or a conductor is an interpreter, holding up the work in a new and coherent manifestation, revealing it in one of its many possibilities, held together like a waterdrop by its own conflict and resolution of forces. Such a model is not incompatible with Hartman's psychoanalytically inspired wish to see in the work of art "the iconoclastic within the iconic," the "stratum of legitimate, sacred, or exalted words purifying a stratum of guilty, forbidden, or debased words." But it does imply an analysis terminable rather than interminable, as every performance of a musical work implies final choices of emphasis and color.

As a polemicist, Hartman presses for that substance which has comforted his own "seduced yet disbelieving" critical mind, and he dismisses — courteously, even apologetically, but ruthlessly — all rival systematic claims, sweeping aside with them that irrefutably stubborn tendency of literature to remain, unlike the other arts, language-bound. We cannot take on German or French as our mother tongue or our mother culture. But if Hartman exhibits the inescapable "blindness of insight," as Paul de Man has called it, he nonetheless puts deadly questions to our present cultural presuppositions and educational arrangements.

4

Defensive Harmonies: On Harold Bloom

Poetry and Repression, published in 1976, completes Harold Bloom's efforts, begun in *The Anxiety of Influence* and continued in *A Map of Misreading* and *Kabbalah and Criticism,* to map out a functional poetics of the lyric. The terms in which the lyric has conventionally been discussed are borrowed, most unsatisfactorily, from the rhetoric invented to describe oratory, an art entirely different from lyric in conception, in purpose, and in effect. And it remains true that the figures of rhetoric, while they may be thought to appear in a more concentrated form in lyric, seem equally at home in narrative and expository writing. Nothing in the figures of paradox, or irony, or metaphor, or imagery — or in the generic conventions of, say, the elegy — specifies a basis in verse.

Consequently, there has been a good deal of difficulty in knowing what it is proper to say about a lyric poem beyond what can be said about human imaginative expression in general. In desperation, incompetent commentators have fastened on the most salient characteristics of the conventional lyric — its phonetic and metrical ground plans — singling out these aspects as the "form" of the lyric, while treating its "content" under various historical, ethical, or metaphysical heads. The true generic history of the English lyric, and a corresponding history of essential distinguishing features of lyric expression, remain to be written.

It has always been recognized, in commentary on literature in general and the lyric in particular, that authors draw on other authors. The extent of such borrowing varies, and its function remains a matter of debate. Students are told that classical "conventions" in poetry were revived in the Renaissance; that they were revived in the Augustan Age; that they were revived by the Romantics; that they

49

were revived by Pound and others in the modern era. But these are descriptive statements, not functional ones.

A functional history of a poem would explain why certain conventions appeared suitable to the poet at this time for use in this poem, why such modifications of the conventions as appear were made, how the various conventions appearing in the poem function with respect to each other and with respect to the tradition from which they were drawn, and the meaning of the sequence of conventional elements in the poem. This is a daunting task to assume for even one poem, and it is generally avoided (in favor of moral summary) except by the most acute, learned, and hardworking critics, whose pages pose these perpetual questions, and at least attempt some answers.

Questions about the function of traditional elements in a poem cannot occur unless the reader agrees that every word or element used is a choice against another word or element, and that to include A means the exclusion of B and C — for a reason; to include A means also to include it for a reason. It may seem absurd that a critic must account not only for the presence of A but also for the absence of the infinite series $B \ldots \infty$, but of course in practice some items in the latter, "invisible" series are more probable than others, and the very presence of A usually hints at what is being displaced, ignored, repressed, or postponed.

Bloom's tetralogy has addressed itself to these questions of critical responsibility. The four books are aimed at an audience which has read most of the canon of English and American lyric, and which remembers most of what it has read, so that no echoes will be missed. I am willing to grant all the objections to Bloom's highly colored prose, which Christopher Ricks once described as "melodramatic," and also the objections which have been made to the rapid proliferation of Bloom's terminology. By my rough count there are now fifty or so terms Bloom is using in his "maps" of poetic process and product. Some of these are old (presence versus absence, fullness versus emptiness), some new (Anna Freud's mechanisms of defense, conflated for convenience into Bloom's magic total of six), some borrowed (from rhetoric, mainly via Kenneth Burke), and some Bloomian (the original six "revisionary ratios" named in "Gnostic exuberance" — Bloom's own phrase for the spirit behind his coinages — *clinamen, tessera, kenosis, daemonization, askesis,* and *apophrades*). Later additions include Hebrew importations from the Torah and Kabbalah, including those naming a sixfold process in "The Primal Scene of Instruction" (*'ahabah, chesed, ruach, davhar, lidrosh,* and revisionism proper) and a threefold process of cosmic creation (*zimzum, shevirath ha-kelim,* and *tikkun*).

These are indeed strange bedfellows to poetry in English. But it will be remembered that Bloom has always wanted a theology to support his literary theory, from his initial use of Martin Buber in his first book to his present wish — understandable to anyone with imaginative hunger or impatience — to see whether we possess other ways of interpreting the cosmos besides our Platonic and Aristotelian ones. The fantasy-creation (as Bloom allegorizes it) found in the Lurianic Kabbalah, which includes God's initial contraction of himself to make a space for creation, a subsequent disruption of the creation or "breaking of the vessels," and a final "restitution," gives Bloom an imaginative model for what he has chosen to present as the *ur*-pattern of all post-Enlightenment lyric — a pattern in which Speculation and her Sixfold take on a suspicious resemblance to our old acquaintance Beginning-Middle-and-End, even if called by the Bloomian names of Limitation-Substitution-Representation.

In the incessant rhetoric of Bloom's pages, the fifty analytic terms and the fifty or so patron saints of Bloom's critical and poetic canon (ranging from Vico to Derrida, from Milton to Ammons) play hide and seek, now obscured in dense allusiveness, now rising in Emersonian aphorism.

Bloom's literary model for his chapters, the lay-sermon, implies that his aim is to win converts to his way of seeing poetry. Though his terminology has not been widely adopted, his notions have exerted powerful influence (and even consequent anxiety, to judge by reviews). Because of Bloom, we can never again refer quite so complacently to "an allusion to" an earlier poet, nor can we speak of the appearance of "Miltonic" or "Keatsian" diction in a later poet without being put on our guard. Such intertextual echoes result, as Bloom has conclusively shown, from the many ways in which a poet manifests his struggle with antecedent style — a struggle which is varied, serious, continued, protracted, and profound, caused by the equal pressures of the apprentice's love (Keats's "Shakespeare and the Paradise Lost every day become greater wonders to me") and the adult poet's self-assertion (Keats's remark on Milton, "Life to him would be death to me"). Though even in the most respectable books about poetry facile metaphors of "adaptation" or "assimilation" by a younger poet of the work of his predecessors still appear, they will be looked on, after Bloom, with a far more critical eye.

Besides alerting us to the intense feelings underlying intertextual reference among poets, Bloom has, notably in this new volume, formulated a theory of the progress of a given poem as the overt or covert expression in language of a series of psychic defense mechanisms. Not everyone will see, with Bloom, these defenses as a self-choreographed sequence, relatively inflexible, always and everywhere the same (except in proportion) in poem after poem. But the problem to which Bloom here turns his attention — what it is that causes a poem to change, from moment to moment, its gait, its mood, its tone, its pattern of images, its type of reference to antecedent poetry, and so on — is the most profound problem in a theory of lyric, and one to which no fully developed answers of a satisfactory sort have been given (though Kenneth Burke, among Bloom's predecessors, pursues the question throughout his work). It may be that not all changes of posture in longer lyrics are most profitably seen as maneuvers of defense on the part of the poet against errant and anxious impulses of his own psyche, but Bloom's is at least a plausible line of thought to follow, and one which any counter-theory must take seriously.

Both of the chief conflicts described in Bloom's account of the writing of poetry — the poet's struggle with his (internalized) poetic models, and his struggle with his own psychic resistances — have the merit of being deduced from visible elements in a text, whether a poetic echo of some sort, or a clear jolt or alteration in the structure or progress of the text. A theory of poetic functions based on identifiable happenings in a text would seem, surely, preferable to a theory based on some putative "reader" (or even "superreader," for such has been postulated) with an even more putative set of "affective responses."

The sort of mind fertile in conceptual organization must inevitably interest itself less in those minute particulars which obstruct themselves as soon as the mind begins to generalize. On the other hand, the opposite sort of mind, one which rejoices chiefly in the infinite individuality of literary data, is helpless to combine them into any workable mass. Bloom's conceptual bent, combined with his uneasy relation to language itself (apparent in his mannered prose) often causes his pages about a text to be, especially by comparison with the exquisite lines quoted, needlessly clotted. His wish to compress his readings of the poems of two centuries leads him to write in what he calls his "shorthand," the metaphor itself suggesting the unreadable:

Let us map *Tintern Abbey* together. The poem consists of five verse-paragraphs, of which the first three (lines 1-57) form a single movement that alternates the ratios of *clinamen* and *tessera*. The fourth verse-paragraph is the second movement (lines 58-111) and goes from the ratio of *kenosis* to a *daemonization* that brings in the Sublime. The fifth and final verse paragraph is the third and last movement (lines 112-159), and alternates the ratios of *askesis* and *apophrades*. To abandon my own esoteric shorthand, lines 1-57 shuttle back and forth between dialectical images of presence and absence and representing images of parts and wholes. Lines 58-111 alternate images of fullness and emptiness, of gain and loss, with images of height and depth. Finally lines 112-159 move from inside/outside juxtapositions of the self and nature to an interplay of images of earliness and lateness. This is of course merely a very rough revisionary pattern, but it is there all right, in *Tintern Abbey* as in hundreds of good poems afterwards, down to the present day.

Such passages alternate with a more relaxed mood in which Bloom juxtaposes poems, not always well. To the sublime central passage of *Tintern Abbey* (in which "the burthen of the mystery" is lightened and "with an eye made quiet by the power / Of harmony, and the deep power of Joy, / We see into the life of things") he compares some modern lines, which begin:

> I am still completely happy.
> My resolve to win further I have
> Thrown out, and am charged by the thrill
> Of the sun coming up.

These lines come, Bloom tells us, from "John Ashbery's beautiful *Evening in the Country,* one of the most distinguished descendants of *Tintern Abbey.*" If these lines seem more distinguished to Bloom than they may to others, it is perhaps because Bloom is delighted to find writers — like Ashbery — who worry in verse about their own "belatedness" with respect to previous poetic achievement. For the same reason, Bloom is "obsessed," as he puts it, with Browning's labored poem "Childe Roland to the Dark Tower Came" because Roland is a "belated" figure who follows a host of failed predecessors. Bloom's estimation of certain passages will strain the agreement of readers who value him for his subtlety in theoretical proposals. When Bloom writes of a poem by Browning, "Eros crowds the poem, with an intensity and poignance almost Shakespearian in its strength," the subsequent quotation will not easily persuade readers to concur in Bloom's judgment:

> Was a lady such a lady, cheeks so round and lips so red
> On her neck the small face buoyant, like a bell-flower on its bed,
> O'er the breast's superb abundance where a man might base his head?

More disquieting in the pages of *Poetry and Repression* is a certain insistence that this "antithetical criticism" must conflict with received ideas about many famous poems. Bloom twice affirms, for instance, that "the youthful Harlot's curse," at the close of Blake's "London," refers not to the syphilis which, contracted by the husband who infects his wife and thereby his unborn child, "Blasts the new-born Infant's tear," but rather to the harlot's menstruation. This reading is not, so far as I can see, in any sense proved, but only, in two passages, asserted:

> The harlot's curse is not, as various interpreters have said, venereal disease, but is indeed what "curse" came to mean in the vernacular after Blake and still means now: menstruation, the natural cycle in the human female . . . I want to reject altogether the customary interpretation that makes "curse" here a variety of venereal infection, and that makes the infant's condition a prenatal blindness. Instead, I want to reaffirm my own earlier interpretation of the Harlot here as Blake's perpetually youthful Harlot, Nature, *not* the human female, but the natural element in the human, male or female . . . [Blake sees] how another curse or ban or natural fact (menstruation) blasts or scatters another natural fact, the tearlessness of the new-born infant.

It is regrettable that passages like this may distract readers from the real excellence in Bloom's formulation of larger questions.

For the most part, Bloom's wider meditations on poetry surprise, enlighten, and invigorate. In my own judgment, the chapters in *Poetry and Repression* on Milton, Blake, Shelley, Yeats, and Emerson are more rewarding than those on Wordsworth, Keats, Tennyson, Whitman, and Stevens. The line of stern public prophetic poets from Milton through Blake to Shelley and Yeats is more congenial to Bloom than the more flexible, inward-looking, and sinuous line of poets from Spenser through Keats and Tennyson to Stevens and Eliot. Wordsworth, while aspiring to belong to the first line, was temperamentally of the second, and therefore also eludes, to some degree, Bloom's grasp. But even when writing about poets less congenial than his Protestant prophets, Bloom makes comments, hears echoes, and sees linkages that powerfully support his central theoretical commitments, and that rebuke less well-read critics. One looks forward to each new book by Bloom as a repository of vivid engagement with poems, with thoughts and arguments springing up on every page, and as a source of provocative ways of thinking about poetry. The running argument in *Poetry and Repression*, for instance, about the appearance of the sublime, while too complex to present fairly in summary, will make readers pause in the future when they come upon passages of poetic sublimity, at once so solacing to the imagination and yet, as Bloom shows, so suspect in their origins. (Briefly put, Bloom's hypothesis is that the more hyperbolical the sublime, the more anxiety it is repressing; Bloom's choice of instances of sublimity, and his unravelings of the amount of psychic material they are at pains to resist, form a small book-within-a-book which is brilliant, revealing, and convincing.)

If Bloom slights, in favor of his "intertextual relations," what Keats called "the holiness of the heart's affections," another undeniable force in the shaping of poetry; if he asserts that he is opposing T. S. Eliot's and Northrop Frye's more gentle view of benevolent "tradition" while in fact he shares, in a more combative way, their emphasis on the interaction between poetic fathers and sons; if he, scrutinizing poems as analogues of each other rather than as distinctive and remarkable separate appearances, neglects to remind us how different each great work of art is from any other one, nonetheless he is pressing us to a fresh look at masterpieces, offering us new ways to view them, and, above all, challenging our familiar responses, readings, terminology, and proprieties.

However, he is adamantly doing all of this entirely on his own terms, and he demands a sophisticated reader who knows how far-reaching a penumbra of literary meaning shades out from every word, every turn of syntax, and every trope in a great poem.

Until the literary meaning of a poem is understood — and about this Bloom is indisputably right — absolutely nothing of worth can be said about its moral or metaphysical or ideological import. One petulant complaint uttered against Bloom in America self-righteously quoted Wordsworth's remark on the poet as a man speaking to men in order to protest, in the name of the human universal, Bloom's insistence on the recognition of literary echoes in reading a poem. In spite of such "humanist" cant, it remains incontestably true that literary language, as used by the greatest poets, is an extremely specialized dialect. The loss of the languages (of the ballads, of the Bible, of Milton) in which Wordsworth, for instance, wrote, as a man speaking to men who knew such languages, means that we must begin, when we are teaching poems, at an extremely simple level; it does not mean that the possession of such languages is no longer indispensable to the competent reader of poems. Bloom possesses to an extraordinary degree a sense of the interactions among the various "languages" in which English and American poetry has been written; his criticism is addressed to those who are interested in such inter-actions and their functional implications.

Such critical and theoretical work, while not designed for the general reader, will eventually find its way into the general literary consciousness, and will help to prevent the reduction, in universities as well as in schools, of poems to "sensuous," moral, patriotic, ethical, or ideological statement. Poems may come to be seen, even in the schools, for what they are, part of a perpetual struggling dialogue between generations, temperaments, wills, and perceptions, all couched in a fraternity of shared and contested language, unin-telligible unless the common usage of that language, and the problems to which it gives rise, are perceived, weighed, and appreciated. The poet-shepherd in "Lycidas," recognizing his obligation to his dead predecessor, hopes that some poet in the future will do for him what he is doing for his friend:

> So may some gentle Muse
> With lucky words favour my destined urn
> And as he passes turn,
> And bid fair peace be to my sable shroud.

Each poet turns in passing, and makes valedictory utterances toward his predecessors, using and revising the languages they bequeathed to him, while charging successors to take up his language made lucky by the Muse's favor. Divested of the linkages between generations, poetry might seem a poor unadorned thing. Nevertheless, it still possesses an independent aesthetic beauty, which is after all what draws even naive and uninformed young readers before they have any sense of the Bloomian revisionary ratios. Bloom does not explain that independent beauty, but he does make certain that his readers can never again ignore the struggles and evasions, poetic and psychic alike, which give rise to the grand motions of the deceptively harmonious surface of lyric.

5

The Medley Is the Message: On Roland Barthes

Roland Barthes died in a street accident in Paris in 1980, at the age of sixty-four. *The Rustle of Language* (1986) and *The Responsibility of Forms* (1985) collect, in English translation, articles and reviews written between 1961 and 1980 — work produced, that is, during the second half of Barthes's publishing life (his first essay, on the *Journal* of André Gide, was published in 1942). These two collections can perhaps provide the pre-text (as Barthes would have said) for a posthumous consideration of this remarkable man, a writer at home neither as a novelist (though he aspired to fiction) nor as a university professor (though he taught university students) nor as an intellectual (though that is the title by which he was known).

Those of us who have felt sympathetic to Barthes over the years have on occasion received a portion of the ridicule directed toward him. "How can you like that silly homosexual?" I was asked by an eminent literary critic in tones of impatience and revulsion, when I ventured to praise Barthes's hymn to reading, *The Pleasure of the Text* (1973). The remark manifested, besides homophobia, a suspicion that Barthes was "not serious." Barthes knew that *les gens sérieux* excluded him from the inner circle of their company, perhaps for the same reason that they excluded his beloved Michelet, the historian on whom he had written a short book in 1954: "Our languages are coded, we must not forget: society is forbidden, by a thousand means, to mingle them, to transgress their separation and their hierarchy; the discourse of History, that of moral ideology (or that of philosophy) are to be kept pure of desire: by not reading Michelet, it is his desire we censure. Thus, because he blurs the discriminatory law of 'genres,' Michelet fails first of all to be given his place: serious people — conformists — exclude him from their reading."

58

As usual, Barthes's language here has oblique sexual and class references; generic miscegenation, linguistic morganatic marriages, are feared by the *gens sérieux,* whose defenses are those of their race, class, and religion. Any wall breached threatens the breaching of all. And yet it is not only the mingling of codes in Michelet that Barthes claims as his own; it is also the opulence of Michelet's sensual language, always ready to "indulge itself" (as the detractors would say). Barthes quotes Michelet on insects, a "purple passage" almost unthinkable in a present-day historian; the insects are "charming creatures, bizarre creatures, admirable monsters, with wings of fire, encased in emerald, dressed in enamel of a hundred varieties, armed with strange devices, as brilliant as they are threatening, some in burnished steel frosted with gold, others with silky tassels, lined with black velvet; some with delicate pincers of russet silk against a deep mahogany ground; this one in garnet velvet dotted with gold; then certain rare metallic blues, heightened with velvety spots; elsewhere metallic stripes, alternating with matte velvet." "Yes, in Michelet the signifier is sumptuous," Barthes concludes, praising that excess in expression visible when the author's pen loses itself in the athletic joy of writing. Because the interminging of codes, and the insertion of vertical metaphor into the horizontal argument, are sins against those virtues of "logic" and "clarity" so highly valued by the French, we can see Barthes's career as a long rebellion against the intellectual and institutional practices in which he was raised — and which, even in his late years, he could never entirely escape.

The intellectual formation of a French child attracted to literature is hardly imaginable to Americans. We are unfamiliar with those sacred French institutions the *cahier* (the notebook in which never a blot can appear), the *dictée* (the oral dictation in which faults of spelling and punctuation are subsequently mercilessly reproved), the *manuel littéraire* (a potted version of literary history) — all the furniture of the school and the *lycée.* Barthes himself knew very well how little he could escape from this training. He amused himself in his late "autobiography," *Roland Barthes* (1975), by setting himself compositional subjects of the sort set for French students: "Arrogance," "Ease," "Money," "Coincidence," "Friends." The characteristic Barthesian fragment — a paragraph complete in itself, unlinked to a longer discourse — arises in part from the *dictée,* in part from the *pensée* (the most French of all literary forms).

The instruction in composition received by the French child derived still, in Barthes's day, from Renaissance methods, with their base in the logic, grammar, and rhetoric of the trivium. The first systematic act in treating any subject was to divide it into manageable parts along some logical axis — temporal, hierarchical, structural. Whence the inevitable beginning of almost any Barthesian essay — "X may be divided into two [or three — rarely four] parts [or divisions, or motives, or effects]." This factitious divisibility-of-everything is counteracted by Barthes in his purposeful use of mélange, often directed by a purely arbitrary principle (he will, for instance, consider together homosexuality and hashish because they both begin with *h*). Because logic — the system of divisibility — voiced itself as the Law in school, it became for Barthes the symbol of patriarchy, violence, the father, while intermixture became the symbol of the mother and of the aesthetic.

In *Roland Barthes,* he wrote about himself, under the heading "Aesthetic Discourse": "He attempts to compose a discourse which is not uttered in the name of the Law and/or of Violence: whose instance might be neither political nor religious nor scientific; which might be in a sense the remainder and the supplement of all such utterances. What shall we call such discourse? *erotic* no doubt, for it has to do with pleasure; or even perhaps: *aesthetic,* if we foresee subjecting this old category to a gradual torsion which will alienate it from its regressive, idealist background and bring it closer to the body, to the *drift.*" But this is a late utterance. Before Barthes could write in such a way, he had to come under the sway of a succession of "Laws" — among them Marxism, semiology, anthropology, psychoanalysis — each of which he would (as he had with logic) in turn appropriate and repudiate, thereby alienating himself from the true believers in each camp. Accepting various discourses first of all as "solutions" or "truths," Barthes came to see them, later, as competing languages in a world made up of those very languages of culture. Other people seemed able to locate themselves within one or the other of these group discourses or sociolects; for himself, he was, as it were, "traversed" by them (he was their traversal, as he said), but they exited as they had entered. Of what, then, was he himself constituted, if not by one or another of these grids through which to see the world? He realizes (in *Roland Barthes*) that he is formed by the mother tongue, by French itself — with all its infinite lexical and discursive variety. "This is not," he points out, "a national love" in the patriotic sense; rather "the French language is nothing more or less for him than the umbilical language."

Now a writer who loves words — all words, single words — for their materiality and for their image-inspiring power is at the furthest remove from someone who loves "ideas." If Barthes became attached to various ideologies, it was perhaps because these intellectual comets bore as their train a cloud of new words, new apparel for the world. The full lexicons of Marxist, anthropological, Freudian, and semiological discourse were at least as much an occasion for the reveling play of his imagination as the systematic ideas of Marx, Freud, or Saussure. Yet if the anarchy of the lexicon appealed to Barthes, so did, paradoxically, the logical austerity of syntax. (He once defined himself as "the dream of a pure syntax and the pleasure of an impure, heterological lexicon.") The logical and "syntactic" side of Barthes made him eager to engage in intellectual debate; the dispersive, "lexical" side made him "spoil" the logic of debate with "digressions" into various discourses, "indulgences" of language, what he called the "skids" and "drifts" of argument. The authors for whom he felt the most intense sympathy reflected one or the other of his two sides: Racine for austerity of syntax, Michelet for sensuality of language, Robbe-Grillet for a prose freed from connotation, Brecht for a superb materiality of staging.

"Received opinion" — what Barthes called the *Doxa* ("Medusa: who petrifies those who look at her") — was his enemy. It is hard to say which Barthes hated more as a young man, the concepts of the manuals of literary history in use in the *lycées,* or the language in which those concepts were expressed. In an excoriating lecture called "Reflections on a Manual" (1969), Barthes sets out the poverty of the all-purpose concepts by which the irrepressible verbal energies of literature are academically codified: "the authors, the schools, the movements, the genres, and the centuries." There is, he begins, "the archetypal paradigm of our whole literature, *romanticism-classicism* . . . occasionally amplified into *romanticism-realism-symbolism.*" He continues, ironically, with the absurd characterizations of the centuries: "The sixteenth is overflowing life; the seventeenth is unity; the eighteenth is movement; and the nineteenth is complexity." The fatuity of these nouns is matched by that of the blanket descriptions offered by the manual: "There is 'exuberant' opposed to 'restrained'; there is 'lofty art' or 'deliberate obscurity' opposed to 'expansiveness'; 'rhetorical coldness' to 'sensibility.'" These stereotypes enraged Barthes by their falsity, as they pretended to encompass all authors equally in their facile "understanding." How adequate is it to say of

François Villon that he manifests "a witty nature concealing a tragic sense"?

But what Barthes (in his quasi-Marxist phase during the 1960s) addresses more savagely than the vapid crudity of the ideas animating French literary history is the censorship visible in the literary manual — a censorship of questions about class, sexuality, the functions (social, symbolic, or anthropological) of literature, and competing literary languages (including the spoken language). He criticizes as well the nationalism that pervades French literary consciousness ("We are presented with a kind of shiny image in which king and literature reflect each other"), and the naive psychology that is presupposed in literary evaluations ("For instance, du Bellay will be praised for having produced certain sincere and personal cries; Ronsard had a sincere and profound Catholic faith; Villon, a cry from the heart, etc.").

As a student, Barthes had been exposed not only to the puerility of the literary history found in school manuals, but also to the prescribed form for writing about literature — the *explication de texte*. When I was myself obliged to practice it, in the late 1950s, the form it took (as I recall) was as follows: one was obliged to detach from the poem its main animating idea (called, significantly enough, the *idée-mère*), then to list the *idées secondaires* deriving from the "mother"; then to give the *fond* (or general content) followed by the *forme* (or prosodic structure).

This improbable recreation of the text as a logical structure of ideas, separated into form and content, would of course eventually be repudiated by anyone of sensibility who had perceived, in literature, the essential inextricability of ideas, content, and form. Barthes's own commentaries on books or paintings combat the *explication de texte* in various ways. In *S/Z* for instance (his commentary on a tale by Balzac), he fragments the text into short phrases, and reads serially, piece by piece — a process that seemed nothing short of deranged to various readers who did not realize that to emphasize the temporal and incremental quality of reading was one way to rebel against the spatial quality of the "structure of ideas" required by conventional French explication. Elsewhere, as in his essays on painting, a delighted discourse glances over the field of vision in a wayward, musing, and irregular way: nothing could be further from systematic exposition.

Though a parallel has often been drawn between Barthes's writing and that of the American "New Critics" (since both were attacking the manuals of an inert and genteel literary pedagogy), in fact Barthes — politically radical, psychoanalytic in his approach, and informed by linguistics and anthropology — resembled very little the New Critics, who were politically conservative, and philological rather than psychoanalytic in their approach to a text. Had he been born in America (futile hypothesis), Barthes would have been protected from the two wars that, in Europe, made life inescapably political. Barthes's father, after all, had died in World War I; and Barthes himself was of draft age (though exempt because of his tuberculosis) during World War II; he had seen the defeat of France by Germany, and the division of France between supporters of Pétain and supporters of De Gaulle. Barthes came to intellectual maturity in the shadow of Sartre; and Susan Sontag has suggested that Barthes's first book, *Writing Degree Zero* (1953) was in fact a riposte to Sartre's "What is Literature?" (1947), rejecting Sartre's notion of style as the servant of content.

Barthes had to find, against Sartre, a way to describe the *engagement* or free ethical commitment of the writer, one that addressed the full exercise of the act of writing, not simply political content. To this end, Barthes argued that the writer encounters two necessities and one freedom. He inherits, as given, both the entire historical past as it is embodied in language and his own personal past as it has issued in the style of his temperament and his personality. "A language is therefore a horizon, and style a vertical dimension, which together map out for the writer a Nature, since he does not choose either . . . In the former, he finds a familiar History, in the latter, a familiar personal past." But beyond history, both past and biographical, the author, according to Barthes, makes a personal choice in the form taken by his writing. He chooses the mode through which he will enter history; his form is committed to certain techniques and conventions, certain ideas of the relation between style and content, depending on "the social use which he has chosen for his form, and his commitment to this choice." Barthes concludes, in *Writing Degree Zero*, that "writing is thus essentially the morality of form, the choice of that social area within which the writer elects to situate the Nature [that is, the historical givens] of his language."

Though this argument from *Writing Degree Zero* can be attacked on several fronts (not least in its separation of "style" from "form," and its singling out of choice as exempt from destiny), it represents

Barthes's will to locate writing — the activity of the writer — in the mobile act of signifying rather than, with Sartre, in the immobile content of what is signified. At this point, Barthes is still conceiving of writing as an authorial production; later, he came to link it far more strongly with the reader, as his interest shifted from the author (that monument consecrated by past literary history) to the Text, for him a shimmering force-field of signifying, into which the reader enters and by which the reader is "traversed."

Through the Text the reader becomes a writer, producing meaning; the reader produces writing of his own only as a response to a previous experience of a Text. Critics are perhaps to be defined, Barthes suggests, in the same way as other writers — as "those who read *in order* to write." The circulating of writing from author to reader, from Text to Text, came to seem to Barthes like the circulation of money, on the one hand, and of desire, on the other, leading him to use about literature various metaphors (of expenditure, of erotic combination, of "cruising") that offended readers accustomed to the decorum of conventional literary language.

His frequent use of metaphor is in fact the first characteristic suggesting that Barthes was more a "writer" than an "intellectual." In "Outcomes of the Text" (1973) in *The Rustle of Language,* he repudiates the denatured, falsely impersonal language of intellectuals as an inauthentic form of writing, to which he gives the pejorative name of *écrivance*: "*Ecrivance,* which is not writing (*écriture*), but its inauthentic form, ordinarily censures [censors] the work of what, in language, is both its center and its excess; have you ever seen a metaphor in a sociological study or in an article of *Le Monde?*" One might not see metaphors in the writing of intellectuals, but one would see them, often at a crucial moment of argument, in Barthes, as in this essay on Brecht: "Have you ever seen a Japanese pin? It is a dressmaker's pin whose head is a tiny bell, so that you cannot forget it once the garment has been finished. Brecht remakes the logosphere by leaving the bell-headed pins in it, the signs furbished with their tiny jingle."

Finding the sequentially argued essay as limiting as denatured *écrivance,* Barthes increasingly turned to the fragment, allying himself thereby with Pascal and Nietzsche — writers, not (degraded species) intellectuals. The arbitrary alphabetical arrangement of topics in both *Roland Barthes* and *A Lover's Discourse* (1977) satisfied Barthes's wish for a combination in which topics would succeed one another in the fixed order A, B, C (so that Art would come before Conscience, for example); but the order would be arbitrary, not logical or narrative, thus breaking with the usual laws of expository writing.

To enumerate all of Barthes's rebellions against the literary training of his youth would be to retell the story of his life. His gadfly instincts precipitated him into controversy, as in the bitter dispute over philological and historical constraints on interpretation that followed his book on Racine and led to his impassioned *Critique et vérité* (a book only recently translated into English), in which he argued the right of every century to interpret the classics anew through the vivifying lenses of new intellectual systems (as he had reinterpreted Racine in the light of anthropological and psychoanalytic speculation).

But though Barthes rose sharply to conflict, it was not conflict that interested him most. Rather, he wished to find a nonideological form of discourse (a utopian desire, perhaps). If ideology (as he defines it in *Roland Barthes*) is "what is repeated and *consistent*," it is by its very consistency, as he continues, "excluded from the order of the signifier," that is, of language-in-process, with its continued search for synonyms and its ambiguity. Counterideology, or ideological analysis (by which one shows the hidden ideological underpinnings of phrases such as "law and order"), is therefore also an ideology. "How escape this? One solution is possible: the *aesthetic* one": and Barthes finds his exemplar in Brecht: "In Brecht . . . counter-ideology creeps in by means of a fiction — not realistic but *accurate*. This is perhaps the role of the aesthetic in our society: to provide the rules of an *indirect and transitive* discourse (it can transform language, but does not display its domination, its good conscience)." We know this solution already from Sir Philip Sidney: "The poet nothing affirmeth, and therefore never lieth." But the "indirect and transitive" discourse of fiction was not available to Barthes (who seems not to have possessed the interest in others' lives inseparable from the fictional imagination). We consequently see him, in all these essays, combating the inherently assertive nature of the sentence itself (which he fully recognized), and trying for a lightness or urbanity of tone, a historical skepticism, and a figurative language that would remove his essays from the earnest assertiveness, uninvaded by irony or figure, inseparable from the systematic intellectuality of ideological writing.

Barthes is a figure of great contemporary interest in his recognition both of the human necessity of belief systems ("mythologies" — what we think with) and of the mortality of such systems (they are what succeed one another). He made lists of his own such belief systems — "He had always, up to now, worked successively under the aegis of a great system (Marx, Sartre, Brecht, semiology, the Text)" — and of his own phases and influences, situating himself within that "intertext" which echoed in his mind. He often quoted, with approval, Brecht's words about the intertext: "He thought in other heads; and in his own, others besides himself thought. This is true thinking." Barthes comments: "True thinking is more important than the (idealist) thought of truth. In other words, in the Marxist field, Brecht's discourse is never a priestly discourse." In addressing the form of discourse, Barthes argues that any urging of *a* truth as *the* truth is only theological discourse by another name. He attacked the medieval notion of signification as a signified kernel of meaning inside a husk of signifier-chaff. To that notion, or the notion of meaning as the pit of a fruit, Barthes opposes his metaphor of the onion, which consists of its successive peelings. Or he compares the braidings of various "codes" in a text to the interweavings of polyphonic music, where no single strand is definitively "the" music. In either case, Barthes argues against the separation of essence from surface — always an aesthetic argument.

The essays collected in these two volumes, then, are the work of someone who believes in the activity of signifying as one of the fields of human freedom, and as one of the processes by which the "human subject," the thinking and feeling mind, is created. The irreducible plurality of signifying is set against ideological consistency. And the Barthesian "pleasure of the text" is above all the joy of the exercise of creative freedom, as the reader cooperates with the printed text to render it alive once more within a human mind. Since any system, no matter how revolutionary to begin with, passes with time into received opinion, the mind (he writes in *The Rustle of Language*) which is committed to freedom and to freshness must forever seek a new way of writing. This prescription will not be unfamiliar to readers of Emerson, Whitman, or Stevens: it is a utopian prescription, as Barthes often remarks, but it is preferable to its opposite, the hobgoblin of theological or ideological consistency, which both creates and maintains ideological interest groups.

Barthes's own consistency lies in his praise of "the great theme proper to the signifier, sole predicate of essence it can actually support, *metamorphosis*." It has also been called *différence*. In this, Barthes is loyal to his own experience: as his commentators have often pointed out, his place in French society was always that of an outsider. He was fatherless, poor in youth, a Protestant, a noncombatant, an inhabitant of a tuberculosis sanitarium, a homosexual, unmarried. (Later, in academic settings, he was a non-*agrégé*, that is, he never took the examination required to teach in secondary schools.) One of the most revealing passages in *Roland Barthes* places him at a Catholic wedding: "Walking through the Church of Saint-Sulpice and happening to witness the end of a wedding, he has a feeling of exclusion. Now, why this faltering, produced under the effect of the silliest of spectacles: ceremonial, religious, conjugal, and petit bourgeois (it was not a large wedding)? Chance had produced that rare moment in which the whole *symbolic* accumulates and forces the body to yield. He had received in a single gust all the divisions of which he is the object, as if, suddenly, it was the very *being* of exclusion with which he had been bludgeoned: dense and hard." Though the exclusion from the social and sexual practice of the French majority was painful to Barthes, yet more painful to him was the linguistic alienation caused in part by his social difference but more intensely by his habitual irony and detachment: "To the simple exclusions which this episode represented for him was added a final alienation: that of his language: he could not assume his distress in the very code of distress, i.e., *express it:* he felt more than excluded: *detached:* forever assigned the place of the *witness,* whose discourse can only be, of course, subject to codes of detachment: either narrative, or explicative, or challenging, or ironic: never *lyrical,* never homogeneous with the pathos outside of which he must seek his place."

Barthes frequently emphasized his later marginality and that of the institutions — not degree-granting ones — at which he lectured. Of course, there was a triumph for him in his very eccentricity's becoming central to modern criticism. But not everyone could follow him into his final skepticism, in which all systematic argument seemed to him finally to follow the same underlying grammar of system, with only the lexicon changed. Human freedom is, within each system, reduced to a poor copy of itself (Barthes called it the human head reduced to the shrunken head preserved by cannibals). Only with each new reopening of the signified to the signifier, that is, to the free activity of signifying, can conscience once again be served. According to Barthes it is, in the end, an ethical impulse that sets the writer to writing; all writing worth the name is the revolutionary effort toward freedom, away from the sterotypes of thought and language inherent in every belief system.

The Responsibility of Forms — the very title suggesting the ethical impulses pressing the artist toward representation — collects twenty-three essays (five of which were previously published in 1977 in *Image–Music–Text*) on photography, cinema, painting, and music. (Barthes played the piano and was an amateur of the visual arts; his last book, *Camera Lucida,* was a meditation on photography.) Though several of these essays are slight book reviews, even they contribute to the underlying subject of Barthes's investigation, which is always what one might call "inventiveness of manner." This quality is brought under scrutiny as it appears in the fanciful alphabet of the fashion designer Erté, in the grotesque seasonal portraits by Arcimboldo (such as a portrait head of Autumn composed out of fruits), in the encrusted paintings of Bernard Réquichot. It is also investigated in Barthes's concern with gesture: so much does gesture seem to Barthes the characteristic act of the graphic arts, that the two long meditations on the art of Cy Twombly included here can stand for Barthes at one theoretical extreme, represented by his interest in the doodle, which he calls "the signifier without the signified."

The best instance here of Barthes's subtlety is the (already famous) essay "The Third Meaning," in which he touches on stray elements in representation: those "left over," those not directly participating in the meaning, "a luxury, an expenditure without exchange," the "truly filmic" (that which is not, strictly speaking, required either by the story or the theme). In the illustrations he takes from Eisenstein, the filmmaker's eye is shown to include various symmetries and moments of visual delight that are not, in any conceivable way, required by the narrative or ideological interests of the film. There, if anywhere, for Barthes, is where the signifier is free, and creativity of the purest sort is possible.

Both in *The Responsibility of Forms* and in *The Rustle of Language,* the typically Barthesian texture of the writing makes itself felt. That texture — delightful to many of us — is composed of the mutual jostling of many (often mutually incompatible) registers of discourse. Linguistics, literature, philosophy, anthropology, mythology, art history, economics, politics, information theory, psychoanalysis, rhetoric, sociology, history, semantics, Marxism — these are only the commonest of the many categories that organize Barthes's thinking. Insofar as Barthes's medley is his message, one can say he exemplifies his own definition of the human person — a consciousness constituted by the available languages of its social and historical era.

The play of differences is for Barthes the definition of linguistic utopia: where all is difference, nothing can be marked off as "different" and therefore to be hated. He takes up this theme at greatest length in his essay on Fourier (*Sade/Fourier/Loyola,* 1981 — Barthes's most provocative title), but it is most intensely displayed in his remarks (in *Roland Barthes*) on homosexuality:

> *Virile/non-virile*: this famous pair, which rules over the entire *Doxa,* sums up all the ploys of alternation: the paradigmatic play of meaning and the sexual game of ostentation . . .
>
> As he said in an article of 1971, "What is difficult is not to liberate sexuality according to a more or less libertarian project but to release it from meaning, including from transgression as meaning."
>
> . . . Once the paradigm is blurred, utopia begins: meaning and sex become the object of a free play, at the heart of which the (polysemant) forms and the (sensual) practices, liberated from the binary prison, will achieve a state of infinite expansion.

Liberation from "the binary prison," the prison of male/female, majority/minority, right/wrong — is it possible? Can there be what Barthes called the Neutral — "a back-and-forth, an amoral oscillation, in short, one might say, the converse of an antinomy." To anyone who does not fit into the binary categories of ordinary social reference (male/female, virile/nonvirile), the Neutral is the only non-imprisoning hope. Barthes stands, then, for the blurring of models, for many-sided meanings, for the oscillation of value, for metamorphosis. But this "drifting," this back and forth, this freedom, must always take place within the social relation ("What other relation is there?" Barthes once asked).

The smallest compass of the social relation is the erotic relation (of which one subclass, for Barthes, was the relation of the reader to the text). In *A Lover's Discourse* and *The Pleasure of the Text,* Barthes assumes this restricted compass of social relation as his own favorite territory. In the same vein, he prefers the lied (in "The Romantic Song") because it is not coded by sex:

The classification of human voices — like any classification elaborated by a society — is never innocent. In the peasant choirs . . . the men's voices answered to the women's voices: by this simple division of the sexes, the group mimed the preliminaries of exchange, of the matrimonial market. In our Western society, through the four vocal registers of the opera, it is Oedipus who triumphs: the whole family is there, father, mother, daughter, and son, symbolically projected . . . into bass, mezzo, soprano, and tenor. It is precisely these four family voices which the romantic lied, in a sense, *forgets*: it does not take into account the sexual marks of the voice, for the same lied can be sung by a man or by a woman; no vocal "family," nothing but a human subject — *unisexual,* one might say.

Such a passage suggests how Barthes longed for occasions when one could be considered "nothing but a human subject" — unmarked by the family romance into which he could not insert himself.

Other passages in *The Responsibility of Forms* reveal Barthes at his most self-effacing, when he becomes the critic so sympathetic to his subject — the music of Schumann, for instance — that he finds words for the most difficult of all art forms:

Schumann's music involves something radical, which makes it into an existential, rather than a social or moral experience. This radicality has some relation to madness, even if Schumann's music is continuously "well-behaved" insofar as it submits to the code of tonality and to the formal regularity of melismata [grace or melodic embellishments]. Madness here is incipient in the vision, the economy of the world with which the subject, Schumann, entertains a relation which gradually destroys him, while the music itself seeks to construct itself . . .

. . . [Schumann's] music, by its titles, sometimes by certain discreet effects of description, continuously refers to concrete things: seasons, times of the day, landscapes, festivals, métiers. But this reality is threatened with disarticulation, dissociation, with movements not violent (nothing harsh) but brief and, one might say, ceaselessly "mutant": nothing lasts long, each movement interrupts the next: this is the realm of the *intermezzo,* a rather dizzying notion when it extends to all of music, and when the matrix is experienced only as an exhausting (if graceful) sequence of interstices.

And so Barthes launches himself into description, as he does with no less expansiveness and interest with any number of aesthetic objects — showing, in these appreciations, his truest and freest self.

The Rustle of Language collects forty-five of Barthes's essays on literature and teaching written between 1967 and 1980. It includes *hommages* to various authors, from Brecht to Proust, and to various scholars, from Jakobson to Kristeva. There are central Barthesian statements about the future of semiological investigation, urging that it go beyond exploring the class interests underlying discourse, and question discourse-making itself. In the opening manifesto, "From Science to Literature" (1967), Barthes makes the distinction, which he will repeat on many occasions, between a language that pretends to objectivity (the "impersonal" language of intellectuality) and a self-reflexive ironic language that puts itself, as well as its subject matter, in question. In all of these essays, the briskness and liveliness of Barthes's style make the work interesting, even when it is repeating, in essence, conclusions from earlier writing.

To my mind, the most unexpected material in this collection comes in the essays on teaching, all written in the early 1970s. How will the master of all ideologies, servant to none (except to a utopian ideology of plurality) see the pedagogical function, the pedagogical atmosphere? Once again, Barthes enters into *constatation* (to use the word of the 1968 intellectual rebellion); this time, he attacks the *cours magistral,* the large lecture class. He decides, in a brilliant fiction, that the teacher before the audience is like the analysand before the psychiatrist, constantly babbling in front of a silent auditor. As we know, if one talks long enough into a void, one begins to hear what one's tonality and import sound like, often to the point of embarrassment. This *dédoublement* (or doubling oneself) is one more form available to Barthesian irony; as he hears himself being an authority, he turns on himself, just as he had when he heard himself being an ideologue. The sound of the lecturer is not a sound he likes: it is the sound of the univocal, the Law, the priest. He recognizes fully the difficulty imposed not only by the professorial role but also by the oratorical sentence; and he comes to prefer the role of *animateur* — instigator — of a seminar, where the assumption of authority can be less imposing than in the auditorium, and where the discourse is a broken, collaborative, circulating one.

Even here, Barthes recognizes the anterior authority ascribed to him as the one among the group *who has already written* (while the others are those *who desire to write*). It will amuse an American teacher to hear Barthes cite, as the greatest of risks, the act of teaching a *subject the teacher has not yet written on*: the American professor, who does this all the time, is thereby made the more aware of how greatly the French teacher feels the obligation of magisterial authority, how little the French classroom has been a theater of tentative exploration.

In the utopian imagining of his essay "Writers, Intellectuals, Teachers," Barthes conjures up the ideal arena of learning: it would not negate the realities of university life (degrees, professional advancement, and so on), but it would diffuse what is too often a coercive and dogmatic teaching: "Within the very limits of the teaching space as given, the need is to attempt, quite patiently, to trace out a pure form, that of a *floating* (the very form of the signifier); such floating destroys nothing; it is content to disorient the Law: the necessities of promotion, professional obligations . . . , imperatives of knowledge, prestige of method, ideological criticism — everything is there, but *floating.*"

Through the notions of a constant free signifying, of metamorphosis, of floating, Barthes embodies his last challenge to the premature and ahistorical assertiveness of the intellectual life. He would have agreed with Keats on the value of negative capability — the capacity to experience "uncertainties, mysteries, doubts, without any irritable reaching after fact and reason." To dwell in reverie and responsiveness, to speak warmly and from within the object — this is the style of Barthes's practical criticism. One feels his wish to linger; to savor, to dilate.

There is, however, a dark other side to this responsiveness; it is the restless intermission between responses, to which Barthes gives the Baudelairean name of Ennui. In a disquieting analogy, he repeatedly compares the quest for an aesthetic object to sexual "cruising"; "Le Nouveau" has a neurotic and sexual hysteria attached to it, perhaps as much learned as innate. If there is a flaw in the Barthesian aesthetic, it is the overvaluing of the hunger for innumerable new objects. There is something of this, of course, in all aesthetic experimentation; and yet there is another aspect to art, that "constancy to an ideal object" (Coleridge's words) that keeps Cézanne obdurately attached to his mountain, Mondrian to his rectangles.

The poet Richard Howard is the translator of these volumes, as of so many others that have brought French criticism and literature across the ocean. Barthes is not easy to translate, and it is a mark of Howard's longstanding comprehension of Barthes's thought that the line of argument is always rendered clearly. Barthes's vocabulary (he was a constant creator of neologisms) presents difficulties that are not always happily solved. Must we have *mathesis, sopitive, semelfactive, edulcorate,* and so on, in English? Perhaps they are unavoidable; but they do mar the English page. *The Rustle of Language* gives a date and citation of the original appearance for each of its essays; its predecessor, *The Responsibility of Forms,* has no citations, though it does offer dates. One would have appreciated, in the case of Barthes's book reviews and art criticism, a citation of the author's or artist's name, and of the book or exposition under review. As things now stand, an essay will refer to "Masson's work" without otherwise identifying Masson, or will speak of "Jean-Louis Schefer's discourse" without revealing the name of the book under discussion.

I have not treated here Barthes's texts as Text — as an interweaving of significations and intertextual citations floating free from the authority of their author and creating a reponsive site in myself as reader. Instead I have seen them as stages of an autobiography in which we can view a French intellectual, made marginal by his own destiny, struggle through the generic life offered his generation, not submitting to a single *prise de conscience,* but instead suffering restlessly all the intellectual currents of his time, finding not a single grid through which to orient himself, but rather locating, over time, a plurality of grids, each offering the advantage of a different "fix" on the world, each proffering a new discourse, a new lexicon, a new mentality. A profound and lifelong appetite for a plurality of languages — by which I mean a plurality of apprehensions — distinguishes Barthes from most of his contemporaries. The compulsion to iconoclasm is always (as he saw) the compulsion toward a new style of writing. "New styles of architecture, a change of heart," was what Auden asked for; "a lust to break the icon" was Lowell's phrase. In his restlessness and desire for change of discourse, Barthes allied himself finally with artists.

Barthes's last pronouncements, after the death of his mother in 1980, turn away from his former distanced view of the Text to an assertion of the commemorative and elegiac powers of literature. Were he to write a novel, he says, he would want it to fulfill three missions:

> The first would permit me to *say* whom I love . . . To say whom one loves is to testify that they have not lived (and frequently suffered) "for nothing" . . . These lives, these sufferings, are gathered up, pondered, justified . . . The second mission . . . would permit me, fully but indirectly, the representation of an affective order . . . It is characteristic of a "modern" sensibility to "conceal its tenderness" (beneath the stratagems of writing); but why? . . . Finally and perhaps especially, the Novel . . . exerts no pressure upon the other (the reader); its power is the truth of affects, not of ideas: hence, it is never arrogant, terrorist: according to Nietzsche's typology, it aligns itself with Art, not with Priesthood.

To say whom one loves, to say that lives do not fall into nothingness, to represent an affective order — this is the discourse of imagination, the promised land toward which Barthes gazed, but which he could never enter. He is the votary of language, rather than of the imagination. His own best self-description closes the title essay of the most recent collection, as he represents himself surrounded by "the rustle of language": "I imagine myself today something like the ancient Greek as Hegel describes him: he interrogated, Hegel says, passionately, uninterruptedly, the rustle of branches, of springs, of winds, in short, the shudder of Nature, in order to perceive in it the design of an intelligence. And I — it is the shudder of meaning I interrogate, listening to the rustle of language, that language which for me, modern man, is my Nature." The type of thinker represented by Barthes will always stand in hostile opposition to "the man whose mind was made up and who, therefore, died" (Wallace Stevens). It has been fashionable in the past to oppose the amoral "aesthete" to the ethical "moralist," the "dandy" to the "thinker." But it is clear, as one reads Barthes entire, that his devotion to the aesthetic was not only a natural inclination but also a fully ethical commitment. The aesthetic, by having an inherent plurality of language, tone, and viewpoint, defends the mind against its own premature anxiety for closure. A mind like that of Barthes, attuned to the aesthetic, accepts its own transiency in the procession of historical belief and rejoices in its own capacity for incorporating, over its lifetime, more than a single truth.

6

The Hunting of Wallace Stevens: Critical Approaches

It is just over thirty years since Wallace Stevens died. Those of us who wrote on Stevens during his lifetime or within the first ten or fifteen years after his death were occupied in sorting out what his wonderful constructions — tempting, seductive, solacing, impertinent, resistant, teasing — were up to. We learned his language, and instructed others in its odd grammar and lexicon. It was a delightful period, in which his poems were still fresh and (especially the later ones) relatively unknown. It was also a time of preliminary evaluations: Was Stevens good? great? original? or reactionary? conservative? derivative? Was he the dandy and hedonist that Yvor Winters thought him? the elephant to which Randall Jarrell compared him?

Opinion has always been rather sharply divided on Stevens, both as a poet and as a man. As a poet, he tends to write second-order poems. First-order poems (this distinction is a crude one) have a first-person, narrative base ("I went out to the hazel wood"); second-order poems reflect on that first-order plane ("Doing a filthy pleasure is, and short"). Indeed the distinction is so crude as to be false, because all good poetry pretending to be first-order poetry ("I did X, I thought Y") is in fact implicitly second-order poetry by virtue of its having arranged its first-order narrative in a certain shape; the shape is the implicit second-order reflection made manifest. Nonetheless, for crude purposes we can say that there are many poems of the pure second order, which either do not exhibit a visible first-order human narrative, or exhibit it in a subordinate or oblique way. Such poems are most digestible when they imitate prose and treat familiar subjects ("The expense of spirit in a waste of shame / Is lust in action"). But they are baffling to the ordinary reader when they enact the thinking of thoughts, or the sensing of sensations, or the supposing of suppositions (activities for which we do not have the usual narrative plots).

Stevens was particularly interested in such activities, and in the moments when things were coming to be or turning away from what they had been. Those "insolid billowings" of change are of course quite as much a part of "life" as narratively marked events, incidents, or endings in the life of action. Stevens loved

> The first wick of night, the stellar summering
> At three-quarters gone, the morning's prescience.

For readers who want to find in poetry robust "real-life" events, decided opinions, political platforms, or wounded outcries, Stevens is disappointing. John Berryman — certainly a man delighted by poetry — could not find it in his heart to give unreserved praise to Stevens. Berryman's own *Dream Songs* made up a long first-order autobiography, a series of explicit disasters accompanied by their own tragicomic outcries. Stevens's preference for the poem as a projection of experience onto another plane, rather than as a narrative of experience, seemed to Berryman to take the force out of poetry, to rob it of its capacity to wound, to take it from the realm of physics to the realm of metaphysics. And Berryman's mixed feelings leave a sting in his elegy on Stevens (#219 of the *Dream Songs*). It is the best short brief against Stevens. (In it Berryman calls Stevens a "crow" because Stevens chose crows, grackles, and blackbirds as symbols of his darkened and angular eccentric music; "Henry" is Berryman's name for his own rueful id; Stevens is a "money man" among the actuaries because he was a successful surety lawyer for an insurance company.) Berryman acknowledges Stevens to be his superior as a poet, but he nonetheless finds Stevens's poems temperamentally uncongenial:

> He lifted up among the actuaries,
> a grandee cow. Ah ha and he crowed good.
> That funny money-man.
> Mutter we all must as well as we can.
> He mutter spiffy. He make wonder Henry's
> wit, tho, with a odd

> . . . something . . . something . . . not there in his
>   flourishing art.
> O veteran of death, you will not mind
> a counter-mutter.
> What was it missing, then, at the man's heart
> so that he does not wound? It is our kind
> to wound, as well as utter
>
> a fact of happy world. That metaphysics
> he hefted up until we could not breathe
> the physics. *On our side,*
> monotonous (or ever-fresh) — it sticks
> in Henry's throat to judge — brilliant, he seethe;
> better than us; less wide.

Berryman's view — "better than us; less wide" — is common even among those who write on Stevens. Something in Stevens seems remote, enigmatic, indecipherable, even inhuman to many readers. I believe this comes from the relative absence in his work of first-order poems.

And yet the necessary distance between a poem and its occasion in life has been constantly explained by poets. Shakespeare and Dickinson both resorted to comparing a poem to perfume; you cannot see the meadow, you cannot see the flower, you cannot see the petals — yet the scent is redolent of the vanished reality. Elizabeth Bishop resorted to the analogy of a map; the poem resembles life as the graphic curved hook called "Cape Cod" resembles Cape Cod. Stevens himself was attracted to Picasso's phrase calling a painting "a hoard of destructions" — a phrase emphasizing the artist's need to dismantle "reality" before rearranging it (in no matter how "life-like" a way) in art. But because mimetic or illusionistic art conceals its destructions and its rearrangements, its immediate, "wounding" nature seems "real," whereas an art exposing its own strategies — and its own nature as second-order arrangement — always seems "cold" or "narrow" or "rarefied" to the spectator preferring the direct impact of successful mimesis. In Stevens, a reflexive intelligence that cannot evade a knowledge of its own processes is always present. Profound feeling, sustained intelligence, whimsical self-derision, and a discipline of aesthetic outline coexist in Stevens, but not in all his readers.

A few years ago, the Huntington Library acquired from Holly Stevens, the poet's daughter, what remains of Stevens's books, manuscripts, and letters (together with family photographs and other memorabilia). A second era of Stevens studies then began, an era in which explication could be aided by scholarship, all of it dependent, of course, on Holly Stevens's own original editing of her father's letters, journals, and poems. Using the Huntington materials and information collected orally (chiefly by the late Peter Brazeau) scholars have attempted new accounts of Stevens, notably a short critical life by Milton Bates, a set of loosely connected essays by George Lensing, and a psychoanalytically flavored biography by Joan Richardson (a first volume of two).

Milton Bates's book, *Wallace Stevens: A Mythology of Self* (1986), is by all odds the most enjoyable of the three. It is stylish, readable, interesting, and refreshingly intelligent. It also corrects various misapprehensions about Stevens — for instance the notion that Stevens was indifferent to the social order. Bates shows, in his careful examination of Stevens's poetry of the Twenties and Thirties and early Forties, the degree of Stevens's awareness of, and changing response to, social reality. (By the time World War II was ending, Stevens was sixty-five, his formative period long behind him; it is not to be expected that he would be so deeply engaged then as in the Thirties, when he had to come to terms with Marxist demands on art.) In the Thirties, Stevens arrived at the position Walter Benjamin articulated in "The Author as Producer" — that ideological content is not the measure of revolution in art. Rather, Benjamin says, it is the new possibilities of technique (arrangement of content in new collocations, montages, juxtapositions, endings) that define a fresh beginning. *"An author who teaches writers nothing, teaches no one"*: "What matters, therefore, is the exemplary character of production, which is able first to induce other producers to produce, and second to put an improved apparatus at their disposal . . . [This train of thought] presents to the writer only one demand, the demand to *think*, to reflect on his position in the process of production." Among the writers to whom Stevens has taught new possibilities, one could name Elizabeth Bishop, Howard Nemerov, Charles Tomlinson, John Ashbery, W. S. Merwin, Mark Strand, Louise Glück, Charles Wright, and Jorie Graham (no doubt there are many others). These writers have explored the imaginative, formal, lexical, and rhetorical possibilities opened by Stevens; they have benefited from his sense of the poem as enacted mental process rather than as statement or narrative.

Bates describes Stevens's life as a search for an adequate "mythology of self." Stevens, he argues, "had perforce to shape his image and likeness from materials that lay ready to hand," and so biographical information is brought to bear, deftly and sensibly, as Bates treats Stevens successively as youth, lover, "burgher, fop, and clown," "pure poet," political poet, and inventor of both "medium man" and "major man" (the heroic ideal, so named by Stevens). Bates calls "major man" (invented by Stevens largely in response to World War II) "the most daring and ambitious of Stevens's personae, the cynosure of his mythology of self," while conceding that major man is not necessarily "the most convincing of Stevens's mythic figures."

There is a will to idealism in Stevens's "major man," a will to nobility remarked on by John Crowe Ransom in a letter quoted by Bates. Stevens refused to let Knopf use Ransom's words as a blurb, taking the position that any defining statement freezes poetry into immobility. For Stevens, to be alive was, above all, to change. "Living changingness" ("Notes Toward a Supreme Fiction") accounted for the several successive selves sketched and illustrated by Bates, as the provincial boy from Reading became, in turn, the Harvard man, the New York man, the legal man, the American poet, *l'homme moyen sensuel,* the heroic man, the filial man. Bates's inevitably simplifying but nonetheless roughly accurate summary reads:

> In the early poetry, Stevens had cultivated a variety of outlandish poses, appearing as aesthete, dandy, and clown or projecting such figures onto the stage of his imagination. These dramatis personae constitute what Joseph Riddel has rightly called "a self (or many faces and gestures of a self) in emergence." Together with the hero of his middle period, they enabled him to surpass or extend his limited experience as the son of a lawyer, later a lawyer himself, living in comfortable middle-class surroundings . . . In the late poetry, he turns from the exotic to the homely, from dandified clowns and masterful heroes to figures resembling his own parents and, as in a glass darkly, the God of his boyhood and youth.

Though one could quarrel with one or the other interpretation in Bates's discussion of particular poems, his sense of Stevens's aim is a secure one. He feels its risks, he measures its daring, he recognizes its triumphs. Perhaps, in seeing it chiefly as a way of *conceiving* poetry, he slights it as a way of *making* poetry. If, as he grants, "major man" is not Stevens's best moment of making, then perhaps a different history of the Stevensian imagination is possible, where the summit of making poetry, not of conceiving it, would be the high point.

Bates's admiration for heroic conceptions, for a dimension larger than the human, makes him decide to give some credence, and even some importance, to the unsupported account by the Reverend Arthur P. Hanley (given a quarter-century after the supposed fact) of Stevens's "conversion" to Roman Catholicism, and his baptism, during the very last days before his death from cancer. (There are no supporting witnesses of this account. Holly Stevens, who was at the hospital daily, knows nothing of its having occurred. The baptism was never recorded, at the time or later, though Catholic baptisms are normally recorded. Stevens was no doubt sedated, as one dying in 1955 of internal cancer was likely to have been. Father Hanley's recollections may be inexact, or exaggerated by the passage of time.)

Father Hanley's explanation for the absence of any record of the baptism, given to Professor Bates, was that "the archbishop of the Archdiocese of Hartford requested that Stevens's baptism not be recorded or made public lest people think that Saint Francis Hospital actively sought to convert non-Catholic patients." But a private record made in a parish registry would not have drawn public attention; and it is not explained how the archbishop would have become aware of the putative happenings in the hospital. Perhaps future biographers will tend to find Stevens's daughter the more reliable witness of her father's last days. In any case, the lifework had been brought to a close before Stevens's last days in the hospital, and any judgment on Stevens's work must find irrelevant those events occurring after it was complete.

Bates's book has real distinction. It is free of cant, padding, and special pleading. It has a shape, and a pace, and a sense of nuance appropriate to the poems it takes up. This book is certainly the first one to give to a new reader of Stevens. "I particularly address these pages," says Bates in his preface, "to students in and out of the university whose interest and good will have been balked by the difficulties of Stevens's poetry and the sometimes more formidable difficulties of Stevens criticism." I hope that a new generation of readers, brought up on this book, will recognize that the naive canards about Stevens — that he was a heartless hedonist, an ivory-tower poet insensitive to social distress, a cold, over-cerebral aesthete, a poetic conservative, and so on — are all untrue. Bates's book rightly describes Stevens as a poet constantly enlarging the self, a revolutionary imagining new aesthetic possibilities not only for himself but for future poets, aware of social unrest, passionately concerned with the accurate way of conceiving the artist's role in the social order, evaluating the claims of Marx, Freud, and Nietzsche long before most members of his generation, a man of restless self-scrutiny and deep feeling.

George Lensing's study, *Wallace Stevens* (1986), which makes good use of the Huntington materials, is subtitled *A Poet's Growth*. After retelling the relatively familiar story of how Stevens became a poet and a modernist, Lensing moves to his central interests — Stevens's "peculiar habits of composition; . . . his use of notebooks, epigraphs derived from reading, and the extensive personal correspondence that brought the world to Hartford, from which Stevens only rarely strayed." Lensing has other valuable chapters (notably one on the importance to Stevens of Harriet Monroe's encouragement in his early, lonely years). But I want to emphasize here his brilliant account of the uses to Stevens of writing and receiving letters. Unsympathetic critics have seen Stevens's requests to his correspondents for Ceylon tea or French art catalogs as the dilettante amusements of a rich man. Lensing sees them for what they were — the authentic food for a starved imagination, longing to know what it would be to stand in a Paris gallery, to see elephants in Ceylon. Stevens's correspondence with a Cuban poet or with a Korean student of poetry permitted him to experience in Hartford what Pound (or even Frost) experienced in Europe and England — the delight of the imagination in unfamiliar things, landscapes, fragrances, pictures, words. As Stevens said in a letter quoted by Lensing: "My experience . . . has taken place in a very limited space. It means a lot to me to know a man in Dublin, to receive letters from a friend in Italy, to look at the map of Spain [where his friend Barbara Church was traveling] and to find that it suddenly becomes as minutely significant as the map of Connecticut." The appearance in the poems of items, landscapes, names, and words from abroad testifies to the nourishment provided by the correspondence. Stevens had longed to go to Europe; prevented first by his father and later by his wife ("a terrible traveler, and constantly carsick or seasick whenever she went anywhere," according to Holly Stevens), he found "the heaven of Europe" in letters and objects.

Lensing's most interesting chapter makes public the contents of a notebook belonging to Stevens entitled "From Pieces of Paper." Lensing makes the reasonable supposition that Stevens jotted down phrases, titles, and *pensées* on pieces of paper, at work or while walking or traveling, and later transcribed them into this notebook. Many of the phrases reappear as titles of published poems. Many others are titles for poems that were never written, or never preserved. How one longs to have the poems called "An American Monster," "The Halo That Would Not Light," "Aultres Dieux," "Revolution against the Rose," "Morgue Near Heaven," "A Jackass in His Own Clothes," "We Are All Indians," "Black Gloves for the Bishop," "Fame & Fright," and "Pax, Ajax, and the Crocuses." There are 361 phrases in all. What the notebook proves is that for Stevens the title was a third-order encapsulation summing up the other two orders — of experience, of poetry — preceding (or following) it. Among the titles he did use, for instance, was "No Possum, No Sop, No Taters." That is the encapsulation of the following second-order scene which opens the poem:

> He is not here, the old sun,
> As absent as if we were asleep.
>
> The field is frozen. The leaves are dry.
> Bad is final in this light.
>
> In this bleak air the broken stalks
> Have arms without hands. They have trunks
>
> Without legs or, for that, without heads.
> They have heads in which a captive cry
>
> Is merely the moving of a tongue.
> Snow sparkles like eyesight falling to earth,
>
> Like seeing fallen brightly away.
> The leaves hop, scraping on the ground.
>
> It is deep January. The sky is hard.
> The stalks are firmly rooted in ice.

These stanzas render a first-order human experience through a second-order image of a frozen field. The first-order experience, we deduce, must have been one of immobility, sterility, mutilation, and muteness. Stevens's characteristic way of writing was to take his worst first-order experiences, find an impersonal second-order vehicle for them ("The field is frozen"), write in the second order as though it (and not his experience) were the governing subject, and then sum up the whole with an ironic, deprecatory, and oblique title (here the rural phrase, "possum, sop and taters" used by Stevens as well in a 1940 letter quoted by Peter Brazeau). The bleak field of broken stalks and captive cries, and the nameless personal bleakness that created it, were both summarized for Stevens in the rough graffito of the title.

If these are the three Stevenses — the ironist of the title, the landscapist of the symbolic weather, and the historic sufferer of inner mutilation and captivity — it follows that a biographer might want to include all three. The known facts of Stevens's life (by comparison, say, to a life like Byron's) are relatively few, though not so few as to preclude a conventional biography. Joan Richardson's two-volume biography attempts to represent the three Stevenses — and it will certainly be the fullest repository, when it is complete, of facts (major and minor) and quotations relevant to Stevens's life. Richardson is really writing three books at once — a factual biography using the Huntington materials and some cultural history (unfortunately of the potted sort); a study of Stevens's sources; and a psychoanalytic reading of Stevens's inner life. The first volume, published in 1986, is entitled *Wallace Stevens: The Early Years, 1879–1923*; it takes Stevens to the publication, at forty-four, of his first book. Since most of the important biographical facts of this period are known (though filled out here with more quotation), Richardson is staking her book on her sensitivity to what Stevens drew from his reading and on her own analytic readings of his letters and poems.

I was glad to have Stevens's reading reassembled from his brief references to it in letters and journals. It is here summarized, quoted from, and linked (sometimes convincingly, sometimes not) to his writings. Some day there will be an intellectual biography of Stevens (based not on the life but on the poems and letters and essays), and the writer of that biography will find Richardson's reminders of Stevens's reading (from Arnold to Buddhism) helpful. Stevens's own intellectual positions are both remarkably elusive and remarkably precise: elusive because concerned with perception and feeling, precise because they fix and meditate on very subtle points of accord and discord which are not categorized in the coarser taxonomy of psychology.

It is not surprising that Richardson's psychoanalytic account comes down to one that we have heard before: Oedipal rivalry with the father and elder brother; a struggle to integrate the female and male principles; a search for the ideal parent in the choice of a spouse; an ambivalence toward the rival claims of internalized parental values. Even if all such deductions were wholly true, they can never seem other than reductive as the history of a mind, an imagination, and a set of original poems. Criticism and psychobiography are fairly incompatible arts, since psychobiography goes from a set of symptoms in language ("a frozen field," "broken stalks") to the emotional cause, while criticism goes from the cursorily perceived cause ("a landscape poem about feeling mutilated and mute") to the differentiated components. The critic asks what Stevens is doing here with the presence or absence of definite and indefinite articles, how he is articulating his chosen objects, why and how the poem is made to shift structural gears, and so on. Of course there is an ideal horizon where these two parallels would converge, but in fact one's interest must tend in one direction or the other, and so a biography of the psyche and a biography of the art can rarely be combined.

Richardson's biography seems to me, for all its earnestness of endeavor, tone-deaf, awkward, and turgid. It is marked, too, by a frequent vulgarity of tone that makes me distrust the author's own ear, and by solecisms that put in question her ability to follow Stevens's use of language, with its seemingly infinite gradations. I will cite a very few samples (the book has almost six hundred pages, and there is scarcely one unmarred by bad writing).

Stevens would not have become the successful lawyer he did, nor would he have been able to set down the subtle arguments folded into his poems like those unheard melodies sweeter still that jazz musicians hear in their mind's ear as they play the riffs around them, had he not honed the tool of reason to murderous possibilities. (p. 20)

To present an in-depth analysis of Stevens's dialogue with any one of these figures would itself be a healthy volume. (p. 23)

[Garrett Stevens, the poet's father, courting his mother Kate] no doubt impressed her as someone to whom she could entrust her spirit as well as her physical well-being. And, as someone having a similar family background as she, Kate could be fairly certain of their fundamental agreement . . . (p. 40)

Her youth and the inadequacy of her education mitigated [*sic*] against her being able to see herself with eyes that did not share the common view. (pp. 232–233)

He filled out . . . his developing thought by nosing into other works . . . [In his journal] there were also illustrations of the use of words from his nosings in the dictionary . . . He had already begun nosing toward the East himself . . . (pp. 236, 241, 278)

Unlike his response to Dickinson, Stevens was at first put off by More . . . He indicated how Christianity's idealization of the eternal feminine extended Plato's eschewing of the senses. (pp. 245, 247)

Though his relative inaccessibility and difficulty were frequently blamed on this, often called his cerebral quality, quite ironically, wanting to make himself as universally accessible as possible was Stevens's implicit intellectual rationale for choosing structures of argument and terms of reference drawn from the vocabulary of pure reason. (p. 472)

These, as Stevens would have said, are merely instances. But they do, with their psycho-speak, their solecisms, their syntactic lumbering, their bathos, and their mixed metaphors, suggest that the mind producing them is not the mind to move along Stevens's sinuous tracks.

What is more serious is Richardson's frequent misunderstandings of Stevens's theoretical positions. I can cite only one: she is convinced that the distinction Stevens draws between the "true subject" of a poem and "the poetry of the subject" corresponds to the psychoanalytic distinction she draws between the infantile kernel (as she sees it) of a poem — "the fears and uncertainties of the boy who still crouched inside him" — and what she refers to as the "surface of his words' appearance." Richardson then sees a discrepancy and concealment between surface and feeling, and describes the construction of a poem as follows: "It allowed him *to hide beneath a 'piano-polished' surface . . . thoughts and feelings that would have been considered indecorous or, at least, inappropriate to one raised as a 'good Puritan.'* This split also reflected the American dissociation of sensibility that began with the first Puritans *giving the rhetorical lie to the truth of their experience.*" (Italics added.) This may be what one kind of psychoanalytic thinking makes of writing poetry — but it is not what poets like Stevens write poetry for. They write poetry to be as explicit as possible, to be absolutely accurate, to make a point-for-point map of a mental form. It would therefore be impossible for Stevens to suggest that the "true subject" was indecorous feelings which he wanted to hide, or that "the poetry of the subject" was the rhetorical lie, the polished surface, enabling the cover-up. In the late essay "The Irrational Element in Poetry," where Stevens draws the distinction between "the true subject" and "the poetry of the subject," the true subject he instances (alluding to a paragraph of Edith Sitwell's) is "the brilliance and color of an impression" that the artist is caught up by. He adds that "the poets who most urgently search the world for the sanctions of life, for that which makes life so prodigiously worth living, may find their solutions in a duck in a pond or in the wind on a winter night." That duck, that wind, are the "true subject." The *rendering* of the duck (alone? with others? still? moving? close up? from a distance? in quatrains? in couplets? elegiacally? comically?) is "the poetry of the subject." Neither the "true subject" (which one might call the elected symbol) nor "the poetry of the subject" (its manner of rendering) has to do, for Stevens, with psychic kernels or any putative boy crouched eternally inside him. Stevens was quite willing to speak of feelings and poetry — but feelings were antecedent, in the emotional life, to either the subject or the poetry of the subject.

It follows that Richardson's book will not satisfy as an account of Stevens as a poet. Nor is it a biography of him conceived in his character as a poet. The extreme heroism of his poetic life — as he abandoned the received poetic of his century, vowed himself to an exhausting accuracy of registration and perception, tested his powers by examining and rejecting work he believed to be inferior, and persisted through solitude and overwork toward the creation of new forms of language — would, if it were the governing concept, produce a very different sort of biography. The heroism of writing is an unthinkable venture into the unknown, as unmapped and frightening as any voyage to the source of the Amazon, as powerful and daring in its conception as the far gaze of Pascal or the abyss of Wittgensteinian skepticism. This could be the premise of a different biography. Its tone would be one of wonder, even amazement, that the wager of genius was won against the odds of provincialism, a lifetime of responsible work, and a trying marriage.

But Richardson does not see Stevens as a hero. Instead, she wants to "follow the evolution of Stevens's consciousness" in a rather neutral way, and see him as part of "a biography of America from 1879 to 1953" (the latter very superficially done, in the event). She wants to include "weaknesses of character, offensive habits or behavior, and intimate details." These boil down to snobbery (including the verbal anti-Semitism common in his era to his class, never reaching to any thought of anti-Semitic action but nonetheless deplorable), more drinking than Richardson thinks was good for him (though she adduces no evidence to suggest it damaged his business life, his marriage, or his art), and his relationship with his wife, in which Richardson tends to sympathize with Mrs. Stevens rather more than seems warranted.

Holly Stevens has written about her mother, in *Souvenirs and Prophecies,* "All her life, at least during the time I knew her, she suffered from a persecution complex which undoubtedly originated during her childhood." Whatever the strains of living with an artist, and they are many, the strains of living with a wife with a persecution complex, unable to function socially, may well be worse. To Stevens's credit, he did not abandon his unsuitable and gloomy wife. Perhaps that is all that can be said about the marriage. Richardson analyzes minutely the idealization, tenderness, didacticism, fantasies, role-playing, and hopes for the future that Stevens expressed in the long letters he wrote to his wife during their courtship. These psychological attitudes seem to me ordinary (if somewhat repellently of their era), and could probably be found, although less elegantly expressed, in the love letters of many of Stevens's contemporaries. His beloved was his distant princess, his Little Bo-Peep, his twin "Buddy," his to-be-docile wife, his beauty on a pedestal, his Arcadian nymph. And Elsie no doubt had equally unrealistic ideas of him during their long-distance courtship, carried on while he was working in New York and she stayed at home in Reading, Pennsylvania. Richardson rightly notes that both partners were unable to compromise and work out a joint life. But surely compromise is stimulated by compatibility; and it is uncertain whether the Stevenses were incompatible in later life because they could not compromise, or whether they were unable to compromise because they were from the beginning incompatible.

One can argue that Stevens, older and better educated, should have perceived the folly of his infatuation with a girl, no matter how beautiful, who was nothing like himself in character, background, education, or taste; but his apparent virginity and lack of social experience made him as naive as his bride. The subtle air of injury maintained by Richardson ("Elsie must have suffered. She was deprived of both his physical presence and his spirit," and so on) is extended chiefly to the female side. We do not read, "Wallace must have suffered. He constantly encountered Elsie's discontented gloom, her poverty of resource, her lack of humor, her suspiciousness, her incomprehension of his language." The real horror, for a genius, of living with an uneducated, limited, suspicious, and provincial person, one who has no idea of the arduousness of his life project, is not evoked in this book. Stevens spoke of this suffering in indirect terms quite often, and it appears nakedly in "World without Peculiarity":

> The red ripeness of round leaves is thick
> With the spices of red summer.
> But she that he loved turns cold at his light touch.

Later in the poem he refers to "the hating woman."

One can see Elsie's point of view without criticizing Stevens. Biographically speaking, he seems to have married unwisely someone whom he could not, at close quarters, love. The error in youthful judgment does not amount, I think, to a fault in character. His response to his error — to withdraw into reading and writing — seems a fundamentally decent one (preferable certainly to reiterated criticism, abandonment, or infidelity). The persistent suggestion in the biography that he could have acted otherwise — could have continued to engage with, respond to, and love Elsie — seems to me sentimental.

The analysis of Stevens's character here appears mistaken or overstated in several respects. Again, I can give only one illustration. Because Stevens found Walter Arensberg's pre-Columbian art "hideous" (a fairly common response, after all, in the early years of this century, from those trained in a European sculptural aesthetic), Richardson concludes: "In terms of the overt bestiality and violence that [Stevens] despised in pre-Columbian art, contrasted with the hidden bestiality and violence in his poetry — and especially evident in *Harmonium* — his harsh judgment [is] very instructive." Since *Harmonium* does not seem to me to have an especial freight of "bestiality and violence" (more than what? than Yeats's plays? than *Les Fleurs du mal*? than Shakespeare's sonnets?), I can only await Richardson's second volume for proof that "the impulse to hurt, punish, chastise, humiliate was with him." Richardson sees this sadistic component as "inverted under the guise of self-sacrifice during his periods of asceticism," and "externalized as the macabre celebration of death and destruction in many of his poems." She also sees Stevens "transform[ing] this impulse into the verbal wit for which he was noted."

There is a slippage here from the Freudian assertion that we all possess sadistic impulses (in which case, Stevens may have had no more wish to hurt and punish than the rest of us) to a psychological reading in which Stevens has more sadism in him than the rest of us. ("The personality trait that Stevens had the greatest trouble managing was his violence, his desire to destroy.") These slippages make this biography hard to engage with. No doubt, humor or asceticism may mask or deflect sadistic impulses; but then some people (and Stevens was one) seem to be born ironists; and we think of many other earnest youths who strove for asceticism in order to be artists — Hawthorne, James, Yeats, all fellow ascetics and fellow ironists in their youth. Some breadth of reference might keep Richardson from reading too much into small details (the psychoanalytic stock in trade, in life as in art). Or perhaps Richardson would say that Hawthorne and James and Yeats are all sadists too, given their asceticism, their celebration of death, their wit and irony. The category thus becomes an empty one — since we could equally well include in it Baudelaire, Kafka, Mann, Woolf, Beckett, and who knows who else. A real biography should be engaged in distinguishing Stevens from others, not in drawing large pictures that could fit any artist from Shakespeare on.

The investigation of Stevens through his life and reading was inevitable, given the opening of the Huntington Library collection. In another hundred years, the ferment will have settled, and the life and writing, the man and the era, will come into a clearer relation. For the moment, it testifies to the power of Stevens's fortitude and originality that more and more of his readers are stirred to write about him. He may never be a popular poet, popular taste usually preferring first-order poetry, full of first-person event and emotion. And he may never be popular with another set of readers, those who mistakenly read him as a prosy poet. Stevens does not juxtapose phrasal images, after the manner of Pound and Williams. He seems to be telling rather than showing, and to a certain modern taste this seems a "conservative" form of writing.

I believe — though this is not the place to make the argument fully — that Stevens is always "showing," though not by images. Rather, he does his showing through his curious words and syntax. His articulation of thought is not (though it may at first look as if it were) Wordsworthian meditation. It is, in fact, utterly unlike Wordsworth. Wordsworth almost always uses words in their common denotative meaning, and he uses syntax for the normal purposes of syntax — momentum and organization. Stevens's words are almost always deflected from their common denotation, and his syntax serves to delay and to disarticulate (Ashbery has learned both of these practices from Stevens). The appearance of "telling" is superficially maintained (there is an iambic sentence, as in Wordsworth, spilling down the page), but one gets nowhere reading Stevens in a Wordsworthian spirit. The assertions, the language, and the syntax are all too preposterous for that:

> We make, although inside an egg,
> Variations on the words spread sail.
>
> The morning glories grow in the egg.
> It is full of the myrrh and camphor of summer
>
> And Adirondack glittering. The cat hawks it
> And the hawk cats it and we say spread sail.

Whatever this is in the Forties, it is not conservative discursive writing. Here, as elsewhere, Stevens's art is always about to refresh itself at the well of nonsense. Sound for him is the locus of the primitive, as sight was for Pound. What an image was to Pound, a syllable was to Stevens. There is no need to judge one form of the primitive to be superior to another. What is certain is that every great poet touches both a primitive and a hierophantic note. And it is that reach in poetry toward a double horizon of language — toward "infant A standing on infant legs" and toward "twisted, stooping, polymathic Z" that readers of all tastes ultimately look for. For some readers — and their number seems to be increasing — Stevens's poetry is one of the places to find it.

II

On Poetry

7

Lionel Trilling and Wordsworth's Immortality Ode

Lionel Trilling wrote more often about prose than about poetry, but he had a deeply felt relation with at least two poets — Arnold and Wordsworth. What he loved in them was their moral insight: in one of the most autobiographical of his essays, he compares the writings of Wordsworth with the *Pirke Aboth*, a collection of Hebrew wisdom-writing that he read as a boy. It is not surprising, then, that when he wrote in *The Liberal Imagination* about Wordsworth's Immortality Ode (as he called it for convenience) his purpose was to defend the Ode from what he regarded as moral misrepresentation. He disliked the view that the Ode is "Wordsworth's conscious farewell to his art": "I believe the 'Ode' is not only not a dirge sung over departing powers, but actually a dedication to new powers." The "new powers" Trilling identifies as a "greater sensitivity and responsiveness" because "the 'philosophic mind' has not decreased but, on the contrary, increased the power to feel." The "new poetic subject matter" which Trilling finds implied in the Ode is tragedy — though he adds that Wordsworth was, in the event, incapable of writing the tragic verse announced in the Ode.

I take up Trilling's essay in part to dispute its conclusions, but also to ask to what degree its assumptions and methods are suited to the art of poetry. What, for Trilling, was poetry? It was — and this is the strangest of his assumptions — something other than, and less than, life. "Those critics," he says with considerable emphasis, "who . . . make the Ode relate only to poetical powers . . . conceive the Ode to be a lesser thing than it really is, for it is not about poetry, it is about life." A poet would scarcely assent to such a distinction; for poets, to make poetry is one of the modes of living, one of the ways in which life manifests itself. For Wordsworth especially, to create is to live, to become that "sensitive being" and "creative soul" for whom the essence of living is responding and creating.

Trilling's second assumption about a poem is that it is at heart a discursive statement, in which the author says what he means and means what he says, line by line: a poem is a statement "about something." The Ode is "about growing up," Trilling decides, and to judge by his description the Ode might be an essay or a homily: "The first [of the two stanzas] *tells us* . . . the second movement . . . *tells us again* . . . the rainbow epigraph also *says* . . . Wordsworth *says* . . . he *says* . . . he *mentions* . . . Wordsworth *is speaking of a period* . . . Wordsworth *is talking about something* common to us all" (italics added). The phrases Trilling uses are proper to a notion of the poem as an utterance *à haute voix,* something close to moral instruction from a pulpit. The objections to such a view are familiar, but I must mention them briefly. Trilling's attitude fails to separate a poet's *intention* (which is often that of providing moral instruction, poets being only human) from his *accomplishment,* an accomplishment which separates the poet from common moral instructors — those who have not, as they uttered their instructions, composed a great poem. Secondly, such a view assumes that a poem is a discourse rather than an action; and thirdly, such a view takes no heed of Lawrence's famous warning — to trust not the teller but the tale. In his trust of his teller, in his use of a static discursive model, and in his failure to distinguish Wordsworth's mode from other modes of moral instruction, Trilling detaches the sentiments of the Ode from the only medium in which they can live, the medium of their language.

Assuming that Trilling is right, and that the Ode is not an elegy for youth but a poem about growing up, why, we may ask, should we prize it or listen to it? Its "message," as Trilling decodes it, is by no means a new one, though it is suffused, in Trilling's presentation, by a then-fashionable Freudian aura. Wordsworth is, like all of us, says Trilling, ambivalent about the losses and gains of growing up: "Inevitably we resist change and turn back with passionate nostalgia to the stage we are leaving. Still, we fulfill ourselves by choosing what is painful and difficult and necessary, and we develop by moving toward death. In short, organic development is a hard paradox which Wordsworth is stating in the discrepant answers of the second part of the Ode." The "hard paradox" of "organic development" is not a new doctrine, but is rather one of the staples of both religious and secular literature. If any version of this "hard paradox" will do, of what particular value is Wordsworth's? Trilling imputes a virtue to Wordsworth's presentation of ambivalence, but when he adds that we find other examples of this ambivalence at leaving Eden (for instance in Milton and his creation Adam) he implies that Wordsworth is simply one of a long line of authors who present us with the pains and rewards of growth.

Adequacy to the complexity of experience is certainly one — but only one — of the criteria by which we judge great literature. It is disquieting how indistinguishable the Ode becomes, in Trilling's description, from an essay by Emerson or a lecture by Arnold. It is true that the moral conception of great art on which Trilling's writing is based is one found commonly among his American and English critical predecessors: "It is not by the mode of representing and saying, but by what is represented and said," says Ruskin in *Modern Painters*, "that the respective greatness either of the painter or the writer is to be finally determined." And yet, for all his insistence on content, Ruskin rarely embarks on a set of remarks about an artist without making us feel the liveliest sense of the individual painter's manner as he perceives it. Here he is on Turner's representations of "the force of agitated water":

> He never loses himself and his subject in the splash of the fall, his presence of mind never fails as he goes down; he does not blind us with the spray, or veil the countenance of his fall with its own drapery . . . Thus, in the Upper Fall of the Tees, though the whole basin of the fall is blue and dim with the rising vapour, yet the attention of the spectator is chiefly directed to the concentric zones and delicate curves of the falling water itself; and it is impossible to express with what exquisite accuracy these are given.

In this description — which praises Turner's capacity to show airy smoke and foam without losing the structural concentric zones and curves behind the spray, and which admires Turner's combination of receptivity with presence of mind, of mimetic power with power of composition — Ruskin, without forgetting the sublimity of Turner's subject, remarks the finest details of Turner's conception and execution. Trilling does not seem to feel a comparable relish; he feels no impulse to delight in Wordsworth's invention or his manner. There is no mention in Trilling's essay of the large aesthetic problems —

of scale, focus, perspective, structure, climax, and dénouement — solved by Wordsworth in the Ode, nor is there any admiring lingering on the smaller means — the registers of diction, the allusions, the internal cross-referencing, the sequence of events — by which local effects are given meaning. By addressing the import rather than the being of the poem, Trilling deprives us of any reason to believe in its assertions. Surely, even in poetry, perhaps especially in poetry, we do not believe assertions because they are asserted. If we are to assent to Wordsworth's "hard paradox" — that (in Trilling's version) "we develop by moving toward death" — it is because something *in the poem* compels our assent. It is not, as Trilling thinks, something in us that compels that assent. Wordsworth, says Trilling, "is speaking of a period common to the development of everyone," and "critics who make the Ode refer to some particular and unique experience of Wordsworth's and who make it relate only to poetical powers have forgotten their own lives." This sort of remark imposes a false criterion of universality upon poetry. It is not necessary that the poet's experience should exactly resemble our own; it is enough if we find some analogy between the growth of the poet's mind and the growth of our own, nonpoetic mind. But we should not be surprised if poetry about the growth of the poet's mind has special reference to the well-being of his creative powers.

If Trilling's method is insufficient to the Ode, what can be presented to supplement it? For I too believe with Trilling that the Ode "succeeds," that we "believe" Wordsworth's assertion that the possession of the "philosophic mind" is a greater good than the former possession of the lost "glory." I differ with Trilling, however, in the interpretation of the nature of the philosophic mind and of its powers. I do not believe that the philosophic mind can be said to have "increased the power to feel." Rather, the philosophic mind has enabled the composition of poetry, a quite different matter. The child who saw the visionary gleam was not a poet; he was not even a writer. He saw; he was; he existed in pure apprehension and pure feeling. I do not believe it to be true that "the knowledge of man's mortality . . . replaces the 'glory' as the agency which makes *things* significant and precious." Rather, the capacity to make natural things into metaphors of human life — the poet's gift, as Aristotle said — confers on those natural things an aura replacing the lost aura of celestial light. What the child cannot do, the poet can do — that is, he can see in every natural phenomenon an echo or mirror of the moral life of the human self:

I love the Brooks which down their channels *fret,*
Even more than *when I tripped lightly as they*;
The *innocent* brightness of a *new-born* Day
                Is lovely yet;
The Clouds that *gather round* the setting sun
Do take a *sober* colouring from an eye
That hath kept watch o'er man's mortality.

The eye that has seen the child "fretted" by its mother's kisses can perceive the brooks as "fretting"; the man remembering his own light tripping as a child can say of the brooks that they too "trip lightly"; the adult who has called a new-born child innocent can transfer the epithets "new-born" and "innocent" to a bright dawn; the eye that has kept a death-vigil can compare the clouds in a sunset to the watchers "gathering round" a deathbed, and can, by the metaphor of the deathwatch, confer a "sober colouring" on a sunset panorama which to the pure seeing of the visionary child would have represented simply a lively play of vivid sky-hues. The child, for all his possession of the visionary gleam, cannot say that the brooks "trip lightly" or "fret," or that the day is "new-born" and "innocent," or that the clouds which "gather round" the sun have a "sober" coloring. Not the knowledge of mortality alone, but the reflective knowledge of one's own life, informs these metaphors. But the truly important thing about them is that they are metaphors. Everything in the world — everything — now reminds the adult Wordsworth of some aspect of human experience. He can no longer see a flower as the child in the Prelude (II) sees it. A fine passage in Trilling's essay describes the child's seeing: "He does not perceive things merely as objects, he first sees them, because maternal love is a condition of his perception, as objects-and-judgments, as valued objects. He does not learn about a flower, but about the pretty-flower, the flower that-I-want-and-that-mother-will-get-for-me . . . but the objects he sees are not in utter darkness." This is probably as adequate a description of the psychological cause of the "glory" as one can give: but Trilling does not remark that the child's perception can as yet have no pathos of self-reference. The child cannot say, "the flower is innocent as I am innocent," or "the flower grows as I grow." Only with the advent of reflectiveness can metaphor arise. And it is the capacity for metaphor — for the drawing of analogies between natural emblems and human events — that is celebrated in the conclusion of the Ode. The child feels intensely — "the fullness of your bliss, I feel — I feel it all," says Wordsworth to the child, protesting too much. Noone can *feel* more strongly than the child. But one can *love* more strongly than the child does. "I love the brooks . . . *even more*," says Wordsworth. As a child he loved them, as he loved the sun, for their beauty; now, as an adult, he loves them more because they remind him, in their light and joyous motion, of his own careless steps as a child. The dawn was lovely to him when he was a child; it is "lovely yet" because it seems the emblem of all new-born and innocent things. "A child, I loved the sun," but now the adult can confer things on nature, not merely receive impressions from it; the clouds take a coloring from his eye. What else is metaphor but a conferral of colors on the neutral world, an introduction of pathos where before there was only fact?

If every object in the adult poet's eye thus becomes weighty with possible meditation, he is no longer a stranger in the world, longing hopelessly for the "imperial palace whence he came." He has become, instead, naturalized in the world, as all its parts become colored by the feeling eye. This new analogizing habit of mind grows up imperceptibly, but eventually it becomes an habitual mode of vision. Wordsworth's aesthetic problem in the ode is to find languages appropriate to each of three stages described in the poem — the stage of "glory" and "obstinate questioning"; the stage of loss; and the stage of metaphor. Ideally he must express — and we must be made to feel — the full reality of each stage. If he fails to do justice to any portion of his psychological journey, then readers, trusting not the teller but the tale, will be tempted to "believe" in one stage more than in another. Those critics whom Trilling wishes to refute — those who see the Ode as a dirge over departing powers — clearly "believe" in the rendition of the stages of glory and loss, but give less credence to the final repossession of the world by metaphor. Trilling's suggestion — that such critics could not read Wordsworth's plain declaration of compensatory value — does not seem credible. It is more plausible to say that those who read the Ode as a dirge have decided that Wordsworth's closing protestations ring false; and not all of Trilling's insistence on the "hard necessity" of "growing up" will convince them if Wordsworth's own words did not.

I should like to look at Wordsworth's "languages" for his three states in order to address this discrepancy of conviction between Trilling and the critics he attempts to refute. It is through religious language that Wordsworth at first describes his childhood: the light is "celestial," the gleam is "visionary," and "there hath past away a glory from the earth" — an ironic echo of Jesus' prophecy, "Heaven and earth shall pass away, but my words shall not pass away." The child comes from *God*, trailing clouds of *glory*; as a youth, he is still attended by the *vision* splendid, and is Nature's *priest*. The child lives with Immortality brooding over him like the Spirit who dove-like sat brooding o'er the vast abyss; his freedom is *heaven-born*; he is a *prophet* and a *seer*, a *Soul* in the "eternal Silence." Now this vocabulary comes from the most powerful cluster of poetic words, images, and concepts in English, the King James Bible (as transmitted, moreover, through Milton). All these lavish resources of language are spent on the initial rendition of the first stage, the stage of glory. It is no wonder that critics brought up — in home, school, and church — to believe this world of religious discourse superior to all others found this part of the poem irresistible. Wordsworth had dared to clothe the experience of his own human childhood in the most sublime of literary modes, the mode of revealed religion. If the earthly paradise has been transformed, in Wordsworth as in Milton, to "a paradise within," it only renders the archetypal loss of Eden more painful. Wordsworth has not been expelled; it is his sight which has been darkened: those things which he has seen he now can see no more. The paradox resides in the double use of "see": the things both are and are not still there. Wordsworth departs from tradition in showing the non-Edenic world not as "wild woods forlorn" but as wholly beautiful to *the neutrally aesthetic eye* which sees only natural forms; at best this eye, a noncreative one, uses personifications well worn into cliché:

> The Rainbow comes and goes
> And *lovely* is the Rose,
> The Moon doth *with delight*
> Look round her when the heavens are bare;
> Waters on a starry night
> Are *beautiful and fair*;
> The sunshine is a *glorious birth*.

The whole substance of the poem lies in Wordsworth's transition from this inherited language, springing solely from the eye, to the language of the concluding lines of the poem, which springs from the heart and is never without human reference. "The innocent brightness of a new-born Day is lovely yet," says the final voice, and we are meant to recognize the difference between the pathos of that statement and one which says that the rose is lovely and that the sunshine is a glorious birth.

In the midst of Wordsworth's religious language describing human childhood, two metaphors stand out in a discrepancy which will become useful in enabling his passage to the stage of loss. The original radiant experience is called a "dream," and our place of origin, elsewhere named "heaven," is represented as an "imperial palace." "Dream," invoking illusion rather than religious vision, hints at the inevitability of waking; the palace, in its haughtiness ("imperial," though suggested by "empyreal," remains a hierarchical word) foreshadows by contrast the humanizing process to come. These slight tremblings of diction away from the religious premise presage the imminent crumbling of Wordsworth's rapt first language of isolation and spectatorship.

A *frisson* of another sort arises as into the pastoral scenery there intrudes a new language like some overture to a later, as yet unannounced, drama of strength in the poem. After the relief brought by the "timely utterance" (which Trilling, for his own "growing up" thesis, decides, without much in the way of support, was not "My Heart Leaps Up" but "Resolution and Independence"), Wordsworth's vista enlarges beyond the lambs, the birds, and the accompanying rose, rainbow, and sunshine:

> I again am strong:
> The cataracts blow their trumpets from the steep;
> No more shall grief of mine the season wrong;
> I hear the echoes through the mountains throng,
> The winds come to me from the fields of sleep.

The resolve — "No more shall grief of mine the season wrong" — is, as we know, premature: but Wordsworth's instinct toward strength (later reappearing in the variant "We will *grieve* not, rather find / *Strength* in what remains behind") shows that the new emotion of resolve required a new scenery — the sublimity of cataracts and "the steep" and mountains and winds, the majestic orchestration of trumpets, over against the pipes and tabors of pastoral joy. The dream, the imperial palace, and this fugitive and mysterious early appearance of the sublime all prepare us for the great analysis of loss which follows the original grieving memory of celestial light.

The analysis of loss is carried on in the middle sections (7, 8, and 9) of the poem, in which Wordsworth uses language of exceptional variety and interest, and invents a series of structures that threaten to rupture lyric convention. The central structure of the poem is the remarkable diptych of the six-year-old "little Child." On the left, so to speak (st. 7), we see the Child wholly in exterior semblance, and the passage is consequently written in a satiric mode. On the right (st. 8) we see the Child in his immensity of soul, and the passage is written in the spiritual mode appropriate to pure substance wholly removed from accident. (Coleridge, who should have known better, in *Biographia Literaria* called this passage an example of "mental bombast or thoughts and images too great for the subject.") Both satire and the *via negativa* of theology are in essence disharmonious to lyric, because lyric requires sympathy *vis-à-vis* its subject, and needs the images of sense for its language. By severing the Child's exterior semblance from his soul's immensity, and by becoming in consequence educational satirist on the one hand and theologian of the inexpressible on the other, Wordsworth risks his whole poem. If the child's exterior is soulless, his interior is lifeless (it is "deaf" and "silent"). Such a dissevering of one human presence into two aspects generates thematic and stylistic tension, and a compensatory will-toward-harmony presses us to reintegrate the separated human principles of the child, his appearance and his soul.

The satiric stanza on the child is rightly compared to the Prelude's mockery of the "model child": in each, Wordsworth's fine eye for human development is grimly accurate. In the Ode, we last saw the child on the lap of his homely nurse, his foster-mother the earth, but at six, the child fatally leaves the nursery behind, repudiates the female lap and maternal kisses, and eagerly prepares to join the masculine world of business, love, or strife. In Wordsworth's symbolic tableau, the child is already expected to be "a little man." He has outgrown his nursery skirts and is dressed in male clothing, which grotesquely makes him appear, to Wordsworth's eye, a dwarfish version of the adult male — "a six years' Darling of a pygmy size." He has discovered how to please his father — by imitating adult transactions. He is annoyed when his mother — who wishes he were still the baby on her lap — makes possessive forays on his attention. The father's approval is all he seeks:

> Behold the Child among his new-born blisses,
> A six-years' Darling of a pygmy size!
> See, where 'mid work of his own hand he lies,
> Fretted by sallies of his mother's kisses,
> With light upon him from his father's eyes!

"Behold, see, see," says our guide in developmental psychology. The scorn of the guide is intervened with the pathos of the sight. Children in their imitative play invariably betray their ignorance of what a wedding is, what funerals entail.

> See, at his feet, some little plan or chart,
> Some fragment from his dream of human life,
> Shaped by himself with newly-learnèd art;
>> A wedding or a festival,
>> A mourning or a funeral.

"His dream of human life" — the voice almost breaks in the judgment of experience on innocence. The little Actor, conning one part after another, plays all the persons "down to palsied Age" — but the voice knows, as the six-year-old child playing the palsied elder does not, what palsy is, what Age is. The voice cries out in protest: the child, says the voice, is socialized by male approval into all these roles and dreams and dialogues, "as if his whole vocation / Were endless imitation." We know that in Wordsworth's lexicon the opposite of imitation is creation, and the true human vocation is not to be imitative, but rather to be "a sensitive being, a *creative* soul."

The ironic vocabulary of the satiric tableau is hard to bear. The true new-born blisses of the visionary gleam are replaced by the "new-born blisses" of social imitation; the child's "celestial light" is replaced by the "light upon him from his father's eyes"; the "glory and the freshness of a dream" is replaced by the child's ignorant "dream of human life"; the joy of the babe who "leaps up on his Mother's arm" is replaced by the little Actor's "joy and pride" as he masters roles under his approving father's glance. Heart, song, tongue, and art are enrolled in the service of "endless imitation." If there is a center of despair in the Ode, it comes in this oppressive tableau of socialization. And yet this too is "growing up." Trilling nowhere dwells on this stanza, but simply abstracts Wordsworth's remark about the weight of custom, and talks about "maturity, with its habits and its cares and its increase of distance from our celestial origin." This is to treat "maturity" as something imposed upon us, with "habits and cares" its inevitable concomitant. But Wordsworth keenly sees the child's own eagerness to "grow up," and emphasizes the paternal role in the socializing of the boy. The tone of this stanza was, I should guess, offensive to Trilling, since it departs from the homiletic and the exalted; and the content, incriminating us in our own loss of the light, despairingly confronting our eagerness to please our parents, was threatening to the value Trilling placed on the "mature" acceptance of the adult role. Consequently, nobody reading Trilling's essay could ever guess that the Ode contains anything like this stanza of satiric externality.

The poetic voice, passing from satire into its own adult pain, the pain of those "in darkness lost, the darkness of the grave," grieves at the child's haste to attain adulthood. But before the poet expresses his anguished wish to halt the child's precipitous striving for adult status, he addresses the child in a second tableau, paired with the first. If it is true that all odes address a Divinity, then the Divinity of this ode is Reciprocity — a mutual Divinity which consists of the child receptive to the Eternal Mind and Immortality brooding over the child. (The demonic or ironic version of this Romantic reciprocity can be seen in Coleridge's "Limbo," where, in the tableau of the blind man with uplifted head in moonlight, the man "seems to gaze at that which seems to gaze on him.") Wordsworth's ironic and satiric language gives way, in this moment of intensest penetration, to the language of inexpressibility. The child is all Eye, all Seer. While the "exterior" child listens to words, frames songs, and fits his tongue to dialogues, this "interior" child is deaf and silent. He "reads" a text at once illimitable and unfathomable, the eternal deep, voluminous in extent and profundity. The paradoxes of the passage are theological: the child is both slave to his Immortality and the possessor of heaven-born freedom; he actively reads eternity but is passively haunted by the eternal mind; he is fixed on the eternal deep but stands glorious on the height of being; he is a prophet but voiceless; he is a philosopher who does not enunciate truths, but on whom truths rest. The Seer *blest*, the Eye among the *blind*, is yet, in the activities of his own socialization, "*blindly* with [his] *blessedness* at strife.*" This last phrase "undoes" the former one, and dissolves the seer-child into one of us. The earthly freight of "custom" or social posture will bury the child, and in exchange for the eternal *deep*, the child will experience that weight "*deep* almost as life."

These two tableaux, which form the center of the Ode, are reactions by *one* mind to *one* object — the six-year-old child. If we consider this child as he strives toward male adulthood, in his misconceived external occupations and games, he is an object of scorn and pathos; but if we consider him in his soul, which is still, through no will of its own, an Eye haunted by an Eternal Mind, he is an object of stricken awe. In neither case is he humanly attractive. It is evident that the pygmy Actor is a repellent, if innocent, form; but it needs to be said as well that the child who is deaf and silent and a slave is also, for all his "blessedness" and "freedom," a deprived form. That child will, in the course of the poem, achieve authentic hearing and speech (which may be contrasted to the false speech of the little Actor). We believe in the acquisition of that true hearing and speech because of our uneasiness at the double portrait of the child who is falsely framing "adult" dramas and language on the one hand, deaf and silent on the other.

Trilling's remarks about this central portion of the poem are odd. In his view the Ode is divided into two large parts, of which the first (1–4) poses the question of the disappearance of the glory. "The second half of the Ode," says Trilling (ignoring the fact that what he calls "the second half" should more properly, in terms of length, be called "the last two-thirds") "is divided into two large movements, each of which gives an answer to the question with which the first part ends":

> The two answers seem to contradict each other. The first (5–8) issues in despair, the second (9–11) in hope; the first uses a language strikingly supernatural, the second is entirely naturalistic. The two parts even differ in the statement of fact, for the first says that the gleam is gone, whereas the second says that it is not gone, but only transmuted. It is necessary to understand this contradiction, but it is not necessary to resolve it, for from the circuit between its two poles comes much of the power of the poem.

I believe that most of what Trilling says in this excerpt is false. In his view, the structure of the poem can be diagrammed, as follows:

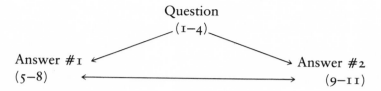

Question
(1–4)

Answer #1   Answer #2
(5–8)   (9–11)

"Answer #1" and "Answer #2" remain opposed, Trilling has said, in a mutually energizing relation. "Answer #2" does not depend on "Answer #1" in this structure — they are autonomous parallel units. I would propose a counterstructure, wholly linear and sequential, divided into thirds, in which the closing stanzas (9–11) stand in a real and final relation to all that has preceded them. Because Trilling chooses not to mention the intensely "naturalistic" language of socialization in stanza 7 and in the close of stanza 8, he can represent the language of the first "answer" as "strikingly supernatural"; because he omits all mention of the race, the palms, the children on the shore of the immortal sea, and the faith that looks through death in stanzas 9–11, he can represent the language of the second "answer" as "entirely naturalistic." In following the fortunes of the gleam, he loses large portions of the poem, which retains its grasp on both ideality and reality throughout, and does not separate itself into "the supernatural" and "the naturalistic." Trilling even misrepresents the fate of the gleam: he says it is "transmuted" (a word not used by Wordsworth) and then, correcting himself, says it "*has not wholly fled, for it is remembered.*" There is no contradiction between something which, itself, has wholly fled and something which is, though gone forever, remembered. Trilling confuses the remembered "truths that wake, to perish never" with the vanished "splendour in the grass, the glory in the flower." Wordsworth says, wholly explicitly, in the very "answer" where Trilling finds "transmutation," that "the radiance which was once so bright" is "*forever taken*" from his sight. That a "primal sympathy" remains is not to say that a gleam or a glory or a radiance remains. Trilling sees metaphor as a convenient way-station toward idea: but metaphor, for Wordsworth or any other poet, *is* idea. Had Wordsworth wished to say that the gleam was "transmuted" he would have said so.

In order to take issue with Trilling's troubling division of the ode into two autonomous "answers," it is necessary to establish the connections that Wordsworth draws between his despair at socialization and his final estimate of the value of the philosophic mind. As I see the Ode, Wordsworth implies, as much by the prior position of the one "answer" to the other as by any other means, that the acquisition of the philosophic mind depends on our participation, as we grow up, in a wedding or a festival, a mourning or a funeral; on those dialogues of "business, love, or strife"; on becoming, year by year, "all the Persons, down to palsied Age / That Life brings with her in her equipage." Wordsworth is saddened and irritated by the child's inordinate anticipation (in desire and act) of those stages: but the poem affirms (by its own schema of Child, Boy, Youth, and Man) that those stages are inescapable. They impose one terrible burden — the chill weight of custom — but they confer, at least on the "sensitive being, the *creative* soul," a benefit, wholly and amply described in the last two stanzas — a humanizing of the soul. Wordsworth's first mention of "the soothing thoughts that spring / Out of human suffering" is a cryptic one, but he subsequently gives convincing instances of those thoughts in his closing stanza.

It should also be mentioned, in contravention of Trilling, that Wordsworth is following, in his ode, the classic proportions of elegy. Every elegy descends to that point of death which is reached by Wordsworth in the weight of custom. The apotheosis or transfiguration which follows aims at the reestablishment of value, whether (in earlier poets) by the affirmation of a continuing life elsewhere or (since Milton, at least) the establishing of some domain corresponding to the paradise within. Trilling can of course choose to find Wordsworth's despair as convincing as Wordsworth's compensatory finale, and so represent them as two equally valid "answers"; but the presence of the elegiac convention suggests that such was not Wordsworth's intent. Rather, he intended (as I believe his language shows) to "cure" the wounds of despair by his subsequent passages, not simply to offer two irreconcilable views of human life.

Wordsworth shows in the Ode a succession of wounds to the spirit. If we are to believe his closing assertions, and so see the poem as a cumulative experience, we must witness the healing of those wounds. Arnold was uncannily accurate in speaking of Wordsworth's "healing power": the Ode is in fact self-therapeutic, and in postulating his "two answers," irreconcilably if energetically coexisting, Trilling denies Wordsworth's therapeutic success. That success — which is a moral one achieved by literary means — rests on a powerfully plotted succession of what I have called "wounds" and "cures." The turn from the description of wounds to the performance of cures comes of course at the exclamation, "O joy!" *Embers* is cured by *remembers*; the cure for the loss of the light that has *died* away is something that doth *live*; the visionary gleam has *fled*, but nature yet remembers what was so *fugitive*; the child reading the *eternal* deep was a seer *blest*, but now memory breeds *perpetual benediction*; the *song* of the birds is replaced by the *song* of thanks and praise; the Immortality which was *master* to the child is, in the adult, the enduring "*master-light*" of recollection; its *cherishing* and *upholding* substitute for the *mother's arm*; its power to make "our noisy years seem moments in the being of the *eternal silence*" takes the place of the child's *silent* reading of the *eternal* mind. The truths that *wake* counteract the *sleep* of birth; the *sight* of the immortal sea and its children cures the *blindness* of adulthood; our ability to *travel* to that sea makes up for the fact that the Youth daily farther from the east must *travel*; the *hearing* of the mighty waters cures the *deafness* of the contemplative child. To join the youthful throng in *thought* becomes the appropriate response in lieu of the earlier strained wish to join in *feeling*; the initial thought of *grief* is refused in the resolve, "We will *grieve* not"; the premature "I again am *strong*" is renewed by the will to find "*strength* in what remains behind"; the "best *philosopher*" acquires the *philosophic* mind; and the faith that *looks through death* could only occur in a poem that had already looked back through birth (with a glance equally piercing a barrier) to "whence" the light flows, to "that imperial palace whence we came." In its great close, the Ode "cures" its own first lines: the meadows, groves, and streams have had added unto themselves fountains and hills; the *fountains* are a thematic and phonemic echo of the earlier *cataracts* in the *mountains*, while the *hills* are a memory of "*the steep.*" In other words, the final landscape contains the sublimity missing in the first childhood pastoral scene, but subsequently incorporated in the first premature assertion of strength. The humanized brooks, day, clouds, and sunset replace the earlier exclusively visual items; the *setting* sun appears to recall "our life's star [which] hath had elsewhere its *setting*"; the *clouds* that gather round the setting sun replace the *clouds* of glory; the *sport* of the immortal children changes to the earnest *race* of the adult soul. We *live*, says Wordsworth, by the

heart, by that something which doth *live* in our embers. Still, Words-
worth has not finished:

> — But there's a Tree, of many, one,
> A single Field which I have looked upon,
> Both of them speak of something that is gone;
> The Pansy at my feet
> Doth the same tale repeat.

The admonitory Pansy *repeats* the *tale spoken* by the Tree and Field
— a transfer of language from the poet to the elements in the land-
scape. The absence of which the landscape spoke must, above all, be
"cured." The *apparel* of celestial light has been replaced by the
coloring conferred on the clouds by the sobriety of the eye acquainted
with the night; but what will, or can, the Pansy now say? Being a
Pansy, it will speak thoughts: but that alone is not enough. There is
a deep fear in the poem that thought has replaced feeling: "we in
thought will join your throng." And yet feeling, the heart, and love
reappear intensely in the final stanza: "Yet in my *heart of hearts I
feel* your might", "I *love* the Brooks . . . even *more*"; "thanks to the
human *heart* by which we *live*." To end his poem, Wordsworth must
place thought and feeling in some final and conclusive relation to
each other; the landscape must be made to speak; and the new
adjustment to "every *common* sight" must be established. Words-
worth generalizes his pansy, intensifies *common* into *mean*, translates
pensées into *thoughts*, cures the weight of custom which "*lies deep*
almost as life" with the thoughts which "*lie deep*" of the philosophic
mind, and substitutes for the sublimity of cataracts which *blow* their
trumpets and for the glory in the *flower*, the pathos of the *meanest
flower that blows*:

> To me the *meanest flower that blows* can give
> *Thoughts* that do often *lie too deep* for tears.

It may be tedious so to anatomize Wordsworth's intense concen-
tration of vocabulary (which I have by no means exhausted — see
his plays on "forever" and "never," on "take" and "give," on "bring"
and "bring back," on closing shades and gathering clouds, on guilt
and innocence, and so on), but his moral import is convincing only
because his homeopathic cure uses the vocabulary of the disease. By

"solving" the answer of despair (deep-lying custom) with the answer of hope (deep-lying thoughts profounder than tears), Wordsworth intends to assert, as clearly as he can, that the feelings of despair are a way station on the path to his ultimate powers of adulthood.

We return to the original question: to what extent is the Ode Wordsworth's dirge over departed powers? Wordsworth's original impulse — which everyone will agree was to lament those departed powers — still begins the Ode and sets an unforgettable tone. The long climb into compensatory complexity — painfully completed in thought during the two years in which Wordsworth left the Ode unfinished — was only completed in words during the composition of the last seven stanzas. Those readers who respond most strongly to the powerful adaptation of religious language at the opening of the ode will continue to feel that the dirge, having the "best" lines, is the "real" subject of the poem. Those who prefer the stoic and reparatory adult tone of the ending may agree with Trilling in rebuking the elegiac partisans. Those who, in conjunction with Trilling, see the weight of custom as an untranscended endpoint, will find an ineradicable pessimism in the Ode. But there is a passage which seems to escape the grasp of all these parties, and which is, nonetheless, the heart of the poem.

This passage, in the ninth stanza, embodies Wordsworth's *second* account of the psychological conditions he recalls from his childhood. Some extraordinary revaluation of his childhood experiences clearly occurred between the initial composition of the first four stanzas and the later completion of the poem. The first recollections had been ones purely of glory, dream, freshness, light, and gleam — the ravishments of sense. Wordsworth (in the Fenwick Notes) is perfectly explicit on the "dream-like vividness and splendour which invest objects of sight in childhood." There is, however, another, separate, and different recollection: "The poem rests entirely upon *two* recollections of childhood, *one* that of a splendour in the objects of sense which is passed away, and *the other* an indisposition to bend to the law of death as applying to our particular case" (Wordsworth to Mrs. Clarkson, Dec. 1814; italics added).

In the Fenwick Notes, Wordsworth speaks of the second recollection as an "abyss of idealism," says he wrote about it in the lines beginning "Obstinate questionings" and so on, and adds that he was "often unable to think of external things as having external existence." De Selincourt cites a letter from Bonamy Price quoting

Wordsworth: "There was a time in my life when I had to push against something that resisted, to be sure that there was anything outside me. I was sure of my own mind; everything else fell away, and vanished into thought" (*Works*, IV, pp. 463–467).

Trilling wrongly conflates these two separate recollections into one, saying, "We are told then, that light and glory consist, at least in part, of 'questionings,' 'fallings from us,' 'vanishings' and 'blank misgivings.'" Wordsworth nowhere says anything of the sort. What is most interesting about the poem is that Wordsworth chose first to recall only the ecstatic component in childhood, and to write a four-stanza lament for its disappearance. We can scarcely doubt that in the two years during which the unfinished Ode was troubling his mind, he thought more profoundly about the nature of his childhood experience, and recognized that besides the ecstatic component clothing the world in light and glory, there was another component, dark, obscure, and subtractive. Nowhere in Wordsworth is there a stranger or more opaque description of human feeling than in the passage in which he declares that he is finally grateful not for childish delight or liberty or hope,

> But for those obstinate questionings
> Of sense and outward things,
> Fallings from us, vanishings;
> Blank misgivings of a Creature
> Moving about in worlds not realised,
> High instincts before which our mortal Nature
> Did tremble like a guilty Thing surprised.

This is, in language, virtually the only "unpaired" or "nonce" passage in the poem. In a work so consciously self-echoing, this characteristic alone marks the passage as one of special interest. In it, Wordsworth turns away entirely from the pictorial and imagistic language used to represent both the celestial light and the compensatory later vision of brooks, day, sunset, and flower. His vocabulary becomes abstract, unidiomatic ("fallings from us, vanishings"), and obsessive (question*ings*, th*ings*, fall*ings*, vanish*ings*, misgiv*ings*, Th*ing*). Commentary falters always before this passage, and perhaps will always fail. But a few observations may be risked. One myth behind the passage is that of our first parents apprehended by God in disobedience, or so I read the strong Miltonic echoes in "our mortal Nature . . . like a guilty Thing surprised." This hints at the difficulty of our attempt to liberate ourselves from "the spell/ Of that strong frame of sense in which we dwell," as Wordsworth put it in one draft of the Ode. Our instinct for the high is in some sense a betrayal of our primary sense experience. The child's first creed has been that of sense; his "obstinate" questionings of sense are those of a heretic or a rebel. As outward things recede, the child feels literally robbed of his own corporeality: the loss of self expressed in "fallings *from us*, vanishings" is unnerving. One can only have "misgivings" where one has before had trust; just as one cannot be "obstinate" unless in the presence of a sovereign principle expecting submission. These are unpleasant experiences, inexplicable disorientations in a shadowy universe. Of course one would rather recall the "splendour in the objects of sense" than this mistrust of the "strong frame of sense," but Wordsworth was able to complete the Ode only by at last recallng the first motions of *non*sensuous instincts as the most valuable of his childhood experiences. The final human value affirmed by the Ode is that of thought arising from feeling. This value belongs rather to the realm of questioning and misgiving than to the splendor of transfigured sense. Had the Ode not contained this passage of awakened "high instinct" there could have been no continuity discovered between childhood and manhood: childhood would have been radiance and sense-experience, manhood the prison-house of waning responsiveness.

The epigraph to the Ode is often misread: it does not say, as an axiom, that the Child is Father of the Man. It says, in painful emotional relief, "The Child *is* Father of the Man; I had long doubted it; I wondered if any continuity of experience could be affirmed; but now I see that I am, in my adult state, descended from that child I once was; and if I should ever cease to feel this to be true, let me die!" Though the visionary gleam is *fled*, though the radiance is *forever* taken away, though *nothing* can bring back the hour of splendor and glory (and Wordsworth is explicit on the absolute disappearance of the *celestial* light), it is clear that the questionings and misgivings have not disappeared: on the contrary, they are the "truths that wake, / To perish never." Wordsworth does not say (as Trilling would have it) that "What was so intense a light in childhood becomes 'the fountain-light of all our day.'" He says rather that the misgivings and questionings of sense and outward things become that fountain-light. And they do so precisely because they are the foun-

dation on which we construct our later trust in that inward affec-
tional and intellectual reality "by which we live."

Trilling also maintains that in stanzas 9–11 Wordsworth "tells us
of the everlasting connection of the *diminished person* with his own
ideal personality. The child hands on to the *hampered adult* the
imperial nature, the 'primal sympathy.'" Nowhere, however, does
Wordsworth suggest that the speaker had his *ideal personality* in
childhood, or that he is now a *diminished person*, let alone a *ham-
pered adult*. The deaf and silent Child-Seer is not describable as an
ideal personality; he has in fact no personality at all. The adult
capable of thoughts too deep for tears, who lives by the human heart,
is not diminished or hampered. In his inexplicable disregard for
Wordsworth's own vocabulary and imagery, Trilling imposes on
Wordsworth his own modernist sensibility. He was reading into
Wordsworth the sort of thing he could find in Stevens:

Now it is September and the web is woven . . .

It is all that you are, the final dwarf of you,
That is woven and woven and waiting to be worn.

This is the sort of tone that Trilling's talk of the "diminished" and
the "hampered" attributes to Wordsworth. And Trilling concludes
his account of the Ode by saying that because Wordsworth was
incapable of tragedy he could not write the poetry promised by his
"bold declaration that he had acquired a new way of feeling."

If it is truer to say, as I believe it is, that the Ode represents the
acquisition of the power of metaphor; that to rest in either the
splendor of sense or in blank misgivings is not to be a poet; that to
join the external world of sense-experience with the interior world
of moral consciousness is to become an adult; that to express that
juncture in metaphor is to become a poet — then all of Wordsworth's
great poetry is the result of the process of the humanizing of sense
and the symbolizing of interior experience described by the Ode.
Affectional feeling (and not, as Trilling says, "the knowledge of man's
mortality" alone) "replaces the 'glory' as the agency which makes
things significant and precious." It is "thanks to the human *heart*
. . . , its *tenderness*, its *joys* and *fears*," that a common flower can
bear a new weight of meaning. In the epigraph to his poem "To the

Daisy," Wordsworth quotes George Wither, who says his *Muse's divine skill* taught him

> That from everything I saw
> I could some instruction draw
> And raise pleasure to the height
> Through the *meanest object's* sight. (Italics added)

It is this capacity of the Muse — absolutely unattainable by the six-years' darling, however blessed his Soul's immensity — that is celebrated in the Ode.

In *The Meaning of a Literary Idea* Trilling proposes to examine "the relation which should properly obtain between what we call creative literature and what we call ideas," and he continues: "When I consider the respective products of the poetic and of the philosophic mind, although I can see that they are by no means the same and although I can conceive that different processes, even different mental faculties, were at work to make them and to make them different, I cannot resist the impulse to put stress on their similarity and on their easy assimilation to each other." "We demand of our literature," Trilling asserts, "the authority, the cogency, the completeness, the brilliance, the *hardness* of systematic thought." And, he adds, "the aesthetic upon which the critic sets primary store is to the poet himself frequently of only secondary importance." These, among others, are the principles which led Trilling astray in his account of the Ode. Of course it was to Wordsworth wholly urgent to speak the truth about human life as he perceived it; but his utterance does not put "the aesthetic" secondary and "truth" primary. His truth lies in his way of speaking his truths. And if the critic is not to set primary store upon the aesthetic, how is he to explain his interest in this utterance at all? As for the cogency and authority and brilliance which Trilling seeks, they must be, in poetry, a cogency and authority and brilliance of expression and disposition of materials, not necessarily of "systematic thought." Trilling's "easy assimilation" of import to poem leads him, paradoxically, to a dispensing with genuine import, since he neglects import's imparting of itself. "My own interests," said Trilling writing *On the Teaching of Modern Literature*, "lead me to see literary situations as cultural situations, and cultural situations as great elaborate fights about moral issues." Perhaps he was uneasy with the lyric because it turns inward, away from polemic, away from any explicit concern with those "great elaborate fights" and away equally from the broad literary effects employed by epic, novel, and satire. Trilling recalled, in his essay on Isaac Babel, that what he had wanted in his youth from the Russian Revolution was "an art that would have as little ambiguity as a proposition in logic." Though his adult self repudiated this boyish wish, something of it remains in his conviction that the Ode presents "statements" and "answers." Such a vocabulary is inadequate to an art devoted, in Wordsworth's view, to "the history and science of feeling." Our thoughts, to Wordsworth's mind, are not the repository of "systematic thought," but are rather "the representatives of all our past feelings." One feels that Trilling could never be quite happy with a work of literature that presents itself, as the Ode does, as a history and analysis of past and present feeling. A "great elaborate fight about a moral issue" was more to his taste; and his essay on the Ode did its best to see the Ode as a Freudian polemic, representing the diminution of the "oceanic feeling" into inevitable subjection to the superego, with a consequent literary commitment to tragedy, a subject unsuitable to its poet. He missed Wordsworth's complexity of presentation and the synthesis offered by *poesis* to the previous thesis and antithesis of childhood and custom. If Wordsworth's Ode means anything to us now, it is not as a convenient illustration of a preexistent schema drawn from Freudian doctrine. It "means" by its hard-won setting of a later scene of consciousness against an earlier one; by virtue of the minutely created antiphonal relation of the later to the earlier; by its refusal to affirm a unity of early and late selfhood without a unity of early and late language; and most of all by its ability to invent, mediating between the language of childhood sense and its mirror-language of adult inwardness, a daring language of disorientation, which conveys the difficulty inherent in the relation of consciousness to sense-experience, that difficulty which the great poetry of the Ode so triumphantly overcomes.

8

Keats and the Use of Poetry

Heidegger asked, "What is the poet for in a destitute time?" I want to depart from Heidegger's premises, though not from his question: What can we say is the use of poetry? Heidegger's premises are those of nineteenth-century nostalgia, a nostalgia for the presence of God in the universe. He writes as one deprived of theological reassurance, seeing emptiness about him, and longing for presence. He suggests that the poet exists to restore presence, to testify to its possibility — or at least, like Hölderlin, to testify to felt absence.

These are premises of a particular moment — the moment of Götterdämmerung. But Heidegger's plangent lament offers only one response to that moment; readers will remember Nietzsche's far more athletic and exulting response to the same moment, and some will recall Wallace Stevens's remark in "Two or Three Ideas":

> To see the gods dispelled in mid-air and dissolve like clouds is one of the great human experiences. It is not as if they had gone over the horizon to disappear for a time; nor as if they had been overcome by other gods of greater power and profounder knowledge. It is simply that they came to nothing . . . It was their annihilation, not ours, and yet it left us feeling that in a measure, we too had been annihilated . . . At the same time, no man ever muttered a petition in his heart for the restoration of those unreal shapes. There was in every man the increasingly human self, which instead of remaining the observer, the non-participant, the delinquent, became constantly more and more all there was or so it seemed; and whether it was so or merely seemed so still left it for him to resolve life and the world in his own terms.

Perhaps we can consider a response like Heidegger's as one dictated not by the facts of the case but by a certain temperament in Heidegger himself. Another temperament, other premises. And in the confidence that the use of the poet, in human terms, remains constant even through the vicissitudes of cultural change, I want to take up the ideas on the social function of poetry expressed by John Keats. Other poets could serve as well, but I choose Keats as a poet I know well whose original position on the question included the lament voiced by Heidegger (see the "Ode to Psyche") but whose final position is one of more sophistication and more buoyancy.

Keats, a resolute nonbeliever and political radical, came into a post-Enlightenment world, it is true, but it was still a world which felt some of those pangs of loss later expressed by Heidegger. Keats too felt a religious nostalgia, and it entered into many of his own meditations on the function of the poet; but he did not confine himself within that framework. I take the case of Keats to be an exemplary one of a modern poet seeking to define his own worth; Keats seems to me to have thought more deeply about the use of poetry than any subsequent poet. And although Keats will be my example, I want to close by bringing the topic into the present day, by quoting two contemporary poets who have reflected profoundly and long on it, the Polish poet Czeslaw Milosz and the Irish poet Seamus Heaney — both of them compelled by their history to inquire into their own social function. But I will begin with Keats as a modern posttheological poet, a forerunner to others contemplating the question of the use of secular poetry.

Keats had hoped, originally, that literary creation could confer therapeutic benefits on its audience. Admirable as the desire is that art could "beguile" Dido from her grief, or "rob from aged Lear his bitter teen" ("Imitation of Spenser"), this concept of art bars it from participation in human grief. Keats later brought this idea of art to its apogee in the "Ode to a Nightingale," where the poet-speaker hopes that the purely musical art of bird notes will enable him to fly away from the world of the dying young, the palsied old, fading Beauty, and faithless Love. We must distinguish Keats's "escapism" (as it has sometimes been called) from an escapism that does not promise a therapeutic result, such as comforting Dido or Lear or Ruth in grief, "charming the mind from the trammels of pain" ("On Receiving a Curious Shell").

Other ends of art early proposed by Keats include the civilizing psychological one of "attuning . . . the soul to tenderness" ("To Lord Byron") and the educative one of expanding the soul, as, by vicarious experience, it strays in Spenser's halls and flies "with daring Milton through the fields of air" ("Written on the Day That Mr. Leigh Hunt Left Prison") — a view of art given its classical Keatsian expression in the sonnet on Chapman's Homer. Keats's concept of the *utile* here is far from the usual didactic one, which emphasizes social responsibility and moral action. To become tender, to expand one's sense of imaginative possibility, are early recommendations consistent with Keats's later program of converting the blank intelligence into a human "soul"; the difference we notice here is the absence of that "world of pains and troubles" which will become the chief schooling agent of the heart in the letter on soul-making.

Keats, in his early poetry, enumerates four social functions of poetry: a historical thematic one, as epic poetry recorded history of an exalted sort, written by "bards, that erst sublimely told heroic deeds"; a representational (if allegorical) one, as Shakespeare gave, in his dramatic poetry, an incarnation of the passions; a didactic one, as in Spenser's "hymn in praise of spotless Chastity" ("Ode to Apollo"); and a linguistically preservative one, which can "revive" for our day an archaic language, "the dying tones of minstrelsy" ("Specimen of an Induction to a Poem"). And yet, Keats perhaps sensed that these functions — historical, allegorically representational, didactic, and linguistically preservative — were not to be his own: these claims for the social functions of poetry are, in his early work, asserted merely, not poetically enacted. A fair example of the feebleness of the early work comes in Keats's epistle to his brother George, where, after describing the living joys of the bard, Keats writes of "posterity's award," the function of the poet's work after he has died, as society makes use of his verse:

> The patriot shall feel
> My stern alarum, and unsheathe his steel . . .
> The sage will mingle with each moral theme
> My happy thoughts sententious; . . .
> Lays have I left of such a dear delight
> That maids will sing them on their bridal night.
> . . . To sweet rest
> Shall the dear babe, upon its mother's breast,
> Be lulled with songs of mine.

These uses of poetry are strictly ancillary; presumably the hero would still be heroic, the sage wise, the maids bridally delighted, and the baby sleepy, even without the help of the poet. In this conception, poetry is chiefly an intensifying accompaniment to life.

Keats's earliest notions of the power of art were concerned chiefly with the theme the poem may embody. The poet's pastoral tale will distract the grieving; his patriotic and moral sentiments will inspire hero and sage; and his love poems will wake an answering echo in the breast of the young. Poems exist to charm the fair daughters of the earth with love tales, and to warm earth's sons with patriotic sententious ideas.

It is to be expected that a poet of Keats's honesty would soon perceive that the embodying of a thematic and didactic intent was not his own sole motive in composing verse. He eventually admitted that in venturing on "the stream of rhyme" he himself sailed "scarce knowing my intent," but rather exploring "the sweets of song: /The grand, the sweet, the terse, the free, the fine; . . . / Spenserian vowels that elope with ease . . . / Miltonian storms, and more, Miltonian tenderness; . . . / The sonnet . . . / The ode . . . / The epigram . . . / The epic" ("To Charles Cowden Clarke"). This avowal of the aesthetic motives of creation, this picture of the artist investigating his medium — its vocal range, its prosodic inventions, its emotional tonalities, and its formal genres — sorts uneasily with Keats's former emphasis on the thematic social service of poetry.

While the emphasis on social service always brings in, for Keats, the relief of pain, the emphasis in descriptions of art itself, in early Keats, dwells always on the pleasure principle, so that even woe must be, in literature, "pleasing woe" ("To Lord Byron"), and poetry must make "pleasing music, and not wild uproar" ("How Many Bards"), full of glorious tones and delicious endings ("On Leaving Some Friends"). In these early poems, Keats expresses the characteristic view of the youthful poet, to whom the aesthetic can be found only in the beautiful.

Keats's first attempt to reconcile his philosophical emphasis on social service and his instinctive commitment to those aesthetic interests proper to composition appears in "I stood tiptoe," where he proposes an ingenious reconciliation by suggesting that form allegorically represents content:

> In the calm grandeur of a sober line,
> We see the waving of the mountain pine;
> And when a tale is beautifully staid,
> We feel the safety of a hawthorn glade.

The myths of the gods are said, in "I stood tiptoe," to be formally allegorical renditions of man's life in nature: a poet seeing a flower bending over a pool invents the myth of Narcissus. This is a promising solution for Keats: that form, being an allegory for content, bears not a mimetic but an algebraic relation to life. But in "I stood tiptoe," this solution is conceptualized rather than formally enacted.

In his next manifesto, "Sleep and Poetry," Keats makes an advance on the thematic level, realizing that his former advocacy of a consoling thematic happiness to cure human sorrow cannot survive as a poetic program. Rather, he says, he must "pass the realm of Flora and old Pan" for a "nobler life" where he may encounter "the agonies, the strife / Of human hearts." With the thematic admission of tragic material, formal notions of power and strength can at last enter into Keats's aesthetic and fortify his former aesthetic values — beauty and mildness — with a new sculptural majesty:

> A drainless shower
> Of light is Poesy; 'tis the supreme of power;
> 'Tis might half-slumbering on its own right arm.

Nonetheless, Keats is still critical of a poetry that "feeds upon the burrs, / And thorns of life," arguing rather for the therapeutic function of poetry, "that it should be a friend / To soothe the cares, and lift the thoughts of man" — an end still envisaged in the later "Ode on a Grecian Urn." The poet is simply to "tell the most heart-easing things"; and the poetry of earth ranges only from the grasshopper's delight to the cricket's song "in warmth increasing ever."

A far sterner idea of poetry arises when Keats hopes that something will draw his "brain / Into a delphic labyrinth" ("On Receiving a Laurel Crown"). As soon as he admits thought, prophecy, and labyrinthine mystery into the realm of poetry, Keats becomes frightened at the interpretive responsibilities that lie before him, objectified for him in the example of the Elgin marbles. He cries out that he is too weak for such godlike hardship, that these "glories of the brain / Bring round the heart an undescribable feud."

But Keats obeys the Delphic imperative and writes his first tragic poem, a sonnet on the death of Leander, forcing his art to describe his worst personal specter, the image of a dying youth whom nothing can save. Keats's chief tragic adjective, "desolate," appears for the first time at this period (in his sonnet on the sea), to reappear in the "Hymn to Pan," the passage in "Endymion" on the Cave of Quietude, and the "Ode on a Grecian Urn." Henceforth, Keats can conceive of poetry as a mediating, oracular, and priestlike art, one which, by representation of the desolate in formal terms, can interpret the mysteries of existence to others.

The long romance "Endymion" marks Keats's first success in finding poetic embodiments for the principles he had so far been able merely to assert. The tale of Endymion is not socially mimetic; rather, it is allegorical of human experiences; however, it is still a "pleasing tale," a pastoral, not a tragedy. Even so, Keats admits in "Endymion" two tragic principles that he will later elaborate: that in contrast to warm and moving nature, art must seem cold and carved or inscribed (a marble altar garlanded with a tress of flowers, the inscribed cloak of Glaucus); and that the action demanded of their devotees by Apollo and Pan is a sacrifice of the fruits of the earth. Art is admitted for the first time to be effortful: Pan is implored to be

> the unimaginable lodge
> For solitary thinkings; such as dodge
> Conception to the very bourne of heaven,
> Then leave the naked brain.

These daring and difficult solitary thinkings and new concepts will become, says Keats, "the leaven, / That spreading in this dull and clodded earth / Gives it a touch ethereal — a new birth."

In one sense, this passage represents the end of Keats's theoretical thinking about the nature and social value of poetry. But he could not yet describe how solitary original thinkings become a leaven to resurrect society. The poem "Endymion," as it journeys between the transcendent Cynthia and the Indian maid, may be seen as a journeying to and fro between the two elements of solitude and society, as Keats looks for a place where he can stand. He would like to avert his gaze from the misery of solitude, where those solitary thinkings take place, but he summons up the courage to confront the necessities of his own writing. Eventually, he arrives at two embodying symbols. The first is the cloak of Glaucus, "o'erwrought with symbols by . . . ambitious magic," wherein everything in the world is symbolized, not directly or mimetically, but in emblems and in miniaturizations. Gazed at, however, these printed reductions swell into mimetic reality:

The gulfing whale was like a dot in the spell.
Yet look upon it, and 'twould size and swell
To its huge self, and the minutest fish
Would pass the very hardest gazer's wish,
And show his little eye's anatomy.

Keats faces up, here, to the symbolic nature of art. Art cannot, he
sees, be directly mimetic; it must always bear an allegorical or em-
blematic relation to reality. Also, art is not a picture (he is speaking
here of his own art of writing), but a hieroglyph much smaller than
its original. However, by the cooperation of the gazer (and only by
that cooperation), the hieroglyph "swells into reality." Without
"the very hardest gazer's wish," the little fish could not manifest
himself.

In this way, as later in the "Ode on a Grecian Urn," Keats declares
that art requires a social cooperation between the encoder-artist and
the solitary decoder-beholder. (Keats thought of the transaction be-
tween the artwork and its audience in private, not communal, terms.)
The prescriptions written on the scroll carried by Glaucus announce
Keats's new program for poetic immortality: the poet must "explore
all forms and substances / Straight homeward to their symbol-es-
sences"; he must "pursue this task of joy and grief," and enshrine
all dead lovers. In the allegory that follows, all dead lovers are
resurrected by having pieces of Glaucus's scroll sprinkled on them
by Endymion. Endymion goes "onward . . . upon his high employ, /
Showering those powerful fragments on the dead."

This allegory suggests that one of the social functions of poetry is
to revive the erotic past of the race so that it lives again. But in the
fourth book of "Endymion," as Keats admits to the poem the human
maiden Phoebe and her companion Sorrow, the poem begins to refuse
its own erotic idealizations and resurrections. At the allegorical center
of Book IV, the narrator of "Endymion" finds at last his second
major symbol of art, the solitary and desolate Cave of Quietude, a
"dark Paradise" where "silence dreariest is most articulate; . . . /
Where those eyes are the brightest far that keep / Their lids shut
longest in a dreamless sleep." This is the place of deepest content,
even though "a grievous feud" is said to have led Endymion to the
Cave of Quietude.

Keats thought that this discovery of the tragic, hieroglyphic, and
solitary center of art meant that he must bid farewell to creative

imagination, to "cloudy phantasms . . . / And air of vision, and the monstrous swell / Of visionary seas":

> No, never more
> Shall airy voices cheat me to the shore
> Of tangled wonder, breathless and aghast.

This farewell to "airy" imagination displays the choice that Keats at first felt compelled to make in deciding on a tragic and human art. He could not yet see a relation between the airy voices of visionary shores and human truth; and he felt obliged to choose truth. "I deem," says the narrator of Endymion, "Truth the best music." "Endymion," uneasily balancing the visionary, the symbolic, and the truthful, had nonetheless brought Keats to his view of art as necessarily related, though in symbolic terms, to human reality; as necessarily hieroglyphic; as the locus of social cooperation by which the symbol regained mimetic force; and as a social resurrective power.

Shortly afterward, in a sudden leap of insight, Keats came upon his final symbol for the social function of art, a symbol not to find its ultimate elaboration, however, until he was able to write the ode "To Autumn." In the sonnet "When I have fears that I may cease to be," Keats summons up a rich gestalt:

> When I have fears that I may cease to be,
> Before my pen has glean'd my teeming brain,
> Before high-pilèd books, in charact'ry,
> Hold like rich garners the full-ripen'd grain . . .

The poet's "teeming brain" is the field gleaned by his pen; the produce of his brain, "full-ripened grain," is then stored in the hieroglyphic charactery of books, which are like rich garners. Organic nature, after its transmutation into charactery (like that of Glaucus's magic symbols) becomes edible grain. By means of this gestalt, Keats asserts that the material sublime, the teeming fields of earth, can enter the brain and be hieroglyphically processed into print. Keats's aim is now to see the whole world with godlike range and power, with the seeing of Diana, "Queen of Earth, and Heaven, and Hell" ("To Homer"), or that of Minos, the judge of all things ("On Visiting the Tomb of Burns").

Still, Keats has not yet enacted very far his convictions about the social function of art. The audience has been suggested as the consumer of the gleaned wheat that the poet had processed into grain; and the audience has been mentioned as the necessary cooperator in the reading of Glaucus's symbols, and as the resurrected beneficiaries of Glaucus's distributed scroll fragments. Now, in his greatest performative invention, Keats decides to play, in his own poetry, the role of audience and interpreter of symbols, not (as he so far had tended to do) the role of artist. This seems to me Keats's most successful aesthetic decision, one that distances him from his own investments (therapeutic and pleasurable alike) in creating. By playing the audience, he approaches his own art as one of its auditors, who may well want to know of what use this art will be to him.

In the odes on Indolence and to Psyche, Keats had played the role of the creating artist; but in the "Ode to a Nightingale" and the "Ode on a Grecian Urn" he is respectively the listener to music and the beholder of sculpture. Each of these odes inquires what the recipient of art stands to receive from art. Keats here represents the audience for art as a single individual, rather than as a collective social group such as his Greek worshippers on the urn. In the absence of ideational content ("Nightingale"), no social collective audience can be postulated; and a modern beholder does not belong to the society that produced the urn. Keats seems to suggest that the social audience is, in the case of art, an aggregate of individual recipients, since the aesthetic experience is primarily a personal one; but what the individual receives, society, as a multiplication of individuals, also receives, as we conclude from the enumeration of listeners to the nightingale through the ages.

In the two "aesthetic odes" proper to the senses of hearing and sight, Keats begins to enact the theories of the social function of art that he had previously only asserted. As the listener to the nightingale, Keats enters a realm of wordless, nonconceptual, and nonrepresentational song. He leaves behind the human pageant of sorrow and the griefs of consciousness; he forsakes the conceptual faculty, the perplexing and retarding brain. He offers himself up to beauty in the form of Sensation, as he becomes a blind ear, ravished by the consolations of sweet sounds articulated together by the composer-singer, the nightingale.

In the "Ode on a Grecian Urn," by contrast, Keats as audience opens his eyes to representational (if allegorical) art and readmits his brain, with all its perplexities and interrogations, to aesthetic experience. In this fiction, one function of art is still, as in the case of the "Ode to a Nightingale," to offer a delight of an aesthetic and sensuous sort — this time a delight to the eye rather than to the ear. But no longer does art, with consolatory intent, ravish its audience away from the human scene; instead, it draws its audience into its truthful representational and representative pictures carved in stone. The fiction of artistic creation as a spontaneous outpouring to an invisible audience — the fiction of the "Ode to a Nightingale" — is jettisoned in favor of admitting the laborious nature of art, as sculpted artifice. And Keats, in the "Ode on a Grecian Urn," establishes the fact that appreciation need not be coincident with creation; he is appreciating the urn now, even though it was sculpted centuries ago. The freshness and perpetuity of art are insisted on, as is its social service to many generations, each of which brings its woe to the urn, each of which finds itself solaced by the urn, a friend to man. The social function of art, Keats discovers here, is to remind its audience, by means of recognizable representative figures, of emotions and events common to all human life — here, lust, love, and sacrifice — which bind generations each to each.

The Elgin marbles, recently installed in England, were Keats's example of his aesthetic ideal — an art that exerts a powerful aesthetic effect even though created long ago, even though the audience cannot ascribe historical or legendary names to the figures represented. This ode declares that art need not be historically based in order to be humanly meaningful; that art, although representationally mimetic, is not directly or historically mimetic; that art works in a symbolic or allegorical order, like that of Glaucus's cloak. It is wrong, therefore, to demand of an artist that he treat directly — autobiographically, journalistically, or historically — of events; his means are radically other than reportage. In fact, unless he pursues things to their "symbol-essences" he will not be able to communicate with ages later than his own.

Finally, in the ode "To Autumn," Keats finds his most comprehensive and adequate symbol for the social value of art. He does this by playing, in this ode, two roles at once. Once again, as in the "Ode on Indolence" and the "Ode to Psyche," he will play the role of the artist, the dreamer indolent in reverie on the bedded grass or the gardener Fancy engaged in touching the fruits of the earth into life. But he will also play the role of audience, of the one who seeks abroad to behold the creative goddess and sings hymns to her activity and her music.

In "To Autumn," in his final understanding of the social function of art, Keats chooses nature and culture as the two poles of his symbolic system. He sees the work of the artist as the transformation of nature into culture, the transmutation of the teeming fields into garnered grain (the gleaning of the natural into books, as his earlier sonnet had described it). Since civilization itself arose from man's dominion over nature, the processing of nature by agriculture became the symbol in Greece of the most sacred mysteries. The vegetation goddess Demeter, with her sheaf of corn and her poppies, was honored in the Eleusinian rituals. And the two symbolic harvests, bread and wine, food and drink, remain transmuted even to this day in the Christian Eucharist.

Keats's autumn ode takes as its allegory for art the making of nature into nurture. The artist, with reaping hook, gleaning basket, and cider press, denudes nature, we may say, but creates food. We cannot, so to speak, drink apples or eat wheat; we can only consume processed nature, apple juice and grain. Since the artist is his own teeming field, art, in this allegory, is a process of self-immolation. As life is processed into art by the gleaning pen or threshing flail, the artist's own life substance disappears, and where wheat was, only a stubble-plain can be seen; but over the plain there rises a song. Song is produced by the steady rhythm of nature transmuted by self-sacrifice into culture. Art does not mimetically resemble nature, any more than cider mimetically resembles apples. But without apples there would be no cider; without life there would be no hieroglyphs of life. In this way, Keats insists again on the radically nonmimetic nature of art but yet argues for its intelligible relation to life in its representative symbolic order, and for its constitutive power in that order.

Keats is the audience for the artist-goddess's sacrifice of herself into food, as she passes from careless girl through ample maternity and into her own death vigil; when all the corn has been threshed, and all the apples pressed, she disappears; nature has become culture. As her beneficiary, Keats is full of an overflowing gratitude — for her generous omnipresence ("whoever seeks abroad / May find thee") and for her elegiac harmonies ("thou hast thy music too"). Her rhythms permeate the whole world until all visual, tactile, and kinetic presence is transubstantiated into Apollonian music for the ear.

We can now put Keats's view over against Heidegger's. Heidegger looks at the world and sees an absence; Keats looks at the world and sees, through the apparition of postharvest absence, a vision of past natural plenty — apples, nuts, grapevines, gourds, honey, and grain. For Keats, the task of the poet is to remember and recreate the immeasurable plenitude of the world and to process it, by the pen, into something which draws from the sensual world but does not resemble it mimetically. The artist must find a charactery, or symbolic order, by which to turn presence into intellectual grain and cider, food and drink. The reaper's hook, the threshing flail, and the cider press are images of the mind at work, processing nature. The work of the mind in aesthetic production is not interrogative or proposition-making (as Keats had thought in the "Ode on a Grecian Urn"), but rather "stationing" — composing symbolic items in a symbolic arrangement until that order bears an algebraic or indicative relation to the order of reality. Only in this way is a vision of reality made intelligible to other minds.

It is not by being a sage or a physician (two roles that appealed to Keats) that the artist produces his result in other minds; it is by his creation of symbolic equivalences arranged in a meaningful gestalt. Once the mind of the audience sees this vision of reality, this shadow of a magnitude, it shares its intelligibility, can "consume" it. The haphazard and unreadable texture of life becomes the interpreted and the stationed. We, as audience, may indeed find ourselves enlightened, solaced, or cured by art; but it cannot be the artist's chief *aim* to enlighten or solace or cure us; he must rather aim to transmute the natural into the hieroglyphic aesthetic, making his music part of a choral harmony contributed to by all his fellow artists. If his art is not music, it has not yet done its work of transubstantiation but is still inert direct mimesis.

By putting the "airy voices" of his choir of creatures (and the "barred clouds") at the end of his ode, Keats places the imaginative (the quality he had thought he might have to forfeit in his quest for reality and truth) in a harmonious relation to the natural. He thus displays the aesthetic principle of music as paramount over even the algebraic or symbolic principle of allegorical representation. Music resembles apples even less than cider does; and yet it is the music of autumn, which arises cotemporally with its transmutations and because of them, on which Keats insists as he closes his ode.

I believe that every poet of substance passes through a course of realizations very like those of Keats. Judging from their juvenilia, artists all begin with an exquisite, almost painful, response to the beautiful, and an equal revulsion against the ugly. In their youth, they often equate the tragic and the deformed with the ugly, and attempt therefore to create an idyllic counterspace. This space is usually not a social one; at most it is occupied only by a narcissistically conceived other, the beloved. As soon as the social scene intrudes into the young artist's poetry — either in the form of history (mythological or actual) or in the form of current political or domestic struggle — the poem is forced into the world of human tragedy. This exemplary process leads to a new aesthetic, in which the dissonant, the mutable, and the ugly must find a place. Usually, a poet writes *about* such disagreeable subjects before he can write *within* them. Later, if the poet can do the requisite work of internalization and symbolizing, there comes the discovery of a virtual order, powerfully organized, through which the complex vision of tragic reality can express itself. The move into the symbolic order always angers those for whom the artist's duty is a historically mimetic one, and for whom the clarity of propaganda is preferable to the ambivalence of human response to the human world. "Art," Yeats said, "is but a vision of reality." In using the concessive "but" and the symbolic word "vision," Yeats argues for the algebraic or allegorical relation between art and reality. One who cannot recognize that algebraic relation, and bring it, by his own gaze, back into "swelling reality," is incompetent to read art.

Those poets who encounter particularly acute political stress, like Czeslaw Milosz and Seamus Heaney, are always urged to be more socially specific in their poetry than poets can be. Poets resist this pressure by offering their own meditations on the social function of the artist faced with the huge and varied questions of the world, and by enacting an aesthetic which embraces social reality in an algebraic way. Imagination, as Stevens says, presses back against the pressure of reality. I want to quote two poems, one by Milosz, one by Heaney, which reaffirm the necessarily symbolic nature of the artist's work and yet repeat and enact its equally necessary connection with social reality.

Milosz's poem, "The Poor Poet," was written in Warsaw in 1944, during the last horrors of the war. It recapitulates the passage that we have seen in the young poet from an aesthetic of joy to an aesthetic of tragedy; it is modernist in its hatred of the mutually tormenting relation between the arranged symbolic order of art and the random tragic scene of life; and it sees the creating of the symbolic order as a form of revenge against the horrors of life. The poet as a man is deformed by the deformations he witnesses; and for all the beauty he creates he cannot himself be beautiful but must share the deformities of the world:

The Poor Poet

The first movement is singing,
A free voice, filling mountains and valleys.
The first movement is joy,
But it is taken away.

And now that the years have transformed my blood
And thousands of planetary systems have been born and
　　died in my flesh,
I sit, a sly and angry poet
With malevolently squinted eyes,
And, weighing a pen in my hand,
I plot revenge.

I poise the pen and it puts forth twigs and leaves, it is
　　covered with blossoms.

And the scent of that tree is impudent, for there, on the real
　　earth,
Such trees do not grow, and like an insult
To suffering humanity is the scent of that tree.

Some take refuge in despair, which is sweet
Like strong tobacco, like a glass of vodka drunk in the hour
　　of annihilation.
Others have the hope of fools, rosy as erotic dreams.

Still others find peace in the idolatry of country,
Which can last for a long time,
Although little longer than the nineteenth century lasts.

But to me a cynical hope is given,
For since I opened my eyes I have seen only the glow of
　　fires, massacres,
Only injustice, humiliation, and the laughable shame of
　　braggarts.

To me is given the hope of revenge on others and on myself.
For I was he who knew
And took from it no profit for myself.

(Selected Poems, 53–54)

Formally, this poem places its one moment of adult "beauty" in one line, recounting the blossoming of the pen and alluding to Aaron's rod. This brief Keatsian moment (with its promise of fruit to come, following the blossoms), is encapsulated, like a kernel, within Milosz's two mentions of revenge: "I plot revenge . . . To me is given the hope of revenge." It is also encapsulated within tragedy ("Joy . . . is taken away") and the common responses to tragedy, whether despair, hope, or idolatry. The poet's "cynical hope" is the penalty for his creation of poetry, and his revenge is directed not only against others but against himself for daring to "insult" suffering humanity with the perfection of form. Milosz's Manichaean spirit poses the problem of content and form in its most violent aspect, as the serenity of form (even here, in the concentric form of this lyric) tortures the anguish of content ("fires, massacres, . . . injustice, humiliation . . . shame"). There can be, according to Milosz, no political poetry that does not aim at the aesthetic equilibrium of form. Art, in its social function, thus enacts for us the paradox of our orderly symbolic capacity as it exists within the disorder it symbolizes.

A poem by Seamus Heaney about Chekhov traces again the young writer's passage from sensuous pleasure to social obligation. The recognition of social obligation by the writer must pass, the poem suggests, not into social activism but rather into symbolic representation. In the poem, as in fact, Chekhov decides to leave his attractive life in Moscow to go to see the penal colony on the faraway island of Sakhalin, off the east coast of Russia below Japan. Though Chekhov is a doctor, he does not go to Sakhalin to minister to the convicts, but rather to observe, and to write a book. He even forces himself to stay to watch a flogging in order to see the full reality of life in the colony. And then he has to find the right tone to write about what he has seen — not tract, not thesis. Once he has admitted the colony to his consciousness, he will never be able to exorcise it; he will carry a second convict-self within him. The parallels with Northern Ireland need no describing; the poet composing this poem has left Northern Ireland and lives in the Republic, but he writes about the reality he has left behind, and he must find a symbolic way to enact its truth.

Chekhov's biographer recounts that, as he departed for Sakhalin, the friends who came to see him off at the railway station gave him a bottle of cognac to drink when he should have arrived (by rail and boat and troika) at Sakhalin, thousands of miles away. The cognac is Chekhov's last taste of uncomplicated sensual joy; henceforth he will be a symbolic convict.

Chekhov on Sakhalin

So, he would pay his "debt to medicine."
But first he drank cognac by the ocean
With his back to all he travelled north to face.
His head was swimming free as the troikas

Of Tyumin, he looked down from the rail
Of his thirty years and saw a mile
Into himself as if he were clear water:
Lake Baikhal from the deckrail of the steamer.

That far north, Siberia was south.
Should it have been an ulcer in the mouth,
The cognac that the Moscow literati
Packed off with him to a penal colony —

Him, born, you may say, under the counter?
At least that meant he knew its worth. No cantor
In full throat by the iconostasis
Got holier joy than he got from that glass

That shone and warmed like diamonds warming
On some pert young cleavage in a salon,
Inviolable and affronting.
He felt the glass go cold in the midnight sun.

When he staggered up and smashed it on the stones
It rang as clearly as the convict's chains
That haunted him. In the months to come
It rang on like the burden of his freedom

To try for the right tone — not tract, not thesis —
And walk away from floggings. He who thought to squeeze
His slave's blood out and waken the free man
Shadowed a convict guide through Sakhalin.

Station Island, 18–19

Heaney's poem implies that the way to write about the condition of the poet in twentieth-century Ireland is to write about a nineteenth-century Russian incident. The indirection proper to art is reflected thematically here in the repudiation of religious tract and political thesis alike: Chekhov's book is detached, descriptive, the book of a novelist, not an evangelist or a social reformer. Heaney's formal refusal to mention any audience for Chekhov's eventual book enacts the one condition for socially effective art — that it be directed, not to the transformation of its putative audience, but to the transformation of the artist's own self. By acknowledging his own past as the grandson of a serf and the son of a grocer, Chekhov can enter the chains of the convict and write powerfully about them. At the same time, he drinks with full relish and intoxication the brandy of his Moscow self, before he turns to "all he travelled north to face." The self-transformation of Keats's goddess of the corn acknowledged a similar death in the self as the condition of an art that could nourish others.

In separate ways, Milosz and Heaney have retraced the steps toward an analysis of art that we have seen in Keats. It is important to each of them to assert that poetry does perform a social function; it is equally important to them to remove it from a direct and journalistic mimesis. The poet indeed witnesses, constructs, and records; but the creation of a symbolic and musical form is the imperative, in the end, which he must serve if his witness is to be believed.

9

Reading Walt Whitman

"When Lilacs Last in the Dooryard Bloom'd" is one of six elegies that Whitman wrote for Lincoln. Two of them were rejected from *Leaves of Grass*; he printed the other four together (1871 Second Issue) under the general title "Memories of President Lincoln." This group title is in fact misleading; there are no "memories" of Lincoln — of his upbringing, character, or actions in office — in the first three printed elegies at all. Only in the last, "This Dust," first published in 1871 (Second Issue), is it said that Lincoln was "gentle, plain, just and resolute" and that under his "cautious hand" the Union was saved (339).* The other three poems, all written in 1865, could well have named Lincoln and attributed to him the preservation of the Union, but they do not. The first of the printed elegies, "Hush'd Be the Camps Today," dated the day of Lincoln's burial, was composed early enough to be included in *Drum-Taps* (1865); the other two elegies, "Lilacs" and "O Captain! My Captain!," were included in the 1865 *Sequel to Drum-Taps.* Against "O Captain" and its appeal to public taste, we set the more private "Lilacs." In both "Hush'd Be the Camps" and "O Captain!" Whitman places himself in a subordinate role; in the one he is a soldier whose commander in chief has died, and in the other he is a son and a crew member on the ship of state whose father-captain has been shot to death. However, the end of "Hush'd Be the Camps" presages the writing of "Lilacs," as the humble "soldier" who speaks the poem charges an unnamed poet to "sing in our name, . . . / Sing . . . one verse, / For the heavy hearts of soldiers" (339). We know what the mourning soldier says and what the grieving son-shipmate says, and even, in

---

* Quotations cited by page number are from Blodgett and Bradley's edition of Whitman. Early poems will be cited from Brasher's edition.

the 1871 elegy, what the orator-eulogist at the grave says — "This dust was once the man" who saved the Union. But not until we come to "Lilacs" do we learn what the poet says, and how it is that a poet says things, and how his words differ from what a citizen-mourner might say, or an orator, or a eulogist, or an historical chronicler.

When, in "Lilacs," Whitman rises to his own utterance as poet, he takes a commanding position, turning away from the frigid public allegory of the ship of state to what he knew much better — the land. He proposed to make what he called "the large unconscious scenery of my land" conscious at last. The slow progress by rail of Lincoln's coffin from the East Coast to the middle of the continent, from Washington to Springfield, Illinois, from city to city through the rural expanses of America, gave Whitman a peculiarly congenial pictorial base to his poem, satisfying his appetite for progressive and teleological movement to a goal and his equal appetite for expanding visual panoramas. But if we ask where he gathered the other materials of his poem, we must look beyond the historical narrative of Lincoln's burial journey, into Whitman's own history and the history of some earlier compositions.

In 1840, when he was twenty-one, Whitman had boasted that America, in contrast to Europe, would never know the evil of political assassination:

> Here at length is found
> A wide extending shore,
> Where Freedom's starry gleam,
> Shines with unvarying beam;
> Not as it did of yore,
> With flickering flash, when CAESAR fell,
> Or haughty GESLER heard his knell
> Or STUART rolled in gore.
>
> Nor let our foes presume
> That this heart-prized union band,
> Will e'er be severed by the stroke
> Of a fraternal hand.
> ("The Columbian's Song," Brasher 13)

The war between the states and the death of Lincoln refuted these naive words, and "Lilacs" is the elegy for Whitman's own untried hopes and for a fantasized America of pure optimism and progressive harmony. Whitman's own past had to be represented in "Lilacs" so that he could base his own present grief and his future resolves upon it; nothing is more touching in the poem than the reprise in it of Whitman's earlier work.

I want to mention first of all those fragments from the past — fragments, we may say, of Whitman's own past perceptions. Out of the voluminous writings that antedate April 1865, Whitman gathered a few crucial passages; in some fashion they were in his mind while he wrote "Lilacs." The first is a group of fragments called "Debris," which he had published in 1860; he never again reprinted those portions of the group I am about to quote, as though he knew he had used them up in "Lilacs." The first is Whitman's beautiful, humorous, and hopeful presentation of himself as a new messiah, holding the happiest emblems he can find from the world of copious nature — a robin's egg, a branch of gooseberries, a scarlet tomato, and a white pebble from the beach:

> I will take an egg out of the robin's nest in the orchard,
> I will take a branch of gooseberries from the old bush in the
>   garden, and go and preach to the world;
> You shall see I will not meet a single heretic or scorner,
> You shall see how I stump clergymen, and confound them,
> You shall see me showing a scarlet tomato, and a white
>   pebble from the beach.   (607)

This passage undergoes a metamorphosis for "Lilacs":

> From this bush in the dooryard,
> With delicate-color'd blossoms and heart-shaped leaves of
>   rich green,
> A sprig with its flower I break . . .
>
> Blossoms and branches green to coffins all I bring . . .
>
> Copious I break, I break the sprigs from the bushes,
> With loaded arms I come, pouring for you,
> For you and the coffins all of you O death.   (329–331)

The young risen god of the egg and gooseberry branch is now a god of a different tonality, perceiving not the annual (the egg, the tomato) but his new emblem, the perennial, the lilac of mourning and heart-shaped tenderness. But above all, and crucially for Whitman, the flower is "the lilac that blooms the first" (331) — first not only temporally, but first in his history of perception. Here Whitman is remembering the autobiography of his perceptual life, "There Was a Child Went Forth" (1855), where the first things mentioned that became part of that child were "the early lilacs" (364). In that verse autobiography, Whitman takes the child from his dooryard (where at his first step outside the house he sees the lilac at the stoop) out to the horizon's edge, but the untried child who sees the lilacs is aware only of their name and color. It is the grieving poet, in a change of perception, who now sees that the leaves are heart-shaped, remarks the delicacy of the lavender color of the blossoms (that lavender which was in dress the color of subdued mourning), and recalls the recurrent stable promise of its bloom — "lilac blooming perennial" (328). The lilies and roses that Whitman adds to his armfuls of lilac represent in their emblematic purity and passion a homage to the language of flowers in literature, but Whitman's heart is not with the cultivated "bouquets of roses" so much as with the domestic sprigs broken from his childhood lilac.

The second borrowing from "Debris" gave Whitman his elegiac "solution" to "Lilacs" — the remarkable image of his walk into the swamp holding by the hand two comrades, whom he enigmatically names the knowledge of death and the thought of death. In "Debris," Whitman envisaged an odd procession by threes in which, in each line, an old man holds two other old men by the hand:

> They are beautiful — the one in the middle of each group
>   holds his companions by the hand,
> As they walk, they give out perfume wherever they
>   walk. (607)

The deliberately nonerotic companionship implied by a group of three coincides, here, with Whitman's imagining this form of association as the appropriate one for the old; any procession of the young would have to be paired off two by two. In reimagining the trio in "Lilacs" and placing himself between two forms of death, Whitman turns definitively away from that erotic self which had dominated *Children of Adam* and *Calamus* and sets himself in the orbit of age and death. This change from walking with an erotic companion to walking in the company of more than one person comes about only by a loss of love; the last vignette in "Debris" (reused and changed in "As If a Phantom Caressed Me" in the 1892 edition of *Leaves of Grass*) reads as follows (the phrase in brackets was added in 1892):

> I thought I was not alone, walking here by the shore,
> But the one I thought was with me, as now I walk by the
>   shore, [the one I loved that caress'd me]
> As I lean and look through the glimmering light — that one
>   has utterly disappeared,
> And those appear that perplex me.   (608)

Those perplexing apparitions, hinted at in 1860 in "Debris," become in "Lilacs" Whitman's death companions.

Other fragments pressed forward in Whitman's mind as he composed. One was his recent question in *Drum-Taps*:

> Must I change my triumphant songs?
> Must I indeed learn to chant the cold dirges of the baffled?
> And sullen hymns of defeat?
>
> ("Year that Trembled and Reel'd Beneath Me," 308)

It was in "Lilacs" that Whitman sought to find a middle ground between triumph and "the mournful voices of the dirges pour'd around the coffin" (330), to find not a sullen hymn of defeat but an acceptable "Burial Hymn" for a man whose life, he was certain, transcended the brutal fact of his death. He wished to find, in the language of perception, an equivalent for transcendence, and he turned to three objects of perception — the star, the flower, and the song of the bird — as ways of exploring that problem of equivalency.

In 1850, Whitman had printed in the *Daily Tribune* a poem about the carnage of the 1848 revolutions abroad; in the 1856 *Leaves of Grass* he had called it "Poem of the Dead Young Men of Europe, the 72d and 73d Years of These States." (In 1850, he had called the poem "Resurgemus"; in the Civil War elegies, there is no mention of resurrection.) At that time, the far-off carnage had seemed to him necessitated by the struggle against European decadence — not a phenomenon that could happen in an America where democracy, as he thought, had been achieved. Now, made ill by his sight of the dead young men of America, he remembered his earlier poem, which declared that the "bloody corpses of young men . . . / those hearts pierc'd by the gray lead, / Cold and motionless as they seem live elsewhere with unslaughtered vitality" (267–268). In 1865 he could no longer affirm the unslaughtered vitality of the dead. He remembered too his "Song of the Banner at Daybreak" (1865), written in the elation of the first days of the Civil War: "Over all, (aye! aye!)" sings the poet, "my little and lengthen'd pennant shaped like a sword,"

> Runs swiftly up indicating war and defiance — and now the
>   halyards have rais'd it,
> Side of my banner broad and blue, side of my starry banner,
> Discarding peace over all the sea and land.　(288)

This star-spangled banner, it is true, presages "slaughter, premature death," but the banner, undaunted, announces a new aesthetic that will blend the peaceful with "demons and death" — "Our voice persuasive no more, / Croaking like crows here in the wind" (289). At the beginning of the poem, the poet had used the "Lilacs" word "twine":

> I'll weave the chord and twine in,
> Man's desire and babe's desire, I'll twine them in, I'll put in
>   life,
> I'll put in the bayonet's flashing point, I'll let bullets and
>   slugs whizz. . . .
> I'll pour the verse with streams of blood.　(285)

This facile aesthetic, in which all perceptions can intermingle simply because the perceiving apparatus is itself single, "a kosmos," is sharply rebuked in "Lilacs," where what is twined together must have a symphonic harmony, even if it includes life and death at once. Whitman's later "twining" of lilac and star and bird is a sober recantation of this earlier flashy twining; his hermit thrush is a recantation of the croaking crow; his pouring of dirges and flowers is a recantation of the pouring of streams of blood. The slaughtered young men of 1848 and the intact banner of 1860 reappear, corrected, in "Lilacs." The battle flags now are "pierc'd with missiles . . . and torn and bloody, / And at last but a few shreds left on the staffs" (336), and the young men have now no unslaughtered vitality; the carnage is complete:

> I saw battle-corpses, myriads of them,
> And the white skeletons of young men, I saw them,
> I saw the debris and debris of all the slain soldiers of the
>   war. (336)

Whitman has resuscitated his earlier title, "Debris," to use not only of the remains of bodies but also of the remains of organic life; the violets of "Lilacs" had been seen "spotting the gray debris" of the woods. From "Song of the Banner at Daybreak" Whitman borrowed also the unrolling scenery of "Lilacs," down to the phrase "measureless light" — but again the perception is corrected, abandoning the original shrill cry of the pennant "Fly in the clouds and winds with me, and play with the measureless light" (285), and adopting a deeper sense of the value and charity of the light: "Lo . . . / the gentle soft-born measureless light" (333). With the correction of various perceptions — of what battle flags are likely to become, of the future of corpses, of the gifts of light — comes a correction of tonality, a modifying depth of reflection, as Whitman reins in his wish to be assertive and boisterous and celebratory — whether of martyrs or war banners or gooseberry branches. At the same time he checks his rebellious "Luciferian" self, which wishes, in defeat, to be baffled, sullen, and vengeful. In the gap between the aggressive perceptions dominated by unmediated visual energies and a defensive optimism, on the one hand, and the balked and despairing perceptions of "thick gloom," on the other, Whitman finds the new tonality of "Lilacs."

Yet another borrowing deserves mention. The "Year of Meteors (1859–60)," as Whitman called it, brought forth a poem by that name in *Drum-Taps*, which recalled a comet that after a moment "departed, dropt in the night, and was gone" (239). The reworking in "Lilacs" addresses the star "where you sad orb, / Concluded, dropt in the night, and was gone" (331). The earlier poem applies the disappearance of the comet to the poet's own envisaged death:

> Year of comets and meteors transient and strange — lo! even
>   here one equally transient and strange!
> As I flit through you hastily, soon to fall and be gone, what
>   is this chant,
> What am I myself but one of your meteors? (239)

The star that drops in "Lilacs" is tinged by this recollection with thoughts of Whitman's death as well as Lincoln's. (Later, in "O Star of France" [1871], Whitman will say of the "dim smitten star" that it is a symbol "not of France alone" but also a "pale symbol of my soul, its dearest hopes" [396]; we may assume the same of the star of "Lilacs.")

Finally, Whitman borrowed from his unpublished early (pre-1855) poem "Pictures," which represented his own skull as a house in which he keeps pictures:

> In a little house pictures I keep, many pictures hanging
>   suspended — It is not a fixed house,
> It is round — it is but a few inches from one side of it to the
>   other side,
> But behold! it has room enough — in it, hundreds and
>   thousands, — all the varieties.   (642)

In turning his picture house into a tomb in "Lilacs," Whitman himself becomes in effect as one "disembodied, triumphant, dead" (506), transformed into his own memorial gallery as well as the decorator of a tomb for his president. Insofar as he is an artist, he is already as one dead; this realization, articulated more completely elsewhere in *Leaves of Grass,* in part enables the song of the bird in "Lilacs."

I have emphasized these "corrected perceptions" present in "Lilacs" because I believe that the pathos of the poem depends in part on them and on our noticing that Whitman included them as he composed the elegy. But the pathos of the poem also depends on what we might call its "mythology of modern death" (to borrow a phrase from Stevens). Whitman was determined not to invoke, for Lincoln's burial hymn, those Christian consolations which were being relied on in the "dim-lit churches" with their "shuddering organs" and "tolling tolling bells' perpetual clang" (331). Whitman's unusual choice of three recurrent keynotes — lilac and star and bird — has often been remarked, but varying symbolic burdens have been attributed to these objects of perception. (Blodgett and Bradley, in their edition of Whitman, call them, respectively, the poet's love, Lincoln, and the chant of death (328). While this may not be untrue, I believe there is more to be said.) It seems to me that Whitman was constrained to his three objects by a wish to represent the three traditional divisions of the universe into the heavens, the earth, and the underworld. A poem was always, for Whitman, both a cosmos and a human body, as the poem "Kosmos" (1860) declares: the poet "out of the theory of the earth and of his or her body, understands by subtle analogies all other theories / The theory of a city, a poem, and of the large politics of these States" (392–393). In "Lilacs," then, the perennial lilac of earth stands between the fateful star above it and the bird singing in the ghostly trees of the swamp, that swamp which, with its water and its dim shore, mimics the geography of Hades. The lilac, broken and offered by the elegist, is governed from above by the celestial star and from below by the unconscious outlet song of life. These are only approximations; but we may also say that fate, free will, and the unconscious are as much invoked by Whitman's tripartite chord of symbols as are heaven, earth, and Hades. The archetype of overworld, this world, and underworld is an ancient one in elegy, and has found both classical and Christian embodiments. Whitman deliberately makes the overworld represented by his star fateful rather than providential and the underworld of the bird one of shades rather than demons; in this he is consciously post-Christian, as he reverts to the Greek myths of fate and the afterlife. He is also post-Christian in imagining the sort of tomb, or burial house, he will construct for Lincoln; he models it after those Egyptian tombs frescoed, on the inside, with scenes of daily life:

> O what shall I hang on the chamber walls?
> And what shall the pictures be that I hang on the walls,
> To adorn the burial-house of him I love?
>
> Pictures of growing spring and farms and homes,
> With the fourth-month eve at sundown, and the gray smoke
>   lucid and bright,
> With floods of the yellow gold of the gorgeous, indolent,
>   sinking sun, burning, expanding the air . .
> And the city at hand with dwellings so dense, and stacks of
>   chimneys,
> And all the scenes of life and the workshops, and the
>   workmen homeward returning.   (332–333)

(It was, we recall, an Egyptian tomb that Whitman seemed to wish to construct for himself, years later, in a final protest against Christian memorial architecture, whether Gothic chantries or New England slates with skulls and crossbones.) The only residue of Christian symbolism in "Lilacs" lies in the majestic sight of the risen wheat —

"the yellow-spear'd wheat, every grain from its shroud in the dark-brown fields uprisen" (330) — but that phrase is so defiantly natu-ralized by its placement among violets and apple blossoms that it becomes as much pagan as Christian. Whitman's idea of an American elegy is one that promises the dead no afterlife, one that celebrates its rite far from those of the churches, and one that ends, as this one does, in the Hades of the mind — "There in the fragrant pines and the cedars dusk and dim" (337).

This is the place where all the Lincoln poems end. In the first of them, Lincoln is the dead commander: "They invault the coffin there . . . / They close the doors of earth upon him" (339). In "O Captain!" he is "fallen cold and dead"; in the last of the poems he is "this dust" that "was once the man." Whitman's youthful poems had made promises of immortality, sometimes bold ones, as in the con-ventional resurrection of "Our Future Lot" (1838):

> That sorrowing heart of thine
> Ere long will find a house of rest;
> Thy form, re-purified shall rise,
> In robes of beauty drest.   (Brasher 28)

Sometimes the promises were more cautious, as in "We Shall Rest at Last" (1840). There, wise men say

> That when we leave our land of care,
> We float to a mysterious shore,
> Peaceful, and pure, and fair.   (Brasher 17)

We can judge from Whitman's unremitting wish to end poems in the affirmative the degree of moral strength and aesthetic purity of in-tention he needed to draw on when he ended "Lilacs" in the shadows.

The "plot" of the elegy is a long resistance on Whitman's part to the experience in the swamp. Finally, he concedes to it, and accepts the brotherhood of the bleeding throat, tallying with his own "outlet song" of death the song of the bird. But before that wordless song can be translated into language by his voice he must undergo an ordeal by silence. He flees forth, with the knowledge of death and the thought of death as companions, entering the triadic social grouping of age, and subjects himself to "the hiding receiving night that talks not" (334). "The night that talks not" is perhaps the strangest of all the strange phrases in the poem. "The hiding receiving night" is formally linked by its participial adjectives to two other forms in the poem: the light "spreading bathing all" (333) and the oceanic "cool-enfolding" "sure-enwinding" death (335). Light, darkness, and the ocean seemed to Whitman the three elemental enveloping mediums that we know — each was capable of taking the whole world in its fluid embrace. Each precludes the others. Light is one facilitating medium, and many things can be seen only through its mercy: "The gentle soft-born measureless light, / The miracle spreading bathing all" (333). But in the night that talks not, in noiseless dreams, all in silence, Whitman is able to see with a sight different from that of his corporeal eye which saw the large unconscious scenery of his land with its lakes and forests. The night, for Whitman, is rarely a time of sleep; rather, it is a time of vigils, of tears, and of insight. In the darkness of the underworld, a different sight is unbound, loosed from the constrictions that paradoxically kept it bound in the upperworld of fulfilled noon: "My sight that was bound in my eyes unclosed, / As to long panoramas of visions" (336).

"And I *saw*" says Whitman. What he sees is that naked vision of the corpse to which all truthful elegists must come. Whitman deflects it briefly by seeing instead the anthropomorphized banners pierced and shredded, torn and bloody, and the staffs all splintered and broken; but he then sees the "battle corpses . . . / And the white skeletons of young men . . . / . . . the debris and debris of all the slain soldiers of the war" (336). It has taken Whitman 180 lines to come in darkness and silence to the heart of his vision. Then, mediating between the spectacularly beautiful sights visible in the medium of daylight and the spectacularly somber visions revealed by the medium of darkness, comes the passage through the medium of water — the carol of the bird, tallied by the voice of Whitman's spirit. Water, for Whitman, is the element of rest, of floating, of buoyancy, of abandon to being without sight or insight; we might say that it was only in the water that he could sleep. The swamp to which he goes is a distinctly watery underworld — he flees "down to the shores of the water, the path by the swamp in the dimness, / To the solemn shadowy cedars and ghostly pines so still" (334).

It is surely the most extraordinary word in the poem, the word "swamp" — doing duty for Hades, for the realm of the ghosts and the shades, and for the domain of the solitary singer. A dark and hidden place of water must here do service for Whitman's more usual turning to the sea, when he needed a final origin and destination.

One source for Whitman's "lovely and soothing death" that "undulates round the world" can be deduced from his earlier version of this passage in "Reconciliation" (1865). It is beautiful, Whitman there says, "That the hands of the sisters Death and Night incessantly softly wash again, and ever again, this soil'd world" (321) — and this passage is a reminiscence of Keats's "Bright Star," in which the North Star sees "the moving waters at their priestlike task / Of pure ablution round earth's human shores." The "soil'd world" of "Reconciliation" was soiled by the hideous spectacles of war that Whitman recorded in *Specimen Days* — the amputations, the gangrene, the typhoid, the gaping wounds, the tuberculosis, the heaps of unburied corpses, the starving prisoners from Andersonville. In the carol of the bird, no soiled earth is mentioned, but from the first note of the carol — the apostrophe to death as "sane" and "sacred" — we sense the implied insanity and profanity that provoke the adjectives Whitman chooses. The same is true of subsequent phrases — "soothing death," "delicate death," "strong deliveress": under these words we deduce an unspoken set of opposites, something exacerbating, something gross, and something forcibly fettering the soul. It is only against these concealed horrors that death reveals itself contrastively to be sane, sacred, soothing, delicate, strong, a deliveress. Against the physical and metaphysical carnage of the war there rises in the aria of the bird a carol not of prophesied affection and victory (as in "Over the Carnage Rose Prophetic a Voice") but rather of ultimate despair of human solutions to violence.

It is, as the poem says, the living who remain and suffer. Only the dead are excused from suffering, insanity, and the gross inflictions of war. With characteristic delicacy, Whitman puts himself in a minor place in the list of survivors: for each dead soldier "the mother suffer'd, / And the wife and child and musing comrade suffer'd / And the armies that remain'd suffer'd" (336). The thrice-repeated "suffer'd" is paired inextricably with the twice-repeated "remain'd" until the two verbs become synonymous: to remain is to suffer. It is only as the song of the suffering remnant, voiced by the musing comrade, that we can read the central aria of the poem. It lies, with the knowledge and thought of death, under that long black trail which now spoils the sky for the suffering remnant. Whitman has understood that neither the "measureless light" (the medium of bodily perception) nor the night sky sorrowful with the black cloud and drooping star (the medium of wakeful grief in the troubled soul) will do as the medium of song. He does not sing in the day; he does not sing in the night. He sings only in the swamp, and the medium of song is the ocean, with its rhythmic rise and fall, its capacity to float things on its motion, its preverbal whisper, its cleansing force, and its capacity to absorb all that it receives. Unlike the land in "This Compost," the ocean gives nothing back. Soul and body are alike "lost" in it; it annihilates what it receives, returns all to a prenatal nonbeing. Nothing in the ocean is "perennial"; nothing returns like the evening star. Whitman's carol is "floated" as the ocean is "floating": by predicating the same verb of each, Whitman encourages us to see his funeral song as comparable to the ocean and to death in its ability to embrace all being — lilac and star and bird and dead president — and to enfold them in an undulating coolness far from the warmth of life. The flood of the bliss of rhythmic language absorbs and annihilates the living panorama of the unconscious scenery of the land. In the intoxication of apostrophe, Whitman loses all means of perception; he recalls that there are such things as cities and fields, but he sees and hears nothing, absorbed in his hymn of praise.

For Whitman, finally, every passage from the lived to the written is a passage from the solid to the fluid, the ethereal, the aerial, or the vaporous: "I am as one disembodied, triumphant, dead" (506). The liquid carol, as death's outlet, becomes one of those eluding and fleshless realities made of words toward which Whitman was always tending: "Human thought, poetry or melody, must leave dim escapes and outlets — must possess a certain fluid, serial character . . . Poetic style . . . becomes vista, music, half-tints, and even less than half-tints. True, it may be architecture, but again it may be the forest wild-wood, or the best effects thereof, at twilight, the waving oaks and cedars in the wind, and the impalpable odor" (Preface to *Leaves of Grass* 1876, Blodgett and Bradley 788).

It is thus, always, that Whitman's perceptions culminate. They diffuse into the oceanic or the impalpable, as they draw further away from the senses and closer to the pure rhythmic utterance of words forming in air. Of course, if the enfolding impalpable "retrievements" were not grounded in radically fresh perception, they could not move us. And it is equally true that if this great American elegy were not rooted in all the most venerable elegiac traditions (the procession of mourners, the decking of the grave, the confronting of the corpse, the eulogy, the dirge, and the hymn) we would not appreciate Whitman's profound de-Christianizing of the form* — his recourse to Egyptian burial customs and Greek mythology, his denial of the customary apotheosis, and his refusal (among all his apostrophes to lilacs, star, bird, and death itself) to address the human subject of the elegy. Lincoln, irremediably dead, can never again be addressed as "you" — in his personal being, he is forever dead and inert, deaf to all voice. To abandon the convention — more moving than any other in elegy — of the address to the one dead, is to risk everything in the service of the true.

Finally, the form of "Lilacs" iself embodies Whitman's deepest feelings. The body of the poem is almost rigidly periodic, with successive heaped-up clauses of suspense finally reaching a human end, those conclusions where the syntactic suspense subsides — "A sprig with its flower I break"; "Night and day journeys a coffin"; "I give you my sprig of lilac"; "you . . . dropt in the night and was gone"; "I knew death"; "I saw they were not as was thought"; "I cease from my song." The periodic "stanzas" of the poem, each long sustained and then dropping to a conclusion, are Whitman's embedded syntactic figure for the temporality of all life and action. But the bird's overarching song is understood to be cotemporal with the whole unfolding, from first to last, of the action of the poem; the poet listens constantly to the bird but cannot tally the chant of the bird with the chant of his soul till he enters the darkness of vision in the swamp. The rhythm of the death carol is not periodic. Rather, like the waves of the ocean or the verses of poetry, it is recursive, recurrent, undulant, self-reflexive, self-perpetuating. While the steady temporal progress of daily life can exist only in a forward direction, there occurs around it and enveloping it, Whitman suggests, another ceaseless rhythm, the perpetual arriving, arriving, of death, in the day, in the night, sooner or later, to all, to each. Suitable to this rhythm are the rhythms of ritual events taken out of the routine linear successions of the hours — serenades, dances, feastings; suitable to the rhythm, too, are geographical expanses beyond the reach of ordinary measurement — the open landscape, the high-spread sky, the myriad fields, the huge night, the ocean shore, the wide prairies.

---

* Though Lincoln died on Good Friday, Whitman refuses any Christian association.

The oceanic current of the immeasurable and the perpetual encircles and bathes, Whitman tells us, the foward-directed current of periodic time. We participate, as we read this poem, so dutifully and bitterly in the prolonged periodic suspense of elegiac time that we feel the expansion into oceanic and cosmic space — and the new recurrent rhythms of the carol — as a grateful release. After moving painfully with the coffin on its journey (even if the landscape is beautiful), after being enveloped by the black cloud, we also find a bliss in being given a rhythm on which to float. Though we recur to the vision of human mortality in the final scene of the skeletons of the battle corpses and though we return to a slow temporal and linear withdrawal with our "retrievements out of the night," we have had as we read the poem not one inner experience but two: one is a funeral journey, one is a floating. We have thus a double sense of life and death alike. In his forsaking of historical specificity (so present in all his prose reflections on Lincoln) and in incorporating elements of earlier poems presaging his own death, Whitman composed not a patriotic exercise but a genuine lyric, as inward and personal as it was occasional and historic and American. If it is true, as I think it is, that "When Lilacs Last in the Dooryard Bloom'd" does not reach that vigor of language which we find in "Song of Myself" or "As I Ebb'd with the Ocean of Life," it remains equally true that even in the fetters of a formal occasion and a formal genre Whitman's voice was not quenched. The slight constraints of a decorum that would honor Lincoln make the piece more stately than other poems more purely lyric, but there is room in it still for Whitman's characteristic gestures — a yearning perception, an intransigent Americanness of borrowed non-Christian mythology, and an eventual dissolution into the impalpability of floating song. We keep these as our retrievements out of the night.

III

On Poets

10

Seamus Heaney

With the publication in 1981 of *Poems: 1965-75* and *Preoccupations: Selected Prose, 1968-1978*, together with the 1979 volume *Field Work*, Seamus Heaney became fully accessible to the American public. In England and the United States, Heaney is usually discussed, understandably enough, as an Irish poet (he grew up in Ulster and now lives in the Republic), but that emphasis distorts the beauty and significance of his work: he is as much the legitimate heir of Keats or Frost as of Kavanagh or Yeats, and the history of his consciousness is as germane to our lives as that of any other poet.

Heaney's world as it appeared in his first books was not a particularly social one; human character was not its focus, and its language avoided conversation and polemic. It was not essentially historical; it remained a world of nature. But circumstances changed as Heaney moved out of rural Ulster into the wider world of literature (he has become internationally known and has taught in Dublin, at Berkeley, and at Harvard) and into the worsening political tensions of Ireland. In 1972, after "Bloody Sunday" and the resumption of direct rule of Ulster from Westminster, Heaney moved with his wife and children from Belfast to Wicklow, becoming, he says, an "inner émigré." Such changes could not fail to influence his writing. Heaney's may be an extreme sequence, but a similar passage from a sequestered childhood to a forcibly socialized adulthood happens to us all: we are constrained to acknowledge evil, violence, and our individual helplessness in history. In the process, as Keats said, our intelligences are schooled into souls; in the case of poets, their intelligences are also schooled into style. Heaney's poems and prose are exemplary documents in both schools.

At first, Heaney aggrandized and consecrated his infant world. It is a silent world (his eight siblings are nowhere in the poetry), and it is pregnant with import. The child hiding from his family in the hollow of a willow tree is an oracle who can hear and speak for mute earth; he is its *genius loci:*

> small mouth and ear
> in a woody cleft,
> lobe and larynx
> of the mossy places.

The child is half Ariel, half an innocent Caliban, living with flowers and frogs as though he spoke their language. He watches, in absorptive stillness, the activities on the farm — digging, thatching, churning, plowing. In the poems he writes later, he makes all the farm processes analogous to the process of writing, as if he could understand or justify the writing of verse only by seeing it as a form of sublime agriculture. The pen is a spade he will dig with; like the thatcher, he will ruminate and measure, then finally stitch all together "into a sloped honeycomb, a stubble patch"; he will turn his verses as the farmer turns his plow round furrow ends; he will lay up poems on his shelves as they coagulate, like butter from a churning:

> Out came the four crocks, spilled their heavy lip
> of cream, their white insides, into the sterile churn . . .
> Their short stroke quickened, suddenly
> a yellow curd was weighting the churned up white,
> heavy and rich, coagulated sunlight
> that they fished, dripping, in a wide tin strainer,
> heaped up like gilded gravel in the bowl.

The aesthetic claim made by a poem like this is that the passage of life can indeed be tallied in a narrative, and that the physical processes of life exquisitely resemble the mental ones, with a fluid sliding of import between them. Fluid signals pass in these earlier poems between the human and the natural as well; the poet is a diviner, feeling in his responsive blood the spring water "broadcasting/ Through a green hazel its secret stations." The early world seems perpetual and inexhaustible; as Heaney says of a cow in calf, "her cud and her milk, her heats and her calves / keep coming and going," and her lowing falls as naturally in the poem as her fertility.

On the other hand, the poverty of every child's restricted early life appears in Heaney as rural restriction — famine, bigotry, and decline. His elegies for a lost terrain are paradoxically rich and stinted at once. It is not, for instance, an easy eye in Heaney that watches, first as seed potatoes are halved and buried in furrows called drills and, later, as the potato crop is harvested and stored. The Keatsian harvest is corrected by a harsh history, and an inherited English amplitude of style is roughened, shortened, and darkened:

> Flint-white, purple. They lie scattered
> like inflated pebbles. Native
> to the black hutch of clay
> where the halved seed shot and clotted
> these knobbed and slit-eyed tubers seem
> the petrified hearts of drills. Split
> by the spade, they show white as cream . . .
>
> To be piled in pits; live skulls, blind-eyed.

Already the pastoral narrative premise is put in question, as Heaney arrests his eye at the perpetual: potatoes have always been, will always be impenetrable knobs of a recalcitrant and obdurate reality. The eye is forced to turn to a horizon wider than the farm, or it will be confined to the coarse and stony reality of these earthy hearts.

In turning outward, Heaney finds in one glance shoreline, insularity, and vulnerability to invasion. Ireland, colonized by successive waves of invasion, is not unlike the body, receiving its constant tides of moving impressions:

> Take any minute. A tide
> Is rummaging in
> At the foot of all fields,
> All cliffs and shingles.
>
> Listen. Is it the Danes,
> A black hawk bent on the sail?
> Or the chinking Normans?

The shoreline expands in other poems into a landscape denuded enough to offer, in place of the earlier idyllic cornucopia, a barer, "adult" aesthetic: "things founded clean on their own shapes, / Water and ground in their extremity." This naked conclusiveness accomplishes the divestiture of self necessary to everyone leaving home, but it is premature and cannot long persist against Heaney's sensual responsiveness. The riches of the farm are supplanted by the riches of the sea, and in an eel-fishing sequence, as the eel arrives from beyond the Sargasso Sea and moves up the shoreline and into riverbeds, Heaney leaves the spectatorship of childhood for the restless, subterranean energy of sexuality:

> Against
> ebb, current, rock, rapids
> a muscled icicle
> that melts itself longer
> and fatter, he buries
> his arrival beyond
> light and tidal water,
> investing silt and sand
> with a sleek root . . .
> Dark
> delivers him hungering
> down each undulation.

Heaney is the sort of poet who, because he is so accomplished in each stage, is begrudged his new departures; we want more of what so pleased us earlier. In his lobe and larynx there seemed to lie the greatest natural talent since Keats for creating between words that "binding secret" (as Heaney has called it) which, although it depends in part on sound, depends even more on the intellectual and emotional consent between two words — a consent surprising and, in retrospect, seemingly inevitable, that rises from an arduous cooperation of mind and feeling and ear.

After his early descriptive writing, Heaney took a detour characteristic of colonials writing in the language of the colonizer, and explored his own version of the binding secret in a series of poems meditating on Gaelic place names. The local vocabulary and speech in Northern Ireland make an Ulster poet effectively bilingual in English, as he hears from childhood the Anglo-Irish accent, with its imitation of the English; the sound of English radio; and the correction of his own accent by schoolmasters. Heaney says of his early reading of Keats's ode "To Autumn": "I had a vague satisfaction from 'the small gnats mourn / Among the river sallows,' which would have been complete if it had been 'midges' mourning among the 'sallies.'" The literary language of English "did not delight us by reflecting our experience; it did not re-echo our own speech in formal and surprising arrangements." That statement explains Heaney's experiments with native sounds, but the extent to which a poet can find his voice through his native dialect varies greatly. (We have only to think of the gap between Frost and Stevens to see two American solutions to the colonial predicament; Eliot offers another example — that of expatriation.) The Gaelic solution, which included the imitation of Gaelic verse forms and sonorities, finally seemed to Heaney too programmatic. He would rather, he said in an interview in 1978, think in terms of a Celtic literary temperature: "The temperature of English poetry, on the whole, is a little bit warmer than the temperature of actual English weather — except for Thomas Hardy, maybe, and a few places in Wordsworth. But the temperature of the Irish language, and the emotional weather in that early Irish verse, is colder. It's purer . . . There's one tuning-fork for that music, I think, in Shakespeare: 'Still through the sharp hawthorn blows the cold wind.'" In describing a poetry of "raindrop on a thorn," unlike the "kindlier, more benign" temperature of English verse, Heaney is defining himself as well as the Irish literary tradition. The eye that after early circumscription looked outward to the shore and downward under the ocean and inward to writing now looks farther down. Below the level of agriculture, below even the silt where the eel swims, there lies Heaney's most fertile level — the primitive and slippery ground where memory and creation lie side by side.

For Heaney, the recesses of recollection and imagination alike find their symbol in the landscape of central Ireland — the peat bog, in which successive cultures have left their sunken traces:

> Every layer they strip
> Seems camped on before.
> The bogholes might be Atlantic seepage.
> The wet centre is bottomless.

No longer possessing the child's confidence in narrative cohesiveness or in the easy single correspondences of emblematic agriculture, or even the eel's confidence in its biological purposiveness, Heaney enters the quicksand, where deepening strata offer no sure footing but a source of treasure at once untouched, fearful, deathly, and rich. The poems grow slow, layered, reflective, deep; the hasty faith of youth in clearly defined forms vanishes in favor of a murkier interrogation of the wet center, and the poems move less straightforwardly ahead. Instead, they tend to send ripples outward from an original disturbance. A primitive goddess in whose honor bodies and gold were deposited in the bog presides over these poems. She is still agricultural, and in that sense linked to the early farm, but she is pre-Christian, and she belongs not to retrospection but to introspection.

Heaney's irreproachable sequence of bog poems appeared in *Wintering Out* (1972) and in *North* (1975). They brought him to public attention, not only because the poems were so accomplished and unfaltering but because they took on political and historical force in the relation — sometimes indirect and sometimes pointed — that they bore to the undeclared war in Ulster. In 1969, Faber (Heaney's English publisher) had brought out, in English translation, a book called *The Bog People*, by the Danish archeologist P. V. Glob, containing pictures of bodies that had been slain in prehistoric religious rituals and preserved by the action of the water in Danish bogs. Heaney's poems postulate an entire violent Northland, of which Ireland and Denmark, Celt and Viking are equally part, where ritual sacrifices, of which the Ulster murders on both sides are simply recurrences, are tribal customs defeating all individual reason or endeavor. The exhumed bodies seem to Heaney, who saw them in Denmark, sometimes victims, sometimes saints; he pores over them as though they could reveal to him something obscured by successive encrustations of civilization, education, religion, and politics. He sees the long, dark body of the Grauballe man, preserved for nearly two thousand years, and almost numbers its bones:

> As if he had been poured
> in tar, he lies
> on a pillow of turf
> and seems to weep

the black river of himself.
The grain of his wrists
is like bog oak,
the ball of his heel

like a basalt egg.
His instep has shrunk
cold as a swan's foot
or a wet swamp root.

His hips are the ridge
and purse of a mussel,
his spine an eel arrested
under a glisten of mud.

The head lifts,
the chin is a visor
raised above the vent
of his slashed throat

that has tanned and toughened.
The cured wound
opens inward to a dark
elderberry place.

If, in the end, the Grauballe man is made to stand, in one of Heaney's anxious moralities, for "each hooded victim, / slashed and dumped," he is also, in the plainness of his utter amalgamation of all being (tar, water, wood, basalt, egg, swan, root, mussel, eel, mud, armor, leather), a figure of incomparable beauty. The poet, in his slow, diagnostic gaze, becomes both a geographer of his country's body (its minerals, its turf, its darkened bog oak, its birds and sea creatures, its swamps, its fruit) and a judge balancing a pair of scales to weigh "beauty and atrocity." Heaney finds in his patient vision of the topography of the dead a linear movement wholly devoid, for moral purposes, of resurrective power. This corpse and the others in Ulster are as dead, and as violently dead, after he has mapped their repose as before.

The bog poems represent Heaney's coming to grips with an intractable element deep both in personal life (insofar as the bog and its contents represent the unconscious) and in history. They lift him free from a superficial piety that would put either sectarian or national names to the Ulster killings, and they enable a hymn to the "ruminant ground," which as it digests "mollusc and seed-pod" is an "embalmer / of votive goods / and sabred fugitives." In words that can stand beside Whitman's "This Compost," Heaney undergoes the tireless cyclic processes of the ground:

> The mothers of autumn
> sour and sink,
> ferments of husk and leaf
>
> deepen their ochres.
> Mosses come to a head,
> heather unseeds,
> brackens deposit
>
> their bronze.

This is a poetry of verbs, where each living form gives up its being in its own singular way. Each figure of decay subsides into another grain in the peat, until all living vegetation is seen to be "a windfall composing / the floor it rots into." The poet, kin to the plants, is only another stem in the expanse of bracken and mosses:

> I grew out of all this
> like a weeping willow
> inclined to
> the appetites of gravity.

He remarks dissolution and change by tasting things as they grow sour, feeling them sink in himself, losing part of himself bubbling in the acrid changes of fermentation.

Heaney's subsequent poems in *Field Work* lie alternately under the deepening ochres of mortality and under the sunlight of appetite as he writes, in turn, elegies for those senselessly dead and lyrics of fine palatal relish. He eats oysters the way Keats swallowed his nectarine, but in the midst of pleasure he feels guilt as he recalls that the conquering Romans had oysters packed in ice brought to them over the Alps:

> Over the Alps, packed deep in hay and snow,
> The Romans hauled their oysters south to Rome:
> I saw damp panniers disgorge
> The frond-lipped, brine-stung
> Glut of privilege.

"The seeming needs of my fool-driven land," as Yeats called them, are never far away, much as Heaney would like to go back to being the lobe and larynx of the mossy or briny places:

> [I] was angry that my trust could not repose
> In the clear light, like poetry or freedom
> Leaning in from sea. I ate the day
> Deliberately, that its tang
> Might quicken me all into verb, pure verb.

But the pure, living freedom of the Wordsworthian child, who as verb simply *is*, is unrecapturable, as is the child's sexual innocence. Earlier in the poem, in a disturbing picture of the opened oysters, yet another source of fracture and culpability is disclosed:

> Alive and violated
> They lay on their beds of ice:
> Bivalves: the split bulb
> And philandering sigh of ocean.
> Millions of them ripped and shucked and scattered.

The poem is agitated by the perception that no sensuality is simple any longer; there is no unclouded day of perfect memory possible. The thorns of conscience and apprehension and moral revulsion prick every repose.

In the elegies of *Field Work,* one friend is recalled whose "candid forehead stopped / A pointblank teatime bullet"; another was blown up in a pub, "his cornered outfaced stare / Blinding in the flash." In each of these poems, Heaney refuses the easy climax of placing death at the end; instead, he puts it squarely in the center, flanked early and late — by life, on the one hand, and memory, on the other. The poems refuse accusation in favor of a steadily widening pool of reflection, question, and recollection. The whole of *Field Work* poses aesthetic questions as well. "You are stained, stained / to perfection," it cries out at one pitch of conviction; at another, it envisages a possible poise "between the tree in leaf and the bare tree"; at yet another, it allows for original rural pieties as well as for a later ambition toward a crystalline arrangement of language, while wanting to make room for a poetry foreign to each:

> There are the mud-flowers of dialect
> And the immortelles of perfect pitch
> And that moment when the bird sings very close
> To the music of what happens.

Writing down "the music of what happens" entails for Heaney poems with a new language and new structures, poems drawing on poets as various as Dante, Marvell, and Wyatt. Heaney wants his social voice to make its way into his poetry, joining that voice of secret brooding in which he first found a poetic self. As Keats said of Milton, he wishes to devote himself rather to the ardors than the pleasures of verse; the attempt seems to be a necessity for every ambitious poet.

The story I have briefly told here — of Heaney's coming of age — is told implicitly in the selected prose (really a collection of *causeries,* since the pieces for the most part began as lectures or radio broadcasts). The first, autobiographical essays — on the farm, on Heaney's boyish reading, on early literary acquaintances, on a Belfast increasingly dominated by "the bankrupt psychology and mythologies implicit in the terms Irish Catholic and Ulster Protestant" — will give American readers a context for the poems. Other pieces take up Irish writers (Kavanagh, Ledwidge, Hewitt, Friel, Montague, Muldoon) and contemporary poets from countries other than Ireland (Mandelstam, MacDiarmid, Stevie Smith, Roethke, Larkin, Lowell, Hill, and Hughes). Against all of these, Heaney is, of course, implicitly defining his own practice, but his finest silent self-inquiry takes place in the major essays here (written between 1974 and 1978) on Hopkins, Wordsworth, and Yeats. In the Hopkins essay, Heaney's youthful recognition of similarity between himself and Hopkins provokes an adult recognition of difference, producing the best essay yet written on the relation between diction and aesthetic in Hopkins. The essay on Wordsworth argues, against a good deal of current opinion, that

Wordsworth conceived of the poetic act as "an act of complaisance with natural impulses and tendencies," and sets this Wordsworthian yielding a trifle too diametrically against the implacable control of Yeats. Yeats is said to have "moved within his mode of vision as within . . . some bullet-proof glass of the spirit," putting "a kind of vitreous finish on the work itself" and offering us "the arched back of English in place of its copious lap." Yeatsian implacability is perhaps less foreign to Heaney than he believes; but Heaney's searching senses, his drifting depths and layers and pools and wells, his tenderness of inquiry, his apprehensions of quickening life are far from Yeats's controlling reins and his "domineering intellect" and "equestrian profile." Yet Heaney, through the example of Yeats, preaches himself a sermon in middle age: "[Yeats] bothers you with the suggestion that if you have managed to do one kind of poem in your own way, you should cast off that way and face into another area of your experience until you have learned a new voice to say that area properly." It is an injunction that Heaney has followed — though he could equally have taken the advice from Keats or Lowell.

Heaney speaks in these discussions to nonpoets, but always as a poet; that is, we find in his essays, as in Keats's letters or Lawrence's *Studies in Classic American Literature,* an instinctual alternative to the criticism written by critics. From Heaney's pages we see a shape of poetry arising. It is something "with the aura and authenticity of archeological finds." It uses words "drowsy from their slumber in the unconscious," and is "delicious as texture before it is recognized as architectonic." In its "slightly abnormal, slightly numinous vision," it offers "continuous invitation into its echoes and recesses," and it accomplishes an "interlacing and trellising of natural life and mythic life" by its words "trawling the pool of the ear with a net of associations." In the course of the book, these notions take on depth and shape as they are fleshed out by example and comparison, and are tested against another conception of poetry altogether — that of Hopkins and Yeats, where the poet is interested in "the way words strike off one another, the way they are drilled, marched, and countermarched, rather than the way they philander and linger among themselves."

In particular judgments, Heaney's premises are generosity and sympathy, but these do not preclude sharp phrases of characterization. He imagines Geoffrey Hill "indulging in a morose linguistic delectation, dwelling on the potential of each word with much the same slow relish as Leopold Bloom dwells on the thought of his kidney." Philip Larkin's "poem about super-annuated racehorses . . . entitled 'At Grass,' could well be subtitled 'An Elegy in a Country Paddock.'" Stevie Smith "chanted her poems artfully off-key, in a beautifully flawed plainsong that suggested two kinds of auditory experience: an embarrassed party-piece by a child half-way between tears and giggles, and a deliberate *faux-naif* rendition by a virtuoso." The pleasure principle is so commandingly strong in Heaney that he is almost too ready to commend; the hunger in his ear is so relieved by the presence of art that he melts in gratitude toward almost any enhancing words: "Keats has the life of a swarm, fluent and merged; Hopkins has the design of the honeycomb, definite and loaded." Heaney is willing to be solaced by either. As for those who are solaced by neither, like the editors of *The Penguin Book of English Pastoral Verse,* who remark with Marxist distaste that "the pastoral vision is, at base, a false vision . . . its function is to mystify and to obscure the harshness of actual social and economic organization," Heaney asks that they think again about the matter they so harshly define: "Now this sociological filleting of the convention is a bracing corrective to an over-literary savouring of it as a matter of classical imitation and allusion, but it nevertheless entails a certain attenuation of response, so that consideration of the selected poems as made things, as self-delighting buds on the old bough of a tradition, is much curtailed. The Marxist broom sweeps the poetic enterprise clean of those somewhat hedonistic impulses towards the satisfactions of aural and formal play out of which poems arise."

Readers of Heaney's poems will find brief commentaries here on many of his own central poems; to trace the difference between commentary and poem, from fact to a woven form still warm with the feeling that entered into its making, is to see the way something random in life becomes (to use two words of Heaney's about Lowell) both representative and symptomatic. The poems — mammalian, amphibious, vegetative — elude, in their tactile and sensual being, the prose even of their own creator.

II

Station Island, also known as St. Patrick's Purgatory, is an island in Lough Derg, in northwest Ireland. It has been a site of pilgrimage for centuries; tradition says that St. Patrick once fasted and prayed there. The island gives its name to Seamus Heaney's purgatorial collection *Station Island* (1985), which contains five years' work. The book reflects the disquiet of an uprooted life — one of successive dislocations. Heaney's life began in Castledawson, in Northern Ireland; he was educated at St. Columb's College, in Derry, and then at Queen's University, Belfast (where he later taught); he moved in 1972 to the Republic of Ireland, first to Wicklow and later to Dublin, freelancing and teaching. A stint of teaching at Berkeley, from 1970 to 1971, began his acquaintance with the United States; now he is the Boylston Professor of Rhetoric and Oratory at Harvard, dividing his time between Cambridge and Dublin. Though these dislocations and uprootings have been voluntary, they could not be without effect, and the title poem of this volume reviews, in a series of memorial encounters, the "stations" of Heaney's life — especially those of his adolescence, hitherto scanted in his work. Throughout the poem, the poet moves amid a cloud of ghosts, familial, sexual, and professional. Some are admonitory, some reproachful, some encouraging. These spirits appear and disappear after the manner of Dante's shades, as the fiction of the poem brings Heaney as one penitent among a crowd of pilgrims to Station Island, where he stays for the obligatory three-day ritual — fasting, sleeping in a dormitory, attending services at the basilica, walking barefoot round the circular stone "beds," or foundations of ruined monastic beehive cells. The difference between Heaney and the other penitents is that he is no longer a believer. One of the shades, a young priest, accuses him:

"What are you doing here . . . ?

. . . all this you were clear of you walked into
over again. And the god has, as they say, withdrawn.

What are you doing, going through these motions?
Unless . . . Unless . . ." Again he was short of breath
and his whole fevered body yellowed and shook.

"Unless you are here taking the last look."

"The last look" — traditionally taken before dying — is not quite what Heaney is up to in this sequence, but he certainly uses the twelve cantos of the poem to look back at many of his dead: Simon Sweeney, an old "Sabbath-breaker" from Heaney's childhood; the

Irish writer William Carleton (1794–1869), who after he became a
Protestant wrote "The Lough Derg Pilgrim," satirizing Catholic su-
perstition; the twentieth-century poet Patrick Kavanagh, who also
wrote a poem about the Lough Derg pilgrimage; an invalid relative
who died young; the young priest, dead after a few years in the
foreign missions; two schoolmasters; the little girl Heaney first felt
love for; a college friend shot in his shop by terrorists; an archeologist
friend who died young; a cousin murdered by Protestants; an exe-
cuted Catholic terrorist; a monk who prescribed as penance a trans-
lation from John of the Cross; James Joyce. All these characters (with
the exception of the invalid young relative) speak to Heaney, and the
poem offers a polyphony of admonitions, ranging from the trite
("When you're on the road / give lifts to people, you'll always learn
something") to the eloquent — Joyce's advice to the hesitant poet:

> "That subject people stuff is a cod's game,
> infantile, like your peasant pilgrimage.
>
> You lose more of yourself than you redeem
> doing the decent thing. Keep at a tangent.
> When they make the circle wide, it's time to swim
>
> out on your own and fill the element
> with signatures on your own frequency,
> echo soundings, searches, probes, allurements,
>
> elver-gleams in the dark of the whole sea."

More striking than any attributed voice is Heaney's own self-
portrait, full of a Chaucerian irony overpainted with Dantesque ear-
nestness. In "Station Island," Heaney is sometimes (as with Joyce)
the abashed apprentice, sometimes (as with his murdered cousin) the
guilty survivor, sometimes the penitent turning on himself with hal-
lucinatory self-laceration:

> All seemed to run to waste
> As down a swirl of mucky, glittering flood
> Strange polyp floated like a huge corrupt
> Magnolia bloom, surreal as a shed breast,
> My softly awash and blanching self-disgust.

Though the narrative armature of "Station Island" is almost staidly conventional — borrowed from Dante, even down to his traditional words for the appearance and fading of ghosts — the writing often moves out, as in the passage I have just quoted, to the limits of description. Heaney has always had extraordinary descriptive powers — dangerous ones; conscious of the rich, lulling seductions of his early verse, he experiments here in resourceful and daring ways with both the maximizing and the minimizing of description. The dream passage about the corrupt polyp interrupts lushness with the surgical slash of the shed breast; the same typical self-correction can be seen in a passage where William Carleton plays the surgical role, interrupting the dreamy language of the poet:

> "The alders in the hedge," I said, "mushrooms,
> dark-clumped grass where cows or horses dunged,
> the cluck when pith-lined chestnut shells split open
>
> in your hand, the melt of shells corrupting,
> old jampots in a drain clogged up with mud —"
> But now Carleton was interrupting:
>
> "All this is like a trout kept in a spring
> or maggots sown in wounds —
> another life that cleans our element.
>
> We are earthworms of the earth, and all that
> has gone through us is what will be our trace."
> He turned on his heel when he was saying this
>
> and headed up the road at the same hard pace.

This small sample will do to show why Heaney's lines are not corrupted by pure linguistic revel — as Dylan Thomas's often were, their simpler phonetic indulgence unchecked by astringency. Heaney works, in Yeats's phrase, to "articulate sweet sounds together" in ways not cloying to the ear, often restraining his delight in the unforeseen coincidences of language, sometimes allowing the delight to break loose. Under the influence of Lowell, Heaney pruned his young luxuriance severely in some of the poems of *Field Work* (1979). The rapturous lyricism of the early poetry, though never lost, adapted itself to a worldlier tone, released in "Station Island" into mordant vignettes of Irish social life. Here Heaney describes the

ordination of the young priest and his visits back to the parish from
the missions:

> Blurred oval prints of newly ordained faces,
> "Father" pronounced with a fawning relish,
> the sunlit tears of parents being blessed.
>
> I met a young priest, glossy as a blackbird,
>
>   . . . his polished shoes
> unexpectedly secular beneath
> a pleated, lace-hemmed alb of linen cloth . . .
>
> "I'm older now than you when you went away,"
>
> I ventured, feeling a strange reversal.
> "I never could see you on the foreign missions.
> I could only see you on a bicycle,
>
> a clerical student home for the summer
> doomed to the decent thing. Visiting neighbours.
> Drinking tea and praising home-made bread.
>
> Something in them would be ratified
> when they saw you at the door in your black suit,
> arriving like some sort of holy mascot."

The village round sketched here would be familiar to anyone raised
in Ireland. Heaney's satiric phrases — "fawning relish," "holy mas-
cot" — defamiliarize the pieties; the sharpness of his eye is matched
in such places by sharpness of tongue. A brave exactness in saying
the socially unsayable appears in Heaney's epigrammatic summation
of the society of his youth. Though the nostalgia for his "first king-
dom" — so evident in his earliest poems — is still present, he has
added an adult judgment on the deficiencies of its people:

> They were two-faced and accommodating.
> And seed, breed and generation still
> they are holding on, every bit
> as pious and exacting and demeaned.

The five adjectives and the four nouns in this passage hold on to
their places in the lines as if they were sentinels guarding a fort. They

cannot be budged (as anyone can discover by trying to put "two-faced" in the place of "demeaned," or "generation" in the place of "seed"). The words act out the tenaciousness of the Catholics of Northern Ireland, surviving in spite of being — necessarily — "two-faced and accommodating." When words fit together in this embedded way, they make a harsh poetry far from the softer verse of Heaney's youth. It is a poetry aiming not at liquidity but at the solidity of the mason's courses.

11

Stephen Spender: Journals and Poems

The publication in 1986 of Sir Stephen Spender's *Journals 1939–1983* and his revised and augmented *Collected Poems 1928–1985* was an event for those of my generation who, in their youth, memorized his poems out of Oscar Williams's anthology and read his autobiography, *World within World*. The separate elements of the writing draw together in the journals, and prompt a reconsideration of Spender's life and work.

A continuous filament running through the journals traces connections among lifelong friends. As Spender puts it in the poem "From My Diary,"

> I go with lifelong friends to the same parties
> Which we have gone to always.
> We seem the same age always
> Although the parties sometimes change to funerals
> That sometimes used to change to christenings.

Though the ungenerous have noted that the journal accounts of lunches and dinners are sprinkled with the names of the rich and famous, such an acquaintance is one that a talented man of Spender's generation in England could hardly have avoided. The closed and class-conscious world of Spender's upbringing sent its sons to either of the two old universities (Spender went to Oxford), where they met the cohort that would become the governors and artists and writers of the next fifty years. What is unusual about Spender is the divergence of his life from the upper-class norm, and the way he played the hand that fate dealt him. The journal is a poignant record of youth lost and kept, a psychological inquiry into a sensibility "odd" but longing to be "normal," and the history of an inner war between innocence and irony, vision and form.

The writing in the journal is unusual in its candor; it aims at self-revelation and self-judgment without the sacrifice of dignity, and it succeeds in self-incrimination, so to speak, without incriminating others. Spender is harsher on himself than most diarists are. The long passages of self-incrimination — for the betrayal of talent, the forsaking of the central for the peripheral — have been called masochistic by some reviewers, and by others have been taken complacently for the truth. To me they seem, rather, the affliction of a writer to whom the perfect has always been more real than the imperfect. There are many writers, from Chaucer to Dickens, who love and relish the imperfect, but there are other writers, chiefly lyric poets, who *see* (it is not too much to say) and love the perfect — the perfectly harmonious, perfectly shaped, impeccable whole. These writers are subject to passionate misery at the spectacle of inharmonious, distracted, and fragmented life (as well as at the spectacle of unsuccessful, partly realized, or unfinished poems). Both the Christian heaven and utopian social schemes have appealed to such writers as imaginative end points for their visions. Deprived of heaven, Spender took to politics.

What attracted Spender was not, of course, realistic domestic and imperial political interests — such as those, for instance, of his father and two of his uncles — but, rather, the utopian dream of Communism. When that failed (with the usual break over freedom to write), Spender did not, however, forsake politics. His continued interest in political causes and events may be a legacy from the males of both sides of his family, or a result of his partly Jewish descent on his mother's side, or a consequence of his youthful love for and subsequent horror at Germany, the country of origin of his mother's grandparents. In any case, Spender could not, and did not, grow up to be an insular Englishman. He could not even return to being an insular Englishman, as Auden so successfully did in New York. Instead, he has had the strange destiny of one who has lived by choice in several places (Germany, England, the United States, France) and takes upon himself the full consciousness of happenings in countries other than his own. For a mind hungering for perfection, nothing more educational, or more calamitous, can be imagined.

In the more intimate sections of the journal, Spender describes his susceptibility to both homosexual and heterosexual falling in love, his marriages, and his long friendships with both the married and the single. Though the young Spender suffers painfully during his protracted experiments in self-definition, the older Spender, with his second marriage firmly and permanently established and his two children growing up to be among his greatest delights, is free to take himself as he is. It is a problematic life that is revealed — one that combines lasting marital love with love directed toward other men. Spender has written often, with truth and insight, about the different rewards of loving someone of the same sex (with whom one feels reassuringly identical) and loving someone of the opposite sex (with whom one is always exploring chasms of difference). Vignettes of the homosexual world of Auden and Isherwood are interspersed here with glimpses of the world of the married; the journal gives unusual documentation of a sensibility at home in both — one that would feel deprived without both.

Spender's extraordinary tolerance is seen at its best during his rootless American stays (in Holiday Inns, motels, dormitories, anonymous apartments). These expose him to various indignities, surprises, and embarrassments of foreign existence such as most middle-aged people take pains to avoid. His inability to say no (for which he chides himself in his autobiography) has at least the advantage, as he realizes, of granting him an accessibility to experience which the single-minded and the reclusive lose. The journal covers a great deal of geographical, social, and personal terrain, with anecdotes varying from the hilarious to the appalling — all noted down with the gentle speculative curiosity and considerable stoicism that Spender brings to existence.

The journal is written rapidly, usually within a few days of the events it describes; the claim it makes on us is one of spontaneity and accuracy of reporting. Here is Spender at thirty, in September 1939, listening to Hitler on the radio: "I have had the wireless on, playing Hitler's latest speech. His voice varies from a cavernous rumbling to the peaks of an exalted hysteria from which he shrieks like a raucous beast of prey, until the whole chorus of his followers breaks into a thunder of triumphant hatred. Undoubtedly there is something disintegrating about that voice, that applause, and everything they stand for. The cities of one's mind seem to be bombarded, as though a threat could make them fall to pieces." At the same time (and this excerpt represents the other half of the journal), he is a young man worrying about his destiny: "[My father] was furiously ambitious for at least two of his sons, and particularly for me. I hated his kind of journalistic ambitiousness, but I was only able to wriggle out of it by substituting an even more difficult ambition of my own. Instead of being a fake great man, I wanted to be a real great writer. I have resisted my own ambition by sabotaging it for years . . . I learned from my father that it was silly to want to be Lloyd George, but how can I learn that it is silly to want to be Beethoven or Shakespeare?"

"I think continually of those who were truly great" — so begins Spender's early poem that so many of us learned by heart. What is touching in the journal is that Spender never forgets the young man he was or loses him in the eminent man he becomes. Revisionary statements keep occurring, like this one, written at seventy: "It is clear to me that I am much more like my father against whom I reacted than I have realized. What characterized him was incomplete activities enclosed by optimistic rhetoric. Writing journalistic books about subjects he hadn't really studied and hoping that feelings, intuitions, sympathies would carry him through . . . I have done likewise. What makes me different from him is my self-distrust. Still that hasn't been sufficient to stop me."

The interest of Spender's journal for the reader lies especially in the continuities and disruptions of personality which it illustrates, and in the encounters it rapidly sketches: in the earlier years, with Auden, Isherwood, the Sitwells, the Woolfs, Eliot; in the later years, with Lowell, Brodsky, Ginsberg, Pinsky. Spender always remains a neophyte in life, capable of being hurt, shocked, surprised; when David Hockney tells him in 1983 about someone who had died of AIDS, he writes, "All this seemed inexplicable, baffling, terrifying" — adjectives we associate more with adolescence than with the eighth decade of life. It is Spender's capacity for being baffled or terrified or dismayed that gives these pages their freshness, and sustains us through the passages of lunches, dinners, reviews to write, visits to pay, lectures to give, proofs to correct, airplanes to catch. "I like to think of life as at least in part a non-stop festivity," Spender writes in his sixties, resisting — with his disarming capacity for joy — fatigue, age, and obligation.

Spender's *Collected Poems* (1986) revises some old poems, adds a few new poems, and omits some pieces included in his previous *Collected Poems*, published in 1955. The critic in me wishes that Spender had included all his poems in their first, unrevised versions, and that he had dated them and arranged them in the order of their original appearance instead of presenting them in an undated, re-shuffled, revised, and thematically grouped set. However, one has to take one's poet as he is; and Spender, ever the Platonist, regards his published poems as "drafts" (as, indeed, less Platonic poets, like Lowell, have also done). The poems are, in short, still subject to tinkering as the poet seeks ideal expression. Such fluidity of becoming is entirely in accord with Spender's yearning sense of life as a per-petual coming-into-being — a process that never (as the journal bears witness) finds a halt. The personal inflexibility, moral deafness, and intellectual self-righteousness of most adults are absent from all of Spender's work. The verbal and rhythmic awkwardness of some of the poetry is, in fact, obstinate testimony to Spender's unwillingness to curb meaning in the service of form. Though many writers (in-cluding Spender at times) regard pure form as meaning or as discov-ery, Spender's poetics tends toward a visionary, idealist position, in which the poet's duty is that of transcribing accurately an insight or gestalt that exists prior to formal composition.

Nonetheless, in rereading the *Collected Poems* I was struck by how much modernity a poet usually considered very precise and unvision-ary — Elizabeth Bishop — had learned from Spender's practice. Consider, for instance, the opening of a characteristic Spender poem, "Seascape," written in the Forties:

> There are some days the happy ocean lies
> Like an unfingered harp, below the land.
> Afternoon gilds all the silent wires
> Into a burning music for the eyes.
> On mirrors flashing between fine-strung fires
> The shore, heaped up with roses, horses, spires
> Wanders on water tall above ribbed sand.
>
> The motionlessness of the hot sky tires
> And a sigh, like a woman's from inland,
> Brushes the instrument with shadowy hand . . .

Here is the beginning of Bishop's "The Map," first published in *Trial Balances* (1935):

Land lies in water; it is shadowed green.
Shadows, or are they shallows, at its edges
showing the line of long sea-weeded ledges
where weeds hang to the simple blue from green.
Or does the land lean down to lift the sea from under,
drawing it unperturbed around itself?
Along the fine tan sandy shelf
is the land tugging at the sea from under?

In "Seascape," also, Spender's phrase "two zig-zag butterflies like errant dog-roses" could be mistaken for one by Bishop. In "The Map," the "softened" pentameter, the hint of submerged old stanza forms (rhyme royal, ottava rima), the musing nostalgia all suggest that by 1935 Bishop had absorbed the early work of Spender, the lyric "discovery" of the Thirties.

Spender's "naive" quatrains also turn up in Bishop. Here is a Spender poem of the early Forties, with wartime searchlights:

Their ends fuse in a cone of light
Held for a bright instant up
Until they break away again
Smashing that image like a cup.

And here, from "The Armadillo," are Bishop's fire balloons:

Climbing the mountain height,

rising toward a saint
still honored in these parts,
the paper chambers flush and fill with light
that comes and goes, like hearts.

Other illustrations are possible. Bishop's debt to Spender's "The Landscape Near an Aerodrome" is clearly visible in "The Man-Moth." This is all very natural, of course; but it does suggest that Spender invented a new, equivocal tone, rapidly perceived as "modern" and adopted by subsequent poets.

Spender himself had begun writing at Oxford under the influence of Auden, and at first he imitated Auden's self-possessed ironies, his determined use of technological objects (which can be seen in Spender's pylons and airplanes). But no two poets can have been more different. Auden's rigid, brilliant, peremptory, categorizing, allegorical mind demanded forms altogether different from Spender's dreamy, liquid, guilty, hovering sensibility. Auden is a poet of firmly historical time, Spender of timeless nostalgic space. Spender has been perhaps too susceptible to styles other than his own. Yet a recognizable Spenderian style exists — in part deliberately *faux-naif*, in part genuinely pellucid. Spender's desire for the weightless, the transparent, the transfigured, the transcendent (I am paraphrasing from his elegy "Late Stravinsky Listening to Late Beethoven") presses his poems to a clarity that is at war, as he perceives, with modernist hermeticism and irony. He says in the introduction to this volume, "I now think that my best poems are those which are extremely clear and that, perhaps without my being fully aware of it, clarity has always been my aim."

It is certainly true that Spender's best-known poems have been those with that simplicity and clarity, from "An Elementary School Classroom in a Slum" to "Elegy for Margaret." In the most arresting of the new poems in this collection, he brings certain clear and isolated moments of the past into the present, not as memory but as actuality. The coexistence (visible throughout the journals) of past and present in Spender's mind arises from his disbelief in the substantiality of time:

> Today, I see
> Three undergraduates standing talking in
> A college quad. They show each other poems —
> Louis MacNeice, Bernard Spencer and I.
> Louis caught cold in the rain, Bernard fell
> From a train door.
>
> Their lives are now those poems that were
> Pointers to the poems they made their lives.
> We read there in the college quad. Each poem
> Is still a new beginning. If
> They had been finished though they would have died
> Before they died. Being alive,
> Is when each moment's a new start, with past
> And future shuffled between fingers
> For a new game . . .

> I'm dealing out
> My hand to them, one more new botched beginning
> There, where we still stand talking in the quad.

Several "diary poems" exemplify the same sort of clarity and particularity. This specificity represents a change from Spender's beginnings, where he intensely wished (or so it seems to me) to blur the boundaries of sexual, class, and national difference. That wish gave his early poems their willfully soft focus, their emphasis on the atemporal, the collective, and the universal. Airmen, slum children, lovers, the war dead, conscripts appeared in Spender's early poems not (in contrast to Auden's) as social categories but as exemplars of universal selfhood. But Spender's mind was neither historical enough nor collective enough, finally, for Marxist poetry. (He has recently tried to define, with reference to the poetry of the young Spanish Civil War poet Miguel Hernández, a poetry about politics "whose truth seems beyond dispute, outside politics, like certain poems of Walt Whitman in 'Drum-Taps'" — a remark that helps to clarify his own early aims.)

Spender remains, in the history of British poetry, a notable love poet and elegist. He is also one of the important poets of the meaninglessness of war, and of the baseness of feeling it engenders, even in civilians:

> That which sent out the pilot to destroy them
> Was the same will as that with which they send
> An enemy to kill their enemy . . .
> They know the dark is filled with means which are
> Men's plots to murder children.

"Men's plots to murder children": the line may be a pacifist's definition of war, but it is also an incrimination of self and others uttered by a man living, with his pregnant wife, through the London blitz. The journals and the poems interpenetrate in the reading, and should be taken together as traces of a rare life journey — rare in its conception of and aspiration toward a life less mean and constricted than the one that history usually offers its children.

12

Donald Davie: Self-Portraits in Verse

The trenchant and pugnacious self visible in Donald Davie's prose is not quite the self we find portrayed in his lyrics. The self-portrait in the lyrics is a truer, more vexing, and more distressing one than the prose portrait of a sturdy dissenter. Of course the two portraits overlap, not only in intelligence and depth, but in a common style — one that prefers a "horizontal" conversational force to a "vertical" address upward, one that emphasizes the urbane over the romantic, one that insists on the precise and the rational (even in religious matters) over the ecstatic. In the prose and poetry alike, these "sane" and "civil" aspects of style resemble the proverbial figleaf; they are adopted by Davie to hide the primordial shame of rage, pain, cruelty, and doubt. (I hasten to add that Davie's poetry not only admits this shame but makes it the substance of his finest poems.)

In the prose, intellect is called to the bar to justify the air of truculence; the sinner's sin, not Davie's secret pleasure in condemnation, is indicted. When Davie says, for instance, of Hopkins (in *Purity of Diction in English Verse,* 1953), "He has no respect for the language, but gives it Sandow-exercises until it is a muscle-bound monstrosity" (*PD* 175), we read the remark for a view of Hopkins. Here, I choose to read it for a view of Davie, as I also read the offense he takes at Galway Kinnell (in *The Poet in the Imaginary Museum,* 1977): "What a fearsome responsibility for the poet, to lead his readers into bestiality . . . a challenge worthy of a titan! So Charles Manson may have thought. Will Galway Kinnell choose to be a titan, or a human being?" (*PIM* 284; Davie's ellipsis). The extraordinary animus in these quotations (examples could be multiplied) suggests that the wish to denounce may be Davie's strongest emotion, that his most burning desire is to be that societal outlaw, the prophet, calling "Woe unto you" to his society. He is not above voicing such a desire:

> The fact that American poets can now cast themselves as the dissident conscience of their nation, just as Russian and Polish and Hungarian poets have consistently done, ought to bring home to the English reader how remote from our current ways of thinking is any such conception of what being a poet means. As for the English poet, he may find himself wishing that the acute but muffled tensions between himself and his society might build up to the point of strain where he too might be able, without stridency or falseness, to speak for the honour of his nation. (*PIM* 149)

However, in recoil from these prophetic and denunciatory impulses in himself, Davie draws a distinction — the single most important for his poetry — between being a prophet and being a poet. He draws it in the context of a discussion of poetic control, criticizing "a dishevelled poetry [where] the poem and the experience behind the poem are . . . manifestly out of [the poet's] control." The passage is a long one, but central to Davie's life and poetic:

> To be sure, "control" is a word that may easily be misunderstood. Yet I think we need it in order to acknowledge how much of the poetic activity in the act of composition can be summed up in words like "judgement" and "prudence". For I should maintain, in the teeth of Kenneth Rexroth, that, as for *prophetic* poetry (which may be, but need not be, confessional poetry also), it is necessarily an inferior poetry . . . The prophet is above being fair-minded — judiciousness he leaves to someone else. But the poet will absolve himself from none of the responsibilities of being human, he will leave none of those responsibilities to "someone else"; and being human involves the responsibility of being judicious and fair-minded. In this way the poet supports the intellectual venture of humankind, taking his place along with (though *above,* yet also along with) the scholar and the statesman and the learned divine. His poetry supports and nourishes and helps to shape *culture*; the prophet, however, is outside culture and, really, at war with it. He exists on sufferance; he is

on society's expense-account, part of what society can sometimes afford. Not so the poet; he is what society cannot dispense with.   (*PIM* 146)

Davie's prizing of the judicious and the fair-minded accounts for part of his lifelong quarrel with Pound, the poet whose "sculptural" aim in verse he most admires. The quarrel stems also from Pound's abolition of syntax — the very quality which (by contrast to perception, which is phrasal and atomistic) enacts in verse, as Davie sees it, the presence of intellect and law:

[Pound] pins his faith on individual words, grunts, broken phrases, half-uttered exclamations (as we find them in the Cantos), on speech atomized, all syllogistic and syntactical forms broken down. Hence his own esteem of the definite lands him at last in yawning vagueness . . .

It would be too much to say that this is the logical end of abandoning prose syntax. But at least the development from imagism in poetry to fascism in politics is clear and unbroken . . . It is impossible not to trace a connection between the laws of syntax and the laws of society, between tearing a word from its context and choosing a leader out of the ruck. One could almost say, on this showing, that to dislocate syntax in poetry is to threaten the rule of law in the civilized community.   (*PD* 99)

Davie's fondness for quarrelsome apodictic statement of this sort — so pervasively characteristic of his essays — might be expected to reappear in his verse. And so, in a way, it does; but what is apodictically stated there is the prevalence — indeed, the inescapability — of moral and intellectual error. This disarming paradox, whereby stormy assertion of the truth of the prevalence of error saves both prophecy and peccancy, is to me the strongest guarantee of Davie's believability as a poet. The particular torment in which rigidity meets errancy is the hallmark of his verse. And because this torment is most visible in his memorable self-portraits (some phrased in the third person but still visibly self-portraits), I want to direct this essay toward a few of these, early and late.

The Davie self-portrait is simplest when stiff resolve and chagrined change of heart are enacted in separate poems, as they are in two poems dealing with Ireland. Davie, with ties to Ireland stemming from his period of teaching at Trinity College in the Fifties, vows in 1969 never again to return to "Ireland of the Bombers." The word to notice in the poem of that name is not the word of offended British patriotism, "innocents," but the two inserted words of self-knowledge, "stiffly" and "empty," and the decisive word "home":

> Dublin, young manhood's ground,
> Never more I'll roam;
> Stiffly I call my strayed
> Affections home.
>
> Blackbird of Derrycairn,
> Irish song, farewell.
> Bombed innocents could not
> Sing half so well.
>
> Green Leinster, do not weep
> For me, since we must part;
> Dry eyes I pledge to thee,
> And empty heart.
>
> (*Selected Poems*, 1985, 117–118)

Eight years later, returning on invitation to Ireland, Davie reproaches himself for inconsistency:

> "Green Leinster, never weep
>   For me, since we must part.
> Dry eyes I pledge to thee,
>   And empty heart."
>
> Travelling by train
>   — For I am a travelling man —
> Across fields that I laid
>   Under this private ban,
>
> I thought: a travelling man
>   Will come and go, here now
> And gone tomorrow, and
>   He cannot keep a vow.

Forsworn, coming to Sligo
  To mend my battered past,
I thought: it must be true;
  The solder cannot last.

But, dear friends, I could weep.
  Is it the bombs have made
Old lesions knit, old chills
  Warm, and old ghosts be laid?

Atrociously, such changes!
  The winning gentleness
Gentler still, and even
  The poets not so reckless.

Twenty-five years at least
  Higher up the slope
That England plunges down:
  That much ground for hope.

After the expression of these hopes and fears, the "stranger," as
Davie calls himself, leaves Ireland. He had called his strayed affec-
tions home to England in 1969, but now "home" has a different
meaning:

Easy pronouncements from
  The stranger, as he leaves!
The truth is, he was home
  — Or so he half-believes.
                    (*SP* 118–119)

The poem ends in temporariness and temporizing, with a home in
Ireland as well as in England.

  When the stiff man melts, one sees "the life that is fluent even in
the wintriest bronze" (Stevens). Something in Davie is reluctant to
manifest that fluent life, because for him it is allied with the treach-
erous and the slippery. And yet life, as it offers itself to inspection,

always betrays that mobility. Davie's chief statement on the subject appears in *Thomas Hardy and British Poetry* (1973):

> Those cast bronzes which Gautier and Pound respond to so eagerly, as showing how art can be durable and rigid, in fact are fashioned out of the most fluid material; the molten bronze is *poured* into the mould. The rigidity and hardness of the end product are in direct proportion to the fluid malleability in the process of production. Most exegesis of Pound's *Cantos* is wide of the mark because by its very nature exegesis pursues what is said, at the expense of *how* it is said; and this means that the exegetes lead us into a world of continual flux and change which does not at all correspond to our experience as readers, of responding to the hard bright surfaces which Pound's language, when he is in control, presents to us as a sequence of images, each sharp-edged and distinct. The exegetes are necessarily concerned with the process, not with the product; with the bronze while it is still molten, not with the rigid surfaces of the finished bust . . . [The individual psyche] is, as we experience it by introspection, a realm above all protean and malleable, a world of metamorphosis, of merging and self-transforming shapes and fluid contours. Not in those subterranean wynds and galleries, nor in the kneaded wax and the poured bronze which seem their natural concomitant, shall we find what some of us will always want more than anything else — the resistant and persisting, the rigid and the hard, everything that poets have yearned for naively in the image of the stone that resists the chisel and confronts the sunlight. (*TH* 176–177)

As exegete, I indeed want to glance at the fluid self in Davie's verse, but I am equally interested in the moulds into which he pours it. The Irish poems that I have quoted make a childlike and archaic choice of the ballad, a deliberate simplification of form in the service of the single vow made and broken, but it is evident that the vow made fits the ballad form, while the vow transgressed — except for the "pure" moment of hail and farewell — fits uneasily into the ballad lilt, and in fact, since Davie is true to the tenor of his own complication, wrests the form from ballad stanza to intellectual quatrain by the middle of the poem.

It is a sign of Davie's intentness as a poet that he has found a large supply of more complex forms into which to cast his anguish of self-contradiction. In the most accomplished of his religious poems, a recent one called "Advent," the formal equivalent for his mutinous bluster (his own admirable words) is a harsh Anglo-Saxon emphatic alliteration: sooner/settled, fearless/flying, loosed/leash, maunders/ mutinous, better/blusters, bustles/business. The formal equivalent of the predictability of his contrariness is strict repetition: no sooner/no sooner/no sooner. The formal equivalent of his absence of social decorum is the irregularity of his seven-line stanza, rhyming unexpectedly and willfully aslant. In spite of the ostentatiousness of these traits of langauge, they do not outshine the bitterly acute self-portrait of a contradictory man, despising both stability and restlessness, impatient with domesticity while requiring it, arrogant in indecorum, self-important even in the light of God's advent, and finally terrified and rebellious at once, an impotent creature tamed at the last not by Christ's power but by Christ's need of him, as Christ "prevents" him, in St. Paul's idiom, "in charity." Here is the whole of "Advent," a spectacular poem of self-knowledge.

> Some I perceive, content
> And stable in themselves
> And in their place, on whom
> One that I know casts doubt;
> Knowing himself of those
> No sooner settled in
> Than itching to get out.
>
> I hear and partly know
> Of others, fearless and
> Flinging out, whom one
> I know tries to despise;
> Knowing himself of those
> No sooner loosed than they
> Weeping sue for the leash.
>
> Some I see live snug,
> Embosomed. One I know
> Maunders, is mutinous,
> Is never loved enough;
> Being of those who are
> No sooner safely lodged
> They chafe at cherishing.

Some I know who seem
Always in keeping, whom
One I know better blusters
He will not emulate;
Being of those who keep
At Advent, Whitsuntide,
And Harvest Home in Lent.

Some who are his kin
Have strewn the expectant floor
With rushes, long before
The striding shadow grows
And grows above them; he,
The deeper the hush settles,
Bustles about more business.

The eclipse draws near as he
Scuttles from patch to shrinking
Patch of the wintry light,
Chattering, gnashing, not
Oh not to be forced to his knees
By One who, turned to, brings
All quietness and ease.

Self-contradictions, I
Have heard, do not bewilder
That providential care.
Switch and reverse as he
Will, this one I know,
One whose need meets his
Prevents him everywhere.

(SP 120–121)

Davie may reproach us for remembering the pitiable scuttling, chattering, and gnashing of content in this poem more than the stability and firmness of its verse, and his rebuke to exegetes for their emphasis on the psychological has of course its virtue: were the scuttling and the gnashing not poised and balanced in art they could not register as their furtive selves.

Even in an elegy for a friend, Davie will insist on the conscious element in the making of poetry. Unless the "smell of death" undergoes an aestheticizing process, the poet's words of grief will not become a poem. Because for Davie aestheticizing means "sculpting" (as it did not for, say, Keats), a taste accustomed to Keatsian "warmth" may see Davie in his minimalist moments as cold, remote, or scant of feeling. Here is Davie's apologia, his self-portrait as elegist:

July, 1964

I smell a smell of death.
Roethke, who died last year
with whom I drank in London,
wrote the book I am reading;
a friend, of a firm mind,
has died or is dying now,
a telegram informs me;
the wife of a neighbour died
in three quick months of cancer.

Love and art I practise;
they seem to be worth no more
and no less than they were.
The firm mind practised neither.
It practised charity
vocationally and
yet for the most part truly.
Roethke, who practised both,
was slack in his art by the end.

The practice of an art
is to convert all terms
into the terms of art.
By the end of the third stanza
death is a smell no longer;
it is a problem of style.
A man who ought to know me
wrote in a review
my emotional life was meagre.

(*SP* 59)

Is there anything to be said for this as a poem? It seems stinting and bare — almost an instance of the reviewer's quoted accusation of meagerness. If we are not to agree with the reviewer that a stinted style is the sign of a stunted soul, we must look into its propriety, seeking in it signs of that excess or redundancy which, in however hidden a way, is the mark of every art, even a "sculpted" one. (Davie himself says in an early poem that in art "all is patent, and a latency / Is manifest or nothing" (*SP* 22). The redundancy of the first stanza of the elegy is that of the repetition of the fact of death and of its verb: not, "Roethke is dead, as are my firm-minded friend and my neighbor's wife," but rather, "I smell a smell of death. / Roethke . . . died . . . ; / a friend . . . / has died or is dying . . . ; / the wife of a neighbour died." The redundancy of the second stanza is that of the verb "to practise": "Love and art I practise; / . . . the firm mind practised neither. / It practised charity . . . / Roethke . . . practised both." The extreme dryness of this double redundancy should not blind us to its deliberateness as it sets death against various practices of life. The conundrum of the middle of the poem seems like an extended syllogism with some mysterious missing terms which I have guessed at and put in brackets:

> I practise love and art;
> My friend practised neither love nor art;
> My friend practised charity
>   vocationally and yet truly;
> Roethke practised love and art
>   and yet his art went slack;
> Practice does not make perfect;
> [I do not practice charity;]
> Death seems neither to increase nor decrease
>   the value of love and art.
> [I will die whether or not I practise
>   love or art or charity.]
> [The relation of art, love, and charity to death is?]

The third stanza elucidates one hidden proposition, claiming that art dissolves the problem of death by turning it into a problem of style. The reflexive aphorism that "solves" the conundrum partakes of the arid excess of the rest of this harsh elegy:

> The practice of an art
> is to convert all terms
> into the terms of art.

There are moments when aesthetic practice, like religious practice, is habitual, almost (one might say) mechanical, or at least stoic. It can be particularly so in elegy, where a complaisance in "sympathy" or "pity" hides voyeuristic dangers, where a too ready "emotional life," eager not to seem "meagre," is both an aesthetic and a personal betrayal.

At the same time, there is something alleviating, something of the solacing and assuaging power of art, visible in Davie's clenched stanzas. Two features soften his lines here: first, the recurrent feminine endings, composing a quick mini-poem within the whole; "London, informs me, cancer, practise, neither, truly, stanza, longer, know me, meagre"; second, the extra syllables lightening the verse. The poem would sound very different with strict lines and masculine endings. We would then hear a stiffer, less grieving voice, something like the following (if I may be forgiven a rewriting):

> By the end of the verse
> death is a smell no more;
> it is a problem of style.
> A man who knows my work
> wrote in a review
> my emotional life was cold.

The "emotional" Davie lurks in the feminine endings and the reluctant syllabic excess supervening over the "dry" repetitions and the "cold" aphorism.

"We could stand the world if it were hard all over," Davie remarks in "Across the Bay" (*SP* 50); but no poem can be "hard all over." What Davie calls, in the same poem, "the venomous soft jelly, the undersides," must (for all his sculpting) show through, be represented, have its voice. When he is not being spiteful toward the soft underside, the merely human, Davie can relent toward it. A child of the stony Yorkshire hills, he finds himself at a loss when he must live in the flat wet Cambridgeshire fens:

> Tedium, a poison,
> Swells in the sac for the hillborn, dwelling in the flat . . .
> But a beauty there is, noble, dependent, unshrinking
> In being at somebody's mercy, wide and alone.
> I imagine a hillborn sculptor suddenly thinking
> One could live well in a country short of stone.

(SP 45)

For all Davie's insistence in prose on the sturdy "dissentient voice" of his dissenting forebears, it is clear that what draws him to Christianity is precisely the meekness of it — "noble, dependent, unshrinking, being at somebody's mercy," the defenselessness of the sacrificial victim. An art of this meek sort finally appeals to Davie less than the art of the fortress; but in some of his self-portraits he does recognize an aspect of his poetry that is unplanned, "gracious" rather than consciously formed, revelatory rather than sought after. He says of poetry:

> This is the assessor whose word
> Can always be relied on;
> It tells you when has occurred
> Any change you decide on.
>
> More preciously still, it tells
> Of growth not groped towards,
> In the seaway a sound of bells
> From a landfall not on the cards.

(SP 43)

However, Davie's more usual self-portrait, especially in the earlier poems, is that of a man and poet at once "disciplined" and obstinate, the archetypal nonconformist, rebellious except in the stern bonds of verse and dissenting Christianity:

The Nonconformist

> X, whom society's most mild command,
> For instance evening dress, infuriates,
> In art is seen confusingly to stand
> For disciplined conformity, with Yeats.

Taxed to explain what this resentment is
He feels for small proprieties, it comes,
He likes to think, from old enormities
And keeps the faith with famous martyrdoms.

Yet it is likely, if indeed the crimes
His fathers suffered rankle in his blood,
That he finds least excusable the times
When they acceded, not when they withstood.

How else explain this bloody-minded bent
To kick against the prickings of the norm;
When to conform is easy, to dissent;
And when it is most difficult, conform?

(*SP* 30–31)

The formal symmetry of "The Nonconformist" (perfect rhymes; no unrhymed lines; each quatrain a sentence; a syntax processional and epigrammatic) is at war with its disruptive lexicon: infuriates, confusingly, resentment, enormities, martyrdoms, crimes, rankle, bloody-minded, kick, dissent, difficult. The poem resists our wish to call its resenting and bloody-minded lexicon Davie's soul, its strict quatrains his intellect, by reminding us that his soul too has its desire for conformity. But Davie here renders the "emotional life" of resentment more vividly, I think, than the emotional life of "disciplined conformity." That is (to use the language of the Russian formalists), the lexicon is "foregrounded" (by the mere rarity in lyric of such truculent words) over the form (the common rhymed pentameter quatrain). Davie, a conscious artist if there ever was one, would not be unaware of this difficulty, and in fact brings it boldly to the fore (without solving it) by repeating, in "Method. For Ronald Gaskell," Gaskell's critique of the combination of violent matter and ordered verse:

For such a theme (atrocities) you find
My style, you say, too neat and self-possessed.
I ought to show a more disordered mind.

(*SP* 18)

Davie's retort, in this early poem, maintained his position:

> An even tenor's sensitive to shock,
> And stains spread furthest where the floor's not cracked.

Davie did not foresee the cracking of the floor, and the unevenness of the tenor, in his two most ambitious later self-portraits, "In the Stopping Train," and "The Gardens of the Savoy," the poems with which I will close this essay. But already, in "Life Encompassed," he had faced squarely the loss of earlier certainties, both of "method" and of feeling:

> How often I have said,
> "This will never do,"
> Of ways of feeling that now
> I trust in, and pursue!
>
> Do traverses tramped in the past,
> My own, criss-crossed as I forge
> Across from another quarter
> Speak of a life encompassed?
>
> Well, life is not research.
> No one asks you to map the terrain,
> Only to get across it
> In new ways, time and again.
>
> How many such, even now,
> I dismiss out of hand
> As not to my purpose, not
> Unknown, just unexamined.
>
> (SP 43)

Later, "Oak Openings" (another poem in the same stiff trimeters Davie has so made his own) justified a change of style without itself embodying one:

It is not as if the attention
Steadily encroaches
Upon the encircling dark
The circle about the torch is
Moving, it opens new
Glades by obscuring old ones.

Twigs crack under foot, as the tread
Changes. The forge-ahead style
Of our earliest ventures flags;
It becomes, as mile follows mile
Inexhaustibly, an exhausted
Wavering trudge, the explorer's.

(SP 72)

Here tread changes to trudge, forging ahead to flagging, inexhaust-
ibleness to exhaustion; and are we obscuring, wavering, or exploring?
All three, the poem suggests; and the tentativeness of all three verbs
is new in Davie. Nonetheless the poem moves with a martial and
Roman tread, rather than enacting its sense of poetry as exhausted
wavering, as flagging exploring. The writing retains the old style, but
the content questions Davie's simpler division of human possibility
into "action" and "reaction," with which he had armed a more
intolerant poem of self-exposure, "Revulsion":

My strongest feeling all
My life has been
I recognize, revulsion
From the obscene;
That more than anything
My life-consuming passion.

That so much more reaction
Than action should have swayed
My life and rhymes
Must be the heaviest charge
That can be brought against
Me, or my times.

(SP 71)

The final witty turn against the time out of joint cannot entirely deflect Davie's morose delectation in his own capacity for revulsion (however he may condemn it). Here self-condemnation, it seems to me, does not entirely escape complacency; and one doubts that a man of Davie's harsh temperament could have found any previous era more to his liking. (It is true that Davie has created, in his *Dissentient Voice (1982)*, a picture of eighteenth-century Dissent as "a vector of Enlightenment" which, however historians finally may judge his argument, serves him as a paradigm of a better era; but inventing or scanning such a paradigm is an imaginative exercise, different from having lived in another era and found it good.)

In the asperities of his earlier verse, Davie could hardly have foreseen the day when he would imagine himself in a comic self-portrait, mocking his own dependencies (alcohol, tobacco, coffee) as much as his own vaunted Rationality:

> (I think
> Either I need, so early, the day's first drink or
> This is what a sense of sin amounts to. . . .)
> Prosopopoeia everywhere: Stout Labour
> Gets up with his pipe in his mouth or lighting
> The day's first *Gauloise-filtre*; then stout
> Caffeine like a fierce masseur
> Rams him abreast of the day; stout Sin
> Is properly a-tremble. . . .
>   and stout
> Love gets up out of rumpled sheets and goes singing
> Under his breath to the supermarket, the classroom,
> The briskly unhooded
> Bureaucratic typewriter. . . .
>
> And that mob of ideas? Don't knock them. The sick pell-
>   mell
> Goes by the handsome Olympian name of Reason.
>   (SP 98–99)

Charming as this ascent into geniality (and self-forgiveness) is, it is less than typical of Davie. The essential Davie is more sardonic. And it is Davie's sardonic poetry, like the nine bitter poems composing

the stunning sequence " In the Stopping Train," that will, it seems
to me, stand as "Davie" in many future anthologies.

A lyric sequence like the "Stopping Train" enables the contradic-
tions and eddyings of personality to lie side by side without mutual
repression. In embarking on this personal sequence, in allowing for
an aspectual, "fluid" form of mental and psychological life, Davie
must, it seems to me, abandon an essential part of his earlier sculp-
tural "method." It could be objected that a "sculptural" aesthetic
allows for the aspectual in the way that one might walk round a
statue, seeing its volumes differently each time. But Davie's sculptural
aesthetic was formulated from the point of view of the sculptor, not
the beholder. The bronze is poured; a rigid mass is created, and
stands still. Not for that method the halting metaphor of the "local"
(as we in America would call it) or the "stopping" train. The stopping
train is a metaphor representing an intolerable prolongation in Time,
not a serene extension in Space, and is consequently, for the spatial
and sculptural Davie, a figure for unmitigated suffering.

The opening poem of the sequence is unnerving in its explicitness
concerning punishment, justice, and torment.

> I have got into the slow train
> again. I made the mistake
> knowing what I was doing,
> knowing who had to be punished.
>
> I know who has to be punished:
> the man going mad inside me;
> whether I am fleeing
> from him or towards him.
>
> This journey will punish the bastard:
> he'll have his flowering gardens
> to stare at through the hot window;
> words like "laurel" won't help.
>
> He abhors his fellows,
> especially children; let there
> not for pity's sake
> be a crying child in the carriage.

So much for pity's sake.
The rest for the sake of justice:
torment him with his hatreds
and love of fictions.

The punishing slow pace
punishes also places along the line
for having, some of them, Norman
or Hanoverian stone-work:

his old familiars, his
exclusive prophylactics.
He'll stare his fill at their
emptiness on this journey . . .

Torment him with his hatreds,
torment him with his false
loves. Torment him with time
that has disclosed their falsehood.

Time, the exquisite torment!
His future is a slow
and stopping train through places
whose names used to have virtue.

(SP 91–92)

Superb in its beginning, the sequence nevertheless ends badly, it seems to me, with the introduction of a red herring in the form of a bearded hippie who takes "some weird girl off to a weird / commune, clutching at youth" — as though that were the only visible alternative to an abhorrence of humanity. Though Davie cannot explain why he "abhors his fellows," one suspects that he does so first of all because he abhors himself. It is with a fascinated interest that one watches the spectacle of an author being so hard on himself, lacking even the lyric exaltation and musicality of Dostoevskian abjectness:

The things he has been spared . . .
"Gross egotist!" Why don't
his wife, his daughter, shrill
that in his face?

> Love and pity seem
> the likeliest explanations;
> another occurs to him —
> despair too would be quiet.
>
> (SP 94–95)

When one's family despairs of cure, and sinks from expostulation to silence, even God, it might be thought, would give up on the sinner. Of the nine poems in the sequence, this, the fifth and central one, is the only one wholly devoid of ornament. It exists as a bald and awful axis on which the rest turn.

To the poet in the stopping train, his underdeveloped senses are a source of anguish, especially in comparison with his monstrous inner overdevelopment of language:

> Flowers, it seems are important.
> And he can name them all,
> identify hardly any.
>
> (SP 94)

The doppelgänger the speaker meets in the train, all eye and no feeling, becomes a Kafkaesque self-portrait:

> Apologies won't help him:
> his spectacles flared like paired
> lamps as he turned his head.
>
> I knew they had been ranging,
> paired eyes like mine,
> igniting and occluding.
>
> (SP 96)

And language, far from existing in sculptural form (or even in the measured dance of Eliot's Quartets) takes on instead the compelled agony of the tarantella. The dancer, poisoned by venom, moves in a dreadful jig, symbolized for Davie by the irrepressible tendency of language toward polyvalence, manifest in the pun. The passenger in the interminable stopping train of ennui feels the word "pain" seeping into the "pane" of his metaphor, and as he does so, there occurs the last collapse of his early "sculptural" language:

The dance of words
is a circling prison, thought
the passenger staring through
the hot unmoving pane
of boredom. It is not
thank God a dancing pain,
he thought, though it starts to jig
now. (The train is moving.) "This,"
he thought in rising panic
(Sit down! Sit down!)
"this much I can command,
exclude. Dulled words, keep still!
Be the inadequate, cloddish
despair of me!" No good:
they danced, as the smiling land
fled past the pane, the pun's
galvanized *tarantelle*.

(*SP* 96)

"In the Stopping Train" is Davie's masterpiece of self-portraiture. In it, forms of relenting (toward pity, toward flowers, toward courage, toward sociability, even toward despair) cohabit with forms of stubbornness in self-torment; placidity aimed at coincides with panic undergone; and stony reiteration (an old resource) goes hand in hand with baffled invention. The poem has for me the stability of ten years' acquaintance, and the power of the unforgettable.

And yet, I am at the moment under the spell of Davie's latest, not entirely successful, but grimmest, piece of self-portraiture, the sequence "The Gardens of the Savoy," printed in *Parnassus* in 1986. There is an explanatory note to the gardens of the title: "In London, between the Strand and the Embankment, frequented by winos and worse." "Come back," calls this new two-part invention (as if echoing the end of "In the Stopping Train") "to the point of pain." Against the social evils of war ("There are no righteous wars"), racism (the Ku Klux Klan, race wars in Africa), and technology (missiles and rockets; Challenger; the poet's grandchildren bearing home to England a toy moon-buggy), Davie sets worship ("our first and last mission"), aesthetic ambition (for "brilliance"), and poetic alienation. He is, he perceives, to take instruction in his sixties not only from the aubade of birds ("birdbrains"), but also from those

derelicts and drunkards that haunt the Gardens of the Savoy, figures
for the "upside-down *elite*" who become artists:

> I am to learn from them,
>   from layabouts
> feeding from garbage in the Savoy gardens? . . .
>
> I am, I am; and let the time show how . . .
>
> A logic not for the many,
>   for the upside-down *elite,*
>   for the self-chosen, cropping
>   plastic and mineral fruit
>   of the garbage of the Savoy,
>   Proserpine's hell-side gardens;
>   not Nature, Art.

This is a Swinburnian moment:

> No growth of moor or coppice,
>   No heather-flower or vine,
> But bloomless buds of poppies,
>   Green grapes of Proserpine,
> Pale beds of blowing rushes
> Where no leaf blooms or blushes
> Save this whereout she crushes
>   For dead men deadly wine . . .
>
> Pale, beyond porch and portal,
>   Crowned with calm leaves, she stands
> Who gathers all things mortal
>   With cold immortal hands . . .
>
>   ("The Garden of Proserpine")

That the stout dissenter should, in his sixties, place himself with
Swinburne and the derelicts of the gardens of the Savoy means per-
haps, in the Yeatsian sense, that "he completes his partial mind."
But there are formal changes to be remarked as well. The ghost of
Pound, whose fanaticism ruined his poetry, haunts Davie both as
mentor and as warning, in "the grand or great / bankruptcy of the
Cantos." Pound (the derelict, the reprobate) had at his best (accord-
ing to this poem) "deeps in him . . . unemphatic." And the word

"unemphatic," introduced as a leitmotiv, grows to become here the aesthetic word par excellence — a strange word for the decisive dissenter to end on, unforeseeable entirely in his early years. The poetic line is to be not epigrammatic, not authoritative, not sententious, but to be "light as a feather," to "fall floatingly," to have "the lightness of . . . release." "The gift: non-emphasis":

> Drunk, *in ecstasis*
> however artificially,
> a man is reaching
> for the ultimate
> lack of emphasis: "Gods
>   or it may be one God moves
> about us in bright air."
> . . . . .
> Brilliance is known in
> what the tired wing, though
> it never so crookedly towers,
> wins at last into: air
> diamond-clear, unemphatic.

As the passage just quoted reveals, Davie has worked to find a verse that will not display the tight, repetitive, alliterative, patterned beats of his earlier "emphatic" style. The tense trimeters, however, wait always in the wings; as I began by saying, the wish to assert apodictically the absence of certainty hovers always behind, and in, Davie's writing. That wish reaches perhaps its most absurd and exploded expression at the end of "The Gardens of the Savoy," in the closing trimeters:

> "Can you tell the down from the up?"
> The unthinkable answer: No.

Are we to understand that the answer is "No," and that that is unthinkable? or that it is unthinkable that one should give "No" as an answer? I am not, myself, sure.

Our trochaic and alliterative British poet — Dón-ald Dá-vie — betrays, in this most recent self-portrait, his affinity with American modernist verse. He has argued, in *Thomas Hardy and British Poetry,* that "for many years now British poetry and American poetry haven't been on speaking terms. But the truth is rather that they haven't been on *hearing* terms — the American reader can't hear the British poet, neither his rhythms nor his tone of voice" (*TH* 184). If Davie is hearable by an American listener, it is in part because he has listened, more closely than most British poets, to American rhythms and tones. It is true, as he says in "Poetry and the Other Modern Arts" (*PIM* 162) that "poetry forces us back inside the iron cage of being of a certain race speaking a certain language" (all of us Pisan captives), but it is also true, as he adds, that English is more than most an international tongue. He has become in it an international poet. And though he says of the poet, "It is certain that he does *not* need a critic!" (*PIM* 163), he may, in his person as a poet, at least tolerate our praise. Among his subjects — political, religious, domestic, and historical — not the least is his thorny, restless, dissatisfied, and seeking self. That we end by knowing that self so well — in the way we know the increasingly perturbed, vexed, and resigned face of Rembrandt — is a testimony to Davie's exploratory, stern, and ceaselessly revised art of the self-portrait.

13

Ted Hughes

The Poet Laureate of England, Ted Hughes, has written a water book, *River* (1984), to match his 1979 earth book, *Moortown*. In *Moortown*, Hughes's animal surrogates were chiefly sheep and lambs; in *River*, they are fish, eels, and insects. Hughes notices in nature what suits his purpose: if he wants to wince at man's naïveté, he writes about the innocent lamb ignorant of its fate; if he wants to write about disability, he describes a dying insect. In "A March Calf," for example (from the 1975 volume *Season-Songs*), Hughes is the knowing speaker observing the lamb for the slaughter:

> Right from the start he is dressed in his best — his blacks
>   and his whites.
> Little Fauntleroy — quiffed and glossy . . .
>
> Hungry people are getting hungrier,
> Butchers developing expertise and markets,
>
> But he just wobbles his tail — and glistens
> Within his dapper profile
> Unaware of how his whole lineage
> Has been tied up.

In "A Cranefly in September" (from the same book), Hughes is the "giant" who watches the crippled cranefly "with her cumbering limbs and cumbered brain." He prophesies that

> Her jointed bamboo fuselage,
> Her lobster shoulders, and her face
> Like a pinhead dragon, with its tender mustache,

And the simple colorless church windows of her wings
Will come to an end, in mid-search, quite soon.

Poems like these imply, as Hughes wishes to imply, that we, too, are
only animals in the universe, and live and die as helplessly and as
unavoidably as any other animal form. But the poems shade rather
too easily into a form of sadism. Hughes no doubt means to include
himself in the human family of deceived lambs; but the writer of the
poem is undeceived, and the irony is tinged with the relish of superior
power, if only the superior power of knowledge. The giant who
watches the cranefly takes the diagnostic tone of a doctor watching
a terminal case: he "knows she cannot be helped in any way." It is
not Hughes's frustration at his own helplessness that the poem illu-
minates but, rather, the triumph of his biological knowledge:

The calculus of glucose and chitin inadequate
To plot her through the infinities of the stems.

For a long time, Hughes has represented himself as the man who
has seen into the bottomless pit of aggression, death, murder, holo-
caust, catastrophe. There, in the pit, he has faced not only the physical
evils of mutilation and extinction but also the moral squalor attend-
ing on the brute survival instinct, the impulse to prey on others out
of self-interest. His earlier surrogate forms, the hawk and the crow
— in *Lupercal* (1960) and *Crow* (1971) — are his vehicles for facing
base instinct. Crow, for instance, watches a suicide; when it is over
"And the body lay on the gravel / Of the abandoned world . . . /
Crow had to start searching for something to eat." The hawk says,
in "Hawk Roosting":

I kill where I please beause it is all mine . . .
My manners are tearing off heads —

The allotment of death.
For the one path of my flight is direct
Through the bones of the living . . .

I am going to keep things like this.

These are the poems of a man convinced that social hypocrisy has prevented such unlovely truths from appearing in poetry except in an "ethical" poetry condemning them. Hughes is determined to unveil these instincts, to show himself and others, through such animal surrogates, in the most predatory and self-serving light. Needless to say, there is a self-sadism here, which, when Hughes splits himself in two — the watcher and the watched — turns into what appears to be sadism toward the foolish lamb and the stumbling cranefly.

In fact, Hughes's gaze has been so relentlessly selective as he looks at the world that all the arguments made against any "naturalistic" writer apply to him. If a hundred lambs are adequately born and one is not, Hughes's poem will savagely concern itself with the exception. His anger against a world containing stillbirths may be his conscious motive for writing; but what reader will not see in "February 17th" (from *Moortown*) Hughes's powerful imaginative appetite for naming and ornamenting disaster? In this explicitly autobiographical poem, Hughes, who has a farm in Devon, tells us that he found one of his ewes with a half-born lamb "looking out" of her "back end":

> A blood ball swollen
> Tight in its black felt, its mouth gap
> Squashed crooked, tongue stuck out, black-purple,
> Strangled by its mother.

After trying in vain to pull the lamb out, Hughes fetched a razor, and

> Sliced the lamb's throat strings, levered with a knife
> Between the vertebrae and brought the head off
> To stare at its mother, its pipes sitting in the mud
> With all earth for a body.

Then, after decapitating the lamb, Hughes reached in to pull out the rest of it; it came (and the poem ends)

> In a smoking slither of oils and soups and syrups —
> And the body lay born, beside the hacked-off head.

To the argument "But that was exactly how it was" one can only put the counterargument: This is a poet who wants to write words like "blood ball swollen" and "sliced . . . throat strings" and "hacked-off head." Poems are, at one level, experiments in getting certain sounds and phrases and grammatical forms down on paper; and Hughes likes violent phrases, thick sounds, explosive verbs.

Hughes grew up, as every commentator on him remarks, with a sense of violence and death. This is attributed by Hughes himself, and by his critics, following him, to his having internalized his father's experience of the First World War. It may be true, as Hughes says, that "the shrapnel that shattered my father's paybook / Gripped me," and that Hughes's writing replays a child's monstrously enlarged imaginings of trench warfare, mutilation, and death. But something more has been added. Hughes mixes sexual intercourse into the brew of war and death, and his blighted imagination, though it occasionally mentions joy, tends to speak even of that with the exhaustion of one who knows all the moves in the erotic battle and finds a perverse fascination in the stylizations of victimage. In the new book, a damselfly who kills her mate during intercourse serves Hughes as a sexual symbol. She appears, in "Last Act,"

> Hover-poised, in her snakeskin leotards,
> A violet-dark elegance,
>
> Eyelash-delicate, a dracula beauty,
> In her acetylene jewels.
>
> Her mascara smudged, her veils shimmer-fresh.

Later, Hughes finds her murdered mate:

> A touch-crumple petal of web and dew —
> Midget puppet-clown, tranced on his strings.

Less violent matings interest Hughes proportionately less; he insists on demystifying "love" into its most aesthetically lethal biological instance. For Hughes, one suspects, it cannot be aesthetic without its fatality.

Hughes has by now found many ways to embody his wounded sense of the world: catastrophe (the stillborn lamb), predatory acts (by the hawk, by butchers) sexual victimage (the damselfly), suicide (Ophelia), and, in *River*, hunting and fishing. He tears off the bandages to expose the "red unmanageable life," the raw flesh of existence. And he must find not only adequate emblems but adequate formal means. For him, this has meant putting the world into parables, which have an air of reducing things to their most basic terms. Here we are, for example, after the nuclear holocaust:

> The demolition is total
> Except for two strange items remaining in the flames —
> Two survivors, moving in the flames blindly.
>
> Mutations — at home in the nuclear glare.
>
> Horrors — hairy and slobbery, glossy and raw.
>
> They sniff toward each other in the emptiness.
>
> They fasten together. They seem to be eating each other.
>
> But they are not eating each other.
>
> They do not know what else to do.
>
> They have begun to dance a strange dance.

This, from the volume *Crow,* is disarmingly entitled "Notes for a Little Play." It uses, in a wholly mistaken portentousness, all the formal means of parable: a minimal number of actors and actions; an exaggerated plot (in which survivors immediately grapple in intercourse); a primerlike vocabulary ("See the mutants. See them slobber. See them fasten. See them dance"); an equally primitive syntax of short, unsubordinated, and atomized declarative sentences; and an impersonal point of view, which assumes that the anecdote has general applicability. The dangers and powers inherent in parables as representations of human life are self-evident; parables have appealed to stylists from Jesus to Kafka as an exercise in producing the greatest resonance with the fewest words. The irreducible child in Hughes, for whom reality is always large and looming, relishes parables as he relishes cartoon images.

In *River,* cartoon appears in "Night Arrival of Seatrout" as a fantasy by a grimmer Disney. It is an autumn night, and Hughes fishes amid menacingly eroticized rural scenes:

> Honeysuckle hanging her fangs.
> Foxglove rearing her open belly.
> Dogrose touching the membrane.
>
> Through the dew's mist, the oak's mass
> Comes plunging, tossing dark antlers.

The seatrout leaps, snarls, and shivers; lobworms couple; earth sings under her breath.

> And out in the hard corn a horned god
> Running and leaping
> With a bat in his drum.

Though this would like to be pagan, it is in fact neo-pagan and symbolist, a "hard," revisionist view of Keats's apparently softer autumn. Hughes's neo-paganism was learned at Lawrence's knee, and his parables are Lawrentian, too. So are his repetitions (a formal means revived by Lawrence and frequent in Hughes):

> The river . . .
> Lay dark and grew darker. An evil mood
> Darkened in it . . .
>
> Its darkness under roots . . .
> Was dark as blood,
> Rusty peaty blood-dark, old-blood dark.

"Dark," "darker," "darkened," "darkness," "dark," "blood-dark," "dark" — all these variants occur in eight lines, as though, in Lawrentian intensification, one could mesmerize oneself further into sensation by reiteration of a single hypnotic word. The hope of simplification through intensity explains as well Hughes's continued attachment to fixed, repeated sentence forms, as though a furrow once plowed could only be cut deeper and deeper.

On the other hand, against these simplifications of form and language, which play, we might say, the role of fate in Hughes's universe (incorporating the immutable, the geometric, the rigid, the reduced, and the physical laws regulating space and time), there appear a number of variable forms, playing, we could say, the role of free will. It was in Hopkins that Hughes first found a model for this variable side of his otherwise obsessive nature — a side both visual and kinetic, and more animal than human. The intellectual side of Hughes is entirely aligned with fate; only his physical, sensual being escapes into freedom. In a remarkable poem on growing old, "October Salmon," Hughes sketches brilliantly the moment of male adolescence, remembering

> The eye of ravenous joy — king of infinite liberty
> In the flashing expanse, the bloom of sea-life,
>
> On the surge-ride of energy, weightless,
> Body simply the armature of energy
> In that earliest sea-freedom, the savage amazement of life.

This pure kinetic energy is often coarsened and brutalized by Hughes, when it is too theatrically tethered to his Celtic, even Scandinavian, gloom, or when it is too orgasmically "spasming" (his coinage) on the page, or when it is too imitatively re-creating Hopkins's larks and kestrels. But at its best, reined in, it gives Hughes's poems their tensile strength. Hughes has found it difficult in the past to moderate his touch. When he presses just hard enough, not too hard, he raises the English pastoral (Hopkins through Hardy through Lawrence) to a sharper and bleaker pitch. In "The Vintage of River Is Unending," the aspects of a Keatsian autumn — the ripeness, the grapevines, the sweetness, the gathered grain and swelling fruit, the weighted boughs, the river, the cider press — find themselves concentrated as in a burning glass in Hughes's praise of the river of being:

> Grape-heavy woods ripen darkening
> The sweetness.
>
> Tight with golden light
> The hills have been gathered.
>
> Granite weights of sun.
> Tread of burning days.
>
> Unending river
> Swells from the press
> To gladden men.

If this vocabulary of praise seems startling coming from the Hughes of wounds and blood, talon and fang, it is no less startling than Hughes's frequent abandonment, in *River,* of the iron maiden of his habitual sentence structure. *River* is altogether a more flexible book, it seems to me, than its predecessors. Hughes is still recognizably himself in the thrust and momentum of his lines, in his choice of the animal world as human mirror, and in his interest in determined biological patterns. But he has readjusted his focus. As Crow, he was predatory and avian; as lamb, he was victim and mammal; now he goes lower on the evolutionary scale, and becomes eel, fish, insect. The cooling of the blood into a subaqueous current tempers Hughes's lines. They are still head-strong, still governed more by a linear sexual drive than by a spatial pooling; but they are driven less by the plunge and drive of instinctual will, more by the rhythms of biological birth and decay. Hughes seems to have decided, somewhat in the manner of Whitman, that if there ever was any death it led forth life. In the baldest statement of the book, Hughes hails, in italics, the river's perpetual "toilings of plasm" as the salmon spawn:

> *Only birth matters*
> Say the river's whorls.

Hughes's new vitalism particpates in the same mystic obscurantism that animated his earlier convictions about rapacity and death. But because it exchanges the drilled bullet-gaze of Crow for a more sensuous, free-ranging, and associative registering of the natural scene, the vitalism seems more comprehensive and more adequate to natural existence, and even to human existence.

Hughes's father's nightmarish sense of war may have caused his son's obsession with death. But it is also possible, as Hughes suggests, that some quirk in his own makeup dictated his deathly sense of life, and drew him to others who carried death within them. In any case, Hughes often seems to have felt that, unlike ordinary people, he could not live but only imitate the actions of the living. "Life is trying to be life," he writes, in a poem of that title, but "death also is trying to be life":

> Death is in the sperm like the ancient mariner
> With his horrible tale.

Here, impersonally told, is Hughes's story of his own childhood, in the personage of "Death":

> It plays with dolls but cannot get interested.
> It stares at the windowlight and cannot make it out.
> It wears baby clothes and is patient.
> It learns to talk, watching the others' mouths.
> It laughs and shouts and listens to itself numbly.
> It stares at people's faces
> And sees their skin like a strange moon, and stares at the
>   grass
> In its position just as yesterday.
> And stares at its fingers and hears:
> "Look at that child."
> Death is a changeling
> Tortured by daisy chains and Sunday bells . . .
> Death only wants to be life. It cannot quite manage.

The subject may be "Death," but it is also Hughes's inner life:

> Death and Death and Death, it whispers
> With eyes closed, trying to feel life.

Perhaps the strenuousness and the forcing that can be felt in Hughes's poetry arise from the strain of death trying to feel life. His terrible emblems of life and death violently jammed together — the half-born dead lamb protruding from its mother, the live fish with a dead one stuck halfway down its gullet — represent the standoff in his own composition between his unusual physical strength and an underlying spiritual terror.

In *River,* Hughes tries to feel life through "the dance-orgy of being reborn," chiefly in the life cycle of the salmon. He writes of eggs and sperm, of salmon spawning, of insect copulation, of "exhumations and delirious advents." He rises to a rhapsody:

> And this is the liturgy
> Of the earth's tidings — harrowing, crowned — a travail
> Of raptures and rendings.

Around that climax are arranged, in this volume, the tatters of man's mortal dress as it is about to be cast aside — leper-cloths, a frayed scarf, a mask, a shroud, the "crude paints and drapes" of death. Man becomes "death's puppet," and "the masks and regalia drift empty."

In the perfection of the river, all evil, says Hughes, is suspended. The river is the "primitive, radical / Engine of earth's renewal," washing everything to the pure ablution of the sea, "back to the sea's big re-think." In his early combination, in *Crow,* of powerful drama and fine-grained observation, Hughes had praised the power of human consciousness to rise above mortality:

> There was finally something
> The sun could not burn . . .
>
> Crow's eye-pupil, in the tower of its scorched fort.

But, on the evidence of his lifework, Hughes makes poems less to praise consciousness or to construct something beautiful than to reverse an evil spell. In "Stealing Trout on a May Morning" (from *Wodwo,* 1967), Hughes wrote down the deepest truth about his own poetic. As he stands deep in a river fishing, a flood of panic seizes him, "tearing the spirits from my mind's edge and from under." He is magically rescued from terror by the leap of a trout, which gets "a long look" at him. At that moment, the charm is wound up:

> So much for the horror:
> It has changed places.

Hughes's evil spirits have been cast out into the Gadarene swine of objectified nature.

Hughes has gone about the world finding vessels in nature for his private horrors; once the poison is emptied into the natural vessel and the poem has fixed it there, the horror has changed places — of course, only for a moment. For the spell to work, the poem has to be adequate to its object, one presumes; but, even so, the aesthetic end is subordinated to the therapeutic one. These priorities need to be reversed if the poems are to bear the strain well and long.

And it does seem as though a certain flagging in the horror has enabled Hughes to detach himself from his compulsive spell-casting and to look, at least sometimes, on his natural images with more reverie than exorcism. The most beautiful poem in *River*, to my mind, is "October Salmon," Hughes's long self-elegy, masked as an elegy for a dying salmon. I have already quoted some of its phrases; here is some of its long flow:

> Four years old at most, and hardly a winter at sea —
> But already a veteran,
> Already a death-patched hero. So quickly it's over!
>
> So briefly he roamed the gallery of marvels! . . .
>
> The mere hull of his prime, shrunk at shoulder and flank,
>
> With the sea-going Aurora Borealis of his April power —
> The primrose and violet of that first upfling in the estuary —
> Ripened to muddy dregs,
> The river reclaiming his sea-metals.
>
> In the October light
> He hangs there, patched with leper-cloths.
>
> Death has already dressed him
> In her clownish regimentals, her badges and decorations,
> Mapping the completion of his service,
> His face a ghoul-mask . . .
>
> Yet this was always with him. This was inscribed in his egg.
> This chamber of horrors is also home.
> He was probably hatched in this very pool . . .
>
> All this, too, is stitched into the torn richness,
> The epic poise
> That holds him so steady in his wounds, so loyal to his
>   doom, so patient
> In the machinery of heaven.

The tonality of "epic poise" is new in Hughes. "October Salmon" was first published in Hughes's *New Selected Poems* (1982), but the tonality it embodies recurs throughout *River*, struggling for its poise against Hughes's equally recurrent, and more typical, violence and victimization. Hughes's remarkable adjectival gift and his propulsive rhythms may find a balance in epic poise. If they do, and if the obsessive rituals of the poetry are harmonized with aesthetic as well as therapeutic ends, Hughes may become an ampler poet of consciousness. Even if they do not, his glare into the machinery of evolutionary law results in a strong contemporary individual scanning of the rites of human life.

14

Czeslaw Milosz

When Czeslaw Milosz was named the Nobel Prize winner in literature in 1980, the consequent wave of publicity made almost everything about Milosz — everything except his poems — become better known. The Nobel Lecture was reprinted in the *New York Review of Books;* Milosz's prose volumes — *The Captive Mind* (1953), *Native Realm* (1968), and *Emperor of the Earth* (essays collected in 1977) — were all reprinted in paperback; and an early novel, *The Issa Valley,* was published in English translation for the first time. Even the *Selected Poems* (published in English by the Seabury Press in 1973 and revised, by Ecco, in 1980) were, in the wake of the Nobel, reviewed less as poems than as the work of a thinker and political figure; the poems tended to be considered en masse, in relation either to the condition of Poland, or to the suppression of dissident literature under Communist rule, or to the larger topic of European intellectual history. Then in 1984 Ecco issued a spectacular new collection, *The Separate Notebooks,* translated by Robert Hass and Robert Pinsky, with Milosz and Renata Gorczynski. The volume contains poems written as early as 1934 and as late as 1980. Its appearance permitted a more extended consideration of Milosz's work as a modern poet.

Like most others writing about Milosz's verse, I know no Polish. But he has been unusually well translated (in part by himself) and has collaborated with his translators. And as he himself has said, in the introduction to an anthology of postwar Polish poetry, he and other modern Polish poets have adopted a form of free verse relatively adaptable to English, unlike traditional accentual-syllabic Polish metres. At least some aspects of Milosz's poetry do seem to be translatable; it is a poetry that even in English both disturbs and satisfies, with a mordant irony and a classical grandeur vying in it for dominance.

What has it lost in translation? Stanislaw Baranczak, a Polish poet now teaching at Harvard, has said (in an article in *Parnassus*) that Milosz not only uses a polyphony of voices but is also as willing to use a "low" word as a "high" one, and "tries to find the most concrete of all possible synonyms." "He wants a language," says Baranczak, "open to every way of speaking, every recess of vocabulary, every possible style." Apparently, there takes place frequently in Milosz's poetry that rise in temperature which comes when two words that have never before lived side by side suddenly mingle — provoking what we feel in English when we read of Marvell's "green thought," Traherne's "orient and immortal wheat," Donne's "unruly Sun," or Keats's "sylvan historian." This breaking down of "natural" compartments is one of the most powerful effects of poetry, which by its concision and free play can represent better than most prose the fluid access of a daring and unhampered mind to its own several regions. Such linguistic versatility — combining words that have never been combined before, but doing it with a sublime justice and propriety, so that the effect is not a jolt but a confirmation of rightness — gives perhaps the highest pleasure that poetry exists to confer. But in reading Milosz we are barred, as foreigners, from knowing that pure bliss of the newly created linguistic object as a reader of the mother tongue knows it. We are also barred from hearing the indispensable falls of sound and cadence.

If we cannot hear Milosz's native euphonies, and if we miss many of the surprising and (we are told) immensely touching effects of his diction as he searches into long-forgotten or darkened corners of the Polish past and brings them, by a word, into an alignment with the present, what can we bear away from a reading of the poems? We find in them, first of all, a truncated autobiography (to be read against the autobiographical essays of *Native Realm*). The poetic autobiographer, like the prose one, is reticent: Milosz says in *Native Realm*, "The passing over of certain periods important for oneself, but requiring too personal an explanation, will be a token of respect for those undergrounds that exist in all of us and that are better left in peace." He is not a "confessional" poet; his voice is, one might say, disinterestedly personal. For Milosz, the person is irrevocably a person in history, and the interchange between external event and the individual life is the matrix of poetry. Like most lyric poets, Milosz was probably not by nature very much a social being, but, given the situation of his life, he cannot help being a historical one. There is an eerie solitude in Milosz; it sometimes seems that he has suffered the twentieth century all alone, vividly aware of historical cataclysms — those he saw in person (the war, the Nazi occupation of Warsaw, the subsequent Russian occupation, and Communist rule in Poland) and those of Europe in general — yet living in catastrophe as a hermit, sounding like Blake's Mental Traveller:

> I travel'd thro' a Land of Men.
> A Land of Men and Women too.
> And heard & saw such dreadful things
> As cold Earth wanderers never knew.

There are two convictions, both of them mentioned in Milosz's introduction to *Native Realm*, that are important for his poems. The first is that "one can get at man only obliquely, only through the constant masquerade that is the extension of himself at a given moment, through his historical existence." All of Milosz's poetry has, even if sometimes unwillingly, this historical grounding: through circumstance humanity is made visible. At the same time, it is the second conviction that seems to me the more important in isolating Milosz's idiosyncrasy as a poet: he says that if the "chaotic richness" of "the particulars of our fate" did not exist "we would not constantly be aspiring to form achieved by a process of elimination." Milosz offers this as an axiom, and for him it is: form is the achievement, by the poet, of a paring away, of a refinement of original multiplicity into elemental leanness. But this is not so for all poets; there are the poets of putting in, as we may call them (with Spenser our preeminent example), as well as the poets of taking out. Milosz is a stern poet; forbidding and austere lines appear in most of the poems. But they rarely occur alone; they are accompanied by a relenting, a thawing mildness. And it is in this perculiar balance between a juridical, frowning severity and a lyrical, melting attachment that Milosz's power to unsettle us lies. Of course, there are other characteristic aspects of his writing; the one most often remarked on is a gift for classical aphorisms. The aphoristic, or gnomic, sentence offers a linguistic form for Milosz's historical irony — an irony that sees, by virtue of historical length and breadth, beyond the individual case, even if that case is one's own. Poets with a tendency to universalize become (at their worst) deprived of an individual voice; poets who forget that their own fate is part of the common lot fall into self-pity. Milosz's grimness has not blunted the antennae of his painful sensibility; and, conversely, his own exposed nerves have not fatally distracted him from the historical events he has recorded almost involuntarily.

Milosz is more intellectually conscious of his own aesthetic than many poets are. He says, for example:

> Particular existence keeps us from the light
> (That sentence can be read in reverse as well).

The struggle between a clarifying, if inhuman, light and the darkness of particular fate underlies everything that he writes, and provides, in fact, an endlessly fertile resource for invention, as particulars and light dispute each other for room in his work.

From the start, Milosz was a natural ecstatic, destined for intense and radiant perception. (One of the aphorisms reads, "From childhood till old age ecstasy at sunrise.") But everything in his life after his childhood was a scourging of his natural temper. Contradiction afflicted him young, forcing his gaze onto war, death, the murder of the Jews, and the moral impossibility of life in devastated cities, where one stole and cheated and lied to live; later he was to know the betrayals of truth and of old loyalties under the Communist regime:

> Since I opened my eyes I have seen only the glow of fires,
>   massacres,
> Only injustice, humiliation, and the laughable shame of
>   braggarts.

This is the fate of "The Poor Poet," in the *Selected Poems*. But the poet's life had begun differently:

> The first movement is singing,
> A free voice, filling mountains and valleys.
> The first movement is joy,
> But it is taken away.

The second stanza continues:

> And now that the years have transformed my blood
> And thousands of planetary systems have been born and
>   died in my flesh,
> I sit, a sly and angry poet
> With malevolently squinted eyes,
> And, weighing a pen in my hand,
> I plot revenge.

Not every poet is temperamentally created for joy, and not all those who are so created are so early blighted — or, if they are, it is by a personal blight rather than the universal ones of war and occupation by a foreign power. Milosz reads like a soul who has received a wound from which he has never recovered: an air of doom now hangs over every moment of joy, so that the simplest happiness appears always as a reprieve or furlough from an evil sure to reassert itself. The precariousness of life and writing is always felt in Milosz; his contemporaries who died or were killed or were silenced (not only in Poland but in all of Europe) contribute to the voice he has become — a voice almost necessarily that of a generation rather than (or as well as) that of a single man. The "I" who speaks many of the poems speaks for all who witnessed the dissolution of Europe:

> I did not expect to live in such an unusual moment.
> When the God of thunders and of rocky heights,
> the Lord of Hosts, Kyrios Sabaoth,
> would humble people to the quick,
> allowing them to act whatever way they wished,
> leaving to them conclusions, saying nothing . . .
> Dispossessed of its objects, space was swarming.
> Everywhere was nowhere and nowhere, everywhere.
> Letters in books turned silver-pale, wobbled and faded.
> The hand was not able to trace the palm sign, the river sign,
>   or the sign of ibis.

The dispassionate tone of this poem, called "Oeconomia Divina" (the pious phrase is used with a savage lack of comment), is in itself both a manifestation of horror and a dissembling of it. Milosz finds transparently simple ways of expressing the evaporation of materiality and spirituality alike. As bombs render one's native streets unrecognizable, and as all codes of ethics fall at once, space swarms and letters flicker and vanish: Milosz's free pillaging of all historical eras opens out his canvas. It is only by such an oblique treatment of the destruction of Warsaw that Milosz succeeds in treating it at all.

As Baranczak points out, Milosz rejects symbols in favor of metonymy and synecdoche, those figures of speech which represent a whole by a thing allied to it or by a part of it. The originality with which Milosz finds the briefest of words for inner events is one of the reasons to read him. "The years have transformed my blood," he says, "and thousands of planetary systems have been born and died in my flesh." As in the best poets, we feel this account to be not figurative at all but the most literally truthful way of saying what has happened. What is this changing set of interplanetary relations but a concise history of a Polish intellectual's inner life from the Forties to the Sixties? The sort of change Milosz wants to describe can only, for him, be described in those terms usually reserved for the life and death of immensely long cycles; what we gain from his language is a sense of indecent speeding up, as one inner galaxy after another is conceived, brought to being, and annihilated.

His own compulsion to write sometimes drives Milosz to bitterness and anger. "The Poor Poet" continues, for example:

> I poise the pen and it puts forth twigs and leaves, it is
> covered with blossoms.
> And the scent of that tree is impudent, for there, on the real
> earth,
> Such trees do not grow, and like an insult
> To suffering humanity is the scent of that tree.

He finds himself condemned to "odious rhythmic speech / Which grooms itself and, of its own accord, moves on." If such passages testify to the guilt of the survivor, they testify as well to the tormenting distance every poet feels between the miraculous Aaron's rod of art and this world "where men sit and hear each other groan."

Milosz's poems, with a few exceptions, have not been dated in the *Selected Poems,* and we cannot be sure from this fragmentary evidence of a life's work (supplemented by *Bells in Winter,* mostly later poems, published by Ecco in 1978, and by the poems in *The Separate Notebooks*) how his speculations on his art have changed during his writing life. But the notion that art's perpetual fragrance is "impudent" and an "insult" to mortal suffering is not the only view that Milosz takes. In the surpassingly beautiful "The World: A Naïve Poem," a sequence of twenty poems written in 1943, Milosz renders a past of depth and profound feeling in the simplest measures and the simplest words available to a poet, as though only the first syllables of the mother tongue could be words deep-rooted enough for the deepest of primal experiences. "The World" is the most opalescent of Milosz's sequences; it exists as pure light against a background of abysmal darkness, preserving that doubleness of perspective — extreme joy recalled in extreme despair — which is Milosz's unique discovery in the art of poetry.

Much of the "naïveté" of the sequence can be seen in the titles of individual poems: "The Path," "The Gate," "The Porch," "The Dining-room," "The Stairs." These are the elements of the child's precious and irrecoverable visual past. In this space we see the godlike parents. "Father in the Library" revives the little boy full of reverence for the father empowered by mysterious words:

> A high forehead, and tousled hair;
> The sun at the window pouring light —
> Father wears a crest of downy fire
> As he opens, slowly, the great book.
>
> His gown covered with devices
> Like a wizard's, he murmurs spells:
> Only one whom God has taught magic
> Could know the marvels his book reveals.

That is the entire poem, left without adult comment as a testimony to the child's spellbound realization of adult power in the word. All of "The World" is written in primer style. It is a style in which, one feels, it is impossible to lie, or even to shade the truth. Blake, one of Milosz's masters, knew this when he wrote his songs.

In "The World," the sweetness of Milosz's recollection passes from the visual and the personal to the religious with three childlike poems on the three highest, or "theological," virtues — faith, hope, and love — which make up the thirteenth, fourteenth, and fifteenth poems of the sequence. After that, the child goes abroad to the forest and sees the skies, the kingdom of the birds, who live in a "free, high, shining place"; here he first grasps the possibility of far voyaging. In the single frightening poem, the child becomes Blake's little boy lost in the forest, but, as in Blake, he is found by his ever-watchful and kind father. The security and beauty of the world as it should be, and as we all feel it could be if it were governed by faith, hope, and love, is the theme of the father's rescue of the trembling child. This poem, the most radiant and sacred of the sequence, is called "Recovery"; it must be remembered that it was written in the devastated landscape of Warsaw in 1943. The father speaks:

> "Here I am — why this senseless fear?
> Soon now the day will come, and night will fade.
> Listen: you can hear the shepherd's horns, and there,
> Look how the stars pale, over a trace of red.
>
> The path is straight, we're almost to the clearing.
> Down in the village, the first bell chimes,
> And roosters on fences have started crowing.
> The sleepy earth, fertile and happy, steams.
>
> Here it is still dark, and you see fog pour
> In black swirls over the huckleberry knolls.
> But dawn on bright stilts wades in from the shore.
> And the ball of sun is ringing as it rolls."

To imagine this steady parental reassurance in the most simple and fundamental words of the mother tongue, in the metres immemorially present in hymn and nursery rhyme, is to remind oneself of what this father's voice must sound like in its original Polish, as it embodies the oldest dream of all, underlying our most primitive infant memories — that the universe is, as Carlyle said, not a charnel house but godlike, and our father's. Since this dream is the mythical projection of a faith in being, of a hope for reality, and of a reciprocal love, the poem stands firmly as an essay in archetypal forms, as a predication of the deepest values, and as an anguished personal memory of an incinerated culture.

Read in the original, this great hymn of commemoration must be a stab to the heart of any Pole. It is "warm, in the way some pictures look warm" (as Keats said he wanted his autumn ode to be). Perhaps "The World" could have been written in this transparently simple way (for all its concreteness, it is a heavenly version of the earth) only by someone steely enough to pass rapidly beyond the anger, horror, hysteria, and denial felt as a childhood world is being lost. He creates instead this crystalline pendant world on a golden chain, preserved in a child's gaze.

It is clear from his three volumes that Milosz has a powerful inner investment in antagonism. In his poetry, cultures are set in opposition; world views clash; existence struggles with annihilation; learning vanquishes, and is vanquished by, ignorance; laughter and weeping succeed each other; contempt vies with grief. Milosz is not a writer of one chief emotion (as we might think of Blake as chiefly a poet of indignant vision, or of Crane as supremely a poet of Platonic longing). It seems sometimes that Milosz's poems should split open from the sheer internal pressure of their confined contents. What is confined is often at the same time both mysterious and intelligible, if hard to acknowledge. The sequence "Album of Dreams" is a striking group exhibiting this pressure. The dreams retold are dated, as if to give them the force of testimony:

November 23

A long train is standing in the station and the platform is
  empty.
Winter, night, the frozen sky is flooded with red.
Only a woman's weeping is heard. She is pleading for
  something
from an officer in a stone coat.

In this brief glimpse, there is both a general emptiness of landscape and a fullness in the tableau of suppliant and officer; there is both purpose (the long train) and negation of intent (the empty platform); there is darkness and yet a suffusion of blood suggested in the red sky; there is the original, silent scene and the shocking intrusion of weeping and pleading; there is the abject humiliation of the woman and the adamant implacability of the stony officer. Such antagonisms are sensually, aesthetically, ethically, and intellectually unbearable. A more sentimental poet might have represented the hopeless woman and the inhuman officer as a tableau of social protest, but in Milosz's dream-logic the woman and the officer represent, philosophically speaking, the irresistible force and the immovable object, and it is that conjunction (philosophically inconceivable) which the aesthetic of the poem must mirror, and does, in its irreconcilable items of presence and absence, reality and surrealism, flesh and stone, silence and the sound of agony. In little, this is the pattern of the best of Milosz's work. To read it is to feel that one's interior being will crack from incorporating such incompatible pressures.

A strong-minded poet of this sort risks an almost vicious power if he permits one force-field to dominate, unmitigated by another; and Milosz's poems of lethal scorn, though memorable, sin perhaps in allowing no shelter from their commination. In "Child of Europe," those who saved their own skins at the expense of the weak speak in their own voice (though, of course, they would not openly speak in this way). "We," they say, "are better than those who perished . . . We, saved by our own cunning and knowledge." The poem continues:

> Having the choice of our own death and that of a friend,
> We chose his, coldly thinking: let it be done quickly.
>
> We sealed gas chamber doors, stole bread.
> Knowing the next day would be harder to bear than the day
>   before.
>
> As befits human beings, we explored good and evil.
> Our malignant wisdom has no like on this planet.

It may be that Milosz includes himself in his sardonic lines; he speaks in another poem of his "debts never paid," his "shames," his "base deeds to be forgiven." The withering sketch of a political conformist ("Keeping one hand on Marx's writings, he reads the Bible in private") is, after all, drawn by one who has undertaken to translate the Bible into Polish, but who rose to diplomatic service in postwar Poland, serving in Washington and Paris before he finally broke with the regime in 1951. Milosz's conviction of evil in himself breaks intermittently through these poems: "What comes from my evil — that only is true . . ." "Pain raved in me with a diabolic tongue." A gnostic distrust renders every element of virtue suspect: devils, he says, "whistle songs / . . . about the moment of our agony / When everything we have cherished will appear / an artifice of cunning self-love."

Under the rubric of "everything we have cherished" can come language, poetry, freedom, intellectual integrity — everything for which Milosz could tell himself he chose political exile. But linguistic exile is for a poet a form of suicide — no matter that there is a community of exiles, no matter that underground writings from Poland can be obtained, no matter that one's language is in its fully formed adult state when one leaves the linguistic home. Although Milosz has said that "no clear-cut division between the poets living abroad and those at home is apparent in Polish literature . . . their present residence is not a decisive factor," only Polish literary history will be able to judge whether Milosz's later poetry has suffered from his living abroad. (The most interesting twentieth-century case of linguistic exile is, of course, that of Joyce, and the question to be asked is whether his attempt to make a polyglot language in *Finnegans Wake* is not a result of that exile; the comparable lyric case is that of Eliot, where the mask of Englishness may have debilitated the Quartets.) Milosz is now Professor Emeritus of Slavic Languages and Literatures at Berkeley. He has published a *History of Polish Literature* and an anthology of postwar Polish poetry; and yet, he laments, the names he recites are "not known to anyone" — "Chiaromonte / Miomandre / Petöfi / Mickiewicz . . . Young generations are not interested in what happened / Somewhere else, long ago."

In constituting himself the abstract chronicle of a dead Europe, Milosz has chosen a method as different as possible from Pound's. Pound's jumble of detail (American as well as European) is presented by an excavator-poet, who finds a quotation, an ideogram, a letter, a broken fortress, a bit of a diary, a fleeting goddess, a set of ruined visual equivalents of the past. Pound's archeological museum, increasingly, has no place in itself for sentences; the diffraction of time permits only glancing syntactic fragments, phrases scattered across the page. "Reality" in Pound's aesthetic (at least, as testified to by the form of the Cantos) consists of infinitely subdivisible matter, as buildings fall to stone, treatises to ideograms, and literary works to snatches of themselves; the reconstruction of the past is a labor of Sisyphus. Milosz's aesthetic refutes such a judgment; what is important about the past, he insists, is its ontological simplicity, the utter beauty of its traditional parts:

> Now he sees his homeland. At the time of the second
>   mowing.
> Roads winding uphill and down. Pine groves. Lakes.
> An overcast sky with one slanting ray.

> And everywhere men with scythes, in shirts of unbleached
> linen
> And the dark-blue trousers that were common in the
> province.

This material is inherently nostalgic, of course, but one suspects that the reason Pound could not write like this about the wreckage of Europe is that he was not European; he had absorbed his Europe as a reader of books rather than as an inhabitant of a settled place. European detail, and even American historical detail, seemed exotica to the enthusiastic provincial American. For Milosz, who has the past in his bones (not only from his childhood in prewar rural Lithuania but from his early study of Latin), all the detail of the life in Christian Rome's farthest province goes without saying and need not be specified; it need only be remembered:

> Riding in a cart, he looked back to retain as much as
> possible.
> Which means he knew what was needed for some ultimate
> moment
> When he would compose from fragments a world perfect at
> last.

It is that "world perfect at last" which Milosz preserves in "The World."

Milosz's later poems — those collected in *Bells in Winter* and *The Separate Notebooks* — incorporate long ruminations on self, body, language, the past, good and evil. They can seem less pure and less corrosive than the earlier poems, though any true comparative judgment could be made only by a Polish-speaking reader. Milosz's dark spirit of mockery lives in them side by side with his racked religious yearning. His gibes and his prayers vie with each other for room, his macabre visual caprices coexisting with his ineffable simplicity of recollection. It is almost impossible to convey the turbulence of mind produced in a reader by such a succession of mental and visual leaps; that turbulence is the aesthetic on which Milosz stakes his claim. In one representative passage, for example, Milosz remembers the old

woman, Lisabeth, who was the servant in the house where he rented
a room when he was a university student long ago. He remembers,
as if it were today (and this is his simplicity), her going to morning
Mass to the sound of bells in winter:

> I could count the years. But I prefer not to.
> What are years, if I see the snow and her shoes
> Funny, pointed, buttoned on the side,
> And I am the same, though the pride of the flesh
> Has its beginning and end.

Just as we are taken by both the photographic detail of the remem-
bered shoes and the prophetic, biblical tone remarking on the cor-
ruptibility of the flesh, Milosz's demonic mockery rises to remind us
that the mind of a worldly older man is composed not only of piety
and recollection. He describes the service in the baroque church, with
the bowing priest in his vestments:

> Pudgy angels are blowing their trumpets again.
> And him, the stooped priest in his chasuble
> I would compare today to a scarab
> From the Egyptian division of the Louvre.

In this coldness, the poem recedes light-years from the "funny,
pointed" shoes. There follows the most bizarre passage in the poem,
one describing the "communion of saints" — the group of all those
who have been saved by having lived a virtuous life. Church, state,
and men — all are incriminated in Milosz's black redefinition of
"sainthood":

> Our sister Lisabeth in the communion of saints —
> Of witches ducked and broken on the wheel
> Under the image of the cloud-enfolded Trinity
> Until they confess that they turn into magpies at night;
> Of wenches used for their masters' pleasure;
> Of wives who received a letter of divorce;
> Of mothers with a package under a prison wall —
> Follows the letters with her black fingernail,
> When the choirmaster, a sacrificer, a Levite
> Ascending the stairs, sings: *Introibo ad altare Dei.*

Ad Deum qui laetificat juventutem meam.

Prie Dievo kurs linksmina mano jaunystè.

Mano jaunystès.
My youth.

This disturbing passage is one of those which strain with their burden of compressed meaning. Its vignettes are, first of all, visual — the buttoned shoes, the pudgy angels of traditional baroque ornament, the torture of witches (the ducking-pool, the wheel) taking place in the past under a medieval painting of the Father, the Son, and the Holy Ghost in glory. (The parallel with modern torture is made, with ironic savagery, in silence.) Secondly, the items of the poem are historically vertiginous, as Milosz conflates the witch trials of the seventeenth century, the feudal *droit de seigneur,* and the modern mother with a package for an imprisoned son. Thirdly, the range of the poem takes in the social hierarchy (the priest and the church, the prison and the state, the masters and the wenches). Fourth, and finally, the passage interweaves the Lithuanian mother tongue (*"mano jaunystè"*), the Latin of the poet's childhood role as an acolyte at Mass (*"juventutem meam"*), and the Polish "my youth," now tranlated into the English of exile. On the whole, the poem offers a succession of purely dissimilar language categories, as in the space of twenty lines we are made to say, in succession, the following improbable group of words: "buttoned," "pudgy," "chasuble," "scarab," "Egyptian," "Louvre," "saints," "witches," "ducked," "cloud," "Trinity," "magpies," "wenches," "divorce," "package," "fingernail," "Levite," *"Introibo," "Dievo,"* "youth." (Only Lowell, among our contemporaries, embarked on a similar forcible yoking of linguistic realms.) The tones jar as noticeably against one another as do the worlds. The homage in the Latin beginning of the Mass is abraded by the sinister image of the scarab used for the priest, by the tortured women confessing to being magpies at night, and by the derisive epithets — "a sacrificer, a Levite" — applied to the celebrant of the Mass.

Milosz's elaborate inner sytem of grids is in one sense the common possession of any European intellectual — the grid of history, the grid of class structure, the grids of manifold visual experience, the grid of plural ethnic and religious allegiances. But in Milosz the grids are curiously permeable to one another, and the mobile flickering of language darts from one to the next, impelled by a rapid and nearly inhuman intelligence keeping a violent welter of feeling just barely in subjection. Milosz speaks both from within the Heraclitean flux and from above it. On the one hand, he is alive in the now, writing about his life in Berkeley; on the other hand, he dwells in the past, and a posthumous voice arises from him as from the Delphic cleft. Finally, he is the voice of historical irony itself, visiting, eons later, his remains in the indifferent museum of time:

> And the city stood in its brightness when years later I
>   returned . . .
> To my home in the display-case of a granite museum,
> Beside eyelash mascara, alabaster vials,
> And menstruation girdles of an Egyptian princess.
> There was only a sun forged out of gold plate,
> On darkening parquetry the creak of unhurried steps.

There are no direct lessons that American poets can learn from Milosz. Those who have never seen modern war on their own soil cannot adopt his tone; the sights that scarred his eyes cannot be seen by the children of a young provincial empire. A thousand years of history do not exist in American bones, and a culture secular from birth cannot feel the dissolution of the European religious synthesis, on which Milosz dwelt in *The Witness of Poetry,* his Charles Eliot Norton lectures at Harvard. But the work of Milosz reminds us of the great power that poetry gains from bearing within itself an unforced, natural, and long-ranging memory of past customs; a sense of the strata of ancient and modern history; wide visual experience; and a knowledge of many languages and literatures. Not, as in Pound, the self-conscious allusiveness of the autodidact returning obsessively to the books of his formative years, but, rather, the living and tormented revoicing of the past makes Milosz a historical poet of bleak illumination.

15

John Ashbery, Louise Glück

It seems time to write about John Ashbery's subject matter. It is Ashbery's style that has obsessed reviewers, as they alternately wrestle with its elusive impermeability and praise its power of linguistic synthesis. There have been able descriptions of its fluid syntax, its insinuating momentum, its generality of reference, its incorporation of vocabulary from all the arts and all the sciences. But it is popularly believed, with some reason, that the style itself is impenetrable, that it is impossible to say what an Ashbery poem is "about." An alternative view says that every Ashbery poem is about poetry — literally self-reflective, like his "Self-Portrait in a Convex Mirror." Though this may in part be true, it sounds thin in the telling, and it is of some help to remember that in the code language of criticism when a poem is said to be about poetry the word "poetry" is often used to mean many things: how people construct an intelligibility out of the randomness they experience; how people choose what they love; how people integrate loss and gain; how they distort experience by wish and dream; how they perceive and consolidate flashes of harmony; how they (to end a list otherwise endless) achieve what Keats called a "Soul or Intelligence destined to possess the sense of Identity."

It is worth quoting once more Keats's description of this world not as a vale of tears but as a vale of what he called "soul-making." We are born, according to his parable, with an intelligence not yet made human; we are destined to the chastening of life, which, together with painful labor on our part, tutors our chilly intelligence into a feeling and thinking soul. "I will put it in the most homely form possible," wrote Keats to his brother George in Kentucky:

"I will call the *world* a School instituted for the purpose of teaching little children to read — I will call the *human heart* the *horn Book* used in that School — and I will call the *Child able to read, the Soul* made from that *school and its hornbook.* Do you not see how necessary a World of Pains and troubles is to school an Intelligence and make it a soul?" In a less passionate tone, Keats added in another letter that the mind in uncongenial company is forced upon its own resources, and is left free "to make its speculations on the differences of human character and to class them with the calmness of a Botanist."

In these passages, Keats writes very generally — in the first with the generality of parable, in the second with the generality of taxonomy. Ashbery, too, is a generalizing poet, allegorizing and speculating and classifying as he goes, leaving behind, except for occasional traces, the formative "world of circumstances," which, as Keats says, by the trials it imposes proves the heart, alters the nature, and forms a soul. Ashbery turns his gaze from the circumstances to the provings and alterations and schoolings that issue in identity — to the processes themselves. He has been taking up these mysteries with increasing density in each of his successive volumes.

I was only one of many readers put off, years ago, by the mixture of willful flashiness and sentimentality in *The Tennis Court Oath* (1962). And I was impatient for some time after that because of Ashbery's echoes of Stevens, in forms done better, I thought, and earlier, by Stevens himself. Ashbery's mimetic ear, which picks up clichés and advertising slogans as easily as "noble accents and lucid inescapable rhythms" (as Stevens called them), is a mixed blessing in *As We Know* (1980) (which has undigested Eliot from the Quartets in it), as in earlier books. But though some superficial poems still appear in these pages, poems of soul-making and speculative classification — evident in *Rivers and Mountains* (1966) and taking expository form in the prose of *Three Poems* (1972) — have been in the ascendant since *Self-Portrait in a Convex Mirror* (1975) and *Houseboat Days* (1977). In the long poem "Self-Portrait," Ashbery gives his own version of the Keatsian soul-making:

> It is the lumps and trials
> That tell us whether we shall be known
> And whether our fate can be exemplary, like a star.

"Bright star, would I were steadfast as thou art," Keats wrote, echoing Shakespeare and Wordsworth. The Ashbery touch comes in the word "lumps," as in "to take your lumps" — the word anchoring the lofty sentiment to our ironic existence in the world.

Increasingly, Ashbery's poems are about "fear of growing old / Alone, and of finding no one at the evening end / Of the path except another myself," as the poem "Fear of Death" (from *Self-Portrait*) rather too baldly puts it. The distinct remove of his subject matter from immediate "experience" also concerns Ashbery:

> What is writing?
> Well, in my case, it's getting down on paper
> Not thoughts, exactly, but ideas, maybe:
> Ideas about thoughts. Thoughts is too grand a word.

Something — which we could call ruminativeness, speculation, a humming commentary — is going on unnoticed in us always, and is the seed-bed of creation: Keats called it a state of "dim dreams," full of "stirring shades, and baffled beams." We do not quite want to call all these things "thoughts." They nonetheless go on. Do we have ideas about them? Well, yes, as Keats did when he thought of them as shadowy stirrings, perplexed shafts of light. Our "ideas" about these "thoughts" that are not thoughts are, as Keats said, the stuff of poetry before it is put into a neater mental order. Intuition, premonition, suspicion, and surmise are the chracteristic forms of Ashbery's expression. Otherwise, he would not be true to the stage of spiritual activity in which he is interested. In Ashbery we find, above all, what Wordsworth called

> those obstinate questionings
> Of sense and outward things.
> Fallings from us, vanishings,
> Blank misgivings of a Creature
> Moving about in worlds not realized . . .

These misgivings and questionings are often put quite cheerfully by Ashbery, in a departure from the solemnity with which truth and beauty are usually discussed. The chaos we feel when one of the truths we hold to be self-evident forsakes us is generally the source of lugubrious verse; for Ashbery, for whom a change of mood is the chief principle of form, "the truth rushes in to fill the gaps left by/ Its sudden demise so that a fairly accurate record of its activity is possible." In short, a new truth sprouts where the old one used to grow, and the recording of successive truths is what is on Ashbery's mind.

A certain coyness attacks poets, understandably enough, when they are asked about their subject matter. It seems too self-incriminating to reply, "Oh, love, death, loneliness, childhood damage, broken friendships, fate, time, death, ecstasy, sex, decay, landscape, war, poverty." Back in 1965, the Interview Press, in Tucson, published *John Ashbery and Kenneth Koch (A Conversation)*, in which the following exchange occurs:

> ASHBERY: I would not put a statement in a poem. I feel that poetry must reflect on already existing statements.
> KOCH: Why?
> ASHBERY: Poetry does not have subject matter, because it is the subject. We are the subject matter of poetry, not vice versa.
> KOCH: Could you distinguish your statement from the ordinary idea, which it resembles in every particular, that poems are about people?
> ASHBERY: Yes, poems are about people and things.

To this playful warding off of banality (all the while including it), Ashbery truthfully adds, "When statements occur in poetry they are merely a part of the combined refractions of everything else." One can't, in short, extract the discursive parts from a poem and think they are the poem, any more than one can substitute the discursive motto "Beauty is truth, truth beauty" for the ode of which it is a part. However, the relation that was agitating Keats in that ode was surely the relation between truth and beauty, between the representational and the aesthetic, and there is no harm in saying so. Similarly, for Ashbery, it is no disservice to his eloquent fabric of "filiations, shuttlings . . . look, gesture, / Hearsay" (*Self-Portrait*) to speak of what the shuttlings are shuttling around, what the gestures are gesturing to.

An eminent scholar once told me, more in sorrow than in anger, that he had read and reread the poem "Houseboat Days" and still he could not understand it. This can happen, even as people read Ashbery with good will, because Ashbery has borrowed from Stevens a trick of working up obliquely to his subject, so that the subject itself makes a rather late appearance in the poem. The poem begins with a thought or image that provides a stimulus, and the poet works his way into the poem by an exploratory process resembling, Ashbery has said, philosophical inquiry. The beginning, Ashbery modestly adds, may eventually not have very much to do with the outcome, but by then it has become enmeshed in the poem and cannot be detached from it. If a reader proceeds past the rather odd and off-putting beginning of "Houseboat Days," he will come to a meditation, first of all, on how little either the mind or the senses finally give us. In youth, we are appetitive, mentally and physically, and are convinced we are learning and feeling everything; as we age, we find how much of what we have learned is corrupted by use, and how fast the surge of sensual discovery ebbs:

> The mind
> Is so hospitable, taking in everything
> Like boarders, and you don't see until
> It's all over how little there was to learn
> Once the stench of knowledge has dissipated, and the
>   trouvailles
> Of every one of the senses fallen back.

After the next meditation (on the insusceptibility of our inmost convictions to reason and argument) comes a meditation on the ubiquitous presence, no matter what your convictions make you praise or blame in life, of intractable pain:

> Do you see where it leads? To pain . . .
> It . . . happens, like an explosion in the brain.
> Only it's a catastrophe on another planet to which
> One has been invited, and as surely cannot refuse:
> Pain in the cistern, in the gutters . . .

Oddly enough, our first response to emotional pain all around us, down in the cisterns, up in the gutters, is to deny we are feeling it; it is, Ashbery muses, "as though a universe of pain / Had been created just so as to deny its own existence." In the manifesto that follows, Ashbery sets forth a Paterian ethics of perception, introspection, memory, art, and flexibility. He argues, given the nature of life, against polemic and contentiousness:

> But I don't set much stock in things
> Beyond the weather and the certainties of living and dying:
> The rest is optional. To praise this, blame that,
> Leads one subtly away from the beginning, where
> We must stay, in motion. To flash light
> Into the house within, its many chambers,
> Its memories and associations, upon its inscribed
> And pictured walls, argues enough that life is various.
> Life is beautiful. He who reads that
> As in the window of some distant, speeding train
> Knows what he wants, and what will befall.

What we hear in these lines, with their ethos of sweetness and Hellenic light borrowed from Arnold, is a syntax borrowed from Yeats: "He who can read the signs nor sink unmanned / . . . May know not what he knows, but knows not grief." But Yeats would not continue, as Ashbery does, by readmitting in the next line a Keatsian melancholy: "Pinpricks of rain fall again." Hope, he says, seems in middle age a futile emotion: "Hope is something else, something concrete / You can't have." Hope exists still, but suppressed, confined to the subterranean life of dream, repressed until the force of desire becomes unmanageable — a tidal wave:

> It becomes a vast dream
> Of having that can topple governments, level towns and
>   cities
> With the pressure of sleep building up behind it.
> The surge creates its own edge
> And you must proceed this way: mornings of assent,
> Indifferent noons leading to the ripple of the question
> Of late afternoon projected into evening.

And what results from the balked torrential surge and earthquake of desire? They find their way much diminished, says the poet, into these poems, these addresses, these needle-tracings of disturbance:

> Arabesques and runnels are the result
> Over the public address system, on the seismograph at
>   Berkeley.

And what do they cost, these houseboat days, our days in this fragile ark, adrift on the Byronic tide? They cost precisely (by a "little simple arithmetic") everything, and they point to the end of the vacation, that "last week in August" which the poem envisages, with not much time left at all, as the rain gathers, and we notice this instant "for the first and last time," as one would notice a place on the dustcover of a book one is closing, "fading like the spine/Of an adventure novel behind glass, behind the teacups." In this light, the mournful beginning of the poem — about a break in a previously healthy surface, about thinking, over the hotel china, at breakfast, about the end of one's stay — is also about the common heresy of thinking oneself immortal and finding the wing of death rushing above, about the tendency of the mind to linger (to "botanize," to borrow Keats's metaphor) on these questions of time and death, and about the equal tendency of life (a dazed daisy, or life "dazed with the fume of poppies," to quote the unrevised ode "To Autumn") to blossom again in its inhospitable environment:

> "The skin is broken. The hotel breakfast china
> Poking ahead to the last week in August, not really
> Very much at all, found the land where you began . . ."
> The hills smouldered up blue that day, again
> You walk five feet along the shore, and you duck
> As a common heresy sweeps over. We can botanize
> About this for centuries, and the little dazey
> Blooms again in the cities . . .

Life for Ashbery, as everyone has noticed, is motion. We are on boats, on rivers, on trains. Each instant is seen "for the first and last time"; each moment is precious and vanishing, and consequently every poem is unique, recording a unique interval of consciousness. This is a consoling aesthetic, since by its standards every utterance is privileged as a nonce affair; it is also mournful, since it considers art as fleeting as life. In an interview he gave to the *New York Quarterly* (reprinted in *The Craft of Poetry,* 1974), Ashbery spoke unequivocally on various topics — his subject matter, his supposed "obscurity," his method of writing, his forms, his influences. There are occasional self-contradictions in the piece, as might be expected in conversation on matters so complex. But, for the record, some of Ashbery's helpful remarks bear repeating:

> All my stuff is romantic poetry, rather than metaphysical or surrealist . . . As far as painting itself goes . . . I don't feel that the visual part of art is important to me, although I certainly love painting, but I'm much more audio-directed . . . French poetry on the whole hasn't influenced me in any very deep way . . . I'm attempting to reproduce in poetry . . . the actions of a mind at work or at rest . . . ["The Skaters"] is a meditation on my childhood which was rather solitary. I grew up on a farm in a region of very hard winters and I think the boredom of my own childhood was what I was remembering when I wrote that poem — the stamp albums, going outside to try and be amused in the snow . . . Also an imaginary voyage prompted by the sight of a label or a postage stamp was again a memory of childhood . . . In the last few years I have been attempting to keep meaningfulness up to the pace of randomness . . . but I really think that meaningfulness can't get along without randomness and that they somehow have to be brought together . . . The passage of time is becoming more and more *the* subject of my poetry as I get older . . . ["Fragment"], like maybe all of my poems, [is] a love poem . . .

The entire interview is a revealing one, and links Ashbery conclusively to the Western lyric tradition. He comes from Wordsworth, Keats, Tennyson, Stevens, Eliot; his poems are about love, or time, or age.

And yet it is no service to Ashbery, on the whole, to group him with Stevens and Eliot; when he echoes them most compliantly, he is least himself. In any case, though he descends from them, he is not very much like them: he is garrulous, like Whitman, not angular, like Eliot; he is not rhetorical, like Stevens, but tends rather to be conversational, for all the world like Keats in his mercurial letters. The familiar letter, sometimes the familiar essay are his models now that he has forsaken the formal experiments of his earlier books. We open *As We Know* already included, by its title, in a complicity of recognition and inquiry. The book clarifies itself over time, and is itself the clearest of all Ashbery's books; his special allusiveness, a private language perfected over the past twenty years, appears in it, of course, but there are long stretches of accessible table talk, so to speak. These appear chiefly in "Litany," a long poem written in double columns, in what I find a somewhat trying imitation of the bicameral mind. It is full of perfectly intelligible and heartfelt ruminations on soul-making in art, life, and criticism. On the whole, it wonders why — placed, as we are, on this isthmus of our middle state — we go on living and doing the things we do: inventing, imitating, and transforming life.

> Earthly inadequacy
> Is indescribable, and heavenly satisfaction
> Needs no description, but between
> Them, hovering like Satan on airless
> Wing is the matter at hand:
> The essence of it is that all love
> Is imitative, creative, and that we can't hear it.

Ashbery, like Coleridge, who found all life an interruption of what was going on in his mind, lives in the "chronic reverie" of the natural contemplative. As often as not, his contemplation is chagrined, reproachful of the world that promised us so much and gave us so little. At times, he even doubts whether we are doing any soul-making at all:

> And slowly
> The results are brought in, and are found disappointing
> As broken blue birds' eggs in a nest among rushes
> And we fall away like fish from the Grand Banks
> Into the inky, tepid depths beyond. It is said
> That this is our development, but no one believes
> It is, but no one has any authority to proceed further.
> And we keep chewing on darkness like a rind
> For what comfort it can give in the crevices
> Between us . . .

These are the dark passages that Keats foresaw and feared, sketched by Ashbery in his characteristically speckled humor.

Ashbery has said that his long poems are like diaries, written for an hour or so a day over long periods, and "Litany" — a "comic dirge routine," like so many of his poems — has to be listened to as well over a long stretch of time. Such a form of composition, he says in a poem at the end of *Houseboat Days,* has to do with "The way music passes, emblematic / Of life and how you cannot isolate a note of it / And say it is good or bad." Nor can a line, or a passage, or an inception or conclusion from Ashbery be isolated as good or bad: "the linear style / is discarded / though this is / not realized for centuries." It is our wish to isolate the line as touchstone which makes us at first find Ashbery baffling; once we stop looking for self-contained units we begin to feel better about our responses, and soon find a drift here, a meander there that feels, if not like our old beloved stanzas or aphorisms, at least like a pause in the rapids. What we find in him (to quote again from *Houseboat Days*) is "branching diversions around an axis"; the axis of loss, or forgetfulness, or remorse, or optimism, or human drama — since we are all, as Ashbery wittily says, "characters in the opera *The Flood,* by the great anonymous composer."

Houseboat Days is the volume containing Ashbery's most explicit short accounts of his own intent. One model there is a tapestry done in the form of a Möbius strip; this metaphor, with its (literal) new twist on an ancient figure for the web of art, coexists with the metaphor of the litany, the chain of words, the sequence of lessons in the heart's hornbook:

> We may as well begin the litany here;
> How all that forgotten past seasons us, prepares
> Us for each other, now that the mathematics
> Of winter is starting to point it out.

As things are reduced, once leafless, to the harsh geometry lesson of winter, we learn the diagrammatic forms of life, and chant its repetitive and lengthening chant. Such is the mournful view. On the other hand, Ashbery is irrepressibly sanguine. Something will always turn up to change the mood, as it does in a sonata. Never was there a "castaway of middle life" (Ashbery was born in 1927) more confident of his daily bread from the ravens:

> Impetuously
> We travel on, life seems full of promise.
> . . . Surely
> Life is meant to be this way, solemn
> And joyful as an autumn wood . . .

Of course, this cannot last, and the wood is "rent by the hunters'/ Horns and their dogs." But a renewal does keep happening: the sun brings, as is its wont, a zephyr, a cowslip.

Not only is Ashbery perennially hopeful, he is perennially generous, especially toward the whole enterprise of art — its origins in experience, the collecting of data that might help it along, its actual, stumbling efforts, its stiffening into print or onto canvas, its preservation by the academies. In "Litany," he is quite willing, for example, for the academy and the critics to exist. After all, his fresco or his "small liturgical opera," this litany, will be preserved by the academy, described by critics, long after the author dies, and even while time threatens to devour everything:

> Certainly the academy has performed
> A useful function. Where else could
> Tiny flecks of plaster float almost
> Forever in innocuous sundown almost
> Fashionable as the dark probes again.
> An open beak is shadowed against the
> Small liturgical opera this time.
> It is nobody's fault. And the academy
> Has saved it all for remembering.

As for critics, they are there, like the poets, to keep reminding people of what is in fact happening to them:

> People
> Are either too stunned or too engrossed
> In their own petty pursuits to bother with
> What is happening all around them, even
> When that turns out to be extremely interesting . . .
> Who
> Can evaluate it, formulate

The appropriate apothegm, show us
In a few well-chosen words of wisdom
Exactly what is taking place all about us?
Not critics, certainly, though that is precisely
What they are supposed to be doing.

The despair of language here is a sign of Ashbery's yearning for a vision less than preformulated, more than foreseeable: for something done by great poets ("and a few / Great critics as well," he adds generously); that is, to

describe the exact feel
And slant of a field in such a way as to
Make you wish you were in it, or better yet
To make you realize that you actually are in it
For better or for worse, with no
Conceivable way of getting out . . .

I quote these lines even though they are not among Ashbery's best — they haven't his eel-like darting — because they show his earnestness about the whole enterprise of art, as he asks for a new criticism, deriving from the actual current practice of poetry, for only in this way do we make our poetry intelligible to ourselves:

It is to count our own ribs, as though Narcissus
Were born blind, and still daily
Haunts the mantled pool, and does not know why.

It is as though poetry were incompetent to see its own image until reflected in the discursive analysis of criticism. And it may be so.

The best moments in Ashbery are those of "antithesis chirping / to antithesis" in an alternation of "elegy and toccata," all told in a style of "ductility, its swift / Garrulity, jumping from line to line, / From page to page." The endless beginnings and endings in Ashbery, the changes of scenery, the shifting of characters ally him to our most volatile poets — the Shakespeare of the sonnets, the Herbert of *The Temple,* the Keats of the letters, the Shelley of "Epipsychidion." He is different from all but Keats in being often very funny. In "Litany," for example, he gives himself mock commands and injunctions:

And so
I say unto you: beware the right margin
Which is unjustified; the left
Is justified and can take care of itself
But what is in between expands and flaps . . .

And in a parody of Blake he goes "bopping down the valleys wild"; the poetry of pastoral, parodied, becomes both touching and ridiculous:

The lovers saunter away.
It is a mild day in May.
With music and birdsong alway
And the hope of love in the way . . .

Then, in a trice, the pastoral grows grim:

Death likes to stay
Near so as to be able to slay
The lovers who humbly come to pray
Him to pardon them yet his stay
Of execution includes none and there lay
Hope aside and soon disappear.

And so the small liturgical opera of "Litany" goes on through three parts, in a Protean masque of genres. Different readers will prefer different arias and, through the device of the double columns, different counterpoints. My current favorite is an ode to love:

It is, then,
Gigantic, yet life-size. And
Once it has lived, one has lived with it. The astringent,
Clear timbre is, having belonged to one,
One's own, forever, and this
Despite the green ghetto that intrudes
Its blighted charm on each of the moments
We called on love for, to lead us
To farther tables and new, surprised,
Suffocated chants just beyond the range
Of simple perception.

This ode continues for nearly forty lines; the part I have quoted is paired, in the other column, with a reflection on solitude, perhaps preceding death:

> The river is waning
> On. Now no one comes
> To disturb the murk, and the profoundest
> Tributaries are silent with the smell
> Of being alone. How it
> Dances alone, in winter shine
> Or autumn filth.

As always in Ashbery, there is a new beginning, an upswelling. Even the end of "Litany" shows us caught in the reel of life, as the naïf speaker earnestly addresses us for help:

> Some months ago I got an offer
> From Columbia Tape Club, Terre
> Haute, Ind., where I could buy one
> Tape and get another free. I accept-
> Ed the deal, paid for one tape and
> Chose a free one. But since I've been
> Repeatedly billed for my free tape.
> I've written them several times but
> Can't straighten it out — would you
> Try?

We all think life's first reel is free; we always find ourselves billed for it over and over; we can never "straighten it out." Never has Freud been so lightly explicated.

The rest of *As We Know* — forty-seven short lyrics — is not any more easily summarized than "Litany." There are poems (I begin this list from the beginning) about growing up, about fidelity, about identity, about death, about (I have skipped two) the permanence of art, about construction, deconstruction, and perpetual creative joy in the face of death:

> We must first trick the idea
> Into being, then dismantle it,
> Scattering the pieces on the wind,

> So that the old joy, modest as cake, as wine and friendship
> Will stay with us at the last, backed by the night
> Whose ruse gave it our final meaning.

One could go on, listing the subjects of all forty-seven poems. They are all "about" something. Some are carried off better than others; some seem destined to last, to be memorable and remembered — none more so than the calmly fateful "Haunted Landscape."

"Haunted Landscape" tells us that we all enter at birth a landscape previously inhabited by the dead. We all play Adam and Eve in the land; we then suffer uprootings and upheaval. We are all — as Ashbery says, quoting Yeats — "led . . . / By the nose" through life; we see life and ourselves dwindle into poverty, and it is only our naïveté (some would say stupidity) that lets us construct castles in air, which of course collapse. Life is both a miracle and a non-event. At the end, we die, and become part of the groundcover and the ground; we become ghosts, as we are told by an unknown herald that it is time to go. The transformation takes place without our knowing how, and our history becomes once again the history of earth's dust. Ths is the "plot" of "Haunted Landscape"; there is no plot more endemic to lyric. I quote the middle lines, about the eternal reappearance and sexual conjunction and final undoing of the arche-typal human couple:

> She had preferred to sidle through the cane and he
> To hoe the land in the hope that some day they would grow
>   happy
> Contemplating the result: so much fruitfulness. A legend.
> He came now in the certainty of her braided greeting . . .
>
> They were thinking, too, that this was the right way to
>   begin
> A farm that would later have to be uprooted to make way
> For the new plains and mountains that would follow after
> To be extinguished in turn as the ocean takes over
>
> Where the glacier leaves off and in the thundering of surf
> And rock, something, some note or other, gets lost . . .

It is from Stevens that Ashbery learns the dispassionate recording of horror, as here the farm is uprooted, the plains are extinguished, and the irretrievable note (of hope, of happiness, of love) is lost, if not under the glacier then in the crash of surf and rock. And what can we look back on? Only the ruined pastoral, our quenched dreams, our diminished life:

> And we have this to look back on, not much, but a sign
> Of the petty ordering of our days as it was created and led
>   us
>
> By the nose through itself, and now it has happened
> And we have it to look at, and have to look at it
> For the good it now possesses which has shrunk from the
> Outline surrounding it to a little heap or handful near the
>   center.

"Others call this old age or stupidity," comments Ashbery. We cannot bear to utter those words of ourselves.

In the meantime, the only heroism, even when life becomes shaming and humiliating, is to attain the eye that misses nothing:

> The wide angle that seeks to contain
> Everything, as a sea, is an eye.
> What is beheld is whatever lives,
> Is wildly unappetizing and inappropriate,
> And sits, and fits us.

With every construction of pleasure, there arises, says Ashbery, a precisely equivalent and simultaneous construct of criticism, and vice versa: "They are constructing pleasure simultaneously / In an adjacent chamber / That occupies the same cube of space as the critic's study." The perplexed relations between these two — pleasure and criticism, beauty and truth — are shown in constant flux in these poems, the question perpetually reexamined:

> The contest ends at midnight tonight
> But you can submit again, and again.

Ashbery is an American poet, always putting into his poems our parades and contests and shaded streets. He sometimes sounds like Charles Ives in his irrepressible Americana, full of "dried tears / Loitering at the sun's school shade." There is nonetheless something monkish in these poems, which, in spite of their social joy and their hours of devoted illumination in the scriptorium, see a blank and blighted end. The poem with the portmanteau title "Landscapeople" sums up our dilemma — the intersection of humanity and nature. It tells us, in brief, all that Ashbery has to say at this moment about our lives, a summary both scarred and sunlit:

> Long desired, the journey is begun. The suppliants
> Climb aboard the damaged carrousel:
> Some have been hacked to death, one has learned
> Some new thing, and all are touched
> With the same blight . . .

It is the blight man was born for, we remind ourselves. We travel in circles on the carrousel, going nowhere:

> And the new ways are as simple as the old ones,
> Only more firmly anchored to the spectacle
> Of the madness of the seasons as it unfolds
> With iron-clad rigidity, filling the sky with light.

The sacred seasons, Keats wrote, must not be disturbed. But they bring the chilly auroras of autumn, as Stevens said, filling the sky with "the color of ice and fire and solitude." At the close of "Landscapeople," Ashbery thinks of Wordsworth's "Immortality" ode, and of his own art as a Rilkean Book of Hours:

> We began in an anonymous sensuality
> And lived most of it out before the difference
> Of time got in the way, filling up the margins of the days
> With pictures of fruit, light, colors, music, and vines,
> Until it ceases to be a problem.

I have been extracting chiefly the more accessible parts of Ashbery, but it is possible to explain his "hard" parts, too, given time, patience, and an acquaintance with his manner. It is possible also to charac-

terize that manner — by turns so free-floating, allusive, arch, desul-
tory, mild, genial, unassertive, accommodating, wistful, confiding,
oscillatory, tactful, self-deprecatory, humorous, colloquial, despair-
ing, witty, polite, nostalgic, elusive, entertaining. It is within our grasp
to schematize his practice, categorize his tics — opaque references,
slithering pronouns, eliding tenses, vague excitements, timid protests,
comic reversals, knowing clichés. We can recognize his attitudes —
the mania for collection, the outlandish suggestions, the fragrant
memories, the camaraderie in anguish. If we ask why the manner,
why the tics, why the attitudes, and we do ask it — at least, I have
sometimes asked it and heard it asked — the answer, for a poet as
serious as Ashbery, cannot be simply the one of play, though the
element of playfulness (of not being, God forbid, boring or, worse,
bored) always enters in, and enters in powerfully. The answer lies in
yet another of Ashbery's affinities with Keats. Keats said that the
poet had no identity of his own but, rather, took on the identities of
other things — people, animals, atmospheres — which pressed in
upon him. "I guess I don't have a very strong sense of my own
identity," said Ashbery in the *New York Quarterly* interview. "I find
it very easy to move from one person in the sense of a pronoun to
another and this again helps to produce a kind of polyphony in my
poetry which I again feel is a means toward greater naturalism." "A
crowd of voices," as Stevens called it, is spoken for by the single
poet; as we feel ourselves farther and farther from uniqueness and
more and more part of a human collective, living, as Lowell said, a
generic life, the pressure of reality exerts a pressure on style — a
pressure to speak in the voice of the many, with no portion of their
language (whether the language of cliché, the language of the media,
the language of obscenity, or the language of technology) ruled out.
Our dénouement is a collective fate; we are "already drenched in the
perfume of fatality." What the poet can do is remind us of "the
gigantic / Bits and pieces of knowledge we have retained," of that
which "made the chimes ring." If anything, in Ashbery's view, makes
a beautiful order of the bits and pieces and the chimes ringing, it is
poetry:

> If you listen you can hear them ringing still:
> A mood, a Stimmung, adding up to a sense of what they
>   really were,
> All along, through the chain of lengthening days.

II

The reflective and discursive verse of paradox represents one extreme of lyric; the opposite extreme is song. Song and reflection are the two sources of lyric, and poems move along a continuum between them. Song alone is tenuous, and reflection alone is ponderous; song requires some ballast of analysis, and reflection requires some leaven of buoyancy. When song and reflection join, lyric is born. All lyrics tend toward one or the other of the extremes, and must be judged according to their kind.

John Ashbery, a reflective poet, and Louise Glück, a writer of lyrics like lieder, can serve as examples of current practice. I must add, to be just, that Ashbery's rhythms are as seductive as ever, and that Glück's poems exemplify Lowell's remark about poets' mental processes — "We thought in images." Glück's weighted images move magnetically toward configurations; they glow toward each other in responsive understanding; they cohere in constellations. Ashbery's sentences are not centripetal; their orbits are long ellipses, full of the irregularities of planetary distraction. Or, like sociable comets, they trail a dispersal of attention behind them that nonetheless assembles into a coda, something visible.

When it was first announced, Ashbery's book *Shadow Train* (1981) had a different title — *Paradoxes and Oxymorons* — that called up Donne's *Paradoxes and Problems* (the usual title for a collection of short pieces circulated privately in Donne's lifetime and posthumously published). Ashbery's witty variation placed propositional impossibility (paradox) next to figurative impossibility (oxymoron) to tell us that he was about to propose the contradictions of life in the contradictions of rhetoric. An oxymoron ("dazzling darkness") is a paradox compressed into a single self-contradicting phrase, and is therefore the show-off among figures of speech.

A poetry composed of paradoxes and oxymorons — whatever the content of either — announces, by its use of these two figures, that things cannot to the will be settled (as Keats put it); that life, when thought about, gives rise to the ultimately frustrating conviction that things are and are not, can be and cannot be, must be and will not be — that life famishes where most it satisfies. The great source book in English literature for paradoxes and oxymorons of Ashbery's sort is Shakespeare's *Sonnets* — where life is consumed with that which it was nourished by, where blackness turns fair, and loathsome canker lives in sweetest bud.

It is easy, on the other hand, to imagine Glück's poems being set to music as a song-sequence; they have the intensity of a chain of emblematically significant moments, fixed in time. Ashbery's paradoxes, though, are composed under the aegis of the goddess he calls Forward Animation (who, with her two sister Fates, presides over the soft-sculpture alphabet of life):

> The tent stitch is repeated in the blue and red
>
> Letters on the blocks. Love is spelled L-O-V-E
> And is echoed farther down by fear. These two are sisters
> But the youngest and most beautiful sister
> Is called Forward Animation.
>
>   . . .Of her it may be said
> That what she says, she knows, and it will always come
>   undone
> Around her, as you are thinking, and so the choice
> Is still and always yours, and yet
>
> You may move on, untouched . . .

This is a characterisitc set of paradoxes: that we are still children spelling out letters in the heart's hornbook, that L-O-V-E and F-E-A-R echo each other in stalemate, but that in any case — whether love conquers the fear of love, or the fear of love defeats the temptation to love — we will find our choice undone by Nemesis, her irresistible foot advancing on through time.

Nemesis is every truth's undoing; as she utters any truth, it dissolves in change. We can choose love, or choose fear, or choose to remain untouched; the one certainty is that we move on. Ashbery shifts into another cliché, the river of time; but just as he revivifies Nemesis by calling her Forward Animation, so he reinvents the Heraclitean flux, making it first a cascade and then a deluge, which as fast as we can define ourselves de-defines us. Nemesis watches our plight; as Keats said, a superior being might be amused by us just as we are by the beasts. The only solution is for us to adopt toward ourselves the godlike indifference of Nemesis:

> You may move on, untouched. The glassy,
> Chill surface of the cascade reflected her,

> Her opinions and future, de-defining you. To be amused this
>   way
> Is to be immortal, as water gushes down the sides of the
>   globe.

The deluge in Ashbery's last line brilliantly transforms the (limited)
cascade into the limitless ocean, the ocean seen from an unnervingly
distant perspective in space, the perspective of the Fates who can
look on terror from afar. Ashbery's paradoxes — of choice vitiated
by necessity, love undone by fear, love and fear alike "dissolved in
the stream of history," history itself "de-defined" in deluge — make
the title of this poem, "Oh, Nothing" perfectly just. "What did you
say?" "Oh, nothing" — since by the time it is said it is snuffed out,
canceled ("those / Now empty pairs of parentheses"), or evaporated,
like a dazzling shower "Sucked back up into the peacock's-feather
eye in the sky / As though through a straw."

Each of the fifty poems in *Shadow Train* resembles a sonnet,
even though Ashbery's "sonnets" (like Meredith's in *Modern Love*)
have sixteen lines each, in four stanzas of four lines. The sonnet form
seems so inescapable in English that every century since the sixteenth
has generated it anew, rhymed and unrhymed, enlarged and dimin-
ished. Stevens wrote fifteen-line "sonnets" in "Sunday Morning" and
"Le Monocle de Mon Oncle," but they often felt more Petrarchan
(falling into two parts) than Shakespearean. Ashbery's four stanzas
make his "sonnets" look Shakespearean, and often they are (though
his quatrains tend to run over to the next line, in his confiding haste).
In these poems, the loquacious poet of "Litany" (Ashbery's long
double-columned poem) is contracted into a stricter narrator of sum-
mary fate. Brevity requires that Ashbery's characteristic sleight-of-
hand proceed even more rapidly than usual. Ashbery's metaphors
rarely connect with one another on a horizontal plane; instead, each
radiates out from a central notion animating the lines. I take a typical
three-line passage as illustration; it reads,

> The endless ladder being carried
> Past our affairs, like strings in a hop-field, decants
> A piano-tuning we feed on as it dances us to the edge.

The kernel sentences here sound surrealistic: "The ladder decants
a piano-tuning"; "We feed on the piano-tuning"; and "The piano-

tuning dances us to the edge": and Ashbery is frequently called a surrealist on such evidence. But surrealism cannot be parsed into sense, and Ashbery can — a process one finds laborious at first, but then increasingly natural, as one gets the hang of it (if my own experience is typical).

Yeats's poetic ladder rose up from the rag-and-bone shop of the heart; Ashbery's ladder (in the lines just quoted) rides modestly sideways. Its rungs (running vertically because the ladder is being carried sideways) are carried past our lives. Instead of seeing us as wheat fields, as Keats had done, Ashbery sees us more Dionysiacally as hop fields; the growing hops are supported by vertical strings, which resemble in their parallel verticality the ladder rungs. The verticality of the stringed plane is rotated to become the horizontal bed of strings of the piano of art, and (by a pun, perhaps, on "descant"), the ladder in the hop fields becomes the brimming intoxicant of life, decanting a well-tempered melody to us on which we feed as we follow its pied piping. It dances us to the edge of the field of life — that edge of doom from whose flatness we fall into nothingness.

Each of the metaphors — the ladder, the hop field, the decanting of an intoxicating drink, the tempering of the piano strings, the harvest-nourishment, the dance of life, the edge of doom — is a perfectly well-known, conventional, and allegorically precise image. It is their nonconnection with one another (however much each is connected radially to the parable of life, love, art, and death) that makes Ashbery's lines sound incomprehensible at first. But the incomprehensibility, in the poems that seem to me most rewarding, does not last; it is soluble; it rides on its own melting (to borrow Frost's phrase).

There are private poems here, and private titles ("Corky's Car Keys," "Penny Parker's Mistake"). Ashbery's deep trust in his own associative processes makes for cases of inaccessibility. But many — even most — of the poems here are based on the pure stuff of myth — or rather myths — conflated and treated with such freedom that they seem something vaguely remembered and always known. "Songs without Words," for instance, tells the story of everyone's life. We went willingly down to an obscure shore expecting life and love; we met people there whom we set about trying to know and understand and on whom we projected our own wishes for love and identity; when dawn came to us we joyfully walked over it, like the gods on their rainbow bridge, from the night of ignorance to the day of experience. And there were ships at the shore, waiting to take us on the journey.

Now, later, we know with the wisdom of hindsight that the country we were taken to was a criminal one, a disaster area, and that we were lured by sirens to destruction, and that the cruel sun melted our frail wings and sent us plunging to our death. But would it have happened otherwise in any other scenario? Here is the poem:

> Yes, we had gone down to the shore
> That year and were waiting for the expected to happen
> According to a preordained system of its own devising.
> Its people were there for decoration,
>
> Like notes arranged on a staff. What you made of them
> Depended on your ability to read music and to hear more
> In the night behind them. It gave us
> A kind of amplitude. And the watchmen were praying
>
> So long before rosy-fingered dawn began to mess around
> With the horizon that you wondered, yet
> It made a convenient bridge to pass over, from starlight
> To the daylit kingdom. I don't think it would have been any
>   different
>
> If the ships hadn't been there, poised, flexing their muscles,
> Ready to take us where they pleased and that country had
>   been
> Rehabilitated and the sirens, la la, stopped singing
> And canceled our melting protection from the sun.

Surely this poem will be anthologized. It makes happen what it describes, and exemplifies Ashbery's tragicomic mode, composed of one part suffering and one part sophistication. Ashbery builds his porch "on pilings, far out over the sand," not on rock; he chooses some patterns ("So many patterns to choose from") and allows them, like excited gases, to collide:

> they the colliding of all dispirited
> Illustration on our lives, that will rise in its time like
> Temperature, and mean us, and then faint away.

He is a tightrope-walker in altitudes "seeing only the ooze of foliage and blue sunlight / Above"; he admits to "signs of fatigue and mended places"; he asks,

> It hurts now,
> Cradled in the bend of your arm, the pure tear, doesn't it?

In Ashbery's "school of velocity," the fatal "shuttle never falters." It is almost by revenge that art gets made; enraged at the slipperiness and unsatisfactoriness of life, the artist determines to put some portion of it down on canvas, where it can be held and possessed. Yet even this act attests to our wild desire to have, not canvas, but the real, the flesh, the heart:

> It seems that all
> Moments are like this: thin, unsatisfactory
> As gruel, worn away more each time you return to them.
> Until one day you rip the canvas from its frame
>
> And take it home with you. You think the god-given
> Assertiveness in you has triumphed
> Over the stingy scenario: these objects are real as meat,
> As tears. We are all soiled with this desire, at the last
>   moment, the last.

Shadow Train is here to be picked up and reread until it yields its full feelings, a process which will take some time. How very transparent Ashbery's poems can become over time will be clear to anyone who now returns to *Rivers and Mountains* or the close of *Three Poems,* his most limpid piece of narration. It was probably inevitable that Freudian "free association" (with its iron, paradoxical, and oxymoronic linkages) should eventually find its poet.

Louise Glück's sense of myth, while as firm as Ashbery's, is less fluid; his retellings of myth tend to be lightly touched and Greek; hers are more likely to biblical, ritualized, and haunted. "The Garden" and "Lamentations" — two mythical sequences in *Descending Figure* — concern the waking into erotic life, and reflect the myths of Eden, Adam and Eve, and the immortality of the soul. In "The Garden" a soul who had earlier refused the dirt, terror, and cruelty of life finally agrees to enter "a field without immunity," and to endure the unions and losses intrinsic to engagement. The soul waits with its body in the garden, among the green willows and the impervious animal statuary, and agrees to the inception of love:

> The garden admires you.
> For your sake it smears itself with green pigment,
> the ecstatic reds of the roses,
> so that you will come to it with your lovers.
>
> And the willows —
> see how it has shaped these green
> tents of silence. Yet
> there is still something you need,
> your body so soft, so alive, among the stone animals.
> Admit that it is terrible to be like them,
> beyond harm.

From this poem we can construe a paradigm of Glück's manner and matter both. The manner is always one of fated recognition, almost of *déjà vu*. The soul does not wonder what the garden intends; she knows. She does not question, she accepts; almost, we want to say, she undergoes. The alternative to choosing life is perfectly clear; it is to be made of stone and to be beyond harm — but also beyond love.

Ashbery's triad of fear, love, and Forward Animation appear here too, except that Forward Animation has become reluctant, hesitant, slowing nearly to standstill. This Psyche waits for Eros with some disgust; like Stevens's mansion "smeared with the gold of the opulent sun," this garden is self-smeared with green, a primitive paradise. Its willows are to harbor love, like Stevens's willows that shiver in the sun for new lovers. But the rigidity of the lines bodes ill for love. In Glück a transfixed idealism is at war with a wish for the natural; and the perfection of the lines, in their measured and conclusive force, imposes a logic inimical to the asserted choice of softness and sexual ecstasy.

Glück has some of Sylvia Plath's willed immobility; but her rhythms are not spiky and hysterical like Plath's. Instead they are mesmeric, trancelike, almost posthumously gentle; about the dead body, buried in the grave, Glück says,

Think of the body's loneliness . . .
Such a long journey . . .
How far away they seem,
the wooden doors, the bread and milk
laid like weights on the table.

The bread and milk lie like weights on the dead, too; the domestic wooden doors and the weighted table are the coffin displaced upward.

It is with no sense of the unexpected, then, that we come on Glück's sequence about anorexia:

It begins quietly
in certain female children:
the fear of death, taking as its form
dedication to hunger . . .
what I feel now, aligning these words —
it is the same need to perfect,
of which death is the mere byproduct.

Glück is not at her best in expository verse, where her hieratic rhythms can begin to sound portentous. But the poem reveals the aesthetic of Glück's verse — or of part of it: the acquiring, by renunciation, of a self. Denying itself the possession of the sacred object, the soul finds identity. Acquiring an object means absorbing it into the soul and losing it from view; renouncing it, the soul keeps it in view forever, and is able to see it clearly, free of projection. The sacred object is exposed, its underlying body visible, its form known in the x-ray vision of desire, which by renunciation is enabled into perception. It is an aesthetic Emily Dickinson would have recognized.

But there is another aesthetic at work in Glück besides this renunciatory one. It appears, this other one, almost unwittingly, in the concession, for instance, that "everything fixed is marred." And yet the unfixed is repellent in its fickleness: "The sea triumphs, / like all that is false, / all that is fluent and womanly." Glück's struggle to find a fluent that is not false is the shadow-twin of her claim that there is a fixed that is not marred. Her wonderfully suggestive poems about art (whether about its governing dreams or its formal expression in a medium) bring her embattled oppositions into their finest confrontation. It is often by means of a luminously enwound syntax that she combines the opposing forces.

Here, for example, is a child in his crib, afraid of nightmares, who stands up and spreads out his arms in the light of the nightlight to ward off the threat of beasts in the dark — and yet his own shadow thrown on the wall is the type and forerunner of those beasts. In making the defensive shadow-gestures of art, the mind creates anew those terrors which are only projections of its own self. Or so a paraphrase of this poem might read. But the poem itself does not read like that; instead, it winds itself immediately and sinuously into the child's experience, into his imperfect understanding, his futilely brave pretenses, his helplessness, his corporeality. Three simple sentences form the narrative skeleton of the poem:

> He knows he will be hurt.
> He spreads his arms.
> He cannot sleep apart from them.

But what unspeakable insinuations envenom the spaces between the simplicities:

Night Piece

> He knows he will be hurt.
> The warnings come to him in bed
> because repose threatens him: in the camouflaging
> light of the nightlight, he pretends to guard
> the flesh in which his life is summarized.
> He spreads his arms. On the wall, a corresponding figure
> links him to the darkness he cannot control.
> In its forms, the beasts originate
> who are his enemies. He cannot sleep
> apart from them.

Glück's poems about her son (of which this seems to be one) are eerily successful in catching the incomprehensions and discontinuities of a childish understanding as yet unformed. Glück has a gift for the skewed perspective, best seen, I think, in another of her reflections on art as death, one linked to the memory of her sister, who died in childhood. The poem takes its title ("The Sick Child") from a painting in the Rijksmuseum; but it is not Glück, looking at the painting, who is the spectator, but rather the mother in the painting holding her sick child at night, willing her not to die. As the mother looks out "into the bright museum" from the painting, Glück begs her to let the child die, so that her other children can live, and can wake to find themselves living children, not objects (as the dying child will be) on a painted canvas. The livingness of the painted mother exists in desperate conflict with the wish to live of her other children, menaced by the deathliness of art. (Art here stands too for the inability to forget; if the mother remains fixed in grieving for the dead child, her other children will feel themselves somehow obliged to die too.)

The Sick Child
— Rijksmuseum

A small child
is ill, has wakened.
It is winter, past midnight
in Antwerp. Above a wooden chest,
the stars shine,
And the child
relaxes in her mother's arms.
The mother does not sleep;
she stares
fixedly into the bright museum.
By spring the child will die.
Then it is wrong, wrong
to hold her —
Let her be alone,
without memory, as the others wake
terrified, scraping the dark
paint from their faces.

The painted Pietà of mother and dead child (matched in another poem, "Pietà," by a pregnant mother's unwillingness to send her unborn child into the disorder and pain of life) exists, in Glück, to be gainsaid — the living children wake (even if terrifed), and the baby is born (even if to the "dark context" in which a single star shines).

A misguided critic has said of *Descending Figure* that it "provides relatively little to engage the intellect," that the poems do not "engage our feelings," that Glück offers "no overall, coherent statement," and that "a poetry this pure makes inordinate demands upon our interest in style and style alone, unsullied by the complications of too great an engagement with reality." This tone is reminiscent of Allen Tate's in his notorious remark about the ode "To Autumn" — "a very nearly perfect piece of style but it has little to say." Such remarks issue from a critical peremptoriness that likes only discursive poetry, the poetry nearest to prose and the furthest from song, icon, or dream. But song, icon, and dream engage reality too — in Glück, the realities (among others) of death, marriage, motherhood, mourning, and the invention of religion. The style in which Glück engages these realities is the style of the rock, rather than the stream, of consciousness. Ashbery's fluidity puts us in the *res cogitans* as it carries on its marvelous observations and retoolings; Glück's sternness reminds us that we have also a precipitate, a residue, from life's fluidity — that which we recite by heart, the immutable, the unadorned, the skeletal, the known.

III

The figures traced in John Ashbery's rich book *A Wave* (1984) have to do with death: in fact, *A Wave* has qualities of a last testament. As I first read the opening poem, "At North Farm" (the Farm is from the *Kalevala*), it seemed to me a poem about the Angel of Death:

> Somewhere someone is traveling furiously toward you,
> At incredible speed, traveling day and night,
> Through blizzards and desert heat, across torrents, through
>   narrow passes.
> But will he know where to find you,
> Recognize you when he sees you,
> Give you the thing he has for you?
>
> Hardly anything grows here,
> Yet the granaries are bursting with meal,
> The sacks of meal piled to the rafters.
> The streams run with sweetness, fattening fish;
> Birds darken the sky. Is it enough

That the dish of milk is set out at night,
That we think of him sometimes,
Sometimes and always, with mixed feelings?

We register at first the clichés, as we read "incredible speed," "desert heat," "narrow passes," "granaries . . . bursting," and "mixed feelings." These trip so easily on the tongue that we understand this drama to be something "everyone knows": and yet at the same time the paradoxes of drought and abundance, sweetness and menace, dread and longing, warn us that this is an almost unimaginable state of affairs. Someone travels furiously toward you (with all the determination of the Post Office) — but will he — and here the poem takes its cue from the catchiness of popular lyric, "know where to find you . . . when he sees you . . . give you the thing he has for you?" Ashbery has said that this is the messenger of love, not death, but perhaps one can call him Fate, of whom we always think with mixed feelings.

No pleasure is sweeter in the ear than something new done to the old. Ashbery's deep literary dependencies escape cliché by the pure Americanness of his diction. A middle-aged American reads "Hardly anything grows here" with immediate recognition, a shock not possible any longer from the mention in a contemporary poem of "stubble plains" or "the barrenness / Of the fertile thing that can attain no more" — words used so memorably that they cannot be reused. Ashbery's gift for American plainness is his strongest weapon: "Hardly anything grows here" disarms us in its naked truth.

At the same time, in barren middle age one has seen too much; there is more experience than one can ever consume in recollection or perpetuate in art — the granaries are bursting with meal. That too, while Keatsian, is American in its "bursting with meal" (in Keats, what burst are clouds, in tears). Ashbery's propitiatory dish of milk for the goblin (to keep him outside the house) is just unexpected enough, as folk naiveté, to throw us off balance (in this Keatsian, Stevensian context); it gives us Fate through the lens of the literary grotesque instead of through the lens of tragicomic destiny (traveling furiously) or the lens of seasonal turn (vegetative barrenness, harvest plenty). Will it keep Fate out of the house if we set milk out for him? (Milton: "The drudging Goblin sweat, / To earn his cream-bowl duly set.") Will it mollify the Goblin if we don't think badly of him? And yet, isn't there as well a hope that he will come and stop for us and give us what he has for us — the horoscope in his hand? Emily

Dickinson, whose air of macabre comedy often resembles Ashbery's, would have read this poem with perfect comprehension.

A few pages later, Ashbery tells the "same" story over again, staged this time at the moment of loss. Sick and shaken, one hears the bad news about one's future:

> It was as though I'd been left with the empty street
> A few seconds after the bus pulled out. A dollop of
>   afternoon wind.
> Others tell you to take your attention off it
> For awhile, refocus the picture. Plan to entertain,
> To get out. (Do people really talk that way?)

The awful thing is that people really do talk that way. To see the very coin of our conversation exposed in the palm of the poem is horrible, but mesmerizing.

Yet once again, Ashbery tells the "same" story. This time he enters it as he realizes the terrible shortness of time, and begins to count the beads of the past:

> Each is a base one might wish to touch once more
>
> Before dying. There's the moment years ago in the station
>   in Venice,
> The dark rainy afternoon in fourth grade, and the shoes
>   then,
> Made of a dull crinkled brown leather that no longer exists.
> And nothing does, until you name it, remembering . . .

But there is no leisure to remember those Wordsworthian spots of time:

> The wrecking ball bursts through the wall with the
>   bookshelves
> Scattering the works of famous authors as well as those
> Of more obscure ones, and books with no author . . .

Ashbery does time justice: old structures die so that new structures of language may come into being. The wrecking ball lets in "Space, and an extraneous babble from the street / Confirming the new value the hollow core has again." The hollow core, the possibility of sig-nification itself, is made by artists into a cultural construct (here, a library); the wrecking ball lets in a new influx of demotic speech, and a new generation will construct the library all over again around that perpetual hollow core. If Ashbery's poetry is made possible only by the wreckage of Romanticism and Modernism, then his own fate and wreckage will empower a new poetry issuing from consciousness, "the light / From the lighthouse that protects as it pushes us away." The potential for culture is protected; the individual is cleared away. (I am translating Ashbery's delicacy into crudity, his narrative into observation.)

And again, Ashbery tells the story, insisting, by his manner, that everything said "in English" has to be written over "in American." If Keats's sonnet reads,

> When I have fears that I may cease to be
>   Before my pen has glean'd my teeming brain,
> Before high-piléd books, in charact'ry,
>   Hold like rich garners the full-ripen'd grain;

then Ashbery will write,

> I think a lot about it,
> Think quite a lot about it —
> The omnipresent possibility of being interrupted
> While what I stand for is still almost a bare canvas:
> A few traceries, that may be fibers, perhaps
> Not even these but shadows, hallucinations . . .

(Keats: "And think that I may never live to trace / Their shadows"; Ashbery: "traceries . . . shadows.") Ashbery does not hide his sources, but he does not replicate them, either. The "educated" reader thinks that "poetry" must sound Keatsian, rhythmic, and noble. But our American language cannot speak in those "noble accents / And lucid inescapable rhythms" (Stevens) without modification. "I think a lot about it" *is* how we now say "When I have fears." And Ashbery expertly winds up his sentence from that flat American beginning, first into American cliché ("omnipresent possibility," "what I stand for") and then into Stevensian qualification ("almost," "may be," "perhaps," "not even these but"), finishing with the hallowed words for art: "canvas," "traceries," "fibers," "shadows," "hallucinations."

Ashbery retells both life and loss with American comic pragmatism and deadpan pratfalls:

> The first year was like icing.
> Then the cake started to show through.

Reading Ashbery, one notices the idiom: when exactly, did "show through" come into common speech in this sense? and "started," too, for that matter? The poem ends with the remark, "And paintings are one thing we never seem to run out of": when did "to run out of something" become our normal way of saying that the supply was exhausted? "What need for purists," says Ashbery, "when the demotic is built to last, / To outlast us?" His campaign (of course, not only his) to write down the matter of lyric in the idiom of America is a principled one. His eclectic borrowing from many past styles — an aesthetic some would like to call postmodern — creates a "variegated, polluted skyscraper to which all gazes are drawn," the style of our century, to which we are both condemned and entrusted, a "pleasure we cannot and will not escape."

I have been writing, up to now, about the first seventeen pages of *A Wave,* simply to give the sense of a reader's first assenting page-turning. It is scarcely to the point, as we turn the pages, to ask what Ashbery "thinks about fate." Of course he thinks the things anyone could, and many have, thought about it. The aesthetic interest is how he makes it new. The duty and pleasure of art is to invent a thousand and one ways of telling the same story (or painting the same Crucifixion, or varying "*Non più andrai*"). Nobody wants a new lyric subject. We want the old subjects done over.

Ashbery's genius for a free and accurate American rendition of very elusive inner feelings, and especially for transitive states between feelings, satisfies our baffled search for intelligibility of experience. Here is Ashbery on the apprehensiveness of dying:

> The parachute won't land, only drift sideways.
> The carnival never ends; the apples,
> The land, are duly tucked away
> And we are left with only sensations of ourselves

> And the dry otherness, like a clenched fist
> Around the throttle as we go down, sideways and down.

There are other dazzling endings here. Each of us, says Ashbery, advances into his own labyrinth,

> Filling the road up with colors, faces,
> Tender speeches, until they feed us to the truth.

An icy hand grips the reader's wrist. There is a moment of flurried protest — "No, now that's just a metaphor, I mean nobody is going to feed me to — feed *me?* —' they? who? — *feed?*" — but the fluster freezes into the shock and glare of undeniability. The horrors of life and death have rarely been conveyed in a more dispassionately comic tone.

Ashbery's corrections in the typescript of *A Wave* sent by his publishers before the book arrived are invariably in the direction of more Americanness of diction. He crosses out foreign words, Anglicisms, and stately formulations (the latter not an easy sacrifice if, like Ashbery, you have learned your syntax from James and Proust). Ashbery has taken his Americanness in part from Gertrude Stein, who turns up in various agreeable echoes:

> What kind is it, is there more than one
> Kind, are people forever going to be at the edge
> Of things, even the nice ones, and when it happens
> Will we all be alone together?

There is a happy inconsequence of phrasing here that Ashbery aims for when he generalizes about life. He deletes passages that smack too much of the preacher. In one such instance of revision, a passage Ashbery deleted from "Destiny Waltz," Eliot's shadow falls and is expunged:

> Save us from the revealed meaning
> And revealing the meaning:
> Somewhere in between
> You shall find it not all bad
> And the questioning meaning may grow again.

Or, as Ashbery puts it in one of his one-line haiku, "You have original art works hanging on the walls oh I said edit." No contemporary poet can have Eliot hanging, too evidently there, on his walls. Ashbery is vigorous but selective in his editing, and one of the rewards of being his reader, as I have said, is to see the glints of his assimilated sources shining on the page.

Ashbery's poems often reflect on the putative reader for whom he transforms days into poems:

> Each day seems full of itself, and yet it is only
> A few colored beans and some straw lying on a dirt floor
> In a mote-filled shaft of light. There was room. Yes,
> And you have created it by going away. Somewhere,
>   someone
> Listens for your laugh, swallows it like a drink of cool
>   water,
> Neither happy nor aghast. And the stance, that post standing
>   there, is you.

Readers have listened for Ashbery's laugh, have swallowed it like a drink of cool water (Bishop, "The Man-Moth": "Cool as from underground springs and pure enough to drink"). In the aesthetic moment (by contrast to the poet's moment of "experience") we are neither happy nor aghast. The poet's own apologia to us is characteristically comic, dealing in sly paradoxes, and yet bleakly true:

> I shall sit on your doorstep
> Till you notice me. I'm still too young
> To be overlooked, yet not old enough to qualify
> For full attention, I'll flesh out
> The thin warp of your dreams, make them meatier,
> Nuttier. And when a thin pall gathers
>
> Leading finally to outraged investigation
> Into what matters next, I'll be there
> On the other side.

Art, for Ashbery as for Keats, is meat and drink, plumping the hazel shell with a sweet kernel. And art is company: feeling with outrage our own mortality (what happens next and what matters most — in Ashbery's portmanteau version "what matters next"), we turn to the poets who have felt the shock before us, and find them there on the other side. On the other hand, nobody stares truth, or art, in the face for long: psychic denial revises mortality, makes it recede, and disingenuously "speaks no longer / Of loss, but of brevity rather: short naps, keeping fit." The scorpion sting of that satiric close leaves its accusatory poison within us.

In this excellent collection there are things readers will be of two minds about. There is a long literary piece called "Description of a Masque" which invokes, for my taste, too many in-jokes. There are some attempts in the demotic ("The Songs We Know Best") that seem to me uneasy in their use of slang. On the other hand, these pieces are only exaggerations (whether on the literary side or the populist side) of Ashbery's search for a renewed idiom. His rewriting of haiku into one line, and his several prose poems called "Haibun" (the poetic prose written by a haiku poet), suggest a restless investigation of form.

Ashbery's major piece in this book, giving its title to the collection, is the long poem (over six hundred lines long) "A Wave," which as I read it is Ashbery's *Prelude*. A Wordsworthian poem of Whitmanesque lines, it ranges from childhood to death, and describes, in the largest sense, the *vie poétique*.

> By so many systems
> As we are involved in, by just so many
> Are we set free on an ocean of language that comes to be
> Part of us, as though we would ever get away.
> The sky is bright and very wide, and the waves talk to us,
> Preparing dreams we'll have to live with and use . . .
>
> We will all have to walk back this way
> A second time, and not to know it then, not
> To number each straggling piece of sagebrush
> Is to sleep before evening, and well into the night
>
> That always coaxes us out, smoothes out our troubles and
>   puts us back to bed again.

There seems to be a general belief among readers that to write about "poetry" is somehow not to write about "life." But "poetry" is the construction by consciousness of an apprehensible world. Every person constructs such a world, and lives in it. When the poets write about poesis, they are writing about what is done every day by everyone. Most of us do not reflect on it as we do it, but we live nonetheless in our construct of the world. Because the poet writes his constructions down, he cannot be unconscious of them: he must reflect on their structures, their idiom. In recording and enacting the process by which we come to consciousness, form an identity, see our selfhood shadowed and illuminated by circumstance, and finally bid farewell to illusions of immortality, Ashbery reveals the nature of personal life in our era. To say that a poem is "about poetry" means, surely, that it is consciously about the way life makes up a world of meaning.

The poets do not write about poesis as a process exclusive to themselves. The arrangements of memory, the articulations of the dreams of the ego, the inventions of culture, are poesis. If we do not understand ourselves as self-constructing animals, we mistake the source of authority, projecting it onto external fictions. The poets, by describing their act of self-making, call us to witness our own processes of soul-making. "A Wave," the account of a contemporary American life from childhood to death, self-composed, calls us to see in it our own self-composing.

Of course "A Wave" will eventually receive long commentaries, and I can give here only the briefest idea of its scope. It issues from "the dungeon of Better Living" and speaks in an imminently menaced environment ("Headhunters and jackals mingle with the viburnum / And hollyhocks outside"). It is Wordsworthian in its belief that "memory contains everything" and that an immense amount of discourse is needed to describe the sensations of life. The task of consciousness goes on, schooling the intelligence into a soul. Only a few (Arnold's "saving remnant") undertake this task with full wakefulness; they will live to see their work carried off in the impersonal wave of death:

> So always there is a small remnant
> Whose lives are congruent with their souls
> And who ever afterward know no mystery in it,
> The cimmerian moment in which all lives, all destinies
> And incompleted destinies were swamped
> As though by a giant wave that picks itself up
> Out of a calm sea and retreats again into nowhere
> Once its damage is done.

Throughout "A Wave," the joyous interplay of experience and memory, memory and expression, is played out in the shadow of death. The poet questions whether it is worth writing his preludes in the light of extinction:

> To be always articulating these preludes, there seems to be
>   no
> Sense in it, if it is going to be perpetually five o'clock
> With the colors of the bricks seeping more and more
>   bloodlike through the tan
> Of trees, and then only to blacken.

But the effort to recognize consciousness, and to give a musical expression to consciousness, is rewarded by the fullness and amplitude of the examined and constructed life. At the moment of execution,

> When they finally come
> With much laborious jangling of keys to unlock your cell
>
> You can tell them yourself what it is,
> Who you are, and how you happened to turn out this way,
> And how they made you, for better or for worse, what you
>   are now,
>
> And how you seem to be, neither humble nor proud, *frei
>   aber einsam.*

"Free but lonely": Asbery writes here, with irony, the epitaph for all the solitaries who have freely made their own souls, and know the souls they have made. The charm of Ashbery's urbane style — so various, so beautiful, so new — persists throughout this long poem, and will induce the rereadings the poem demands. It is a style that resists, in its glowing reflectiveness, the approaching darkness of the cimmerian moment.

16

Allen Ginsberg

Allen Ginsberg's *Collected Poems 1947–1980* contains, according to Ginsberg's preface, "all his poetry books published to date re-arranged in straight chronological order to compose an autobiography." The late Fifties brought "Howl" (1956) and Ginsberg's fame; the early Sixties brought "Kaddish," Ginsberg's great elegy for his mother; and from then till now Ginsberg has been an original voice in American poetry, helping to change public consciousness, as he justifiably says, "from provincial wartime nationalist-history-bound egoic myopia to panoramic awareness of planet news, eternal view of both formal charm and empty nature of local identity." This idiosyncratic summary exhibits Ginsberg's way with a phrase. It is hard to think of another author who would so debonairly have suggested "formal charm" as one of the attractions of nationalism. As usual, Ginsberg's verbal wit has a keen edge of social truth.

Perhaps because I came to "Howl" in 1957 fresh from reading Blake's long "prophetic books" in the revelatory classroom of Northrop Frye, I never found Ginsberg outlandish. It seemed quite natural that he should pour out headlong obituaries of "the best minds" of his generation":

> who sang out of their windows in despair, fell out of the subway window, jumped in the filthy Passaic, leaped on negroes, cried all over the street, danced on broken wineglasses barefoot smashed phonograph records of nostalgic European 1930s German jazz finished the whiskey and threw up groaning into the bloody toilet, moans in their ears and the blast of colossal steam-whistles.

This representative passage, part farce, part tragedy, suggests Ginsberg's comic rage, or raging comedy. "Howl" delights by its tonal range. Its obituaries expand into cartoons ("who created great suicidal dramas on the apartment cliff-banks of the Hudson"); its accounts of protest actions ridicule themselves ("who threw potato salad at CCNY lecturers on Dadaism"); its madnesses ebb in anticlimax ("who . . . overturned only one symbolic pingpong table, resting briefly in catatonia"); its visions recoil from their own pretentiousness ("Dreams! adorations! illuminations! religions! the whole boatload of sensitive bullshit!"). The violent poetry of the outsider, which Ginsberg had learned from Blake, is married in "Howl" to the teasing self-mockery of Whitman.

In the work of Ginsberg, Whitman's erotic dream of American brotherhood turns on itself in outraged disappointment, and yet the disappointment itself is comic. During the Fifties, Cold War America seemed to Ginsberg preposterous — sunk in its primitive xenophobia, attributing to the Russians its own paranoia, applying to them the same ethnic stereotypes it had already applied, in cowboy movies and popular folklore, to American Indians and to blacks:

> America it's them bad Russians.
> Them Russians them Russians and them Chinamen. And
>   them Russians.
> The Russia wants to eat us alive. The Russia's power mad.
>   She wants to take our cars from out our garages.
> Her wants to grab Chicago. Her needs a Red *Reader's
>   Digest*. Her wants our auto plants in Siberia. Him big
>   bureaucracy running our fillingstations.
> That no good. Ugh. Him make Indians learn read. Him need
>   big black niggers. Hah. Her make us all work sixteen
>   hours a day. Help.
> America this is quite serious.
> America this is the impression I get from looking in the
>   television set.

Ginsberg's exuberant comedy strips from all the patriotic icons of America their inviolable solemnity. As a Jew and a homosexual, Ginsberg is doubly an outsider in America; as someone who himself once had a "nervous breakdown" and knew confinement in an asylum, he is triply an outsider; by his family's Communist sympathies, he even began life as an outlaw. If it is chiefly by means of marginality that one comes to consciousness, then Ginsberg's break into consciousness was at once more difficult and more widely distributed than that experienced by most of us. Ginsberg's awakening, as he tells it in various interviews, occurred in successive moments of aesthetic realization and psychological insight. He perceived, first, that poetry was about himself (he was Blake's "youth pined away with desire") and, second, that everyone, without exception, knows the truths of consciousness, even though most people spend most of life denying and concealing them.

To my mind, the poem characteristic of Ginsberg, the one he writes over and over, is seen in its purest form in the faultless "American Change" (1958). Here Ginsberg situates himself at the margin of American society. He is returning from Europe on the S.S. *United States,* and as he enters New York Harbor he reaches into his pocket and brings out a handful of American money. From a visitor's perspective he scans the iconic forms (usually so familiar as to be invisible) on our coins and bills alike: "Legal Tender (tender!)." The poem displays Ginsberg's inimitable mixture of public history, immigrant history, personal history, sharp-eyed detail, mockery of political authority, and a haunting sense of vanished things. Here, in a long scherzo, is the buffalo nickel seen by the Jewish son of a lost Viennese culture, an American repudiating his rabbinic fathers, a young man remembering what a nickel could buy in the candy stores of Paterson:

> Held in my palm, the head of the feathered indian, old
> Buck-Rogers eagle eyed face, a gash of hunger in the cheek
>   gritted jaw of the vanished man begone like a Hebrew
> with hairlock combed down the side — O Rabbi Indian . . .
>   but now with all the violin music of Vienna, gone into the
> great slot machine of Kansas City, Reno —
> The coin seemed so small after vast European coppers
> thick francs leaden pesetas, lire endless and heavy,
>   a miniature primeval memorialized in 5¢ nickel candy-
> store nostalgia of the redskin, dead on silver coin,
>   with shaggy buffalo on reverse, hump-backed little tail
> incurved, head butting against the rondure of Eternity,
>   cock forelock below, bearded shoulder muscle folded
> below muscle, head of prophet, bowed,

vanishing beast of Time, hoar body rubbed clean of
wrinkles and shining like polished stone, bright metal in
my forefinger, ridiculous buffalo — Go to New York.

This affectionate and amused descriptiveness, this leisurely and smil-
ing play, this fidelity to domestic origins and equal fidelity to actuality,
this rueful and colloquial exchange of pain and pleasure — all these
are marks of Ginsberg's best writing. It is hard to believe that eleven
years earlier, in 1947, he had been writing pseudo-metaphysical verse
in the English manner:

> The argument our minds create
> We do, abed, substantiate;
> Nor we disdain, in our delight,
> To flatter the old Stagirite:
> For in one speedy moment, we
> Endure the whole Eternity,
> And in our darkened shapes have found
> The greater world that we surround.

Ginsberg's conversion to Blakean "vision" and his liberation into
satire seem to have happened simultaneously, and his subsequent
writings have brought satire and vision together in a way poetically
new. As kibitzer and prophet, Ginsberg wanders in his poetry the
streets of America, afoot with his vision of historical absurdity. It is,
in one poem, midnight on May Day of 1978, and Ginsberg, out to
get the *Times,* passes "a dark'd barfront, / police found corpses under
the floor last year, call-girls & Cadillacs lurked there on First Ave-
nue." Newspapers blow around "battered cans & plastic refuse
bags," and a workman is repairing a gas main. On this "Manhattan
May Day Midnight" (as the poem is alliteratively called), while the
rest of the city sleeps, Ginsberg the poet hurries through the streets
"thinking Ancient Rome, Ur." This recent poem, written twenty
years after "American Change," exhibits Ginsberg as the outsider
still — unmated, awake when others sleep, launching an imaginative
filament to Ur and Rome, looking at America with his wonted mix-
ture of affection and disgust, humor and hopelessness, conjecturing
that the ancient citizens of imperial Ur were just like us:

>Were they like this, the same shadowy surveyors & passers-
>by
>scribing records of decaying pipes & Garbage piles on
>Marble, Cuneiform,
>ordinary midnight citizen out on the street looking for
>Empire News?

Again, two years later, in Colorado, studying Buddhism with his guru, Ginsberg is no more at home than he is in New York; he is, as his lines suggest, no more than "mist drifting between water and sky":

>Trapped in the Guru's Chateau surrounded by 300 disciples
>I could go home to Cherry Valley, Manhattan, Nevada City
>to be a farmer forever, die in Lower East Side slums, sit with
>no lightbulbs in the forest,
>Return to my daily mail Secretary, *Hard Times*, Junk mail
>and love letters, get wrinkled old in Manhattan . . .
>Here I'm destined to study the Higher Tantras and be a slave
>of Enlightenment.
>Where can I go, how choose? Either way my life stands
>before me,
>mountains rising over the white lake 6 A.M., mist drifting
>between water and sky.

These "Reflections at Lake Louise" (1980), like the reflections on American change and on midnight in New York, would be of only momentary interest if they pertained to Ginsberg alone. But Ginsberg insists that the unease and pathos of his own social displacement are universal, and that the absence of a providential sanction for human restlessness makes our common homeless predicament alternately farcical and touching. Every so often, it is true, Ginsberg moves out of his usual comedy and arrives at a vast field of bleakness (notably at the end of "Kaddish"), but even that field represents nothingness, a void, rather than tragedy.

It is tempting to place Ginsberg in a specified historical moment, to say that he exemplifies the generation of Jews who were too young to fight in the Second World War, who hurtled from immigrant households through Columbia, who came to adulthood in the heartless economic boom and mindless anti-Communism of the postwar period, whose youth coincided with the availability of drugs; to say also that he came of age when homosexuality began to be more visible and when, finally, the intellectual verse of the Fifties, so dependent on Eliot, was being superseded by a new populism taking its inspiration from Williams. And it is possible to see in him the prophet of several social phenomena — a secularized Judaism, an emergent gay protest, an antiwar movement, and a quest for states of altered consciousness. Since no American poet of his generation has been more topical than Ginsberg, it is tempting to read him historically and leave it at that. But this would be to make his lesser poetry too central.

There are three aesthetic pitfalls for Ginsberg (all of them marked by an absence of humor). The first is a too topical journalism, literally borrowed from the newspapers and baldly emphasized by Ginsberg's preaching to us that this is the language of our day:

> Continued from page one   area
>   after the Marines killed 256
>   Vietcong captured 31
>   ten day operation Harvest Moon last
>   December
>   Language language
> U.S. Military Spokesmen
>   Language language
>   Cong death toll
>   has soared to 100 in First Air
>   Cavalry.

The second pitfall is sexual bathos, most evident in Ginsberg's imitatively Blakean songs:

> Then Love put his face
> in my tenderest place
> where throbbed my breast sweet
> with red hot heart's heat.

And the third pitfall is populist verse, too simpleminded to be taken seriously (Ginsberg is not simpleminded, but his attempts at singable chants sometimes are):

> Too much Police
> too much computers
> too much hi fi
> too much Pork.

I think it true to say of Ginsberg, on the evidence of the *Collected Poems,* that he is a descriptive rather than a topical poet, that his strengths are geographical and domestic rather than erotic, and that at his best he is a rueful intellectual, and not a populist. Yet, much as one wanted Ginsberg to see the messianic mania behind his too freely offered advice to the State Department, one is sorry to see him, in his recent "Ode to Failure" (1980), come to every prophet's end:

> My tirades destroyed no Intellectual Unions of KGB & CIA
>   in turtlenecks & underpants, their woolen suits & tweeds
> I never dissolved Plutonium or dismantled the nuclear Bomb
>   before my skull lost hair
> I have not yet stopped the Armies of entire Mankind in their
>   march toward World War III
> I never got to Heaven, Nirvana, X, Whatchamacallit, I never
>   left Earth,
> I never learned to die.

A bitterness at human folly and vice impedes Ginsberg's humor in these recent years, as his historical experience grows and his buoyancy fades. The death of his father saps his energy; his elegy for his father, "Don't Grow Old," a memorable poem, ends in a tableau of resignation and failure.

Ginsberg has always been a spontaneous and prolific writer, courageously printing (it seems) whatever he thinks. "'First thought, best thought,'" he writes in his preface. Following Whitman ("Spontaneous Me"), he continues to claim, perhaps somewhat disingenuously, that "spontaneous insight — the sequence of thought-forms passing naturally through ordinary mind — was always motif and method of these compositions." He has been tirelessly persistent in protesting censorship, imperial politics, and persecution of the powerless. His usual poetics assumes that the poet can subvert the rational and evade the censor:

> Eliot's voice clanging over the sky on upper Broadway
> "Only thru Time is Time conquered"
> I am the answer: I will swallow my vomit and be naked.

But Ginsberg's very copiousness and generosity of language, and his outpourings against censorship, struggle constantly against the death that waits as silent antagonist to his "mind breaths." Death gives the hysterical edge to Ginsberg's poems of sexual contact, the least convincing utterances since the remarks of Lawrence's Mellors. And Ginsberg censors, even more than the fact of death, his own intellectuality and his wide readings, writing in a voice resolutely populist in tone but recondite in allusion. What he does not censor, and what ornaments the poetry, is his remarkable perception, always mischievous, always relishing the appearances of the world: the "scattered stoopfuls of scared kids frozen in black hair," the "old lady with frayed paper bags/sitting in the tin-boarded doorframe of a dead house." These two vignettes come from the poem "Mugging," written in 1972; the vigor in them visits Ginsberg less often now. His Poundian tirades of political invective died, by and large, with the Vietnam War. The archaism, especially in the erotic poems, does not wear well ("Belly to Belly and knee to knee. / The hot spurt of my body to thee to thee"); the consciously naïve love poems seem to confuse love and sex. But the weary record of celebrity is authentic. "I Am a Victim of Telephone" proves what it says, and the tired inventory of political reality in "Kral Majales" also rings true:

> And the Communists have nothing to offer but fat cheeks
>   and eyeglasses and lying policemen
> and the Capitalists proffer Napalm and money in green
>   suitcases to the Naked,
> and the Communists create heavy industry but the heart is
>   also heavy . . .
> and the Capitalists drink gin and whiskey on airplanes but
>   let Indian brown millions starve.

Ginsberg's best poetry requires an unstable moment, in which perception, passion, and humor combine in the right proportions. In many ways, he came of age at a lucky moment. A loosening of inhibition (at first enabled by drugs) let the long-breathed visionary emerge from the good student who had imitated Donne and Crane. The ethnic chant of the Hebrew psalms came into fragile conjuncton with Whitmanian enumeration. The demotic speech rhythms of Williams and his insistence on material objects gave the visionary Ginsberg permission to notice "the real world." Pound had opened the door of lyric to history. Eliot, Tate, and Ransom offered handy targets for iconoclasm.

Ginsberg's claim on us has been staked in the realm of the imagination; he wants us to imagine a planet without national hostilities, with ethnic tolerance, with pity for the oppressed, and with a Blakean approval for the lineaments of gratified desire. The ironic opposite to this vision of community is Ginsberg's personal loneliness, more emphatically sketched in the recent poetry than ever before. The autobiography of an idealist may always end with a tableau in which the doubly unaccommodating worlds of mortal matter and state authority tyrannize over the conquered visionary. In the short run, at least, death and tyranny always win. The despair that is the enemy of political hope has visited Ginsberg many times. "Yes and It's Hopeless" is the title of one poem (written in 1973):

> All hopeless, the entire solar system running
>   Thermodynamics' Second Law
> down the whole galaxy, all universes brain illusion or
>   solid electric hopeless emptiness.

The earth on which the visionary walks in an unredeemable slaughterhouse:

> Under the world there's broken skulls, crushed feet, cut
>   eyeballs, severed fingers, slashed jaws,
> Dysentery; homeless millions, tortured hearts, empty souls.

Yet "over & over thru the dull material world the call is made"; Whitman's call in the midst of the crowd is still Ginsberg's mantra. Ginsberg's poetry copes with political disappointment through the invoking of Buddhist meditations. But the poet's Buddhist ascription of suffering to ignorance sits uneasily with his Jewish ethic of righteous exposure of the unjust, and his native volubility seems ill-adapted to Buddhist meditative silence. The poetry (derived from the mother, according to "Kaddish") wins out finally against the desire for a paternal religious discipline.

Ginsberg is responsible for loosening the breath of American poetry at midcentury, influencing poets more formal than he, such as Lowell and Rich. He has made major poetry (especially in "Kaddish") out of the deracinated American Jewish experience. The desperate focus given by his mother's life and death brought "Kaddish" to a concentration that I miss in his taped cross-country travelogues. However, those travelogues, from "Wichita Vortex Sutra" to "Ecologue," represent the largest attempt since Whitman to encompass the enormous geographical and political reality of the United States. Most of all. Ginsberg has demonstrated that there is nothing in American social and erotic reality which cannot find a place in American poetry. The epigraph to "Howl" came from Whitman's "Song of Myself": "Unscrew the locks from the doors! / Unscrew the doors themselves from their jambs!" It was not a bad slogan with which to counter the example of Eliot; and Ginsberg's powerful mixture of Blake, Whitman, Pound, and Williams, to which he added his own volatile, grotesque, and tender humor, has assured him a memorable place in modern poetry. His readers will welcome the detailed notes — biographical and topical — appended to the *Collected Poems,* which also contains some Buddhist diagrams, a few photographs, and all the original epigraphs, dedications, and jacket copy of Ginsberg's individual volumes. As current events become history, "mind breaths" require footnotes; the fragile City Lights books in which his contemporaries once read Ginsberg have now been replaced by this handsome, much-needed, and yet unbohemian canonical volume.

17

Sylvia Plath

The *Collected Poems* of Sylvia Plath finally appeared almost twenty years after Plath's suicide on February 11, 1963. Nothing in the introduction written by her former husband, the British poet Ted Hughes, quite explains the long delay in the publication of this collection. Before Plath died, she had prepared the volume called *Ariel* for the press, but "the *Ariel* eventually published in 1965 was a somewhat different volume from the one she had planned," Hughes tells us; it incorporated poems she had planned to keep for a subsequent book, and omitted "some of the more personally aggressive poems from 1962" — those concerning her husband's infidelity, which led to the dissolution of the marriage and to Plath's move from Devon to London. Her daughter, Frieda, was two at the time of the move; her son Nicholas, not yet a year old. Less than a month after his first birthday, Plath was dead. She had managed to live and to write after previous attempts at suicide, but, like Pavese (to cite a comparable case), she continually needed to find reasons *not* to kill herself, rather than a reason to do so.

Until recently, most of the writing about Plath has been psychologically or politically motivated. The time of her fame coincided with a widespread acceptance of the Freudian myths of selfhood (which she also embraced) and with the rise of feminism. Plath's life seemed a text book illustration of the "Electra complex" (as she herself called it, schooled by her therapists and her college reading in psychology), and she also seemed an instance of the damage done to gifted women by social convention. Plath's language — a heady cross of *Kinder, Küche,* Freud, and Frazer — found an audience that already knew and shared its world of reference. An electric current jumped between *Ariel* and a large (mostly female) set of readers, and

272

from then on the poetry of Plath became a part of the feminist canon. *Crossing the Water* and *Winter Trees* were published in 1971; they, together with *The Colossus* (the only volume published in Plath's lifetime, in 1960) and *Ariel* made up the Plath poetic canon until the 1982 *Collected Poems*.

Plath scholars will know most of the work published here. Ted Hughes and his sister Olwyn (of whom Plath was bitterly jealous) have been publishing, bit by bit, small groups of the poems in limited editions in England (all royalties are assigned to the two children). The poems not previously published in any form are mostly very early; the few later ones in this category are undistinguished. For the general reader, however, this volume for the first time conveys the whole of Plath's work, arranged chronologically by date of composition. Fifty very early poems are printed in an appendix; the chronological arrangement begins with the year 1956, when Plath, who was born in 1932, was twenty-three. But the memorable poems do not begin until she turns twenty-four — after her marriage in June 1956. She had six years of mature writing before she died, at thirty. Those years included her second year as a Fulbright fellow at Newnham College, Cambridge; a year of teaching at Smith, where she had been an undergraduate; a year in Boston, where she audited Robert Lowell's writing class at Boston University; and her return to England. In London, after she and Hughes had decided to give up teaching and to live as writers, she had, in succession, a child, a three-month miscarriage, and an appendectomy. There she also wrote her autobiographical novel *The Bell Jar* (published in England under the pseudonym Victoria Lucas). In 1961, she and Hughes moved from London to Devon, and she had her second child. Then came the separation from Hughes, which produced a remarkable spate of writing: in the thirty-one days of October 1962, Plath finished twenty-five poems (while in the entire year of 1960 — which included the last three months of her first pregnancy, the birth of her daughter, and her first months of motherhood — she wrote only twelve).

The events of Plath's life during these years — though some, like the transatlantic move, are slightly unusual — are on the whole those which many women have lived through, not excepting marital disappointments, the discovery of infidelity, and finding oneself a single mother. These events, banal to everyone except the one experiencing them, have been the occasion in the twentieth century of any number of banal poems. As subjects, they are as well worn as the subject of parents (Plath's other topic). What is striking, and satisfying, about reading this volume is how well Plath holds her own, and how firmly she transforms the topics she masters — how her best poems maintain themselves in passion without lacking a strict informing intelligence. In some of the poems (notably the early ones), intelligence averts its eyes from feeling or overcontrols feeling; later, the balance sometimes tips in the other direction, and Plath becomes merely vituperative or spiteful, angrily refusing the acuteness of reflection present in her best work. Her piercing strength when intelligence and feeling cooperate is not easily forgotten.

Plath seems very young now to any older reader, and her career seems cruelly self-aborted. Remembering ourselves at thirty, we wish she could have had the years of living that would inevitably have provided her with new views of her past and, in consequence, new views of herself. Her suicide, for all her attempt to dress it in Greek necessity, seems an unhappy accident — a failure of social resource, a failure of medicine (a hospital bed could not be found for her), and even a failure of weather (she hated the cold, and died in London's coldest winter in sixteen years). We are more conscious now of the physiological causes of (and remedies for) depression, thanks to poets like Lowell, who have expressed considerable irony about the sedulous efforts of therapists to ascribe to environmental causes what turns out to be a lack of lithium.

By the time she died, Plath had written at least two scenarios of her life. In the first scenario, her father, Otto (an entomologist who died, when she was eight, of willfully uncared-for diabetes), is a doting parent, a hero, and a god, and she is his mourning daughter; her mother, Aurelia, is a heroine who keeps Plath and her brother alive by working as a teacher of secretarial skills. (Plath's devotion to her mother and Aurelia Plath's to her daughter appear in the incessant letters they exchanged; some of Sylvia's were collected in *Letters Home,* published in 1975). In the second scenario, Otto Plath becomes an incestuously seductive father, a Nazi, and a vampire; and Sylvia is his victim, a Jew in his concentration camp. Aurelia Plath in this scenario is a tentacular mother, a barnacle obsessively clinging to her daughter, a "blubbery Mary." Plath's scenarios about Ted Hughes underwent comparable changes, as he metamorphosed from fertility god into monster; and Plath's fictions about herself changed, too — she changes from the fruitful bride of the sun, "quick with seed," bearing a king as she couches in the grass, into Lady Lazarus who eats men like air. Eventually, if Plath had managed to stay alive, all the scenarios would probably have revised themselves; she would have seen her parents in yet another guise, and perhaps her ex-husband, too. Certainly she would have seen both herself and her children differently. As she writes about them, her children are infants, pure and poignant, untroubled by their mother's anxieties:

> Your clear eye is the one absolutely beautiful thing.
> I want to fill it with color and ducks,
> The zoo of the new
>
> Whose names you meditate . . .

When, in the future, her children became contrary and baffling adolescents, Plath would have needed to find another fiction for them, and for herself.

The one thing that recommends Plath to us most strongly now is her ability to change her mind when she saw a new truth. She was on the lookout for new truths; never one to receive the world passively, she hunted for accuracy and excoriated herself for her failures. She changed her mind, when it was necessary, in a violent way, repudiating her previous position with all the force of her daunting energy. She had no Keatsian capacity for maintaining two contrary truths at once. But it is not impossible that in middle age she might have come to entertain her scenarios as plural truths, to find some of the equilibrium granted, late, to Lowell, who ended by seeing his parents less harshly. Sylvia Plath, when she died, had at last begun to recognize a monstrousness in herself. If her father was a vampire, so was she. She had also begun to realize that "there is no terminus," no point at which the world is arranged permanently, with all its truths established:

> There is no terminus, only suitcases
> Out of which the same self unfolds like a suit
> Bald and shiny, with pockets of wishes.
> Notions and tickets, short circuits and folding mirrors.

This realization could be the chief principle of interest in life — more wishes, more notions, more tickets — but to Plath, in her tiredness, it seemed a nightmare.

What is regrettable in Plath's work is not the domestic narrowness of her subject matter (Dickinson and Herbert made faultless poetry out of matter putatively as "narrow") but the narrowness of tone. She has wit and sardonic irony; she has blank despair; and she has neutral judgment and observation, and even, at the end, tenderness. But she veers from zero to one hundred like a dangerously swinging needle; she has none of the ravishing variety of tone that colors Herbert's colloquies with God. Plath has another narrowness, too — her scrupulous refusal to generalize, in her best poems, beyond her own case. She will not speak about the human condition, in the way Emily Dickinson emboldened herself to. Dickinson had an acute, generalizing mind as well as an eye for minute particulars; in Plath we miss the sudden, illuminating widening of perspective that Dickinson learned from Emerson. Plath was stubbornly truthful, and she may have felt herself the exception rather than the rule. But her sense of herself as exceptional often prevented her from seeing herself as one of many.

There are two hundred and twenty-four mature poems in this collection, and those after *The Colossus* are better (as most critics have said) than those composed for that volume. Plath assiduously worked and worked on poetry as she had worked on academic subjects; no poet has worked harder. Either marriage and childbearing alone or the encouragement and help of Ted Hughes — or, more probably, both — changed her style. She discovered ways to make lines seem inevitable, not only in sound but also (her most interesting discovery) in looks. She had worked hard at imitating Dylan Thomas, and had early mastered certain coarse sound effects. But in a late line like "The shadows of ringdoves chanting, but easing nothing," she has given up on a bald imitation of Thomas and has found her own voice. Some of the binding devices in such a line are familiar — the parallel of "chanting" and "easing," the repetition of words of two syllables. But what is more unusual is the matching of "nothing," though it is not syntactically parallel, with "chanting" and "easing." Such ear-rhymes are a true binding and a false binding at once, setting the words aslant. The last half of the word "shadows" — "-dows" — almost matches the "doves" of "ringdoves" in the same witty way. Plath's later style is full of such cunning; her eye-rhymes (often without any aural equivalent like that in "doves" and "-dows") continue vigorously to the end of her career, and replace her earlier, self-conscious overwriting for the ear. We require of a poem that the words spring toward each other in magnetic attraction, but we are offended when the trick is done obviously. Plath's later rapprochements seem almost casual by contrast with her obtrusive early rhymes and rhythms, but they are far more premeditated. She began keeping drafts, Hughes tell us. Eventually, they may be published, and testify to the angle of revision she favored. The later poems, at their best, bear witness to Plath's painstaking work to make their parts fall into place and lock.

When Plath began to be able to find adequate language for her feelings, she redid a great number of her earlier themes. Here is early (pre-1956) Plath writing about the moon, always for her the presider:

> The choice between the mica mystery
> of moonlight or the pockmarked face we see
>   through the scrupulous telescope
> is always to be made: innocence
> is a fairy-tale; intelligence
>   hangs itself on its own rope.

"Intelligence hangs itself on its own rope" is a formulation better than what turns up in most college verse, but the language of this poem is Audenesque, prematurely "disillusioned," and arch. (Auden must have been the recommended intellectual model at college in those days; he is equally present in early Rich.) Only the end sounds particularly vigorous; "the mica mystery of moonlight" (in a poem alliteratively named "Metamorphoses of the Moon") shows off Plath's easy alliteration, which in fact does *not* draw the words together but pushes them apart, by calling attention to its own flashiness.

This, by contrast, is from "The Moon and the Yew Tree," written in 1961, just before Plath's twenty-ninth birthday:

> The moon is no door. It is a face in its own right.
> White as a knuckle and terribly upset.
> It drags the sea after it like a dark crime; it is quiet
> With the O-gape of complete despair.

The complacency of the earlier poem is replaced by a distraught but tenacious appropriation of both the world and earlier poetry. (The "gape" is from the gape of Niobe mourning her children in Keats's

Endymion.) This appropriation comes as much from the poet's staring at the moon and staring at a particular line of Keats as from her staring at herself. In any case, the merely fashionable is cast aside, and Plath now seeks out her own affinities — helped, it seems clear, by Hughes.

Plath's phrasemaking went from strength to strength in her last two years, and it is a steady instruction to see her exact eye (with "no preconceptions," as she said of a mirror) attempt to take in reality afresh. An owl cries "from its cold indigo," and the chill lies in the matching c-o-d-i-d-i-g-o, where the *c* and the *g* are only variants of one sound. Under Plath's clinical gaze, her lungs are "two gray, papery bags"; at a funeral, as the open grave yawns, "for a minute the sky pours into the hole like plasma"; the buzz of bees in a bee box is a "furious Latin"; the glittering snow is "marshaling its brilliant cutlery" (a theft from Emily Dickinson); the darkness of a storeroom is "the black bunched in there like a bat," and the compression of "bunched" hides a beast waiting to spring; the flesh of a cut thumb is, as a detached eye takes a cool look, "red plush"; glistening worms are "sticky pearls" (with the shock coming from the sudden endowing of the inorganic word "pearls" with gluey life); a calla lily displays "cold folds of ego" (the "cold indigo" trick again, but with the added surprise of a pairing like "sticky pearls"); and on the farm in winter Plath sees "the barbarous holly with its viridian / Scallops, pure iron," matching the holly leaf's shape with scallops, viridian with iron, and erecting a stiff, bristling fence of *r*'s — "barbarous," "viridian," "pure," "iron." These are all virtuoso phrases, and no poetry could be made up of such things exclusively, but they reassure us that in her most violent moments Plath's eye and ear could remain undisturbedly, and even laboriously, accurate.

Plath used to berate herself for not remembering everything in detail — a room she had seen, or what a person had been wearing — and in her journal (of which only a small but impressive part has been published, in the prose collection *Johnny Panic and the Bible of Dreams*) she noted things down with meticulous exactness. When the journal is published complete, we will know a truer Sylvia Plath. She apparently deceived all of Cambridge into seeing her as a gushing, if intelligent, American coed, but it is to her credit that she could not deceive herself. "That is the latent terror, a symptom: it is suddenly either all or nothing; either you break the surface shell into the whistling void or you don't," she wrote in the journal in 1956. The terse, diagnostic language authorizes the experience even to those of us who may not have had it: "The horror is the sudden folding up and away of the phenomenal world, leaving nothing. Just rags. Human rooks which say: Fraud."

The poems of Plath's last years find a way of giving illustration to that folding up of the phenomenal world. For her, the poems also filled the void: "If I sit still and don't do anything, the world goes on beating like a slack drum, without meaning," she says in the journal. The best of her poems illustrate both the fullness and the emptiness of the universe: how it is filled with complicated, rich, obdurate, and significant forms — yew trees, Gothic letters, blackberries — and how these forms are shadowed by others, diaphanous, elusive, obscuring, and blank, whether moonlight, fog, cloud, or ocean. This dialectic of forms is brought at times to an almost supernatural beauty. For example, under the threatening veils of "a sky / Palely and flamily / Igniting its carbon monoxides" there open the poppies in October:

> O my God, what am I
> That these late mouths should cry open
> In a forest of frost, in a dawn of cornflowers.

That is from a poem written on her thirtieth birthday, the same day as "Ariel," with its equally riveting balance of "substanceless blue" and "the red / Eye, the cauldron of morning."

A bleaker version of form appears in "Blackberrying," where the organic is both beautiful and disgusting:

> I come to one bush of berries so ripe it is a bush of flies,
> Hanging their bluegreen bellies and their wing panes in a
>   Chinese screen.

A "last hook" in the downward path through the blackberry brambles takes Plath from the overdetermined berry/fly bushes to the obscure emptiness of the sea:

> A last hook brings me
> To the hills' northern face, and the face is orange rock
> That looks out on nothing, nothing but a great space
> Of white and pewter lights, and a din like silversmiths
> Beating and beating at an intractable metal.

The resistance of experience to meaning, expressed here in the word "intractable," appears in comparable words all through Plath's poetry: I note, at random, "indefatigable," "irrefutable," "irreplaceable," "irretrievable," "inaccessible," "invisible," "untouchable," "inexorable," "unbreakable," "impossible," "indeterminate," "unintelligible," "indigestible," "unidentifiable," "incapable," and "ineradicable" — a family of barriers to soul, mind, and body. Against those glassy barriers Plath heroically went about her business of constructing meaning, both psychic and literary. She knew enough to choose "The Colossus," a poem about this wearing struggle, as the title poem of her first book. The poem resembles the anxiety dreams Plath had as a child, about tasks too large ever to be done adequately. She addresses, in the poem, the broken statue of her father:

> I shall never get you put together entirely,
>
> Pieced, glued, and properly jointed . . .
>
> Thirty years now I have labored
> To dredge the silt from your throat.
> I am none the wiser.
>
> Scaling little ladders with gluepots and pails of Lysol
> I crawl like an ant in mourning
> Over the weedy acres of your brow
> To mend the immense skull-plates and clear
> The bald, white tumuli of your eyes.

The many poems about Plath's father, including the famous bee poems (Otto Plath had written a book called *Bumblebees and Their Ways*), take up many myths of explanation, including Freudian diagrams, folk myths, fairy tales, and religious analogies. While we may all need such myths to approach the enigmas of family relations, Plath not only, with new insights, replaced one myth with another but also changed her style to fit the myth. The sacrificial victim of the bee poems speaks in a style of obedient, paralyzed sentences, in a dead-toned drama. Occasionally, it modulates to melodrama ("I have a self to recover, a queen"), but that melodrama never quite finds its style in the bee sequence. It awaits its cold and controlled derangement in "Lady Lazarus" and in "Daddy," where style turns to slashing caricature of Freudian self-knowledge:

> Every woman adores a Fascist,
> The boot in the face, the brute
> Brute heart of a brute like you.

Gone are the elegant vicissitudes of rhyme, slant rhyme, and syllabics, and all the genteel college-writing-class conventions:

> But they pulled me out of the sack,
> And they stuck me together with glue.
> And then I knew what to do.
> I made a model of you,
> A man in black with a Meinkampf look

> And a love of the rack and the screw.
> And I said I do, I do.

This *Threepenny Opera* style is an effect usable only once; the violence done to the self here (provoked by the violence Plath suffered under the shock of Hughes's desertion) is the substance of the jeering style. Plath lashes out at her former idolatry of her father and at her subsequent idolatry of her husband, but she also demolishes the noble myths of her own earlier poems, turning the Freudian-Hellenic colossus into a "ghastly statue with one gray toe / Big as a Frisco seal."

"Lady Lazarus," written in the same feverish thirtieth-birthday month that produced "Daddy" and "Ariel," is a mélange of incompatible styles, as though in a meaningluess world every style could have its day: bravado ("I have done it again"), slang ("a sort of walking miracle"), perverse fashion commentary ("my skin / Bright as a Nazi lampshade"), melodrama ("Do I terrify?"), wit ("like the cat I have nine times to die"), boast ("This is Number Three"), self-disgust ("What a trash / To annihilate each decade"). The poem moves on through reductive dismissal ("the big strip tease") to public announcement, with a blasphemous swipe at the "Ecce Homo" ("Gentlemen, ladies / These are my hands / My knees"), and comes to its single lyric moment, recalling Plath's suicide attempt in the summer before her senior year at Smith:

I rocked shut

As a seashell.
They had to call and call
And pick the worms off me like sticky pearls.

Almost every stanza of "Lady Lazarus" picks up a new possibility
for this theatrical voice, from mock movie talk ("So, so, Herr Dok-
tor. / So, Herr Enemy") to bureaucratic politeness ("Do not think I
underestimate your great concern") to witch warnings ("I rise with
my red hair / And I eat men like air"). When an author makes a sort
of headcheese of style in this way — a piece of gristle, a piece of
meat, a piece of gelatine, a piece of rind — the disbelief in style is
countered by a competitive faith in it. Style (as something consistent)
is meaningless, but styles (as dizzying provisional skepticisms) are all.
    Poems like "Daddy" and "Lady Lazarus" are in one sense demon-
iacally intelligent, in their wanton play with concepts, myths, and
language, and in another and more important sense not intelligent at
all, in that they willfully refuse, for the sake of a cacophony of
styles (a tantrum of style), the steady, centripetal effect of thought.
Instead, they display a wild dispersal, a centrifugal spin out to further
and further reaches of outrage. They are written in a loud version of
what Plath elsewhere calls "the zoo yowl, the mad soft / Mirror talk
you love to catch me at." And that zoo yowl has a feral slyness about
it, which rises to a heated hatred in the poems about Hughes and
about Plath's rivals (as she saw them) — her mother, Hughes's sister
Olwyn, and Hughes's mistress. The distress of these poems unbal-
ances them aesthetically. When Plath turns her loathing back on
herself, she instantly resumes control of structure, and the newly stoic
poems recover shape and power: "The heart shuts, / The sea slides
back, / The mirrors are sheeted."
    Plath's cold verdict on her own choices admits the irreconcilables
in her psychic constitution: "Perfection is terrible, it cannot have
children." Her drive toward perfection (of which she had such a clear
and distinct idea, and toward which she slaved) was incompatible —
or so it seemed to her in her depleted state — with the act that had,
along with poetry, brought her real happiness: the bearing of chil-
dren. The verdict of the poems is against perfection and for children.
This conviction enlarged and deepened her last poems, in which she

alternated, pitiably, between a deathly resignation and a despair that envied the narcissistically appetitive flowers:

> The claw
> Of the magnolia,
> Drunk on its own scents,
> Asks nothing of life.

There is more outrage and satire and hysteria in some of the last poems than there is steady thought, especially steady thought evinced in style. Plath, for whatever reason, could not rise to the large concerns of tragedy in a Keatsian way. Her unevenness recalls Hart Crane, but she did not have Crane's open generosity of vision. She did possess — and it gives her a claim on us — a genius for the transcription in words of those wild states of feeling which in the rest of us remain so inchoate that we quail under them, speechless.

18

Elizabeth Bishop

Elizabeth Bishop (1911–79) wrote in her fifties a revealing set of monologues attributed to three ugly tropical animals — a giant toad, a strayed crab, and a giant snail. These prose poems contain reflections on Bishop's self and her art. The giant toad says,

> My eyes bulge and hurt . . . They see too much, above, below, and yet there is not much to see . . . I feel my colors changing now, my pigments gradually shudder and shift over . . .
> [I bear] sacs of poison . . . almost unused poison . . . my burden and my great responsibility.

The crab says,

> I believe in the oblique, the indirect approach, and I keep my feelings to myself . . .
> My shell is tough and tight . . .
> I admire compression, lightness, and agility, all rare in this loose world.

The giant snail says,

> I give the impression of mysterious ease, but it is only with the greatest effort of my will that I can rise above the smallest stones and sticks . . . Draw back. Withdrawal is always best . . .
> That toad was too big, too, like me . . . Our proportions horrify our neighbors . . .

Ah, but I know my shell is beautiful, and high, and glazed, and shining . . . Inside, it is as smooth as silk, and I, I fill it to perfection.
My wide wake shines, now it is growing dark. I leave a lovely opalescent ribbon: I know this.
But O! I am too big. I feel it. Pity me.

It is Bishop's opalescent ribbon or glazed shell left behind that we find in the *Complete Poems* (1983) — or so we might say if this were her only metaphor for verse. But, remembering the toad, its sacs of poison, and its shuddering pigments (Keats's "chameleon poet" metamorphosed), we must not take too simple a view of her achievement. Her objectivity and beauty have been praised by many; the pain under the limpid surfaces has more recently been drawn out for observation; but Bishop's self-criticism (on the order of the poison, the deformity, the timidity) has been left rather aside, especially in the commentary following her death.

Many of Bishop's poems take a sinister view of what a poem is. In one famous poem, it is an iceberg, manufacturing jewelry of ice from the graveyard of the sea. Even in a more sympathetic poem, "The Man-Moth," the radical solitude of the poet is emphasized. The moth (a male version of Keats's Psyche-moth) has an eye of depthless night:

> If you catch him,
> hold up a flashlight to his eye. It's all dark pupil,
> an entire night itself, whose haired horizon tightens . . .

When he closes the eye,

> Then from the lids
> one tear, his only possession, like the bee's sting, slips.

The tear — round, pure, tensely concentric, a small reflecting globe, a secretion of pain — is Bishop's most justifiably famous definition of a poem and is linked, by its analogy to the bee sting, not only to the toad's sacs of poison but also to Keats's pleasure "turning to poison while the bee-mouth sips." Though Bishop's figure of a tear-drop comes from the Christian use of the dewdrop to represent the soul, the tear is meant not for God but, somewhat obliquely, for an audience:

> if you're not paying attention
> he'll swallow it. However, if you watch, he'll hand it over,
> cool as from underground springs and pure enough to drink.

Such metaphors (like Shakespeare's "summer's distillation," Keats's "last oozings," and Dickinson"s "attar of the rose") insist that poetry is a natural secretion but insist as well that it must be processed in a painful way before it is valuable or drinkable. Bishop's intimation of secretiveness in the poet and the slight hint of bullying in the audience ("If you watch, he'll hand it over") suggest her correction of her literary predecessors and her more ironic attitude toward the poetic "tear" or "drop." Like the toad and snail, the man-moth suffers from being physically unlike other creatures: he comes out of his subterranean home only at night and is alone in the populous city. It is tempting to see in this physicality that is alienated from its neighbors a metaphor for sexual difference, and Adrienne Rich has suggested that Bishop's "experience of outsiderhood" is "closely — though not exclusively — linked with the essential outsiderhood of a lesbian identity." But the painful eyes of the giant toad are a burden equal to his abnormal size; the spiritual singularity of artists sets them socially apart, in the long run, whether they are sexual "out-siders" or not. Baudelaire's albatross, powerful in the air but ludi-crous on deck, is the prototype of Bishop's socially unacceptable beasts.

Thus, though Bishop attempted to take an interest in the life of those not afflicted with a singularity like her own, her poems about them (whether about a burglar hiding from the police or about a house servant) tend to be patronizing — at least to my ear. For her, the general run of people remained a group "talkative / and soiled and thirsty," wanting only their necessary drink of water ("Under the Window"). Under the tap the peasants drink from, there is a ditch; around the edges of the waste water there is an oil slick; the oil "flashes or looks upward brokenly, / like bits of mirror — no, more blue than that: / like tatters of the *Morpho* butterfly." We can read the allegory: the Psyche-moth-butterfly is in tatters; the artist works on the edge of the unregarded.

Bishop's talent had relatively few subjects, in the objective sense; her best poems were about the two places where she felt most rooted — Nova Scotia (the home of her mother's family) and Brazil, where she lived in the Fifties and Sixties. There are memorable poems on other topics (a notable elegy for Robert Lowell among them), but long after Bishop left Brazil, and even longer after her life in Nova Scotia, the two places — one the permanent place of her displaced childhood, the other the permanent place of her middle age — continued to be the repositories of Bishop's deepest feelings, at least of those successfully brought into the light of art. More superficial feelings were all too easily dismissed by Bishop's habitual irony: when she was only sixteen, she saw herself impatiently as "full of my tiny tragedies and grotesque grieves" ("To a Tree").

Bishop was both fully at home in, and fully estranged from, Nova Scotia and Brazil. In Nova Scotia, after Bishop's father had died, her mother went insane; Bishop lived there with her grandparents from the age of three to the age of six. She then left to be raised by an aunt in Massachusetts, but spent summers in Nova Scotia until she was thirteen. Subsequent adult visits north produced poems like "Cape Breton," "At the Fishhouses," and "The Moose"; and Bishop responded eagerly to other poets, like John Brinnin and Mark Strand, who knew that landscape. Nova Scotia represented a harsh pastoral to which, though she was rooted in it, she could not return. Brazil, on the other hand, was a place of adult choice, where she bought and restored a beautiful eighteenth-century house in Ouro Prêto. It was yet another pastoral, harsh in a different, tropical way — a pastoral exotic enough to interest her noticing eye but one barred to her by language and culture (though she made efforts to learn and translate Portuguese and was influenced by the Brazilian poet Carlos Drummond de Andrade). Foreign abroad, foreign at home, Bishop appointed herself a poet of foreignness, which (as Rich justly says) is, far more than "travel," her subject. Three of her books have geographical names — *North and South, Questions of Travel,* and *Geography III* — and she feels a geographer's compulsions precisely because she is a foreigner, not a native. Her early metaphor for a poem is a map, and she scrutinized that metaphor, we may imagine, because even as a child she had had to become acquainted through maps with the different territories she lived in and traveled back and forth between. In the poem "Crusoe in England," Bishop's Robinson Crusoe, shipwrecked on his island, has nightmares of having to explore more and more new islands and of having to be their geographer:

> I'd have
> nightmares of other islands
> stretching away from mine, infinities
> of islands, islands spawning islands,
>
> . . . . .
>   knowing that I had to live
> on each and every one, eventually,
> for ages, registering their flora,
> their fauna, their geography.

This recurrent anxiety marks the end of one of Bishop's earlier dreams — that one could go home, or find a place that felt like home. In *A Cold Spring,* a book recording chiefly some unhappy years preceding her move to Brazil, there had yet survived the dream of going home, in a poem using the Prodigal Son as surrogate. He deludes himself, by drinking, that he can be happy away, but finally his evening horrors in exile determine him to return:

> Carrying a bucket along a slimy board,
> he felt the bats' uncertain staggering flight,
> his shuddering insights, beyond his control,
> touching him. But it took him a long time
> finally to make his mind up to go home.
>
> ("The Prodigal Son")

The poem (except for the drinking and the "shuddering insights," which recall the toad's shuddering pigments) is not believable, because it cannot envisage any home for the Prodigal to return to. Bishop's mother, confined for life in a hospital for the insane (Bishop never saw her after her departure), remained the inaccessible blank at the center of all Bishop travel. A foreigner everywhere, and perhaps with everyone, Bishop acquired the optic clarity of the anthropologist, to whom the local gods are not sacred, the local customs not second nature.

What Bishop said she admired in her favorite poet, George Herbert, was his "absolute naturalness of tone." Of course, a foreigner tries unfailingly for this effect so that he will not be convicted of oddness or of being a spy: one suspects a long history in childhood of Bishop's affecting to be a child like other children, while knowing herself shamefully unlike, unable to answer those questions about parents that other children pryingly put. Bishop could taste for herself, each time she found another environment, her own chilling difference from it. Into no territory could she subside gratefully and grip down into native soil. Instead, she was a cold current washing above the native stones; her thoughts, like the ocean, coursed over and against the land without ever being joined, eroticized in an endogamous way, put at rest:

> I have seen it over and over, the same sea, the same,
> slightly, indifferently swinging above the stones,
> icily free above the stones,
> above the stones and then the world.
>
> ("At the Fishhouses")

Whatever knowledge Bishop owned, it was the knowledge of the homeless and migrant,

> drawn from the cold hard mouth
> of the world, derived from the rocky breasts
> forever . . .

Our myths about such displaced persons have tended to create male theatrical characterizations like the Ancient Mariner, the Wandering Jew, or Robinson Crusoe. Bishop repudiates (after "The Prodigal Son") that stereotype, lightening the portrait of the exile. In refusing melodrama and aiming for that "naturalness of tone" that she often succeeded in finding, Bishop was helped by her humor. Even in the dark poem I have been quoting, "At the Fishhouses," she can divert herself at the ocean's edge with a companionable seal:

> He was curious about me. He was interested in music;
> like me a believer in total immersion,
> so I used to sing him Baptist hymns.

In anthropomorphizing the seal, Bishop suggests that people are only a different mammalian species; she uses of the seal exactly the sort of words she could use of an acquaintance. Bishop's own "total immersion" takes place in the bitter Atlantic of an icy truth:

> If you should dip you hand in,
> your wrist would ache immediately,
> your bones would begin to ache and your hand would
>   burn . . .

And yet the curious seal is at home in the water; perhaps (Bishop's humor suggests) one can get used to total immersion. The seal is, one might say, Bishop's characteristic "signature" here; her radical isolation and skepticism are rarely presented without such a moment of self-detachment and self-irony. At her best, she is never entirely solemn. Even the elegy for Lowell mocks, although gently, his compulsive revising of his poems:

> Nature repeats herself, or almost does:
> *repeat, repeat, repeat; revise, revise, revise.*
> . . . . .
>   — you've left
> for good. You can't derange, or re-arrange,
> your poems again. (But the Sparrows can their song.)
> The words won't change again. Sad friend, you cannot
>   change.
>
>   ("North Haven")

As any quotation from Bishop will suggest, one of her formal aims was to write in monosyllables for a substantial amount of the time. (In this she was imitating Herbert's great successes in this mode.) She became an expert not only in the short monosyllables every poet loves ("cold dark deep and absolutely clear," she says of water, rivaling Frost's account of the woods "lovely, dark and deep") but also in what we might call "long" monosyllables — past participles, like "bleached" or "peaked"; consonantally "thick" adjectives, like "sparse" or "brown"; and interestingly shaped, quasi-symmetrical nouns, like "scales" or "thumb." The advantage of using monosyllables is that they sound true; the occasionally polysyllabic grace notes (like Bishop's "absolutely" and "immediately" in "At the Fish-houses") set the monosyllables in musical boldface by contrast.

Against the monosyllables (a legacy from Bishop's dissenting Protestantism) we may set her polysyllabic passages, the province of the eye — as though, compared with the plainness of truth, the world of appearance were treacherously plural:

> The big fish tubs are completely lined
> with layers of beautiful herring scales
> and the wheelbarrows are similarly plastered
> with creamy iridescent coats of mail,
> with small iridescent flies crawling on them.
> > ("At the Fishhouses")

This is visibly Keatsian, resembling

> Fast fading violets covered up in leaves;
> > And mid-May's eldest child,
> The coming musk-rose, full of dewy wine,
> > The murmurous haunt of flies on summer eves.

And the old man at the fishhouses, scraping off herring scales with his knife, is the hermit-in-nature we know chiefly from Wordsworth (who inherited him from Milton). He has to be old, since he is experience itself:

> Although it is a cold evening,
> down by one of the fishhouses
> an old man sits netting,
> his net, in the gloaming almost invisible,
> a dark purple-brown,
> and his shuttle worn and polished.

From him, and the complex organic beauty and decay of the ancient fishhouses, the poem withdraws to the shore and the seal; then, leaving even the seal behind (and with him the human and animal community alike), it immerses itself totally into the icy waters of the sea, saying,

> It is like what we imagine knowledge to be:
> dark, salt, clear, moving, utterly free,
> . . . . .
>   and since
> our knowledge is historical, flowing, and flown.

This is the briny knowledge of Bishop's origins. She cannot, as happier orphans might, forget her historical griefs; nor can she anchor in conventional or social bonds; nor can she evade the knowledge of knowledge flown. She had once thought that poetry could be "artlessly rhetorical" ("The Imaginary Iceberg"); it is now darkly historical. The later poems, which bear that historical weight, are not always oceanic enough to be dark, salt, clear, moving, utterly free — but the ambition of Bishop's poetics is evident in those tidal adjectives. She wanted to come to bedrock and ocean as her aesthetic ground — those places that belong to no country — and to write something as essential as ogham or runes, "the admirable scriptures made on stones by stones." And, in musicality, she wanted the pure unmeaning of the Keatsian swallows:

> thousands of light song-sparrow songs floating upward
> freely, dispassionately, through the mist, and meshing
> in brown-wet, fine, torn fish-nets.
>
>   ("Cape Breton")

The ocean and the sparrows have in common their dispassionateness and their freedom; but knowledge is unbound and song is not. The "fine, torn fish-nets" that catch the song at Cape Breton are those matrices of English verse that Bishop still uses, though in the torn form she had learned from Spender, among others; her rhymes are often slant, her rhythms irregular, her stanzas disproportionate, her comedy often a violation of genre, her allusions oblique; but we see in these rents in the mesh her intimate knowledge of the fabric she works in.

When Bishop fails, it is sometimes because she takes herself less than seriously — the defect, as we would expect, of her virtues of understatement and irony. Some of the brittle poems in *A Cold Spring,* as John Ashbery has remarked, are disappointing. But more often she fails because the feeling in the poem seems shallow or forced, as it does in some of the poems of social concern. When she admits complicity in social evil, she is more interesting. Her own possession of Brazil, she suspects, has something in it not unlike the plunder and rape of the Conquistadors, who came "hard as nails, / tiny as nails, and glinting / in creaking armor" to the New World, a tapestry of vegetative and human attraction:

> Directly after Mass, humming perhaps
> *L'Homme armé* or some such tune,
> they ripped away into the hanging fabric,
> each out to catch an Indian for himself —
> those maddening little women who kept calling,
> calling to each other (or had the birds waked up?)
> and retreating, always retreating, behind it.
>   ("Brazil, January 1, 1502")

To the foreigner, the tropical scene and its inhabitants are a scrim behind which there lies another scrim, and so on forever:

> Is it right to be watching strangers in a play
> in this strangest of theatres?
>   ("Questions of Travel")

The foreignness of land drives Bishop to postulate a deeper region, where she feels more at home, until the alien Amazon tidal estuary feels like a kinder, purifying version of the salty ocean at Cape Breton:

> everything must be there
> in that magic mud, beneath
> the multitudes of fish,
> . . . . .
> with the crayfish, with the worms
> . . . . .
> The river breathes in salt
> and breathes it out again,
> and all is sweetness there
> in the deep, enchanted silt.
>   ("The Riverman")

The notion of poetry as a tidal river that can welcome the inrush of the undrinkable sea and yet exhale it, preserving a freshwater sweetness in which its flora and fauna can live, is a late hope in Bishop, contradicted perhaps by the unsuccessful but revealing 1979 poem about a naked female "pink" dog, hairless, with scabies, that runs the streets of Rio. Warning the dog that society kills its outsiders, Bishop tells it to don a carnival costume as a concealment: "Dress up! Dress up and dance at Carnival!" Otherwise, the dog will meet the fate of other pariahs:

> how [do] they deal with beggars?
> They take and throw them in the tidal rivers.
>
> Yes, idiots, paralytics, parasites
> go bobbing in the ebbing sewage, nights
> out in the suburbs, where there are no lights.
>
> ("Pink Dog")

Even this hideous subterfuge of the suburbs carries the characteristic Bishop joke:

> In the cafés and on the sidewalk corners
> the joke is going round that all the beggars
> who can afford them now wear life preservers.

This mordant poem implies that Bishop's poems may be her life preservers, her carnival dress: Would society have accepted her without them? The physical self-loathing of the giant snail is reproduced in more candidly female terms here, but, perhaps because of its very outspokenness of social protest, the poem rings hollow. The tidal river here can do nothing for the pariahs thrown into its current; they cannot find its silt "sweet" or "enchanted." Poetry makes nothing happen, not at this level, whatever it can do for the soul that creates it.

Because of Bishop's dislike for the explicitly "confessional" and her equal dislike for the sectarian of any description, her poetry resists easy classification. She always refused to be included in any anthology containing only poems by women: she did not want to be a "poetess" (the old-fashioned term) or a "woman writer" (the current term). Equally (though her landscapes come from North and South America) she resists the label "American poet": there is in her work no self-conscious rebellion against English genres, or even English attitudes, of the sort we find in our poetry from Whitman and Dickinson on. As far as she was concerned, she was happy to be in the company of Herbert, Wordsworth, Keats, and Hopkins.

But in one crucial way she is not of their company; she is a creature of her own century, and her poetry represents one of the attempts made in our era to write a poetry no longer dependent on religious or nationalist feeling — a poetry purely human, refusing even Keats's mythological resources. Religious nostalgia was, of course, still present in Bishop:

> Why couldn't we have seen
> this old Nativity while we were at it?
> — the dark ajar, the rocks breaking with light,
> an undisturbed, unbreathing flame,
> colorless, sparkless, freely fed on straw,
> and, lulled within, a family with pets
> — and looked and looked our infant sight away.
> ("Over 2,000 Illustrations and a Complete Concordance")

The opposite pole to this wishfulness must be, in the nature of things, death unredeemed by any meaning:

> I saw what frightened me most of all:
> A holy grave, not looking particularly holy,
> . . . . .
> An open, gritty, marble trough, carved solid
> with exhortation, yellowed
> as scattered cattle-teeth;
> half-filled with dust, not even the dust
> of the poor prophet paynim who once lay there.

The open grave, vacant even of its proper dust, owes something to Herbert's "Church-monuments": it was, I think, the echo of Herbert that called up the Nativity that ends this poem, perhaps Bishop's best. The wish for the Nativity concludes a succession of scenes, the disparate experience afforded to this solitary poet by a life of travel — a scene in Nova Scotia, a scene in Rome, a scene in Mexico, a scene at the ancient North African ruins at Volubilis, a scene in

Ireland, and then, directly after a lesbian brothel near Marrakesh, the open grave. "Everything only connected by 'and' and 'and.'" So much for experience. If meaning cannot be sought in experience itself ("the pilgrimage of life," "a citizen's life," or some other formula affording a ready-made pattern to which one subscribes), then one is left with the mind and the shapes it can confer upon the chain of "ands."

As far as we can gather from the poetry, Bishop began at a very early age to try to connect the "ands," not so much from deliberate choice as from sheer fear. There is a curious poem, frail and steely at once, called "First Death in Nova Scotia" (published when Bishop was fifty-four) that concerns itself with the death of her "little cousin Arthur," but we may guess that it deals implicitly with the earlier death of Bishop's father and with the very idea of death as the principle of disconnection. The poem is written out of a sensibility in shock, that of a child unable to take in the reality of death and unable, in consequence, to subordinate or blot out apparently irrelevant perceptual "noise." The "noise" consists of all the things in the family parlor surrounding the confined corpse: the chromographs of the royal family, the lily in little Arthur's hand, and a grotesque stuffed loon with red glass eyes, shot by the father of dead little Arthur. The poem goes steadily, but crazily, from little Arthur in his coffin to the royal pictures to the loon to Arthur to the child-speaker to the loon to Arthur to the royal pictures. This structure, which follows the bewildered eye of the gazing child trying to put together all her information — sense data, stories of an afterlife, and the rituals of mourning — is a picture of the mind at work. It will not change, in its essentials, throughout Bishop's poetry. The frightened child makes up three helpless fictions, trying to unite items of the scene into a gestalt. In the first, she fears that the loon might want to eat up Arthur and his coffin together, because the loon must share her metaphor for the coffin, brown wood topped off with white lace:

> Arthur's coffin was
> a little frosted cake,
> and the red-eyed loon eyed it
> from his white frozen lake.
>> ("First Death in Nova Scotia")

The second fiction tries to account for little Arthur's fearful pallor by conjecturing that Jack Frost had started to paint him, got as far as his red hair, but then "had dropped the brush / and left him white, forever." The third fiction is an attempted consolation, making up an afterlife more agreeable than the Christian Heaven of which the child has been told; Arthur will join the royal couples in a place warmer than the freezing parlor:

> The gracious royal couples
> were warm in red and ermine;
> their feet were well wrapped up
> in the ladies' ermine trains.
> They invited Arthur to be
> the smallest page at court.

But this childish invention of a fictive paradise for little Arthur is itself immediately questioned, as Bishop replicates for us that skepticism that was a natural motion of her mind (at least, so the poem implies) even in her earliest years:

> But how could Arthur go
> clutching his tiny lily,
> with his eyes shut up so tight
> and the roads deep in snow?

Wherever Arthur (or perhaps Bishop's father) has to go, the child feels terrible apprehension and confusion, displaced onto her mute observation of the parlor and its awful central object, and displaced as well onto her helpless social obedience ("I was lifted up and given / one lily of the valley / to put in Arthur's hand"). A poem of this sort suggests that Bishop's habit of observing and connecting was initially a defense invented against ghastly moments of disconnection and that it was practiced throughout childhood even before it found a structure in poetry.

Abstracting from particulars to make a coherent sketch of social reality seems to Bishop very like what mapmakers do when they rise above the ups and downs of physical terrain in order to represent the earth. Though Adrienne Rich has said that she found "The Map" (the first poem in Bishop's first book) "intellectualized to the point of obliquity," in it Bishop is simply describing her idea of what a poem must do to make experience accessible. In the map, experience is held still for inspection, and rendered palpable to the touch (though under glass); names are given to towns and cities. However, the printer of the map betrays the excitement of creation:

> The names of seashore towns run out to sea,
> the names of cities cross the neighboring mountains
> — the printer here experiencing the same excitement
> as when emotion too far exceeds its cause.

Eliot's famous criticism of *Hamlet* — that it did not work as an "objective correlative" of its author's presumed feelings because Shakespeare's emotions had been too intense for the invention constructed to contain them — hovers behind Bishop's remark here, as she defends the tendency of the work of art to run beyond its own outlines: why should not the names of cities run across the neighboring mountains, if excitement makes them do so? Experiences far too large for human comprehension are rendered attainable by the map:

> These peninsulas take the water between thumb and finger
> like women feeling for the smoothness of yard-goods.

The ending of the poem is an apologia for Bishop's own detachment of treatment:

> Topography displays no favorites: North's as near as West.
> More delicate than the historians' are the map-makers'
> colors.

One can see in this praise Bishop's own early disparagement of "historical" poetry — verse that deals with a social or personal chronicle unelevated into the abstract topographical status of a map. The fact that her own last book allowed for more personal chronicling than had been her habit earlier perhaps means that as Lowell learned from her, so she learned from him.

The attitudes in Bishop that I have dwelt on here — her sense of deformity, her cold capacity for detachment, her foreignness in human society, her suspicion that truth has something annihilating about it, her self-representation as observer of meaninglessly additive experience, her repugnance for social or political or religious association, her preference for mapping and abstraction — are those that are particularly well-sustained, thematically and formally, in the *Complete Poems*. Each of these attitudes had consequences. They led Bishop toward certain genres (landscape poetry, poetry about sky and ocean, travel poetry) and away from others (historical poetry, religious poetry, poetry of social enumeration). They led her as well to certain moments that recur in her verse: the moment of existential loneliness ("The Waiting Room"), the moment of epistemological murk or vacancy (the yawning grave in "Over 2,000 Illustrations"), and the moment of abstraction ("The Monument"). And they ensured Bishop's avoidance of closure through certainty or through social solidarity, in favor of closure in questioning, loss, or inscrutability. Bishop made a new sort of lyric by adhering to a singular clarity of expression, simplicity of effect, and naïveté of tone while making the matter of her poetry the opacity and inexplicability of being. Without her sense of deformity, estrangement, and even murderousness (the poisoned toad, the dangerous iceberg) as central matters of art, she could not have felt the benign contrast of her apparitional moose. Had she not had the greatest admiration for artists (Herbert, Cornell) who used very common means for very subtle effects, she would not have couched her conviction of the opacity of existence in words of such limpidity of effect. The combination of somber matter with a manner net-like, mesh-like, airy, reticulated to let in light, results in the effect we now call by her name — the Bishop style.

19

Anne Sexton

The unevenness in Anne Sexton's writing makes her work hard to judge, but the publication of the *Complete Poems* (1981) demands some attempt at judgment. Many of these poems are by now famous or infamous, but a clear sense of Sexton's talent — its extent and its limitations — has yet to appear. The Sexton legend not only haunts the poems, but is unhappily perpetuated in the ladies'-magazine tone of the introduction to this volume by Sexton's generous friend Maxine Kumin. The introduction begins with a description of Sexton, "tall, blue-eyed, stunningly slim, her carefully coiffed dark hair decorated with flowers." Later we hear that "the frightened little girl became a flamboyant and provocative woman; the timid child who skulked in closets burst forth as an exhibitionist declaiming with her own rock group; the intensely private individual bared her liver to the eagle in public readings." This melodramatic and sentimental style, infected by Sexton's own hyperboles, can perhaps do no harm; but neither can it do any good. Kumin's devoted kindness to Sexton is well known, and perhaps a friend's elegiac tribute is not the place to look for a dispassionate appraisal. Still, the poems do appear within this frame; and the lavish terms of Kumin's essay tend to coerce the reader into a somewhat single-minded view of the poet whom Kumin embarrassingly names "this gifted, ghosted woman."

The introduction is determinedly and sometimes vulgarly feminist: the earlier world view of the poet as "the masculine chief-of-state in charge of dispensing universal spiritual truths" (Diane Middlebrook, *The World into Words*) has eroded. Surely no one could write (Middlebrook) or quote (Kumin) such a reductive vulgarization of Shelley's "poets are the unacknowledged legislators of the world" without an obstinate incomprehension of what Shelley meant in his defense of poetry. Kumin adds that women poets owe a debt to Anne Sexton because she "shattered taboos": she wrote openly about menstruation, abortion, masturbation, incest, adultery, and drug addiction at a time when the proprieties embraced none of these as proper topics for poetry. Such a sentence itself enacts a new (and illogical) definition of what women poets want to, or need to, or should be allowed to, write about. After all, adultery, incest, and drug addiction are not new topics in literature — they are a staple set of Romantic properties. As for biology per se, it does not interest poetry, though the feelings solicited by menstruation or masturbation or abortion do. But lyric poetry has never demanded that the occasion for a poem be named in the poem: masturbatory fantasy, for instance, has taken many literary forms. Taboo-breaking is not in itself a poetic task. No poem is improved by having a shattered taboo in it, or an abortion in it either. It is an absurd stereotyping of women that would charge them to be priestesses of the biological, or shatterers of taboos. "Anne delineated the problematic position of women — the neurotic reality of the time," says Kumin, "though she was not able to cope in her own life with the personal trouble it created." I am not sure to what the "it" here refers, but I assume Kumin means that it was the problematic position of women that created the personal trouble in Sexton's life.

Such a claim is both true and false, and in any case irrefutable. Was it "the problematic position of men — the neurotic reality of the time" that created the personal trouble in Berryman's life? The biographies of Berryman and Sexton have a good deal in common: both poets were intelligent, gifted, married, parents, multiply addicted to pills and alcohol, and often (if not always) in the care of hospitals and therapists until their respective suicides. Both cases seem resistant to simple analyses (it was the pills and drink; it was the original alienating poetic gift; it was childhood guilt; it was unloving parents; it was "the problematic position" in society of women/men). No lived reality is so easily characterized. Nor will it do to hail any poet, finally, as a "woman" poet (or a "gay" poet). Every poet is in the end only one sort of poet — a poet of the native language. The poet does well by perception in vesting it in language, or does not. The poem finds a language for its experience, or it does not. Sometimes Sexton found that language.

Kumin gives valuable testimony to Sexton's industry (even though couched in cliché — "Our sessions were jagged, intense, often angry, but also loving"). Sexton, as the earlier poems show, was eager to master all the prosodic and stanzaic variations she could find useful; Sexton's lack of success does not usually (until the latter part of her life) result from lack of labor. Sexton worked hard for her teachers — among whom I include her therapists as well as her mentors (John Holmes, Robert Lowell) and her fellow poets (Plath, Starbuck, Kumin). She worked hard too for her students, who were grateful to her for her intense advice about their writing.

What, then, did Sexton have; and what did she lack? The second question should perhaps be raised before the first.

She did not have an education. Emily Dickinson had no more formal schooling than Sexton but she did have her father's library, and a precocious appetite for poetry. Kumin takes a peculiarly American point of view when she remarks, "Untrammeled by a traditional education in Donne, Milton, Yeats, Eliot, and Pound, Anne was able to strike out alone, like Conrad's secret sharer, for a new destiny." Needless to say, the poets of the past never thought of a traditional education as a set of fetters. Their notion, on the whole, was that in reading your great predecessors you were learning the language of poetry. So Milton read for seven years at Horton after leaving Cambridge; so Hopkins did classics at Balliol; so Keats translated Virgil in high school and read his way, underlining, through Spenser and Shakespeare and *Paradise Lost* and Chapman's *Homer*. It is anyhow an odd view of a "traditional education" that would sum it up as "Donne, Milton, Yeats, Eliot and Pound." In any case, Sexton is said to have read "omnivorously and quite innocently whatever came to hand and enticed her." According to Kumin's list, rather little that enticed her was poetry. Kumin lists "popular psychiatric texts" (Reik, Rieff, Deutsch, Erikson, Bettelheim), and says that after Sexton took a course in Dostoevsky, Kafka, and Mann, she went on to read novels by Saul Bellow, Philip Roth, and Kurt Vonnegut — a sequence that tells something about Sexton's taste, since someone else might have gone on to Tolstoy, Flaubert, and James. Kumin concludes the remarks on Sexton's reading by saying, "But above all else, she was attracted to the fairy tales of Andersen and Grimm . . .; they were for her, perhaps, what Bible stories and Greek myths had been for other writers." Kumin does not raise the question whether Grimm and Andersen can possibly rival as imaginative sources the Bible and Greek mythology — but the question is important in thinking about Sexton.

It was not the ethical parables of the Bible, or the fertile sugges-
tiveness of Greek myth, but the grim tit-for-tat of fairy tales — where
the unsuccessful suitors are murdered, or the witch is burned in her
own oven, or the wicked wolf is himself sliced open — that appealed
to Sexton's childlike and vengeful mind. Fairy tales and folk tales
put forth a child's black-and-white ethics, with none of the complex-
ity of the Gospels, and none of the worldliness of the Greeks. It is
characteristic of Sexton that she did use the myth of Prometheus —
which reads like one of her folk tales, with a rebel hero, an avenging
father-god, and a grotesque evisceration by a vulture.

Sexton looked, usually in vain, for ways to stabilize her poems
outside her increasingly precarious self. She based one sequence on
horoscope readings, another on the remarks of her therapist "Doctor
Y," another on the life of Jesus, another on the Psalms, another on
beasts. The only group that succeeds more often than it fails is the
group *Transformations,* based on folk tales. The tales — Snow White,
Rapunzel, Cinderella, Red Riding Hood, the Frog Prince, Briar Rose,
Hansel and Gretel, and others — gave Sexton a structure of the sort
she was usually unable to invent for herself, a beginning, a middle,
and an end. Her poems tend, on the whole, to begin well, to repeat
themselves, to sag in the middle, and to tail off. She had an instinct
for reiteration; she wanted to say something five times instead of
once. Her favorite figure of speech is anaphora, where many lines
begin with the same phrase, a figure which causes, more often than
not, diffuseness and spreading of effect rather than concentration of
intensity:

> I will conquer myself.
> I will dig up the pride.
> I will take scissors
> and cut out the beggar.
> I will take a crowbar
> and pry out the broken
> pieces.

This is a form of poetic backstitching or, to change metaphors, a
way of letting the poem get stuck in one groove. The folk tales, by
the necessary forward motion of plot, gave Sexton a momentum and
shape that, on her own, she seemed to have no instinct for.

The tales, as I have said, matched her infantile fantasy; they gave her a clean trajectory; they turned her away from the morass of narcissism. But most of all, they enabled her as a satirist. Kumin in her introduction speaks disapprovingly of a draft of a poem which she disliked. It had, Kumin says, "what seemed to me a malevolently flippant tone." And Kumin urged that it be rewritten; and it was. But Sexton's aesthetically most realized tone is precisely a malevolently flippant one, however distasteful it might seem to others. Sexton herself preferred the maudlin or lachrymose or (on other occasions) the winsome or the babyish. But in the Grimm transformations all her sharp-eyed satire was unleashed. "Snow White," for instance, indicts the bourgeois cult of hypocritical virginity:

> No matter what life you lead
> the virgin is a lovely number:
> cheeks as fragile as cigarette paper,
> arms and legs made of Limoges,
> lips like Vin Du Rhône,
> rolling her china-blue doll eyes
> open and shut.
> Open to say,
> Good Day Mama,
> and shut for the thrust
> of the unicorn.

"Rumpelstiltskin" looks sardonically at the myth of maternal doting:

> A son was born.
> He was like most new babies,
> as ugly as an artichoke
> but the queen though him a pearl.
> She gave him her dumb lactation,
> delicate, trembling, hidden,
> warm, etc.

"One-Eye, Two-Eyes, Three-Eyes" casts a cold eye on the social role of the deformed:

The Thalidomide babies
with flippers at their shoulders,
wearing their mechanical arms
like derricks.
The club-footed boy
wearing his shoe like a flat iron.
The idiot child,
a stuffed doll who can only masturbate.
The hunchback carrying his hump
like a bag of onions . . .
Oh how we treasure
their scenic value.

When a child stays needy until he is fifty —
oh mother-eye, oh mother-eye, crush me in —
the parent is as strong as a telephone pole.

This painfully graphic sketch is written by a person who is not "nice." What is occurring in such writing is not so much the shattering of taboos as the expression of an extremity of nonparticipatory vision. If Keats took part in the existence of the sparrow at his window with what we might call an objective sympathy, he could not have refrained from extending that same sympathy to the repressed virgin or the nursing mother or the hunchback. But a satirist feels under no obligation to extend sympathy. Sexton feels a slashing glee in her perfect vignettes. We see, for instance,

the night nurse
with her eyes slit like Venetian blinds,
she of the tubes and the plasma,
listening to the heart monitor,
the death cricket bleeping,
she who calls you "we"
and keeps vigil like a ballistic missile.

Sexton threw off phrases with reckless bounty. The death cricket and the ballistic missile in this passage are shafts that fly straight and true; and the night nurse enters literature. In these fiendish cartoons, Sexton is most unlike Lowell. Too often, in her poems about family

members and asylum experiences and exacerbated states, she sounds
entirely too much like an echo of Lowell, and a bad one:

> That was the winter
> that my mother died,
> half mad on morphine,
> blown up, at last,
> like a pregnant pig.
> I was her dreamy evil eye.
> In fact,
> I carried a knife in my pocketbook —
> my husband's good L. L. Bean hunting knife,

There is far too much of this sort of thing in the *Complete Poems*,
especially in the dreadfully imitative sequence "The Death of the
Fathers."

Sexton's poems read better as a diary than as poems. They then
seem a rather slapdash journal stuck with brilliant phrases. Even the
most formally arranged poems have, underneath their formal struc-
ture, no real or actual structure: they run on, they chatter, they moan,
they repeat themselves, they deliquesce. Or, conversely (as in the
famous "Her Kind"), they stop without any particular reason — they
could have been shorter, they could have been longer. If, as A. R.
Ammons once said, a poem begins in contingency and ends in ne-
cessity, the trouble with Sexton's poems is that they lack that necessity
— the conviction that they were meant to be just as they are, with
just these words and no others, extending to just this length and no
other, with each part pulling its weight. Dickinson and Bishop often
make us feel that necessity; Edna St. Vincent Millay — like Sexton
a facile and prolific writer — does not.

Necessity appeals to some readers more than others, needless to
say, and most of Sexton's readers have read her as a gripping jour-
nalist of the strained and difficult in life. One knows her very well
by the end of this book. In that sense, she succeeded as a diarist, if
not as a poet. Through this diary we come to know this third daugh-
ter whose two elder sisters laughed at her; she is the daughter of a
rich alcoholic father who behaved toward her with sexual posses-
siveness, and of an unloving mother obsessed with enemas and clean-
liness. The daughter defended herself by taking on a wooden lack of
feeling, from which she was released by therapy after a postpartum

depression. But she then thought of herself as composed solely of excrement. If she saw herself as an animal, it was as a rat.

These feelings were never to disappear. Giving up her children while she was in the asylum exacerbated her guilt. She confused writing poetry with therapy, expression with restructuring. The restructuring never seemed to take hold, though the writing, like the analysis, became obsessive. She saw that she was a perpetual, avid child, "a baby all wrapped up in its red howl," demanding that her family and friends mother her. "I need food / and you walk away reading the paper," became her reproach. She recognized, and was cruelly frank about, her compulsions; but she was unable to change her insatiable nature, her "greed for love." She defined herself as "a woman of excess, of zeal and greed," and nobody could have said worse things of her than she said of herself:

> Do I not look in the mirror,
> these days,
> and see a drunken rat avert her eyes?

Eventually, she was able to work less well at revision. The fantasies spun out of control; the dreams and hallucinations began to float around in disorder, and the masochistic poems about Jesus assumed disagreeable proportions:

> Jesus slept as still as a toy
> and in His dream
> he desired Mary.
> His penis sang like a dog . . .
> with His penis like a chisel
> He carved the Pietà.

In the poems, Sexton seems only fraily connected to anything outside herself. Her children, husband, and friends have a shadowy existence here, along with various unspecified lovers, who seem temporarily valuable as means to make Sexton feel loved. There are occasional mentions of war. But the relentless centrality of the "I" — almost always indoors alone, contemplating its own anguish (even if sometimes in farcical terms) — is finally exasperating. It drives us to comparison with other "I" poets of extreme psychic states —

Dickinson and Berryman come to mind. Berryman, besides his humor, possessed a perfect, even icy, recognition that Henry, his libidinal self, was just that — one restricted portion of his entire self. Berryman's intellectual self took on the derelict Henry as a case study. Berryman's moral self looked on in disapproval, and offered, in blackface, quiet judgments and calm sympathy for Henry's distracted sins. Sexton's own intellectual mercilessness saves many poems. But she had no moral sympathy for herself; and she, more often than Berryman, lost herself in tragic attitudinizing and melodrama. Dickinson had the great gift of observation — not of the freaks of the world, making common cause with them, like Sexton (the witches, the old, the sick, the winos, the crippled), but rather of the cosmos, a universe strict, impersonal, beautiful, dangerous, and indifferent. Dickinson felt acutely the scale of the whole creation, the nature of its imperial design. When she saw human beings, she saw them in that frame:

> Grand go the Years — in the Crescent — above them —
> Worlds scoop their Arcs —
> And Firmaments — row —
> Diadems — drop — and Doges — surrender —
> Soundless as dots — on a Disc of Snow.

Dickinson's "I," though as insistently present as Sexton's, is always placed in a context — religious, philosophical, cosmic, or social — larger than itself. When Dickinson goes mad, she does not take her madness as normative; she says, "And then a plank in Reason broke." There is a normative sanity present to measure the vertigo of psychic instability. Sexton's fantasies are often self-indulgent; only rarely can she include a plumb line by which to estimate her own slant out of equilibrium. In Sexton's poems we miss the complexity contributed by the double vision of fever taking its own pulse, being at once physician and patient. This was a double vision especially rigorously practiced by Sylvia Plath at the end of her life. But Plath, unlike Sexton, had a violent need for structure and containment; chaotic inner states, however exciting, did not in her view suffice to make a poem.

As Sexton passes into the anthologies, the more obviously "feminist" poems will no doubt be chosen, and there is no reason not to represent them:

> Am I approximately an I. Magnin transplant?
> I have hair, black angel,
> black-angel-stuffing to comb,
> nylon legs, luminous arms
> and some advertised clothes.

But the evil eye (as Sexton put it) should be in the anthologies too. This "evil," unsympathetic, flat, malicious, gleeful, noticing eye is neither male nor female, but it is Sexton's most distinguishing characteristic:

> The big fat war was going on.
> So profitable for daddy.
> She drove a pea green Ford.
> He drove a pearl gray Caddy.

> In the end they used it up.
> All that pale green dough.
> The rest I spend on doctors
> Who took it like gigolos.

This is of course superlatively unfair to the doctors and to Sexton herself. But that was Sexton's flair — a knack for the flat, two-dimensional cartoon. Some of that shrewd caricature should make its way into the anthologies too.

20

A. R. Ammons:
Dwelling in the Flow of Shapes

In the mid-nineteenth century, William Dean Howells came east from Ohio for the first time and visited the birthplace of one of his literary heroes, Nathaniel Hawthorne, only to find that the citizens of Salem took a dim view of the writer who had indicted their civic past. With characteristic irony, Howells remarked in his literary reminiscences:

> The advantages to any place of having a great genius born and reared in its midst are so doubtful that it might be well for localities designing to become the birthplaces of distinguished authors to think twice about it. Perhaps only the largest capitals, like London and Paris, and New York and Chicago, ought to risk it. But the authors have an unaccountable perversity, and will seldom come into the world in the large cities.

A. R. Ammons exhibited just that unaccountable perversity of genius in contriving to come into the world in the rural hiddenness of Whiteville, North Carolina. Because of his coming, the literary map has changed, and as we have the New York of Whitman, and the Pennsylvania of Stevens, and the Massachusetts of Lowell, we now have the North Carolina of Ammons. There are states, many of them, still without a genius of the place. In celebrating the sixtieth birthday of A. R. Ammons, one celebrates as well the birth of North Carolina in his poems. But although Ammons is a poet of his place of birth, he is also a migrating nomadic spirit. The finding of self through place is his most characteristic invention, and it has not stopped with North Carolina. He possesses in Ithaca, as someone said, the most famous back yard in the world, tirelessly examined and freshly loved.

310

Like most writers, Ammons could not remain where he was born. Almost all artists find it necessary to migrate to capital cities or university towns — places with books, reviews, presses, students, fellow writers. And yet the universe remains measured outward from home. We all remember that the young Stephen Dedalus inscribes in his book an outward-looking series of locations going from Clongowes Wood to the universe. Ammons will inscribe, in his "Essay on Poetics," a modern version of such a series:

    subatomic particle
    atom
    molecule
    cell
    tissue
    organ
    organ system
    organism
    species
    community
    living world

Ammons can locate himself, imaginatively, at all these levels of at-home-ness, from the invisible world of the quarks to the ecosphere of the cosmos.

We might see North Carolina, then, not as the beginning of an Odyssean journey that has ended in another Ithaca, but as the central shape in a series of concentric circles, forming that sphere reaching out to an infinite circumference. And we would be justified in preferring the figure of concentric circles to the linear figure of a journey because of Ammons's own frequent return to the material of his boyhood as something always within himself, never something he has left behind. The sublime poem "Easter Morning," Ammons' "Elegy in a Country Churchyard," tells us as much:

    I have a life that did not become,
    that turned aside and stopped,
    astonished:
    I hold it in me like a pregnancy or
    as on my lap a child
    not to grow or grow old but dwell on

> it is to his grave I most
> frequently return and return
> to ask what is wrong, what was
> wrong, to see it all by
> the light of a different necessity
> but the grave will not heal
> and the child,
> stirring, must share my grave
> with me, an old man having
> gotten by on what was left.

These lines, I am certain, will be as familiar in a hundred years as Wordsworth's "There was a time when meadow, grove, and stream, / The earth, and every common sight, / To me did seem / Apparelled in celestial light / The glory and the freshness of a dream." The arrested, blocked sadness of Ammons's lines makes us share a death — the death of those possibilities in himself that were brutalized and stunted by events of his youth.

To write of home has never been simple for Ammons — home was too mixed, too harsh, and too painful to be the subject of simple nostalgia. Even the early poems of home face squarely the savagery of country life. No one can easily forget "Hardweed Path Going," the poem of the butchering of the boy's pet hog. The objects of affection in the country are few — a bird, a hog. The pet bird is set free before the hard weather sets in. Only Sparkle, the pet hog, is left. The iron routines of country life continue:

> don't forget to slop the hogs,
> feed the chickens,
> water the mule,
> cut the kindling,
> build the fire,
> call up the cow.

In the midst of dreary chores, there brightens the moment of affection: "Sparkle . . . / You hungry? / Hungry, girly?" Then the hog is killed. The parent senses the son's distress — "She's nothing but a hog, boy" — but the poem ends with no happy ending:

Bleed out, Sparkle, the moon-chilled bleaches of your body
    hanging upside-down,
hardening through the mind and night of the first freeze.

Ammons, like the other poets of the Sixties, was engaged in revising his predecessors. Sparkle the hog could not have appeared, I think, in a poem by Frost, nor could the words , "Hungry, girly?" — Frost's classicism would not have permitted it. In fact, it is when we read Ammons that we see how distant Frost is from his rural characters, even when they are adapted from his own experience. We recognize, by the contrast with Ammons, how much Frost becomes the narrator, rather than the sufferer, of his poetry. Ammons's poem on Nelly Myers is suffered rather than narrated:

I think of her
    but cannot remember how I thought of her
as I grew up: she was not a member of the family:
I knew she was not my mother,
    nor an aunt, there was nothing
visiting about her: she had her room,
    she kept her bag of money. . . .
    she never went away, she was Nelly Myers, we
    called her Nel,
small, thin, her legs wrapped from knees to ankles
in homespun bandages: she always had the soreleg . . .
mother, not my mother, grandmother, not my grandmother,
slave to our farm's work, no slave I would not stoop
to:
I will not end my grief, earth will not end my grief,
I move on, we move on, some scraps of us together,
    my broken soul, leaning toward her to be touched,
listening to be healed.

These early poems of Ammons's are obstinate commemorations of reality, tributes determined in their obligation of exactness to hog-killing, soreleg, and hardship. Whitman gives them some of their courage, but they are homelier and more domestic than Whitman's work tends to be. They embody, in fact, a new style declaring itself. They are written perhaps in revolt against the more allegorical pieces that Ammons had been writing in his twenties, and to which he would return. Even as he writes these early realist pieces, something in him knows that the historical specificity of home is not the only truth about home. The rest of Ammons's work is a struggle between the trawling net which gathers in every detail of home (down to the latest car-repair bill) and the planetary telescope that takes a galactic view of, among other things, home.

Writing of home raises the question of language. Frost had brought the sentence-sounds of his own speech so powerfully to the fore that no subsequent American poet could afford to neglect his comparable cadences. The language of home appears early in Ammons, in the "First Carolina Said-Song" and the "Second Carolina Said-Song," both of them apparently "found art," one spoken by an aunt, the other by a patient in a veterans' hospital in Fayetteville. The aunt's begins:

> In them days
> they won't hardly no way to know if
> somebody way off
> died
> till they'd be
> dead and buried
>
> and Uncle Jim
>
> hitched up a team of mules to the wagon
> and he cracked the whip over them
> and run them their dead-level best
> the whole thirty miles to your great grandma's funeral
> down there in
> Green Sea County . . .

And it ends, after a comic anecdote,

> we got there just in time to see her buried
> in an oak grove up
> back of the field:
>
> it's growed over with soapbushes and huckleberries now.

If there was, for Ammons, a music of home, it lay in this sort of language, and the truest image of home in Ammons's poetry remains,

I would say, in the ongoing voice — musical, humorously paced, rhythmic, inexhaustible — that we associate especially with his long poems. These are poems without periods, halted only by the suspensions of colons: they resemble the melting spring water, flowing down into river and sea, to which Ammons compares lyric itself. In the long poems, Ammons abstracts the music of the tireless southern voice from the dialectical and lexical forms visible in the Carolina said-songs, but the voice is no less, however, a product of that dialect. Something else in Ammons may also be a product of southern talk — a willingness to digress and to expatiate, rather than to conclude and to straighten. In "Corsons Inlet," Ammons discovers that openness, not closure — whether of thought or of form — is the necessary condition of his poetic:

> no arranged terror: no forcing of image, plan,
> or thought:
> no propaganda, no humbling of reality to precept:
>
> terror pervades but it is not arranged, all possibilities
> of escape open: no route shut, except in
> the sudden loss of all routes:
>
> I see narrow orders, limited tightness, but will
> not run to that easy victory:
> still around the looser, wider forces work:
> I will try
> to fasten into order enlarging grasps of disorder,
> widening
> scope, but enjoying the freedom that
> Scope eludes my grasp, that there is no finality of vision,
> that I have perceived nothing competely,
> that tomorrow a new walk is a new walk.

The new walks that Ammons has been taking ever since he made this joyous claim on existence have led to many homes, from the smallest parcel of back yard to the whole United States, a country whose motto, *E pluribus unum,* enunciates one of Ammons's basic paradoxes, the relation of the many and the one (as he says in "Sphere"). Beyond the continent, home extends out to the planet, to the galaxy, and even to the universe. Because poetry must express through form what it says in content, each of the shapes delineated as a dwelling place bestows on the self and on language a different contour. "Dwell[ing] in the flow of shapes" — a phrase from "Sphere" — might be thought of as a variation on the Wordsworthian dwelling in spots of time. But where Wordsworth stabilizes time as a spot in space, Ammons propels space into temporal flow. The temporality, and temporariness, of any dwelling makes it alive, quick with possibility; destination would, for Ammons as for Wordsworth, be death.

The mind tends to wall itself in with a home; therefore, says Ammons in "Sphere," contradict that tendency, force mind out into the universe: "force mind from boxes to radiality." If American poetry, to Ammons's anxious eye, is becoming a poetry of boxes, it too should be forced into a different sort of home:

> most of our writers live in New York City
> densely: there in the abstractions of squares and glassy
> floors they cut up and parcel out the nothingness they
>
> think America is: I wish they would venture the rural and
> see that the woods are undisturbed by their bothering
> reputations and that the brooks have taken to flowing
>
> the way they always have and that the redwing pauses
> to consider his perch before he lights in a cedar.

Ammons does not say explicitly what he expects New York poets to learn from the flowing of the brooks and the pauses of the redwing, but we deduce that it has something to do with a poetry that would not be cut up and parceled out. The unpredictability of natural movement, which is always "uncapturable and vanishing" like a brook, is the rural and organic intuition, brought from home, that governs the motion of Ammons's lines. "While a leaf," he says, "may not answer one's questions, it waves, a / nice language, expressive and complete" ("Hibernaculum"). Though there is a whimsicality in such a salute, Ammons is serious in his claim that the natural brotherhood of gesture unites the poet and the moving world, roots the poet kinesthetically in the cosmos. "My brotherhood's immense," the poet continues, "and if the gods / have vanished that were never here I do not miss them."

At the other extreme from the back yard, as I have said, is the planet; and Ammons, in one of his less successful moments of didacticism, addresses it (in "Extremes and Moderations") as a home already polluted, about to die choked with waste:

> the
> artificial has taken on the complication of the natural and
>   where
> to take hold, how to let go, perplexes individual action: ruin
> and gloom are falling off the shoulders of progress: blue-
>   green
>
> globe, we have tripped your balance and gone into
>   exaggerated possession:
> this seems to me the last poem written to the world
> before its freshness capsizes and sinks into the slush.

This passage comes from the later Ammons, a poet who, increasingly turning from the domestic to the cosmological, makes his home everywhere.

But I want to return for a moment to the famous dwelling in the shape of North Carolina. I have said that Ammons turned to home events and characters — the hog-killing, the memory of Nelly Myers — and to home language, its music and its lexicon, heard in the said-songs. These, however, are largely mimetic efforts — a transcription of what is in some sense already "there." But in every poet's life there comes a moment in which the poet must forsake mimesis, must decide to impose inner motions on outer material. At this moment, Ammons begins to compose an idiosyncratic and masterful score which his thematic and lexical material will obey. This important moment comes for Ammons in his early composition "Four Motions for the Pea Vines." The musical intent is clearest in the last of these four musical movements, which compose a rural suite. I want to quote the whole of this fourth movement to give an idea of the rhythms Ammons has here made the masters of his subject-matter:

> slow as the pale low-arcing sun, the women move
>   down windy rows of the autumn field;
> the peavines are dead:
> cornstalks and peapods rattle in the dry bleach
>   of cold:

the women glean remnant peas
    (too old to snap or shell) that
got past being green; shatter from skeletal vines
    handfuls of peapods, tan, light:

bent the slow women drag towsacks huge
    with peas, bulk but little
weight: a boy carries a sack on his
    shoulders to the end of the rows:
he stoops: the sack goes over his head

to the ground: he flails it with a tobacco stick,
    opens the sack, removes the husks, and
from sack to tub winnows
    dry, hard crackling peas: rhythms reaching through
seasons, motions weaving in and out!

The Keatsian gleaning and winnowing, the Hopkinsian boy, the Williamsesque exclamations are signs of early influences on Ammons. But beyond and above these we see the musical composition of a North Carolinian genre scene. The present-tense rhythm moves from the dead pea vines and the slow stopping women to the active boy, with an arousal into energy characteristic of Ammons, who summons here a network of sounds bringing to life the shattering handfuls, the sack on the shoulders, the flailing stick, the husks and the tub, the crackling peas. In these sounds and motions of home, home lives again in an aesthetic world, one shaped to Ammons's rhythmic measure. One of Ammons's earliest poems had prayed for such a firm personal possession of the real: the title, "This Black Rich Country," refers at once to the soil of home and the earth of mortality, and though the poem enunciates a refusal of "symbolic forms," its own verse rhythms are such a form:

Dispossess me of belief:
between life and me obtrude
no symbolic forms:
· · · · ·
leave me this black rich country,
uncertainty, labor, fear: do not
steal the rewards of my mortality.

Through his mimetic stubbornness, his musical exactness as he varies from stops to quavers, his scientific metaphysics, and his syntactic amplitudes, Ammons constructs a rich poetic universe to serve as home, a universe at once mimetic and allegorical.

Sometimes Ammons's vertiginous sense of the many-leveled world (at once cosmically enormous and minutely particular) dismays even his own imagination. In his famous poem-of-the-whole, "Cascadilla Falls," he tells us that he once picked up a stone and "thought all its motions into it":

> the 800 mph earth spin,
> the 190-million-mile yearly
> displacement around the sun,
> the overriding
> grand
> haul
>
> of the galaxy with the 30,000
> mph of where
> the sun's going;
> thought all the interweaving
> motions
> into myself.

The poem ends with the dismay of consciousness at its own limits:

> Oh
> I do
> not know where I am going
> that I can live my life
> by this single creek.

Ammons's wish to think with the mind of the universe, to comprehend reality not simply with anthropocentric vanity but truly from within, to put the motion of mind among all other physical motions, to become not a single vector but the resultant of all vectors, is his most ambitious aim. He is, I think, the first poet to have the conceptual equipment (gained in his own early scientific training) to think this way. Wordsworth, who had, like Ammons, a sense of the large motions of the universe, foresaw the day when a poet to whom scientific concepts were not foreign or unnatural would write a new sort of poetry:

> If the labours of Men of science should ever create any material revolution, direct or indirect, in our condition, and in the impressions which we habitually receive, the Poet will sleep no more than at present; he will be ready to follow the steps of the Man of science . . . If the time should ever come when what is now called science, thus familiarized to men, shall be ready to put on, as it were, a form of flesh and blood, the Poet will lend his divine spirit to aid the transformation, and will welcome the Being thus produced, as a dear and genuine inmate of the Household of man.   (Second Preface to *Lyrical Ballads*, 1850)

The Household of man, thus defined, is, to Ammons, "home" in the widest sense. "Our being's heart and home," said Wordsworth in *The Prelude* (VI), "is with infinity, and only there": the sense of that infinity is strong in "Cascadilla Falls" and in many of Ammons's long poems, which by their very ebb and flow give us the motions of oceans, of winds, of the drift of continents and the sedimentary accretions of time.

Ammons does not deny the perils of magnitude: the self can get lost in infinity. In a short wry poem called "Concerning the Exclusions of the Object," he wonders whether he has not lost his own small self in his galactic concerns (both physical and metaphysical). "head full of stars, / cosmic / dust in my teeth," "how," he asks, "can I expel these roomy stars?" The journeying up and down between two elements — earth and sky, the particular and the general — animates so many of Ammons's poems that it could be said to be their *modus vivendi,* and in some it is. But I sense in others where this vertical journey might seem to be at issue, an odd twist or spin put on the poem which in itself denies that the vertical polarities of small self and cosmic dust, particular and general, ground and air, can really be separated. The poem does not begin at A and go to B, or begin at A, go to B, and then go back to A. Rather, its structure is cunningly confused. It will consider its own *process* in either direction, and a process is neither A nor B; next it will poise itself on a *hypothesis* which, neither A nor B, resolves itself into a question about the *value* of journeying from A to the furthest B; that will be succeeded by a *hypothesis* of journeying from A to a place less than maximum B; in the end, the poem will praise the "interval designed,

/ apparently, for design." I want to quote the poem I have been describing, "Two Possibilities," to exemplify this twist, because to describe Ammons's theme of "home" without showing, if only briefly, the paradoxical and perplexing structures of "home" would be to simplify his labyrinths.

Coming out of the earth and going
into the earth compose
an interval or arc where
what to do's

difficult to fix: if it's
the coming
out that answers, should one with all
thrust come out and

rise to imagination's limit, leaving
earthiness, maximally
to mark the change, much below:
if it's

going in, should one flatten out on
coming, lie low
among bush
and rock; and keep the residence

near the palm of the hand, the
gross engrossed and palpable:
Well, there is an interval designed,
apparently, for design.

"We have an interval," says Pater in the conclusion to *The Renaissance,* "and only an interval," — but he does not tell us whether our gem-like flame is to burn at a great altitude or close to earth with the gross engrossed and palpable. Ammons's use of the Paterian word may not be an allusion, but it does ask where our being's heart and home is, where we should, in this world, keep our residence. By teasing and twisting our conflicting impulses toward transcendence and immanence, Ammons suggests that in the twist itself, and in its manifestation as design, lies the human home least distorted by transcendence.

I have spoken of Ammons's home of origin, rural North Carolina; and I have spoken of the home of consciousness, the maximal universe of human physical, geological, and organic knowledge; but one must also, in speaking of Ammons, look to the metaphysical home of the ideal and of the affections, which he calls, in one of his most famous poems, "The Eternal City," borrowing Saint Augustine's notion of the City of God. The poem could not perhaps have been written before the annihilation of the world became an imaginative fact. Ammons envisages here the destruction of everything we know as civilization, and the efforts of those who must begin to construct their home anew. It is a poem that suggests many interpretations; it could be about the ruin of a love, or a family, or a home, or an ideal — anything in which one could have placed one's faith and one's affection. What interests Ammons is the human determination to build home afresh, even in the wake of ruin. To that end he places us in a consciousness that moves ingeniously even in cataclysm; it remembers the past as a model, it acknowledges the devastated present, and it envisages a restored perfection in the future:

> After the explosion or cataclysm, that big
> display that does its work but then fails
> out with destructions, one is left with the
>
> pieces: at first, they don't look very valuable,
> but nothing sizable remnant around for
> gathering the senses on, one begins to take
>
> an interest, to sort out, to consider closely
> what will do and won't, matters having become
> not only small but critical: bulbs may have been
>
> uprooted: they should be eaten, if edible, or
> got back into the ground: what used to be garages,
> even the splinters, should be collected for
>
> fires: some unusually deep holes or cleared
> woods may be turned to water supplies or
> sudden fields: ruinage is hardly ever a
>
> pretty sight but it must when splendor goes
> accept into itself piece by piece all the old
> perfect human visions, all the old perfect loves.

Ammons's home is composed, as this poem suggests, of the minutely practical and the sublimely ideal; his actions range from taking an interest in splinters to the reconstruction, with Wordsworthian resolution and veneration, of a former splendor.

It is not surprising the the final home, for Ammons, claims a theological, or (if I may coin a word) theopoetic dimension. As the human will reaches out, like Whitman's spider, for a first frail belief, and then for the first word articulating the first belief, a web of faith and language is constructed across the void:

> to lean belief the lean word comes,
> each scope adjusted to the plausible: to the heart
> emptied of, by elimination, the world, comes the small
>
> 17
>
> cry domesticating the night: if the night is to be
> habitable, if the dawn is to come out of it, if day is ever
> to grow brilliant on delivered populations, the word
>
> must have its way by the brook, lie out cold all night
> along the snow limb, spell by yearning's wilted weed till
> the wilted weed rises, know the patience and smallness
>
> of stones: I address the empty place where the god
> that has been deposed lived: it is the godhead: the
> yearnings that have been addressed to it bear antiquity's
>
> 18
>
> sanction: for the god is ever re-created as
> emptiness, till force and ritual fill up and strangle
> his life, and then he must be born empty again.
>
> ("Hibernaculum")

The resurrection of joy in the face of emptiness and death, of which Ammons has been speaking in this poem, can be seen in the end of "Easter Morning," to which I shall return.

In Ammons's most paradoxical moments of faith, he declares that our home is nowhere but in motion itself. It is not in our place of birth, because we leave that place of origin; it is not in our affections, because we can forsake them and they us; it is not in knowledge, because knowledge evolves always by its own perpetual self-destruction; it is not in a god, because the god is forever becoming emptied of significance. "Can we make a home of motion?" he asks in "Sphere," and answers, "Motion is our place":

> If
> nothing shaped stays and shapelessness is dwellingless, where
> can we dwell: as shapes (bodies) we dwell only in the flow
> of shapes, turning the arcs of mortality: but the imagination,
> though bodiless, is shaped (being the memory or imagined
> memory of shapes) and so can dwell in nothingness: the
>   human
> being is as inscrutable and unformulable as a poem, or, if
>   possible, more so.

In the flow of shapes, real or imagined, our body and spirit, it would seem, can find an unformulable home. But recently, in a more reckless moment, Ammons has thrown shape itself aside as "hateful exactitude" rather than "shapely assertion," claiming rebelliously that only "nothingness's / wide amplitude / makes his place" ("On Being"). If the human condition is one of motion into continual approximation, then home is one of our delusional systems, and we live forever not at a center, but on an expanding periphery. Foxes have holes, and the birds of the air their nests, the gospel tells us; ships have their stopping points, and so even do tigers, says a recent Ammons poem, but the creatures of consciousness do not. "I run on," says the poet in "Coming Round" (a poem of 1983),

> ruffling the periphery,
> the treadmill's outwheel,
>
> declining center
> or any loss of it
>
> and no longer
> crying help.

The creation of a centerless periphery in form has been Ammons's most original formal invention, seen in a spectacular way in the long poems, in a fiercely experimental way in *The Snow Poems,* written in his fiftieth year. But what I would like to notice particularly here is how little these various forms of home form a hierarchy in Ammons's mind. They are, rather, points of orientation through which he circles again and again: the home of origin, the home conceived by scientific knowledge, the home of metaphysical value, the home of the reconstituting of the sacred, the home found in motion, the home in nothingness, the decentered home on the treadmill's outwheel. If, in the early moments of the long poem "Hibernaculum" (quoted earlier), it is the home of the sacred at which Ammons pauses, he will circle back, later in the poem, to the home of origin, as he decides that he does not want to be buried in New York State, but rather in North Carolina:

> I don't think I want to be buried here in these rocky
> hills: once underground, how could I ever get my arms
> free of the silk and steel, how could I ever with those
>
> feet travel through the earth to my sweet home country
> where all the flesh that bore me, back through grandfathers
> and grandmothers, lies, and my little
>
> brothers and my little sister I never saw, born before
> me and dying small.

In thinking of these matters in the work of A. R. Ammons, we recall his line of self-definition in "Sphere": "Grief is all I know and joy all I understand." For Ammons, the thought of his own burial underlies "Easter Morning." The first part of the poem says, "Grief is all I know of home," as the ravages of a harsh childhood are retold — not only the life that did not become, but the shocks encountered and withstood without help to mitigate their terror:

> The child in me that could not become
> . . . stands there by the road
> where the mishap occurred, crying out for
> help, come and fix this or we
> can't get by, but the great ones who
> were to return, they could not or did
> not hear and went on in a flurry and
> now, I say in the graveyard, here
> lies the flurry, now it can't come
> back with help or helpful asides, now

we all buy the bitter
incompletions, pick up the knots of
horror, silently raving, and go on
crashing into empty ends not
completions, not rondures the fullness
has come into and spent itself from.

But the poem, after saying, "Grief is all I know" in its first part, says
in its latter moments, "Joy is all I understand," as the inscrutable
but beautiful communications and motions of migrating birds convey
"a sight of bountiful majesty and integrity." The dance of nature's
motions, at the end of "Easter Morning," is said to be "permanent
in its descriptions / as the ripples round the brook's / ripplestone,"
the beautiful Emersonian type of the joy which, in the Heraclitean
conflagration of all things, balances the terrors and incompletions of
life. The flood of extinction sweeps over all forms of home, but for
Ammons, as for Wordsworth, there is nonetheless something that
remains:

                                        the
        seventeen-year-old self is gone and with it the well and

                            84

wellsweep, chinaberry tree, the mother and father, the two
sisters, living but lost back there, and Silver, Doll, all
the jonquils, the smokehouse, mulberry tree, but when I was

last by, the pecan tree's still standing, the same one, big,
the lean growths and lean shades vanished: more death done
than to do, except that memory grows, accumulating strata
    of

change, and the eyes close on a plenitude, suddenly, directly
into nothingness.

Plenitude and nothingness — as two words for home — coexist in
every adult mind. Ammons conceives of plenitude and nothingness
in a single word, adding to the American canon a poetry of home at
once North Carolinian, American, and universal. We find in this
poetry of tenderness and rueful humor the intimate structures of
home — the house, the people, the landscape, the graveyard; the

feelings of home — the yearnings, the affections, the failures, the
fears; and the speculative metaphysical extensions of home — shapes,
centers, identities, memories, gods. To imagine for a moment the
disappearance of all the poems I have been quoting is to realize that
in addition to describing home, these poems are themselves a home
that sixty years ago had neither been conceived nor constructed. But
now the poems are here, through the genius of the poet who, choosing
North Carolina to be born in, has become the genius of that place
and of many others. Some of us have found, in these poems, a home
for our own spirits, words for intimations we were unable to artic-
ulate alone. In this way, language becomes a habitable place, and
place finds a home in language; American poetry enlarges its canon,
and a new universe — the *Collected Poems* of A. R. Ammons —
becomes, to use Elizabeth Bishop's phrase, "a mirror in which to
dwell."

II

A classic poem, when it appears, comes not as a surprise but as a
confirmation:

> I have a life that did not become,
> that turned aside and stopped,
> astonished:
> I hold it in me like a pregnancy or
> as on my lap a child
> not to grow or grow old but dwell on
>
> it is to his grave I most
> frequently return and return
>
> to ask what is wrong, what was
> wrong, to see it all by
> the light of a different necessity
> but the grave will not heal
> and the child,
> stirring, must share my grave
> with me, an old man having
> gotten by on what was left.

This is the beginning of A. R. Ammons's revelatory poem "Easter Morning." The central sentiment is not altogether unprecedented — Robert Lowell said, "Always inside me is the child who died" — but Lowell was speaking of a younger self continuous in some way with his adult self ("Always inside me is his wish to die"). Ammons is talking about a self that stopped, that never became, that is buried in a grave that does not heal. And yet that self is not dead; it is a "child, stirring." Robert Frost talked, more distantly, of a road not taken in the past; Ammons's metaphor of the child — buried, or in a womb, or on a lap — is alive with pain and quick with dismay. Ammons's lines rivet us where we stand and we find ourselves uttering them as though our own life had suddenly found its outlet-speech: "I have a life that did not become . . . the grave will not heal." Ammons's arrow strikes straight to the heart, and to the unhealed grave in it. "How did you know," we ask Ammons, "when we didn't know, ourselves, till you told us?" This is a poetry of eerie power, dependent not so much on the particular circumstances of Ammons's life as on his unsettling skill as an allegorist. Anything he tells us about his life ("I have a life that did not become") turns out to be true of everyone: he is a poet of the universal human condition, not of particular idiosyncrasy. This great poem, "Easter Morning," turns out to be about the damage which every child undergoes as members of his family — a sibling, an aunt, a grandparent — die. It is an elegy in a family churchyard. When Ammons now goes back to North Carolina, the relatives he knew are dead:

> when I go back to my home country in these
> fresh far-away days, it's convenient to visit
> everybody, aunts and uncles, those who used to say,
> look how he's shooting up, and the
> trinket aunts who always had a little
> something in their pocketbooks . . .

The catalog goes on to include uncles and teachers and Ammons's mother and father — all in the churchyard, dead, their world gone. And Ammons remembers himself as a child, shocked and blighted and deflected out of ordinary growth by these deaths:

the child in me that could not become
was not ready for others to go,
to go on into change, blessings and
horrors, but stands there by the road
where the mishap occurred, crying out for
help, come and fix this or we
can't get by, but the great ones who
were to return, they could not or did
not hear and went on in a flurry and
now, I say in the graveyard, here
lies the flurry, now it can't come
back with help or helpful asides, now
we all buy the bitter
incompletions . . .

In the desolate market of experience where none come to buy (as
Blake said) Ammons stands, with his uncanny plainness of speech,
the lines running on like an explanation and an apology at once,
heedless and pell-mell, every so often stopped by a pulling-up-short,
a bewilderment, an obstacle, an arrest in emotion:

I stand on the stump
of a child, whether myself
or my little brother who died, and
yell as far as I can, I cannot leave this place, for
for me it is the dearest and the worst
it is life nearest to life which is
life lost: it is my place where
I must stand and fail.

I am not sure whether the strange and complex resolution of the
poem (in which Ammons watches the flight of eagles, and is grateful
for perennial natural patterns and fresh insights alike) serves to res-
urrect the dead on this "picture-book, letter-perfect / Easter morn-
ing." And I wonder whether the long anguish of the poem can be
excerpted at all. But to write about Ammons's volume *A Coast of
Trees* (1981) is first of all to give notice of the existence of "Easter
Morning" as a new treasure in American poetry, combining the
blankest of losses with the fullest of visions. It is a poem which

should be published all alone, in a three-page book by itself; it is so complete it repels company.

Nevertheless, it has company, and distinguished company, in this collection of short poems. Ammons always oscillates interestingly between the briefest of brief lyrics ("Briefings," "Uplands") and the longest of long poems ("Sphere," "Tape for the Turn of the Year"). Ammons's bedrock is his conviction of the absolute interconnectedness of all phenomena. The atmosphere (so to speak) over his bedrock is formed by his quick, almost birdlike, noticing of all epiphenomena constantly occurring in the universe — a flight of moths here, a rill of snow-melt there. The short poems record the noticings; the long poems offer the metaphysics of multiple connection. Yet even this description is too divisive. Even in the short poems, Ammons's metaphysics of multiple connection is present in an abbreviated form, represented sometimes by syntax, sometimes by rhetorical figure (notably repetition of a word or a word-root in syntactically significant positions). For instance, Ammons writes about the difficulty of putting a name, or names, to reality — and about the attendant paradox that the closer the approximation of the name to the event the more acutely one feels the frustrating gap between what has been achieved and what absolute fidelity to reality would be. Using his favorite dense repetition, he grieves, "the name nearest the name / names least or names / only a verge before the void takes naming in."

The sound of the writing verges on riddle, and hovers near theological paradox, but the sentiment is neither a riddle nor a mystification. It is a precise denomination in a series of self-joining words: "the name nearest the name names least or names only . . ." This statement of a divergence takes on itself semantically the form of an obsessive connection. And though the creation of the formal barrier of art excludes "reality," it is surely a wonderful mutual relation that makes the terrain of the excluded ("cast out") exactly equal, as a two-piece verb, the terrain of the included ("shut in"): "when the fences foregather / the reality they shut in is cast out." Almost every statement of fear or loss in Ammons occurs in a line that paradoxically consolidates a strict, practical linguistic gain — often as simple a gain as a word humming in resonance with another word, or a triumphant conclusion to a long syntactical suspension. The suspended syntax arises from Ammons's inexhaustible wish to explain; he is the poet par excellence of the bifurcating line of argument, a line that is interspersed with "I suspect" or "well, maybe" or "in fact" or "after all" or "that is" or "probably" or a sequence of "but's." To that extent his poetry is the utterance of that endless rhetoric he calls "reason":

> Reason can't end:
> it is discourse, motion
> to find motion, reason to
> find reason to abandon
> reason.

But against the straight "thruway" of reason Ammons sets another formal motive, which he calls "shape": shape wants to wind discourse up, to give it a rondure, a closure. The shapeliness — almost spherical — of so many of Ammons's short lyrics asserts that a moment or a mood has its own being to proclaim in a determinate form. If that form is violated, something else is produced — even another poem perhaps, but not the original one, which, in being amended, is forever gone. The shape of a poem is inviolate:

> it is as
> it is: it can't be cast
> aside except to cast
> shape aside, no part in it
> free to cast free any
> part.

The rigidity of this verse defies us to shift a single word, to misplace a single "it" or "cast." The verse rejoices in its imperviousness to tinkering: it braces its "no" against its "any," its "free" against its "cast free," its "part" against "part," creating a wind-proof, storm-proof shelter against the inversions of chance. Ammons's loquacity of "reason" so plays against his geometry of "shape" that the exhilaration of the combat of the two motives equals in interest the plangent tales he tells of the life of the spirit.

These are twice-told tales; Ammons moves easily in the line of our poets. Like Traherne, he calls a poem "Poverty"; like Herbert, he sees a silk twist (in Ammons, "silk lines") coming down in radiance from heaven; like Keats, he stands (in the majestic poem called "Swells") on the shore of the wide world till love and fame sink to nothingness. Like Yeats, he feels the pull of the balloon of the mind (Yeats tried to tether it; Ammons says, "I have let all my balloons aloose"); like Emily Dickinson, he feels an affinity for that "neglected son of genius," the spider, working like the poet "airy with radiality"; like Oliver Wendell Holmes, he writes "An Improvisation for the Stately Dwelling"; like Williams and Hopkins, he offers perpetual praise of the world of sight. In Ammons these earlier poets have found the ideal reader — the reader who himself writes a new poem as a variation on the older one.

Ammons's own newness — it bears repeating — lies in his finely calibrated sense of the actual, nontranscendent motions of the natural world. He is not in a hurry, as most of his predecessors (Emerson, Whitman, Dickinson, Hopkins, Moore) have been, to move from natural fact to patriotic or religious or philosophical enthusiasm. Ammons is true to himself in ending "Easter Morning" with the natural fact of bird-instinct, seen in a new configuration, rather than with the transcendent resurrection of the body in spirit. The natural universe is so real to Ammons's imagination that his poem about the earth rolling in space is spoken with an ease foreign to most efforts to "imagine" a cosmic perspective. Only Wordsworth had a comparable iron sense of fact:

> We go around, distanced,
> yearly in a star's
>
> atmosphere, turning
> daily into and out of
> direct light and
>
> slanting through the
> quadrant seasons: deep
> space begins at our
>
> heels, nearly rousing
> us loose: we look up
> or out so high, sight's
>
> silk almost draws us away.

(Frost, who yearned for vision, said we can look "Neither out far nor in deep"; Ammons, in his love of sight, is silently corrective.) Ammons is tugged between sentiment and stoicism, and the play between those two motives is as entrancing as the play between the flow of discourse and the shape of poetry. He is as tender as Keats and as harsh as Keats, reaping some of the same benefits. He does not rise to Wordsworth's full bleakness, but he has more humor and more waywardness than Wordsworth.

"Swells" gives full range to Ammons's sentiment and stoicism alike, to his precise sense of physical motion (in this case, wave-motion), and to his firm momentum-rounding-into-shape. When hundreds of conflicting motions are assimilated into one wave, a paradoxical calm results:

> The very longest swell in the ocean, I suspect,
> carries the deepest memory, the information of actions
> summarized . . .
>   so that the longest swell swells least.

Ocean floor and mountain are alike places where gigantic motions have been summarized into a near stillness:

>   I like to go
> to old places where the effect dwells, summits or seas
> so hard to summon into mind, even with the natural
>
> ones hard to climb or weigh; I go there in my mind
> (which is, after all, where these things negotiably are)
> and tune in to the wave nearly beyond rise or fall in its
>
> staying and hum the constant, universal, assimilation.

To climb the summit or find that summary so hard to summon to mind, and there to hear the hum (as Stevens called it) of the universal pantomime, might be in another poet a forgetful sublimity. But Ammons, like Keats, cannot forget the world where men sit and hear each other groan; he ends his poem by saying he has sought out the summit for "rest from the ragged and rapid pulse, the immediate threat / shot up in a disintegrating spray, the many thoughts and / sights unmanageable, the deaths of so many, hungry or mad." Mortality swells so agitatingly into presence at the end of the poem that the hoped-for-contemplative calm is shaken and bruised. The ills of the body and of the spirit are all there are; we die hungry or mad, our pulse ragged or rapid. In nature, of course, there is nothing "unmanageable"; the word is meaningless in the cosmos, and takes on meaning only through human will, afflicted by thoughts and sights too painful to be borne. If only, like the geologic strata or the ocean floor, we could manage "the constant, universal assimilation: the / information, so packed, nearly silenced with majesty." But we do not, and cannot, for long. The possibility, and the impossibility, of psychic assimilation are held in equilibrium in the long oceanic swell of this Stevensian poem — which should be read with Stevens's "Somnambulisma" and "Chocorua" as its predecessors.

It is a mark of Ammons's variety that it is very hard to generalize about his practice in *Coast of Trees*. Almost every poem has a distinctive shape and a set of new strategies, imitating the variety of nature:

> a dance sacred as the sap in
> the trees, permanent in its descriptions
>
> as the ripples round the brook's
> ripplestone: fresh as this particular
> flood of burn breaking across us now
> from the sun.

Ammons matches his loneliness and his freshness to the solitary, permanent, and renewed acts of nature; and in his "central attention" he keeps the universe alone. The poems enable us to watch this poet going about the business of the universe, both its "lost idyllic" and its present broken radiance. He has been about this business for years now, but I notice in reading this collection how much more secure his language has become. Once, he was likely to err both in amassing scientific words too lavishly and in affecting too folksy a tone. Now the scientific world in Ammons is beautifully in balance with the perceptual one, and the tone is believably, and almost perfectly, colloquial. The lines are as near as we could wish to the ripples round the ripplestone.

III

Ever since Schiller distinguished naive from sentimental poetry, we have been worried by the pathetic fallacy (as Ruskin named it). It is the aesthetic version of the tree falling in the woods; does it make a sound if nobody is there to hear it? Is nature hospitable of itself to meaning (by its rhythms and its orders, its catastrophes and its variety), or are our symbolic uses of it truly abuses, a foisting of our sentiments onto an inert and indifferent scenery? This question has become one that no modern "nature poet" from Wordsworth on can avoid addressing in a perfectly conscious way.

Hopkins, because he was a religious poet, at first assumed an authenticating God transmitting symbols through the book of the creatures:

> These things, these things were here and but the beholder
> Wanting; which two when they once meet,
> The heart rears wings bold and bolder
> And hurls for him, O half hurls earth for him off under his
>   feet.

This rapturous confidence in the Keatsian "greeting of the spirit" could not persevere in Hopkins's ultimately dualistic moral world, where ethics took a necessarily higher position than the aesthetic. At the end, all the diversity of the world (and with it, all its symbolic potential) had, for Hopkins, to be wound onto two spools, parted into two flocks, the elect and the damned:

> Lét life, wáned, ah lét life wind
> Off hér once skéined stained véined varíety / upon, áll on
>   twó spools; párt, pen, páck
> Now her áll in twó flocks, twó folds — black, white; / right,
>   wrong; reckon but, reck but, mind
> But these two; wáre of a wórld where bút these / twó tell.

Stevens's great explorations into the question of the pathetic fallacy (beginning with "The Snow Man," itself a variant on Keats's "In drear-nighted December") occupy him throughout his life, as he meditates the plain sense of things, the bare particular of the natural rock, and the fictive leaves that cover the rock and are a "cure" of it. Ashbery's poems (to cite a contemporary example) are full of jokes on the pathetic fallacy: but jokes are a way of using the convention, even if in a climate of gentle irony. In all these cases, the coincidence of nature with feeling or insight is the problem: is it a trick we play on ourselves, or a means of understanding — even a secular equivalent of grace?

I have written before on Wordsworth's magisterial (and in certain ways conclusive) meditations on this subject in the Immortality Ode: Wordsworth decided that our ability to use transferred epithets bestowing human adjectives on natural scenes ("the *innocent* brightness of a *new-born* day") was a way of objectifying our own feelings about innocence and birth, an activity necessary if we were to think about innocence and birth at all. ("We thought in images," says Lowell of poets.) The intercourse between soul and nature, in Wordsworth's view, clarifies the soul to itself and also endears natural sights (previously merely visual) as they become repositories of a moral and personal gestalt:

> The clouds that gather round the setting sun
> Do take a sober coloring from an eye
> That hath kept watch o'er man's mortality.

Once the habit of reciprocal looking and feeling is formed, looking taps feeling just as feeling transfigures looking: nature then appears to be an originating lamp rather than a reflecting mirror.

In the poetry of A. R. Ammons, the question of the pathetic fallacy is raised again and again, most luminously and painfully in his great poem "Grace Abounding," where the title makes explicit his claim that in states of inchoate feeling he finds a relief so great in the clarification offered by a visual image chanced upon in nature that the feeling corresponds to that which Bunyan named "grace abounding." We recall that in the biblical formulation, where sin abounds, grace will the more abound: in Ammons's frame of things, the emphasis changes from sin to misery. In the poem, where he is trapped in a vise of misery, the sight of a hedge completely encased and bound down by ice so strikes him that he realizes that it is an image, perfectly correspondent, of his inner anguish, the more anguishing because his misery had as yet remained unimaged, unconceptualized, and therefore indescribable. The relief felt when the hedge strikes his eye, and his state is at last nameable, is grace — not offered by Ammons as an "equivalent" to Bunyan's grace, but as *the same thing,* a saving gift from an external source. A poet who has felt that unexpected solace will seek it again.

Ammons looks literally for sermons in stones, books in the running brooks. He has been reproached for the minuteness of his detail, for scrutinizing every letter of the natural alphabet, even every syllable in the genetic code, seeking to extract from each item its assuaging human clarification. If a hedge of ice can explain him to himself, why so can a pebble (and it has) or a wave (and it has). "Grace Abounding" is a critical poem in Ammons's canon because it tells us his habitual state — one of a mute congestion of burdened feeling that must go abroad, baffled, letting the eye roam aimlessly, if minutely, until it feels the click that tells it, when it sees the hedge of ice, that that visual form is the mirror of its present feeling. Of course, while the eye is performing its apparently aimless scrutiny, before the connection can be made, before the appropriate image catches the eye, the work seems dull, even servile. This tedious phase of ruminative watching occupies the first part of Ammons's "Meeting Place," published in *Poetry* (October 1982). The creek water (says Ammons in "Meeting Place") has motions, yes; the wind contributes its motions, yes; the falls also does. These are, Ammons grants, "indifferent" actions. So much for the truths of modernity. After that, the poem turns atavistic, suggesting that all matter shares deep affinities of behavior. From subatomic particles to forms determined by physical law (the sphere of a waterdrop, the body's extensional limits in dance) our human motions obey the same tendencies as nature's motions. Ammons both affirms and questions this axiom of "ancestral" actions in the second part of his poem: "is my / address attribution's burden and abuse? . . . have I / fouled their real nature for myself / by wrenching their meaning, if any, to destinations of my own / forming?"

No poem becomes significant solely by asking questions about *poiesis* and the pathetic fallacy. But when we follow the course of "Meeting Place" we see that it enacts the meeting itself. The apparently random and tediously prolonged inquiry into the most fugitive motions of the creek is Ammons's becoming "multiple and dull in the mists' dreams," his version of Keatsian "indolence." By the time Ammons reaches the end he is claiming the powers of the magus: "when I call out to them . . . / an answering is calling me." The second surprising word in the poem, after "dull," is "howling": the spirits that arise in "Meeting Place" arise from a place like hell ("A minist'ring angel shall my sister be / When thou liest howling!"). These spirits would remain fettered and imprisoned forever without the releasing spell of "figures visible." In making the imprisoned figures ancestral ones, Ammons is being not only Freudian but Christian: Adam and Eve were the first figures released in the harrowing of hell.

The utter congruence between Christian grace and *poiesis* in Ammons is nowhere clearer than in the other new poem printed in the same issue of *Poetry,* "Singling and Doubling Together," a colloquy with God (or with a divine immanence in all things, after the Buddhist model). The simplest way, perhaps, to think about Ammons's central assertion in this poem is in terms of the Christian doctrine of the Incarnation — that God "risked all the way into the taking on of shape / and time." I have here made the verb into an active one ("God risked"), but Ammons has written it as a participial adjective, skirting the problem of voluntariness in God's circumscription of himself; Ammons's "you," risked into time, "fail and fail with me, as me" (Hopkins: "I am all at once what Christ is, since he was what I am"). But Ammons's ecstatic Hopkinsian ode to a presence in leafspeech and bush-snappings and pheasant-flight is deliberately undoctrinal and intimate, reminding us of Whitman's equally lyrical, but entirely sensuous, doublings of self. Ammons originally thought to call this poem (as the typescript shows) by a religious title, "Communion": it defines *poiesis* as Herbert defined it: "It is that which while I use / I am with thee." Ammons's single long sentence composing the ode contains no surprises like "dull" or "howling" in "Meeting Place": cast in the form of a love poem (Stevens: "And for what, if not for you, do I feel love?"), "Singling and Doubling Together" requires the decorum of unclouded praise. The poem deliberately takes the form of spherical perfection, as its first line — "My nature singing in me is your nature singing" — engenders, having come full circle, its close — "changed into your / singing nature, when I need sing my nature nevermore." By ending with its poet's death rather than with the transcendent persistence of an immanent singing, the poem is true to its earthly origins rather than to its religious antecedents; but in fact the beauty of the poem lies in its intertangled breaths of hymn and observation, of grace and birds and bushes. Its incantatory tonality is utterly different from the tones of the sedulous naturalist at the opening of "Meeting Place" (the poems meet, of course, in their endings).

It is odd to turn from these high lyrics to the epigrams of Ammons's 1982 collection, *Worldly Hopes*; the contrast reminds us that Ammons is always oscillating between his expatiations and his "briefings" (as between, from another angle, his hymnody and his nihilism). The short poems here are more of Ammons's experiments in the minimal. The question is, how few words can make a poem, and how densely can a few words be made to resonate. Here is "Providence":

> To stay
> bright as
> if just
> thought of
> earth requires
> only that
> nothing stay

"To stay bright as if just thought of / Earth requires only that nothing stay" — Ammons's art in brevity forbids this sort of rewriting (which all bad poems can sustain). The couplet that I have turned the poem into robs the poem of the doomed *rime riche* of its first and last lines, its form of measure (two words per line), and the wit of the line-breaks ("bright as — " turns out not to be "bright as day" but "bright as if," a curl of thought). My couplet (which of course will not scan, either) also loses Ammons's philosophic emphasis on the "trivial" words "as," "if," "just," "of," and "only" — the sort of words whose insidiousness interested Wittgenstein, too.

"Providence" trembles, with the lightest of touches, toward some reminiscences (Frost: "Nothing gold can stay"; Stevens: "Required, as a necessity requires"). And like many of Ammons's short poems, it burdens itself with a title of overwhelming philosophical or religious significance (others in this volume include "Righting Wrongs," "Subsumption," "Epistemology," "Oblivion's Bloom," "Immortality," and "Volitions"). "Providence" — the word is religiously defined as God's loving care for us — represents Ammons's grafting of an American Protestant mentality onto Keats's discovery of the ambiguous mercy of mortality. In its seven lines (formal "perfection" would demand eight), the poem recalls various early poems of Yeats in which the eighth line is designedly dropped to symbolize loss.

Even Ammons's simplest lyrics have points to make of the sort I
have mentioned in "Providence." An ingenious and eccentric angle
of vision or play of metaphor in them catches the eye; but something
also catches the breath:

>   I went back
>   to my old home
>   and the furrow
>   of each year
>   plowed like
>   surf across
>   the place had
>   not washed
>   memory away.

The backdrop of this poem ("I Went Back") is essentially Shakes-
pearean (the furrow of time, the obliterating sea, the memory of the
poet). But rewritten, the poem takes on another cast:

>   I went back to my old home,
>   And the furrow of each year,
>   (Plowed like surf across the place),
>   Had not washed memory away.

There is something Blakean about the poem-as-quatrain ("I was
angry with my friend . . . : / And it grew both day and night. / Till it
bore an apple bright"). (This may be an irrelevant comparison; but
we grasp at straws in trying to describe poetic effects.) Once again,
here, Ammons departs from the eight-line "norm" to suggest, by
adding a ninth line, the persistence of memory beyond the "natural"
term of its physical moment. The energizing phrase of the poem is
clearly "plowed like surf across the place," said of the furrow: the
other phrases are far more conventional. In a complex image the
furrow (singular) of each year (of an aggregate many), plowed (as of
earth) like surf (as of ocean) across the place, is said to have failed
to obliterate memory. This image is like a triple exposure in photog-
raphy: first, there is the physical family farm (home); second, there
is its spiritual form plowed as far as the eye can see by the furrows
of Time; third, the plowed form is washed over by a new form of
deluge, a surf of inner oblivion that has an intent to drown and erase

the past. A fourth form, memory, then comes to replace the first, at least in the poem; but the memory being identical to the physical farm revisited, they join and merge.

If these brief forms seem constricting at times, it is because we know Ammons's discursive amplitudes. I have not found any poem in *Worldly Hopes* to equal the sublime "Easter Morning," which appeared in *Coast of Trees*. There are new versions here of themes Ammons has touched before: they range from the artist's defense of his life (a fairly savage and sardonic version called "The Role of Society in the Artist") to exercises in pure verbality ("Shit List"). Science, as always, provide apt metaphors ("Precious Weak Fields," "Reaction Rates," "Working Differentials") and the antagonisms of writing are made ever more cunning.

In Ammons, the compulsion to form lurks as a danger. When he says that a poem "begins in contingency and ends in necessity" he is of course right, but necessity need not always wear a necessitarian aspect; it can assume an openhanded stance too, as it sometimes does in Williams or Stevens: "rooted they / grip down and begin to awaken"; "It was like a new knowledge of reality." As Ammons packs words ever more densely and punningly, perhaps necessity begins to usurp some of the place of contingency.

If we step back, after reading Ammons's account of the alternate burgeoning and collapse of "worldly hopes" (as religion would call them) as well as his hymns of thanksgiving for "grace" with which we began, we can see in him a representative figure for the persistence of the Protestant vein in American poetry. He uses the strategy of religious language with much of Dickinson's attachment to it, but he preserves, as Dickinson did not, the tonality of genuine prayer (resembling in this Stevens above all). If this were all he offered — religious language, religious tonality — Ammons would be simply a poet of religious nostalgia, a whited sepulcher. That he is not, we must attribute to two virtues of style which coexist with the religious elements and counterbalance them. One is the grounding of reality in the seen (like Williams, he finds his ideas in things). And the other is his stubborn inclusion of the recalcitrant detail, the hard ragged edge resisting the spherical sheerness of ultimate religious vision. In his naturalist speech, in his untroubled admitting of the psychic origins of the pathetic fallacy, Ammons is modern; in his willingness to substitute the word "grace" for the poetic experience of nature in lieu of the words "pathetic fallacy," he argues, like all poets, for the primacy of feeling in the naming of inner response. If the clarification conferred by the natural world — there is one in almost every poem by Ammons — feels like what Bunyan named "grace," then it *is* grace. What does not feel like a fallacy cannot be truthfully called one. Ammons is sure that the number of fluid inner states is infinite, and that the only matrix of possibility ample enough to correspond with the inner world is the massively various outer world. and the only mediating instrument between the liquid currents of mind and the mountains and deserts of matter is language, that elusive joiner of rivers to rock:

> I tangled with
> the world to
> let it go
> but couldn't free
>
> it: so I made
> words
> to wrestle in my
> stead and went
>
> off silent to
> the quick flow
> of brooks, the
> slow flow of stone

Words are the scapegoat in the fiction that Ammons here names "Extrication": they wrestle with the angel of matter for us.

IV

Recent Writing

21

James Merrill

From the First Nine: Poems 1946–1976 (1982), by James Merrill, brings together the poems Merrill has decided to save (a few of them reworked) from thirty years of writing. They are as ravishing in the rereading as in the reading. (Atheneum, the publisher of this volume, has also issued Merrill's complete trilogy-in-verse, *The Changing Light at Sandover,* but since the trilogy has received the lion's share of attention I am confining myself here to the lyrics, Merrill's "chronicles of love and loss," which in any case I prefer.) Eventually, there will be a *Collected Poems,* with variants and juvenilia and a chronology; even now there is a need for a concordance; but, putting scholarly wishes aside, one can have no complaints with such a profusion of deeply satisfying poems.

In spite of Merrill's limits, real or putative (of which more later), no reader of this book can depart from it without a sense of a firmly idiosyncratic poet writing, ever since his twenties, at the top of his form. Merrill's own metaphors for his work, which are unusually discerning ones, suggest that it is a festive combination of a banquet, a *son et lumière,* a theatrical performance, a travel narrative, and an embrace. The "sense of the sleight-of-hand man," to use Stevens's phrase, accompanies Merrill's lines. Often, perhaps even too often, Merrill refuses the potential transparency of the written word, and reminds his readers that this is writing they are reading, not a window they are privileged to see through. This is in part a form of honesty, but also a defense against the magic realism of writing. In his attacks of honesty, Merrill would almost have us believe that there is something of chicanery in all fictions, and that the more realistic the fiction the more suspect it becomes. In his cruelest exposure of the mimetic "charade" of art, Merrill describes an entire fake tribal childbirth that was staged for him and another credulous foreigner in Isfahan: they watch while in the dark the "mother" shrieks in pain; then she rises, totters forward with a swaddled shape in her arms. But this "mother" is a male house servant, the "baby" is the house puppy, and the impresario of this trick is Merrill's host (for whom the poem, "Chimes for Yahya," is an elegy). If this episode exposes an unexpected barbarity in the otherwise sophisticated host, it is no more, Merrill suggests, than the barbarity of the author of any fiction, who would have us believe that he is feeling pain or giving birth when in reality he is concocting puns.

Merrill's "postmodern" insistence on the conscious artificiality of his art is one way of avoiding bad faith and illusionist deception, and it is by no means a postmodern invention, since Merrill's version of it comes straight out of Byron's *Don Juan*. However, Merrill has it both ways — by also representing himself, over and over, as the erotic innocent who is taken in yet once more by the heart's deceptions. Or, at least, such was his characteristic posture well into his forties. It may remind some readers of George Herbert's recurrent portrait of himself as the naive sinner who, though he knows better, falls again and again into vanity and sin. Like Merrill, Herbert lets his reader know, by his intricate verse texture and his backward looks, that writing is art's jeweled reprise of life's bloody page; such self-conscious artists are especially unsettling to readers who want art to offer them the pleasure of dissolving in an (apparently unmediated) alternative experience.

No doubt we all begin as naive consumers of art, and there are certainly versions of every art which exist to provide direct substitutive experience. But every art, not only literature, has an inescapable reflexivity built into its constituting medium. Sculpture, the most mimetic of the arts, is — in a shock frequently exploited thematically by sculpture itself — unmoving and cold to the touch, thereby belying its imitation of flesh; painting, by its frequent incorporation of maps, windows, and mirrors, reflects on its own impenetrable plane; music, by its occasional departures into narrative "program," places more plainly in relief its basic programlessness, its own independent, intramusical code. Of all the arts, though, literature is the least susceptible to unreflective versions of itself, since its medium, language, is the medium by which we do our second-order thinking about primary-level experience, or, to put it differently, the medium by which we constitute the flux of first-order perceptions.

Most of the resistance to Merrill comes from those who hate reflexivity in art and its attendant irony. When the sleight-of-hand man unmasks his effect, the spectator is offended; when irony becomes "camp" (that is, disintegrative and humorous, and even arch), it causes real discomfort to the earnest reader, who is far more receptive to sardonic or vengeful forms of irony than to airy and self-deprecating ones. Merrill's case, for these readers, is not helped by what they are likely to refer to as his tendency to "coterie verse," by which they mean a verse freely referring to anything Merrill happens to have seen or read about — chiefly things they have neither read about nor seen. The discreet but open references to homosexuality make yet other readers uneasy, and the absence of any but casual references to world events makes some readers suspect that Merrill is not serious. Our American sense of poetry is still deeply Arnoldian, and Arnoldian poetry does not flaunt its own confection. Merrill, for better or worse, takes his constitution as a writer from his habit of going in and out of his illusionist effects while, as a character in his own fictions, he falls in and out of love, hope, travel, and belief. The two phases are roughly proportional: the medium is "transparent" during sensual, religious, or intellectual intoxication but becomes "opaque" and "visible" in the aftermath, when analysis succeeds experience.

The typical curve of experience in Merrill follows the pattern of Romantic illusion and disillusion which we know at its bitterest in "La Belle Dame Sans Merci." But because Merrill is, unlike Keats, a poet of comic and social forms, the castles in air so catastrophically destroyed often take on the brittle or dissolving atmosphere of ironic comedy. In this characteristic passage, for example, a withered romantic past briefly dreams itself alive again and then declines into a dry Hardyesque toast to the future:

> Book by loaf a whole life dreams itself
> From the foundation, from that withered rose
> Mounted in antlers, up past the first morning
> Glory's grasp of lightning rod,
> Labor, cost, frostbite, bedazzlement,

Down to the last friend's guitar and stories,
Name called in sleep, fingers unclenching
In a long bath, its tepid amber inch
And dry bouquet — the future, gentlemen!

This headlong collapse represents Merrill's knowingness, an aspect of his work necessarily more apparent in age: "Tomorrow's cabin, who knows where, will seem / A shade sobered." But an opposite tendency — to warm the past in his hands until it shines, glows, and lives again — is equally strong in Merrill, and becomes the source of a powerful tenderness.

"Lost in Translation" (1976), Merrill's most brilliant mature lyric, brings together with remarkable ease his detached reflectiveness and his lyric kindling of the past; as he often does, he moves serenely in and out of rhyme. In this mid-length poem (six pages), Merrill can bring into play his gift for a rich contextual fabric — here the fabric of his own half-privileged, half-impoverished childhood as the son of rich but often absent parents. Alone for a summer with his half-German, half-English governess — she is the widow of a Frenchman and is herself pretending to be French, because this is 1939 — he awaits the arrival of a promised rental puzzle ("a thousand hand-sawn / Sandal-scented pieces"). Finally, it comes, and he and his polyglot Mademoiselle put it together, musing over its many shaped pieces: "witch on broomstick, ostrich, hourglass" — the limited repertoire of the puzzlemaker. Eventually, in a process recalling the way in which words with identities of their own become subsumed in the verbal universe of the poem, these shaped pieces lose their anterior identity as they become part of the blue sky or the yellow tent of the puzzle. The subject of the puzzle (as of all art) is scandalous: something about "a Sheik with beard / And flashing sword hilt" and "a dark-eyed woman veiled in mauve," who arrives to join his harem — "hardly a proper subject for the Home." The world of sheik and houri (part of that Byronic Orientalism which Merrill adopts as an alternative to both America and Europe) is summoned up in a passage of elegant *aaba* quatrains, marked by a reduction in scale alerting us to a framed "view" — "that piece of Distance deep in which lies hid / Your tiny apex sugary with sun, / Eternal Triangle, Great Pyramid!" Dynasties dwindle to the tiny compass of the eye in this poem-within-a-poem, the visual puzzle within the verbal puzzle. The puzzle picture is itself the reduction of a history painting by "a minor lion attending on Gérôme," that painting, in turn, the miniaturization of a full-scale event in life. Even words on a page are not the ultimate reduction, Merrill suggests, as he recalls a poem by Valéry translated by Rilke (and later translated by Merrill himself), a poem about a coconut palm. In order to be faithful to the outline and meaning of the poem, Rilke, in translating into German, had to strip the poem of its alluring Romance words; and this process mimics the translation — by Merrill himself, among others — of life into art:

> [I] know
> How much of the sun-ripe original
> Felicity Rilke made himself forego
> (Who loved French words — verger, mûr, parfumer)
> In order to render its underlying sense.
> Know already in that tongue of his
> What Pains, what monolithic Truths
> Shadow stanza to stanza's symmetrical
> Rhyme-rutted pavement. Know that ground plan left
> Sublime and barren, where the warm Romance
> Stone by stone faded, cooled; the fluted nouns
> Made taller, lonelier than life
> By leaf-carved capitals in the afterglow.
> The owlet umlaut peeps and hoots
> Above the open vowel. And after rain
> A deep reverberation fills with stars.

The bittersweet afterglow of cooled passion, where tears turn to stars, represents for Merrill a danger that he does not always avoid — the danger of the sentimental or the self-enhancing. But it is easy, remembering the sentiment, to forget Merrill's admirable harsher side, his irritable moments of contemptuous self-exposure. The commerce of his "love" with bribery is not omitted, for instance. In another poem, Merrill's Greek ex-lover, once the blindness of romance has died, is rendered in full vulgarity, exposing his greed and Merrill's mortification:

> "Remember what you wrote
> In answer to my asking for a loan?
> I tore up your address — though you were right! —
> Then sold the cufflinks and the black trenchcoat."

And the whole transaction of "love" is summoned up in the central
aphorism of "Days of 1964":

> Her face was painted
> Clown-white, white of the moon by daylight,
> Lidded with pearl, mouth a poinsettia leaf,
> *Eat me, pay me* — the erotic mask
> Worn the world over by illusion
> To weddings of itself and simple need.

Passages like these are Merrill's armor against melting remembrance.

Merrill's poetry is unashamedly literary. For all its allusions to
foreigners (Proust, Cavafy, Rilke, Valéry, Baudelaire, Goethe, and so
on), it is squarely English and American (out of Herbert, Pope, Byron,
Poe, Auden, Eliot, and James). Until recently, Merrill lived for part
of each year in Greece, and his international self ("exotic at home
and American abroad," he once said in an interview) gives him
somewhat the air of one of James's shocked innocents abroad. (One
poem is called "Flying from Byzantium," as though that were what
any respectable American would do, no matter what golden Irish
poets might recommend.) But an effervescent Byronic comic relish of
social variety tends to mitigate the corruption of the Old World.
These qualities are mixed in Merrill with an Audenesque love of
aphorism, a punning wit that would not be out of place in *The Rape
of the Lock,* and a Herbertian plangency; when these notes are
sounded in sequence or almost in unison, the mixture becomes less
any of its elements and more a new compound, which we can call
Merrillesque. This style is sometimes too gently tempered, or too
precious in its pathos; it has, in short, the defects of its manners. It
wants to be, above all, courteous, and not to have the sun go down
on its wrath. There is a mention of tirades torn up and never sent;
tirades are outside the aesthetic of Merrill's verse — they would
break its eardrums. The lessons of his trilogy, he writes with self-
deprecating modesty, are given "at the salon level"; and conversation
— Merrill's model for this exquisitely written verse — can only be
conducted "at the salon level" as well.

There are, of course, other dimensions to poetic utterance —
prophecy, meditation, commination, and so on — but these are not
the languages one uses to a moral and social equal. Merrill presumes

a listener with whom the only possible wavelength of communication is the assumption of perfect equality. (In this, he is far more "democratic" than many of our hortatory poets, who presume to tell us our sins.) In a sense, Merrill can tell his reader nothing that the reader does not already know, and this tone is a great compliment to us. We are meant to understand the jokes, the puns, the allusions, and the level of experience invoked. We are not being exhorted, instructed, or condemned; we are being conversed with. The effect of reading Merrill's lyrics — so companionable, so touching, so vivid — is to make many other poets seem either loud and brutal, on the one hand, or parsimonious and pallid, on the other.

Merrill's language, always witty and mercurial, has become denser and less explicitly "pretty" over the years. There are several interestingly "difficult" poems in the later books, daunting, or even confusing, at first reading (though lucid, I find, in the long run). A few of these dense poems have American settings, as though Wyoming or New Mexico — those unfamiliar and harsh landscapes — provoked a new tension in rendering. I prefer these poems ("In Nine Sleep Valley," "Under Libra: Weights and Measures") to ones that too predictably melt to a reconciling sunset. To draw the poem out to an elegiac sweetness of sleep, or music, or twilight has been Merrill's temptation in closure, but these poems resist sweetness. It may be true that "all things in time grow musical," but they should not do so too soon. Merrill is, of course, ahead of us in self-criticism — as in the excellent poem "Yánnina," where in a magician's tent a woman is sawed in two and then miraculously emerges whole:

> A glittering death
> Is hefted, swung. The victim smiles consent.
> To a sharp intake of breath she comes apart . . .
> Then to a general exhalation heals
> Like anybody's life.

In his trilogy, Merrill has taken more time with what does not heal, notably death, and yet his prolongation of death into an afterlife of high conversation (the past recaptured) serves also to refuse the tragic, re-forming it into the comic pathetic and the vivacious sublime of divine comedy. Just as his buoyant sense of life — helplessly buoyant, even against his will — rebukes the gloom of much writing, so he is himself rebuked, externally, by the pure abruptness of tragedy, which refuses to have dealings with the social, and instead deals with absolutes. Tragedy and comedy cannot cohabit, because they are mutually displacing or alternative modes. There is no sustained tragedy in Merrill, though there is a great deal of pathos, together with tragic moments encapsulated in the general comedy.

As a historian of the phases of sensuality, Merrill is unequaled in our century. His best poetry (a prism of the opalescent spectrum of the sensual) describes moments so elusive to specification that his having found a music for them is a genuinely startling act. Episodes of intense sensation are extinguished as passion but sustained as art. Flashing with ironies and inventions, rapid in movement, intricate in language, these poems dazzle before they convince, and convince, subsequently, because of their dazzle (the right way for a poem to work). In "Willowware Cup," for instance, love undergone becomes a tattoo

> like ink in flesh, blue anchor
>
> Needled upon drunkenness while its destroyer
> Full steam departs, the stigma throbbing, intricate —
>
> Only to blend into a crazing texture.

In "Syrinx," art is like a flute passage

> Whose silvery breath-tarnished tones
> No longer rivet bone and star in place
>
> Or keep from shriveling, leather round a stone,
> The sunbather's precocious apricot
>
> Or stop the four winds racing overhead
>   Nought
>   Waste   Eased
>   Sought

In such a passage we recognize echoes of Ovid, of pattern-poetry, of Herbert's "shrivelled heart" and his "I ease you," together with Shakespeare's "waste" of lust and something either French or Tennysonian in the extraordinary *trouvaille* of the precocious apricot as the sexual image.

Merrill's diction, though it can be fully literary, is also colloquial and topical, and in that way, though he generally writes in meter, he writes in the current language of America. His many sonnets rank with Auden's and Lowell's in this century, and his rhymes are the cleverest the language has seen since Byron. His lyric work is remarkably free of conspicuous lapses and has improved over time (a gift reserved to a happy few — think of the later careers of Frost, Moore, Pound, and Roethke, to name only a few of the unfortunates). His long trilogy has occupied Merrill for several years, though not to the absolute exclusion of the lyric, since several notable lyrics — especially the beautiful "Samos" — are to be found within the long work. Merrill's plays and his early flirtations with the novel form — *The Seraglio, The (Diblos) Notebook* — revealed him as a poet not satisfied to be simply lyric; he is, like so many other lyric poets, overcome by a hankering for a longer form and a larger canvas. The trilogy is a stubborn return to that play of voices possible only in a form more social than the lyric, governed by that conversation in which Merrill believes.

But it seems to me that Merrill's greatest gifts lie in that solitary form the lyric, where shimmer and light become native to words, and where the myth of the sensual or the solitary, rather than the myth of the social, animates the content. After all, Merrill's originating myth was that of Eros and Psyche. Readers who have not yet found Merrill's very Keatsian retelling of that myth (in "From the Cupola") might well begin their reading of his poetry there:

> Psyche, hush. This is me, James,
> Writing lest he think
> Of the reasons why he writes —
> Boredom, fear, mixed vanities and shames;
> Also love.

II

At the heart of James Merrill's collection of lyrics *Late Settings* (1985) lies his farewell to Greece, where he used to spend part of each year. Merrill urges a grace in losing "Greece itself," a Greece no longer what it was:

> Corrupted whites and blues,
> Taverns torn down for banks, the personnel
> Grown fat and mulish, marbles clogged with soot . . .
> Things just aren't what they were — no more am I.

The leavetaking, commemorated in a poem called "Santorini: Stopping the Leak," is done under the aegis of various lurking horrors. Merrill has just undergone five sessions of radiation to destroy a plantar wart, and the radiologist's waiting room offers vistas of future cancer; a servant in Greece recalls her brother's drowning; the island of Santorini brings up the legend of the destruction of Atlantis by an earthquake. A wave of self-doubt enters Merrill's praise of poise in endings:

> We must be light, light-footed, light of soul,
> Quick to let go, to tighten by a notch
> The broad, star-studded belt Earth wears to feel
> Hungers less mortal for a vanished whole.
> Light-headed at the last? Our lives unreal
> Except as jeweled self-windings, a deathwatch
> Of heartless rhetoric I punctuate,
> Spitting the damson pit onto the plate?

The recommendation of lightness is made more serious by its own final self-interrogation. Joy's grape is burst, as in Keats, upon the fine palate. But in Merrill the metaphor has soured until it fastens no longer on the flesh of the fruit, but rather on the pit. Keats's deathwatch beetle has become the deathbed vigil and also the ticking timepiece of meter, its motive force the jeweled self-winding of the writer. Merrill's stanza in this poem is a version of Yeats's (and Byron's) ottava rima. Merrill adds a fourth rhyme for English ease, but keeps the terminal couplet, its finality clamping each stanza shut.

Throughout the poem "the vanished whole" — youth, love, and a country lost — is treated with comedy, irony, and pathos. In the nightmarish middle of the poem, Merrill has a vision of himself being drained of all existence through the "leak" in his irradiated foot. Other existences, borne in images, begin to invade his consciousness, thousands of other potential beings eager to take his place in the universe, as his own vitality seeps away. The press of images toward embodied being is like the press of a crowd to be admitted to a restaurant:

> Vignettes as through a jeweler's loupe descried,
> Swifter now, churning down the optic sluice,
> Faces young, old, to rend the maître d's
> Red cord, all random, ravenous images
>
> Avid for inwardness, and none but driven
> To gain, like the triumphant sperm, a table
> Set for one — wineglass, napkin, and rosebud.

A passage like this one tests the reader's affinity for Merrill. Those of us who find in him something that nobody else now writing affords us would have to point to the combination, visible here and frequent in Merrill, of savagery and civilization. Merrill mixes the demands of biology, blood, and nerves (the optic sluice, the ravenous bodily appetites, the triumphant sperm) with their utmost ritualizing in formality (the stylizations with which a restaurant surrounds appetite, the scrutiny, at once magnifying and miniaturizing, of the jeweler's eyeglass). Both are here imitated by the verse, beginning in observation, accelerating in momentum, and then brought up short by the absurd and yet touching tableau of the formal table set for one — a metaphor for existence conceivable only in Merrill.

But this is all written, as I have said, in the service of fear — the fear of existence leaking away. Throughout *Late Settings* Merrill faces his own extinction, and suggests fantasies of survival:

> Could a soul that clung
> To its own fusing senses crawl at last
> Away unshriveled from the holocaust?

In fact, in the poem on Santorini, Merrill does survive. A small moth — Psyche — appears, reassuring him that his soul still lives, and a familiar pain in his foot tells him that the plantar wart has begun to grow back, "stopping the leak":

> In gloom the peevish buzz
> Of a wee wingèd one-watt presence short-
> Circuiting compulsively the panes

Gone white. My drained self doesn't yet . . . yet does!
From some remotest galaxy in the veins
A faint, familiar pulse begins. The wart,
Alive and ticking, that I'd thought destroyed.
No lasting cure? No foothold on the void?

"The last kiss," Yeats wrote, "is given to the void," but Merrill has
not quite reached that point. Life and the wart start up anew.

Other poems exhibit a less comic resolution of the shadow of
death. All sorts of death take place here, notably in three short lyrics
grouped under the title "Topics." In the first, a poem about terrorism,
a woman tourist is shot dead. In the second, the governments of
Russia and the United States survive in their bunkers after an atomic
war. In the third, a poem on knowledge, man has traded earthly
happiness for the knowledge of nuclear fission. For this last lyric,
Merrill borrows Shelley's and Yeats's prophetic four-beat closed qua-
trains, and retells, with a Frostian force, the origin and ultimate glory
of the universe before the earth blew itself up. (The poem is called
"Caesarion," after the son of Caesar and Cleopatra, who was put to
death by Octavian.)

A glow of cells in the warm Sea,
Some vaguest green or violet soup
Took a few billion days to loop
The loops we called Eternity.

Before the splendor bit its tail
Blake rendered it in aquatint
And Eddington pursued a glint —
Recoil, explosion — scale on scale.

What stellar hopefuls, plumed like Mars,
Sank to provincial rant and strut,
Lines blown, within the occiput?
Considering the fate of stars,

I think that man died happiest
Who never saw his Mother clasp
Fusion, the tiny naked asp,
By force of habit to her breast.

Merrill's pen turns to such subjects with a degree of anger, an anger turned even against writing itself (that the sign of vivacity should become the sign of extinction). This anger turns even against his own poetic masters, who were too quick to praise the word as moral and life-giving. In a poem about the bombing of Beirut, death appears again:

> By noon, fire from the same blue heavens
> Had half erased Beirut.
> *Allah be praised*, it said on crude handbills,
> *For guns and Nazarenes to shoot.*
> "How gladly with proper words," said Wallace Stevens
> "The soldier dies." Or kills.

Merrill's quarrel with Stevens's aphorism marks a change in our twentieth-century perceptions of government. Stevens's words were written in the idealism of World War II, an idealism about war impossible for Merrill, who quarrels too with Yeats's admiration for Renaissance Italian dukes:

> Above
> Lie field and vineyard, castle built
> To nurture intellect, art, love
> Together with, let's face it, guilt,
> Deception, strife.

The same consciousness of disintegration, catabolism, entropy ("Coils of shot film, run-down DNA") quarrels with Rilke's idealization of art in the archaic torso of Apollo, which spoke to him in shining potency, saying, "You must change your life." Merrill's exhumed Greek gods have a different more impatient message:

> *Expect no*
> *Epiphany such as the torso*
> *In Paris provided for Rilke. Quit*
> *Dreaming of change. It is happening*
> *Whether you like it or not,*
> *So get on with your lives. We have done.*

Merrill's art, so apt for sensuality, travel, and domesticity, recently passed through the purgatorial trial of *The Changing Light at Sandover* (1982), a long three-part poem that consisted of conversations with the dead. That poem now seems to be a threshold over which Merrill had to step in order to translate himself from one of the living to one of the (potentially) dead. The punning title of the present volume, *Late Settings*, looks toward a jeweler's art, a last music, a final banquet, and a setting sun. The sober coloring of the sunset diffuses itself through the book, sometimes glimmering in afterglow, sometimes flashing in fission.

Merrill's Herbertian variety of technique appears here in experiments variously successful, but always interesting to watch. Merrill can imagine, for instance, a stanza like a house of cards for a poem ("An Upset") about the collapse of a table that had belonged to his grandfather. Everything falls on the floor, "ashtray, lamp, magnifying glass," books:

> Whew. A disaster zone
> Facing therapy: sandpaper, clamps and glue,
> Jetsam and overflow's diversion to shelves
> Unbuilt, if not to plain
> Oblivion . . .
> Another "flood" behind us,
> Now to relearn
> Uprightness, lightness, poise:
> First things — the lamp supposes, prone
> Yet burning wildly on.

The interleaving of five-, four-, three-, and two-stress lines (marked by differing marginal indentations) is as "upsetting" as the disorder on the floor; and yet the very order of the indenting reflects the lamp of intellectual light, inquisitive even in disaster, "prone" and almost rhymeless, but "burning wildly on."

Throughout this book, things burn and are burned, scorched, irradiated. The divine Greek sun even burns a hole in Merrill's film. The smallest sparks of burning in the collection shine in the poem that is placed first. They come from the marijuana cigarettes lit in the dark "between Earth and Venus" — two other spots of light in the night sky — as Merrill and his companion stand on the courthouse lawn at dusk. The poem, a small prospective self-elegy in dimeter, is called, innocently enough, "Grass":

> The river irises
> Draw themselves in.
> Enough to have seen
> Their day. The arras
>
> Also of evening drawn,
> We light up between
> Earth and Venus
> On the courthouse lawn,
>
> Kept by this cheerful
> Inch of green
> And ten more years — fifteen? —
> From disappearing.

Here, and elsewhere in this volume, Merrill returns to some of his earliest experiments in rhyme: rhyming two words of which one has an extra falling syllable ("irises" with "arras"); rhyming two words by their penultimate syllables alone ("cheerful" with "disappear-ing"); rhyming aslant ("seen" with "in"); keeping a single rhyme going throughout a whole poem ("in," "seen," "between," "Venus," "green," "fifteen"). There are graceful nonsignifying "rhymes," like the internal orthographic resemblance between "*river*" and "*irises*," and the phonic resemblance between "*even*ing" and "*Ven*us" (the evening star). Merrill is still fond of zeugma, the figure that links two unlikely words in syntactic twinship (here "inch" and "years": "We are kept from disappearing into the earth by this cheerful inch of lawn and by ten — or fifteen? — more years"). Zeugma is the figure most emblematic of the comic union of body and soul; the body stands on (and smokes) the grass, the soul extends itself into certain and uncertain future time. As in this case, Merrill's formal figures almost always carry meaning; his metaphors brim with signification. His allusions are not inert, but transformative. He remembers, for instance, the *Rubáiyát*:

> The Moving Finger writes; and having writ,
> Moves on: nor all your Piety nor Wit
>   Shall lure it back to cancel half a Line,
> Nor all your Tears wash out a Word of it.

Merrill's grim and witty reversal of Fitzgerald, in which the Writing
Finger becomes the Erasing Snail, is spoken by one of the anthro-
pomorphized fish in the sonnet called "Think Tank":

> At our best we were of one mind,
> Did our own sick or vital things
> Within a medium secured by trick
>
> Reflections over which, day, night, the braille
> Eraser glided of the Snail
> Our servant, huge and blind.

   In the past few years Merrill has substituted Florida for Greece
during the winter, and many of these poems take a wild new energy
from the contradictions of the Florida scenery. The most remarkable
among this group is a poem about Palm Beach, to which I will come
in a moment. But first I want to mention, as an example of Merrill's
"Florida writing," a poem about innocence being caught by experi-
ence. Tropical fish are being caught from a pier by fishermen using
other fish as bait; young prostitutes are being hauled into court.
These two narratives are combined, at the end of the poem, with a
reminiscence of Merrill himself, at the age of eight, entering into
experience. Here are the central stanzas, full of brilliant concision:

> These floozy fish —
>
> Ceramic-lipped in filmy
> Peekaboo blouses,
> Fluorescent body
> Stockings, hot stripes, . . .
>
> Jailbait consumers of subliminal
> Hints dropped from on high
> In gobbets none
> Eschews as minced kin;
>
> Who, hooked themselves — bamboo diviner
> Bent their way
> Vigorously nodding
> Encouragement —

Are one by one hauled kisswise, oh
Into some blinding hell
Policed by leathery ex-
Justices each

Minding his catch, if catch is what he can,
If mind is what one means —
The torn mouth
Stifled by newsprint, working still. If . . . if . . .

The little scales
Grow stiff.

This lyric imagining of "The bite. The tug of fate" is what poets can do to bring the various foci of perception (nature, others, self) into one point of attention. Caught fish, street crime, growing up are not three subjects in the poem, but one, and the distress in the disintegration of meaning ("Minding his catch, if catch is what he can, / If mind is what one means — . . . / If . . . if . . .") finds its visual embodiment in the torn mouth of the fish, and the callous reporting in newsprint of police-blotter scandal.

Merrill's fusion of levels of perception at high emotional temperature is brought off most brilliantly in "Palm Beach with Portuguese Man-of-War," an elegy of sorts for Merrill's wealthy thrice-married father (who is buried, as a note tells us, in West Palm Beach). The poem uses no punctuation, letting its images rise surrealistically untethered. The title suggests a tropical painting like those of Martin Johnson Heade, in which an exotic object like a hummingbird or an orchid is set against a carefully rendered landscape: Merrill's object is the "baby gorgon," a man-of-war jellyfish blown ashore on the long spine of sandy beach, waiting to be reclaimed by the Whitmanian sea. The poem owes a good deal to Hart Crane's and Elizabeth Bishop's tropical poems, but is nonetheless wholly Merrill's own in its anatomy of tycoons, their female hangers-on, their sexual and social forays, their eventual tombs. The poem offers no editorial explanations for its processional images. It begins with the virgin beach itself:

A mile-long vertebrate picked clean
To lofty-plumed seableached incurving ribs

Poor white the soil like talcum mixed with grit

The beach is then colonized, irrigated, built up:

> But up came polymorphous green
>
> No sooner fertilized than clipped
> Where glimmerings from buried nozzles rose
>
> And honey gravel driveways led
> To the perpetual readiness of tombs

Tombs and rooms are indistinguishable in Merrill's Florida:

> Shellwhite outside or white-on-white
> A dropping bird motif still wet
>
> Pastel and madrepore the shuttered rooms'
> Nacreous jetsam wave on wave

The poem turns satiric on the subject of the newly divorced and lustful aging tycoon at dinner parties:

> Having swept our late excrescences
> The wens and wives away to mirrorsmoke
>
> Place settings for the skin
> Diver after dark the extra man
>
> Drowning by candlelight whose two minds reel
> How to be potent *and* unsexed
>
> Worth a million *and* expendable
> How to be everybody's dish

The poem envisages the tycoon's destruction by women as an underwater holocaust by cannibal fish:

> And not to have seen through the glass visor
> What would be made of him some night
>
> By the anemone's flame chiffon gown
> Like those downtown in the boutiques
>
> By razor labia of hangers-on
> To territories this or that
>
> Tiny hideous tycoon stakes out

The destruction takes place on a coral reef:

> Empire wholly built upon albino
>
> Slaves the fossil globules of a self-
> Creating self-absorbing scheme
>
> Giddy in scope pedantic in detail

Over the coral reef float the jellyfish:

> Over which random baby gorgons
>
> Float without perception it would seem
> Whom their own purple airs inflate
>
> And ganglia agonizingly outlive
> Look out! one has been blown ashore
>
> For tomorrow's old wet nurse to come
> Ease from the dry breast and sheet in foam

Hatred and pity coexist in this impersonal elegy. Merrill has so often written in the first person that this chilling drift of images unanchored to a personal speaker is the more noticeable. The poem makes no concessions; and while this may annoy some readers (those who want personal speech, autobiographical narrative, explicit editorializing, "communication"), I think it is a proof of strength in Merrill to resist the temptation to annotate his images. After all, all intelligible poems become understood in time.

There is no poem in this volume that is not worth reading. Some are slight, grace notes and observations. Some are chapters in Merrill's continuing verse autobiography (notably the genial "Clearing the Title," on acquiring a house in Key West); some continue the exploration of Merrill's favorite images (the soul-moth, the peacock, the Greek world). Merrill has added yet one more poem to his "Days of . . ." series (the title borrowed from Cavafy) with "Days of 1941 and '44," a fierce sonnet sequence in which we see Merrill at fifteen ("in those days less than nothing, / A shaky X on panic's bottom line") experiencing his aesthetic conversion:

> In vain old Mr Raymond's sky-blue stare
> Paled with revulsion when I spoke to him
> About my final paper. "Jim,"
> He quavered, "don't, *don't* write on Baudelaire."

But Merrill does write on Baudelaire ("Faith rose dripping from the false"), and goes on to enter the army, where he reads Proust ("basic training") and hears of the death of a schoolmate who had, a few years before, tormented him:

> The nightmare shower room. My tormentor leers
> In mock lust — surely? — at my crotch.
> The towel I reach for held just out of reach,
> I gaze back petrified, past speech, past tears.

Now the tormentor is killed in battle, and the eighteen-year-old Merrill does not know how to absorb that death: "The nothing you'd become took on a weight / No style I knew could lighten." The oblique and beautiful ending of the sequence shows a third-person Merrill in battle-training under real fire:

> Beneath unsimulated fire he'd crawl
> With full pack, rifle, helmeted, weak-kneed,
> And peeking upward see the tracers scrawl
>
> Their letter of atonement, then the flare
> Quote its entire red minefield from mid-air —
> Between whose lines it has been life to read.

As the poet-to-be reads between the lines of the tracer bullets and perceives the entire red minefield of life, baffled by the death of his schoolmate who has been transformed from the tormentor into the tormented, lines of life and art begin to intertwine, as hatred ("you were my first true hate") and atonement converge.

Merrill is not often praised for concision; he is considered an elaborate, and elaborating, writer. Yet his lines, here as in "Palm Beach," tell a great deal in a short space. His drive toward the concise is, interestingly, not a drive toward the aphoristic or the epigrammatic, the two modes toward which concision tends. On the contrary, it is a drive toward the complex and dense image that will be per-

ceptual, personal, social, and philosophical at once ("the floozy fish
. . . subliminal jailbait . . . hauled into some blinding hell policed by
ex-justices"). Such images become impatient of syntax, of commen-
tary, even of punctuation (as in "Palm Beach"). A "cinéma-men-
songe," as Merrill calls it in "Santorini" — a free-floating film of
hallucinatory imagery — replaces, as objective correlative, the too
logically articulated process of explanation. The *mensonge inconti-
nent* of poetry has here been brought to a level of high inner artic-
ulation, so much so that it explains itself by its consummately ac-
curate choice of substantive and epithet.

I would not trade this rendered essence for the more conversational
séances of Merrill's trilogy. But I am glad that traces of Merrill's
poignant early style remain, not least in a triumphant poem about
Proustian memory (reductively called "The House Fly"). In earlier
volumes there were love poems to a Greek named Strato; later there
were angry, ironic, and bittersweet adieus to him. Now, in a poem
at once factual, comic, touching, and ghostly, Strato is named and
remembered, the earlier bliss and the later blight of love both sub-
sumed in the ritual of memory provoked by the annual return of the
house fly, a "low-mimetic" version of Merrill's psyche, the winged
soul. The first stanza compares past kisses to the present kisses of
the house fly, and utters the poet's psychic malaise:

> Come October, if I close my eyes,
> A self till then subliminal takes flight
> Buzzing round me, settling upon the knuckle,
> The lip to be explored not as in June
> But with a sense verging on micromania
> Of wrong, of tiny, hazy, crying wrongs
> Which quite undo her — look at that zigzag totter,
> Proboscis blindly tapping like a cane.

Merrill says somewhere in *Late Settings* that he wants a tone that
avoids both levity and leadenness, and this stanza will serve as an
example of what he means, in its portrait of the self-as-pensioner —
fretful, tottering, blind, obsessive in complaint.

The second stanza shows us a more frightful self — the middle-
aged self as compulsive artist, unable to leave off the rhythmic self-
grooming motions that have become a habit. The house fly resumes
her "grand toilette":

> Unwearying strigils taken to the frayed,
> Still-glinting wings; the dull-red lacquer head
> Lifted from its socket, turned mechanically
> This way and that, like a wristwatch being wound.

These passages, with their irritable and bitter Popian accuracy, are the best in the poem, and may be taken to represent Merrill's sense of having been unwittingly deprived of motive while still in the habit of motion. Stevens called this state "desire without an object of desire," and diagnosed it bleakly. But Merrill, for better or worse, does not end his poem in the desert of the present. Instead, he turns gratefully back to memory and its assuaging images, telling us that the fly-Pysche is still worthy of her cult:

> Downstairs in this same house one summer night,
> Founding the cult, her ancestress alit
> On the bare chest of Strato Mouflouzélis
> Who stirred in the lamp-glow but did not wake.
> To say so brings it back on every autumn
> Feebler wings, and further from that Sun,
> That mist-white wafer she and I partake of
> Alone this afternoon, making a rite
> Distinct from both the blessing and the blight.

This daring passage evokes at once the utter foolishness of love — its symbol a fly on the chest of someone absurdly named Mouflouzélis (who is nonetheless the sleeping Eros of the lampglow) — and its utter imprinting of existence, so much so that we are all willing to take that "last communion in the haze" (Dickinson) of the Indian Summer sun. Merrill insists on the value and meaning of early love in later life, even if memory brings it back on ever-feebler wings.

Those of us who read Merrill to know what to do with our sentiments, even to know what our sentiments are (since poets are more expert than the rest of us in human diagnosis), are told by this poem — on the level of its last message — that the infection of general disappointment and dismaying mechanical habit of middle age is not particular to us. The poem suggests that the erotic idealizations of the past are not entirely invalidated by the frayed and fretful present. We may agree or disagree, but the question has been put, and an answer of sorts given, in the homage to memory.

The poem puts its question and answer in painfully particular terms — "tiny, hazy, crying wrongs," a "proboscis blindly tapping," "unwearying strigils," "the dull-red lacquer head," "the bare chest of Strato Mouflouzélis," all of them at once exactly descriptive and either grimly or absurdly ironic. Aside from the experience reenacted in the little personal drama of the poem — the annual return of the house fly and the earlier self it calls to mind — the poem belongs to the classical tradition of autumn elegy and of cult celebration, at once revising these forms in an ironized modernism, and paying tribute to their staying power in the lyric tradition. If the forms remain, perhaps eros remains as well; under the mechanical turnings of the tired head, something stirs in the lamplight. It comes as a balm that Merrill should suggest as much. But for me it is a greater balm to see the baffled proboscis and the weary dull-red head put into words, the ultimate relief of poetry being the knowledge that such tenuous states of feeling are finally expressible. And though *Late Settings* is, as I have said, full of holocausts and upsets, apprehensions and irritabilities, it shows undiminished luster in its still-glinting wings of consummate expression.

22

Adrienne Rich, Jared Carter, Philip Levine

Because Adrienne Rich's poetry is so decisively social and psychological, and so forthright in its manner, it is tempting to review its arguments rather than its poetic character. But issues wax and lapse, and poetry, if it is good poetry, remains interesting after the topical issues it has engaged are dead letters. I will try to reflect here on the sort of poetry Rich has undertaken to write.

Rich decided, fairly early, to write in a common voice, "to do something very common, in my own way." She belongs, by this choice, to the school of William Carlos Williams — the school of poets who, however well read, refuse obvious learning a place in their lines. (This is equally the school of George Herbert.) Eliot, Auden, Pound, Crane, Moore, Lowell, Merrill — and even such unlikely poets as Ammons — write often, if not always, above the level of comprehension of the common reader; books, books, and more books underlie their vocabulary and their allusions, not to speak of their assumptions about culture. Authors who vow, like Rich, to speak for, and be readable by, the unliterary, move away from the learnèd side of language and lose thereby a rich, beautiful, and powerful part of themselves and of literature. They think the loss well worth the gain:

> Who says that fictions only and false hair
> Become a verse? Is there in truth no beautie?

Just as Herbert identified ostentatious learning with sterile "divinity" or theological hairsplitting, which he thought far from the true end of piety, so Rich seems to have identified the hermetic and "instructed" side of language with male institutional life, the life of churches and academies, a life historically unavailable to women. (Williams, the child of foreigners, abjured learnèd diction as too "European"; Whitman, closer to Rich, abjured it as undemocratic.)

In any case, Rich belongs to the school of plain-style poets, those who distrust, as evidence of mystification and hierarchy, ornament and embellishment in poetry. Plain-style poets ask to be judged on effectiveness, rather than on conventional ideas of "beauty": they make scant use of the elaborations of rhetoric, preferring the "horizontal" connections of contiguity to the "vertical" connections of metaphor. Though they affirm that their gaze is fixed on the actual and the historic, they are often utopian, and see the actual and the historic outlined against a Platonic social ideal. Their vision of a better world is entirely reactive, conceived as the opposite of the unjust world they perceive in the here and now. They are not lost in visionary radiance, and their language is not ecstatic but aggrieved.

Plain-style poets belong to the long chronicle of English and American Protestant dissent, with its history of political and religious reform. When Rich finds her own literary ancestors, she quotes women who used this Protestant voice (Susan B. Anthony, Jane Addams); she could equally well have named men like Thoreau in *Civil Disobedience*, William Lloyd Garrison, and Frederick Douglass. We find this voice in Protestant autobiography with its heightened rhetorical polarities of damnation and election, in Protestant sermons with their tides of rebuke and exhortation, and in the oratory and essays of social reform, secular descendants of the religious genres. In using this voice, Rich is writing in a central American tradition.

It is true of all literary voices that they have had fewer women than men practitioners. But in the case of the voice Rich uses, the disparity arises not solely from the relative numbers of male and female writers. Rather, it is caused chiefly, as many women writers have said, by the existence of a competing voice, one thought more "suitable" for women than this voice of Protestant personal and public drama, command, and reprobation. The competing choice is the one that Dickinson, Moore, Bishop, Sexton, and Plath repudiated as strongly as Rich repudiates it. It is the voice of girlishness, erotic pining, winsome coyness, religious submissiveness, and sentimental motherhood, the voice of the nineteenth-century woman poet. (Elizabeth Barrett Browning, because she experimented with a public voice, became the exception that proved the rule.) Even when a religious or social imperative was admitted, only positive sentiments were acceptable in a woman's writing:

But bring not thou the battle's stormy chorus,
 The tramp of armies, and the roar of fight,
Not war's hot smoke to taint the sweet morn o'er us
 Nor blaze of pillage, reddening up the night.

O, let thy lays prolong that angel-singing,
 Girdling with music the Redeemer's star,
And breathe God's peace, to earth 'glad tidings' bringing
 From the near heavens, of old so dim and far!

This self-adjuration by Sarah J. Lippincott is clear enough; the "angel in the house" is to make angelic song.

Dickinson repudiated the "female" voice by blasphemy and pride; Moore, by learning and "observations"; Bishop, by homelessness and skepticism; Sexton, by parody and wildness; Plath, by anger and geometric chill. No one of these women, however, took upon herself the public voice of the political activist. (Perhaps Muriel Rukeyser is Rich's nearest predecessor in that respect.) The voice of "power" — a word Rich uses over and over again about writing — is a voice social in intent. And indeed, Rich's poetry is often treated as social poetry. I find Rich more often a personal poet, psychological rather than social (at least by comparison with Williams, for instance).

Rich's is a poetry of conversion. Like many writers who have undergone a conversion, she wants the process she has felt to be repeated in others. What we call, from the outside, a "conversion," is often seen, by the person experiencing it, not as a change from an old self to a new one, but as the discovery of the authentic self that had been there all along, but had been forced into hiding by pressure from familial or social structures, structures experienced as intolerably powerful, even annihilating. Hence the subsequent quest of the converted for power, enough power to destroy, in turn, those structures which had proved so inhuman.

It could be argued, against Rich, that the structures she found repressive might not have been so for others. Could any social structures invented by an unoriginal heterosexual tribally grouped majority ever have been fostering ones for a child half-Jewish, half-Christian, destined to be an original writer, on the one hand, and a lesbian, on the other? Rich is only one of thousands of "outsiders" or "outlaws" (known to all social communities) who find the expectations of the herd impossible for themselves. The herd is of course — and it is the "of course" to which Rich, perhaps vainly, objects — cruel to the outlaws. Those among the "marginal" who become writers often unleash an entirely realistic anger against "the system" — variously conceived as the established church, or *usura*, or the class structure, or the warmongers. For Rich the oppressive rule is the rule of "compulsory heterosexuality," by which she means that most women have to buy economic survival by marriage. Reformers imagine that once the offending structures have been removed, people will be free — or at least freer than they were before.

The activist view of a better reality struggling toward rebirth is profoundly opposed to the more pessimistic Freudian view in which no perfect originating structure can be imagined for the psyche, which is always wounded by its psychologically dependent status in childhood. Its repressions and Oedipal reenactments ensure the perpetuation of social conventionality and tribal hostilities. Hence the strain, in Rich, between two poetries. One is an introspective and psychologically framed poetry which retells, many times, the story of her own rebellion and struggle for self-liberation (she sees her story in those terms). The other is a more public poetry of protest, the poetry which aims at political "power." I find the first poetry — the autobiographical poetry of Protestant conversion — the more powerful.

Most of the poetry in Rich's *The Fact of a Doorframe* (1984) has been previously published in book form. There are six new poems, and a few old "lost" or uncollected poems. The new poems, of which the most memorable is "In the Wake of Home," continue to reexamine what Rich names the two poles of her nature, "anger and tenderness." It is the anger that has chiefly defined her as a mature poet, as her own private rage gradually attached itself to various oppressed groups — women, poor women, black women, lesbian women. (It is clear that she knows that there are other oppressed groups, but that she cannot generally feel the identity with them that would provoke writing.)

Rich's own original rage, even if generated by an inborn temperament, was emotionally attached to her relationship with her father: she remembers "my Jewish father writing me / letters of seventeen pages / finely inscribed harangues / questions of loyalty and punishment / . . . And I . . . walking to my wedding / . . . a bad daughter . . . a bad sister." Her own solution has been not only to remember her primal anger but to bring it to bear on all other conceivable wrongs suffered by women at the hands of men. One wonders where Rich's anger would have led her if she had had a kind father, and a cruel mother. It is a question one wants to have her intelligence address. She looks hard and long at her own past, but she has not looked at it dispassionately, not yet. Political strategy insists that one must privilege one's own arguments; but intelligence sees no privileged suffering, and no privileged arguments. It sees only what Yeats called "the desolation of reality" — of all reality. Such a view is not congenial, of course, to social hopes, or to reforming temperaments, which do, it is not to be doubted, great good in the world.

"In the Wake of Home" asks, once again, the question John Stuart Mill put to himself in 1826:

> "Suppose that all your objects in life were realized; that all the changes in institutions and opinions which you are looking forward to could be completely effected at this very instant: would this be a great joy and happiness to you?" And an irrepressible self-consciousness distinctly answered, "No!" At this my heart sank within me: the whole foundation on which my life was constructed fell down. All my happiness was to have been found in the continual pursuit of this end. The end had ceased to charm, and how could there ever again be any interest in the means? I seemed to have nothing left to live for.

Rich writes of the woman for whom "home" has been unsatisfactory. Such a woman tries to believe that some homes are successful, that family burial plots and family albums reflect some long fidelity and love, "that once at least it was all in order / and nobody came to grief." Perhaps, she thinks, the time when things were all right was in the anthropological past:

> You imagine an alley   a little kingdom
> where the mother-tongue is spoken
> a village of shelters   woven
> or sewn of hides   in a long-ago way
>
> You imagine the people would all be there
> fathers mothers and children
> the ones you were promised would all be there
> eating arguing working
> trying to get on with life
> you imagine this used to be
> for everyone   everywhere

The woman for whom "home" has been unsatisfactory takes on, as a substitute family, all the homeless of the earth:

> What if I told you your home
> is this planet of warworn children
> women and children standing in line or milling
> endlessly calling each others' names
> What if I tell you, you are no different
> it's the family albums that lie —

So far the voice is the voice of political solidarity. But then the voice breaks:

> — will any of this comfort you
> and how should this comfort you?

The last section of "In the Wake of Home" is a reprise of the rest. Rich scans once again "the rush of purpose to make a life / worth living past abandonment," her own long effort:

> The child's soul carries on
> in the wake of home
> building a complicated house
> a tree-house without a tree
> finding places for everything
> the song the stray cat the skeleton
> The child's soul musters strength
> where the holes were torn
> but there are no miracles;
> even children become exhausted
> And how shall they comfort each other
> who have come young to grief?
> Who will number the grains of loss
> and what would comfort be?

This is the Freudian question, posed again; and it is Mill's question, too. The early wound can be patched but not healed; and no amount of political (or intellectual, or poetic, or pedagogical) action can restore primal loss. That is an ache one will carry to the grave, incurable by love or action.

"In the Wake of Home" is written in a voice usable by everyone who can enter the "you" of Rich's general address. The danger of this "collective," "usable" address is that it can become so general as to be stereotypical, as I think happens when Rich invokes those ancillary figures of childhood who supplemented our unsatisfactory parents:

> And what of the stern and faithful aunt
> the fierce grandmother   the anxious sister
> the good teacher   the one
> who stood at the crossing when you had to cross
> the women hired to love you

Rich is here as far away as possible from Lowell's idiosyncratic, not to say eccentric, family figures in *Life Studies*. Her aesthetic is stubbornly communal, "responsible," and "accountable" (her words in "North American Time"). Though she has irony, and knows personal exhaustion, she has no humor, and no historical skepticism about political effort. Her sternness, the sternness of a secular homilist, cannot allow humor; it is to Anne Sexton or Elizabeth Bishop that one looks for that. Rich's great virtue is her long struggle for authenticity. It has been endangered by self-pity and by writing for a cause, but she repeatedly has returned to self-scrutiny and acknowledged her findings. She will be remembered in literary history as one of the first American women to claim a public voice in lyric. And it is not only a political audience that she possesses (though she has that too). I have read, and not for political reasons, almost everything she has written. What Rich said of Emily Dickinson is true of herself; she has had to "retranslate her own unorthodox, subversive, sometimes volcanic propensities" into poetry. That is always an impossibly difficult translation, the more so since (as Rich says elsewhere, sounding like Wallace Stevens) "There is no 'the truth,' 'a truth' — truth is not one thing, or even a system. It is an increasing complexity." From a poet who believes this, all things are to be hoped.

II

American poets have, on the whole, a distrust of fantasy or fictions; they tend to give even invented stories a coat of circumstantial and gritty realism, full of aggressive details — identifiable, limiting, specified items. Jared Carter's well-written book *Work, for the Night is Coming* (1981) specifies down to the fingers the look of men doing make-work in the Depression:

> They had their shirts off,
> Down on their knees — old scars
> Flared in the sunlight, tattoos
> Glistened on their arms. Men
>
> With no teeth, with noses
> Turned and bent, fingers missing.

Without a break, the poem veers from the shirtless, scarred, tattooed, toothless, gap-fingered men to the equally carefully specified bricks:

> The bricks were tan-colored;
> Each had a picture on the bottom:
>
> A scene of ships, a name, a date.

The import subliminally conveyed by such fine brushwork is the metaphysical significance of the men (individuated) and the bricks (faithfully rendered, underside and all). Since the poem is about the *un*importance, in worldly terms, of the men and the bricks (the anonymous men, out of work, being employed by the government to give each anonymous brick in the street a quarter-turn and replace it), the aesthetic choice of multiple detail implies that poetry exists to rescue the otherwise-forgotten humble and despised things around us. Carter's is a poetry of a resolute middle distance, firmly of this world: between the dust under the earth and the dust of space there exists the place that the poem can illumine:

> What light reveals
> Here, in this room, is the grain of the bare oak floor
> And the shadows of leaves moving with the grain.

Carter trains a steady gaze on this middle ground of nature and architecture. But he is pulled away from it in two opposite directions — one more "realistic," the other more "symbolic." He tries, in some poems, to speak as a historical character, endowing his own present-day voice with "realistic" historical weight by speaking, say, as John Dillinger; in yet other poems, the apparently realistic surface proclaims itself, by open declaration, as in fact the façade of a symbol. The forced quality of Carter's conscientious "historical" realism is visible in Dillinger's speech:

> I stick in your craw, O Hoosier Commonwealth,
> Because I made it look easy.
> I cleaned out your tinhorn banks and arsenals,
>
> I bamboozled your redneck sheriffs and jailers —
> And yawned.

Precisely why the yawning and bamboozling and sticking in the Hoosier craw seem so unconvincing in the mouth of this "desperado" (as Carter's headnote calls Dillinger) is a little hard to say. We feel perhaps that Dillinger would not say "O Hoosier Commonwealth" like some latter-day Whitman; the poem consequently becomes an utterance without a credible speaker — like most, if not all, poems written recently in an "historic" voice.

The technique is now a favorite one among poets looking for a topic: you find an old military diary, or the journals of a pioneer, and you write about the Great Fire of '08, or the deaths in the Pass, or crossing the Divide, or some taxing endeavor. History — "true" history — seems truer to these poets than the imagination (whatever one may mean by that) or than the imprecise and unfinished chaos of their own lives. And history seems to offer a way to choose sides, to come down on the side of proven virtue, the side of daring or stoic fortitude:

> It took three days for me to bleed to death.
> People crowded around the shack
> Where they had me, but I never talked.
> If a man knows anything
> He ought to die with it in him.

Thus the hard-bitten words of Sam Bass ("train robber and outlaw," says Carter's headnote, but Bass is a hero in the poem nonetheless). Since Carter does not comment authorially on these tintypes of his, we take his silence for moral consent. (I should add that the present rage to imitate historical voices does not always mean approval of them: Hitler and his subordinates have also entered the gallery of reproduced voices in contemporary American poetry.)

There is a pathos of self-mistrust in the belief that history, unlike autobiography, is "objective," and that the lyric poet should subordinate himself to this "objectivity." An alternative doctrine of "objectivity" recommends subjecting oneself to the impersonal presence of nature — but however useful these disciplines may be, the poet has no recourse other than to hope that both history and nature will, while remaining themselves, become doubles of himself (as they did, for instance, in Lowell). "Objectivity" is a trap for the lyric; all lyrics are fatally subjective, even when most objective in appearance — especially when most objective in appearance.

It is entirely understandable that a poet should wish to escape the predictability of the single voice, the confines of the personal life. Carter's "symbolic" poems turn away from personal narrative, and make circumspect and lightly touched points about transiency or happiness:

> Then all turned dim —
> Grass holding to the seams, redbud scattered
>
> Across the cliff, dark pool of water
> Rimmed with broken stones, where rain, now
> Falling steadily, left no lasting pattern.

This passage (from Carter's title poem) is Japanese in its economy of parts and in its lending of the eye, via the redbud, from cliff to pool to stones. In this clarity of beauty and dissolution, Carter knows how to leave well enough alone.

Sometimes, though, Carter draws his allegorical morals too explicitly, as he does at the end of a gifted reminiscent poem about laborers, called "At the Sign-Painter's." Carter's belief in the power of detail to render a scene justifies itself fully here: he sees (he is a child at the time)

> tables caked and smeared
> And stacked with hundreds of bottles and jars leaking color
> And fragrance, coffee cans jammed with dried brushes,
>   skylight
> Peppered with dead flies . . .

The scene converges on the sign painters themselves:

> those solemn old men with skin
> Bleached and faded as their hair, white muslin caps
> Speckled with paint, knuckles and fingers faintly dotted —

This is finely done, as the old men bleach out almost into colorlessness, their skin and hair and muslin caps pale against their leaking colors. But the poem goes on to make its drift explicit; the sign painters become like poets, and the poem ends in praise of their signs as "words / Forming out of all that darkness, that huge disorder." Such an ending implies a distrust of the realist premise summoning up the muslin caps. The disjunction between words and things becomes complete in the last line of the poem, where the world is "disorder" and signs are the presumed light in the "darkness."

The earlier premise of the transparency of writing — that through those words "muslin caps" we see the things themselves — is dishonored as the poem becomes self-reflexive and self-conscious, as though "realism" could not take it as far as it wanted to go. The poem would have been better had it stayed within its descriptive faith, leaving the symbolic weight of sign painting to declare itself implicitly. As it is, the faith in description, in art as a miror, suddenly turns into a faith in art as a hieroglyph needing an explicit gloss. One cannot, with any aesthetic consistency of treatment, have it both ways.

Both Philip Levine and Adrienne Rich, too, distrust fantasy and invention, or perhaps I should say the look of fantasy and invention. (Since I am not in any position to know how much either is telling autobiographical truth, my point is that everything, even if invented, has, they feel, to be made to look "real.") Lyric of course must start as the self's concentration of itself into words; but (as Keats said about Shakespeare's sonnets) a poem can be full of fine things said unintentionally in the intensity of working out conceits. What Keats meant is that the process of composition, by its own interest, intensity, and demand, often draws the poet away from the original autobiographical or narcissistic impulse, even away from the original matter that concerned the poet. The most famous modern comment on this process was made by Yeats: he wanted in 1917 to write a poem on the Russian revolution, and took as his symbol the birth of a new era from the conjunction of Zeus and Leda. But as he wrote, "bird and lady" took over the poem, and the Russian revolution faded from his mind.

Nothing so wayward seems to happen to Rich and Levine. They are stern, even grim, ringmasters to their poems, and the hoops, once aligned at the beginning, remain in place in the poem for all subsequent jumps. One longs, reading Rich's *A Wild Patience Has Taken Me This Far* (1981), for the poem to take an unexpected byway, to reverse itself, to mock itself, to question its own premises, to allow itself, in short, some aesthetic independence. In Rich, the moral will is given a dominating role that squeezes the lifeblood out of the imagination. Rich deserves the rebuke of Schiller to Rousseau: "No doubt his serious character prevents him from falling into frivolity; but this seriousness does not allow him to rise to poetic play. Sometimes absorbed by passion, at others by abstractions, he seldom if ever reaches aesthetic freedom." The moral will is deplorably given to stereotypes. So Rich's mother-in-law appears as the stereotype of the discontented idle older woman who lives "on placebos / or Valium," and who appears incapable of understanding her son's strange and restless wife, whom she addresses in placating clichés:

A cut lemon scours the smell of fish away
You'll feel better when the children are in school

One might see these sentences as symbolic gestures of understanding, mutely, if awkwardly, helpful; but they do not satisfy Rich, who has an unholy desire to say the baldly exposed things she finds truer than deflected symbolic interchange:

Your son is dead
ten years. I am a lesbian,
my children are themselves.
Mother-in-law, before we part
shall we try again? Strange as I am,
strange as you are?

Though this seems even-handed (in the admission that they both are strange) the only true even-handedness, the only true imaginative play, would be for Rich to stop setting her own terms for family intercourse. She writes the script for what she wishes her mother-in-law would say to her (instead of the present vague "Tell me something"):

> *Tell me something*
> you say
> Not: What are you working on now, is there anyone special,
> how is the job
> do you mind coming back to an empty house
> what do you do on Sundays

But these casual, and even prying, questions ("Is there anyone special?") are not the common coin of our mothers' more formal era; why should older women have to come into our own far too intrusive "confessional" mode? "Do you mind coming back to an empty house?" and "What are you working on now?" could surely both be construed as cruel questions, at least by someone feeling unloved or unable to work. A poet who could conceive a topic other than autobiographically might have written the poem imagining *herself* as mother-in-law one day, when some daughter-in-law would find no easy way to address her inaccessible poet-mother-in-law, and vice versa.

I take up this instance only to raise the question of Rich's inflexibility of stance. Elsewhere in these new poems we meet, as before, the innocent victimized woman, the brutal sadistic cop: "he pushes her into the car / banging her head . . . he twists the flesh of her thigh / with his nails / . . . he sprays her / in her eyes with Mace / . . . she is charged / with trespass assault and battery." And, as if to affix a stamp of authenticity, "This is Boston 1979," says the poem — as if the only attestation to the genuineness of art is a newspaper dateline.

This sort of propaganda poetry generates a counterproductive aesthetic result: the reader, comically enough, becomes an instant partisan of policemen and mothers-in-law. It is for the sake of Rich's own good intentions — to show the gulf between women of different generations, to protest the helplessness of the wrongly arrested citizen — that I wish she would consider more closely her aesthetic means.

Stereotypes (the uncomprehending mother-in-law, the vicious cop) not only exist, but exist in sufficient numbers to have given rise to the stereotype; but they have no more place in art in their crude state than the grasping Jew or the drunken Irishman. Shylock, in Shakespeare's imagination, grows in interest and stature so greatly that he incriminates the anti-Semitism of Belmont: the dialectic of mutual violence (criminals to police, police to criminals — a system in which the brutalized police brutalize the innocent along with the guilty) is less present in Rich than it would be in a writer of more comprehensive imagination. In the sentimental black-and-white terms of these poems, men are exploiters, women helpless pawns who never chose their role:

> . . . when did we ever choose
> to see our bodies strung
> in bondage and crucifixion across the exhausted air
> when did we choose
> to be lynched on the queasy electric signs
> of midtown when did we choose
>
> to become the masturbator's fix

This, from the title poem, begs many questions of biology, history, economics, and social change. But even if we assume that evolutionary roles (and women's complicity in them) could be changed overnight, this passage assumes that in the present women no longer (by seeing themselves as bargainers with sex) have any complicity in how men see them; and it equally assumes that men are always the victimizers, never the victimized. Later in the poem Rich has a chance to reflect on Christ as victim, male though he was; but she chooses to think only of his mother in her iconic form as Pietà. There follows an unrelenting indictment of form in art as a mystification of violence. If, Rich argues, a Pietà (or a Passion) has been rendered beautiful, art has performed a disservice; a disguise has been imposed, by a pattern "powerful and pure," on the reality of blood and sacrifice:

> I can never romanticize language again
> never deny its power for disguise for mystification
> but the same could be said for music
> or any form created

> painted ceilings beaten gold worm-worn Pietàs
> reorganizing victimization frescoes translating
> violence into patterns so powerful and pure
> we continually fail to ask are they true for us.

There is, as anyone can see, something wrong with this argument. In her first book, Rich had, rather wrong-headedly, praised Bach for his austerity, asserting that "a too-compassionate art is half an art." Now the argument claims that a too-beautiful art is half an art. This position would admit as proper art only the tortured and twisted crucifixions of the more gruesome Spanish masters, not the hieratic crucifixions of, say, the Byzantine tradition. The adamantly realist aesthetic of the on-the-spot news photo ("This is Boston 1979"; "This is Judea 33 AD") leaves out a great deal (chiefly the mediation of reflective thought) in its fascination with transcription *tout court*.

The dangers of unmediated transcription are accompanied, in this volume, by the dangers of self-dramatization. To call a poem "Integrity," to begin it with the theatrical sentence "A wild patience has taken me this far," to add that the "anger and tenderness" breathing in oneself are "angels, not polarities" — this is to make oneself one's own heroine. There are dangers in the melodramatic enshrining of one's own capacities, of "these two hands":

> they have caught the baby leaping
> from between trembling legs
> and they have worked the vacuum aspirator
> and stroked the sweated temples

In a moment of distraction, Rich misreads a title, THE HISTORY OF WOMAN SUFFRAGE, as THE HISTORY OF HUMAN SUFFERING, and ratifies her mistake:

> OF HUMAN SUFFERING: borne,
> tended, soothed, cauterized,
> stanched, cleansed, absorbed, endured
> by women

The last line is incomplete: it should read "by women and men" — otherwise it is a lie. Whitman tending the Civil War dead; Keats tending his dying brother; Arthur Severn tending the dying Keats;

these and all their innumerable male counterparts rise to refute the
sort of history Rich here retells. Truth has its claims. And though
Rich adapts Whitman's line, "I am the man, I suffer'd, I was there,"
to her own "I say I am there," her great predecessor said it of the
sufferings of men and women alike, of runaway slaves, of the old
and of children, of the ill and the deformed. It is hard to believe in
an empathy reserved for one segment of humanity alone.

Rich's form in this volume is essentially the form of realist oratory.
She presses points, she pursues an argument, she cites instances, and
she pitches her voice above the conversational or narrative level —
not always, but more often than not. Conscience, as she says, hurls
questions at her; she hurls, in her turn, accusations at society. Her
fierce Utopian desires are at their best when most unsettled, as in a
poem which looks back to the days when she thought of the con-
stellation Orion as a king or brother. In "Orion" (1969) she had
written:

> Far back when I went zig-zagging
> through tamarack pastures
> you were my genius, you
> my cast-iron Viking, my helmed
> lion-heart king in prison.
> Years later now you're young
>
> my fierce half-brother, staring
> down from that simplified west.

Twelve years have passed, and Rich's perceptions have become more
rash and violent:

> Orion plunges like a drunken hunter
> over the Mohawk Trail   a parallelogram
> slashed with two cuts of steel
> . . . . .
> All the figures up there look violent to me
> as a pogrom on Christmas Eve in some old country

Then, in a turn unusual for Rich, the poem settles for the knowable
earth, both in its present state and in our attempts to know it and
ourselves:

> I want our own earth not the satellites, our
> world as it is   if not as it might be
> then as it is: male dominion,
>   gangrape, lynching, pogrom
> . . . . .
> The world as it is: not as her users boast
> damaged beyond reclamation by their using
> Ourselves as we are   in these painful motions
>
> of staying cognizant: some part of us always
> out beyond ourselves
> knowing   knowing   knowing

The painful motions of staying cognizant are, as they always have been, alive in Rich. Her impatience, her railing, her scorn, her brusqueness, her didacticism, have been in her poetry from the beginning. One of her earliest poems envied the fanatic who believes himself touched by God into truth and prophecy. She did not reprint, in her 1975 *Poems: Selected and New,* the 1951 sonnet "A Revivalist in Boston," but it has in it the germ of her own vocation, as she says of the obsessed preacher:

> Something loosed his tongue and drove him shouting
> Compulsion's not play-acted in a face,
> And he was telling us the way to grace.

The compulsion is real; but not everyone wants to be told a single mandatory way to grace. Inner lights differ, after all.

The line-form Rich uses in most of the new poems derives more from the older English alliterative line with a heavy pause in the middle than from the old seamless Norman pentameter. Rich's lines usually stop somewhere in the middle, halt, add a thought, pause at the end of the line, and take up the skein of thought anew as the line turns around. This halting progress suggests, interestingly enough, an intellectual process rather different from the one which produces Rich's intransigent diction and social cartoons; it may win out in the long run over more programmatic agitations. There are many more poems here than I can mention; all of them (and I do not except the poems putatively about "other people") strenuously pursue what it is to be Adrienne Rich in middle age — her investigations, her commitments, her memories, her outrage. I wish these poems were not so exclusively bound to that single realist vision.

Philip Levine is, though it may seem odd to say so, in the same camp as Rich, believing that realism is the only credible base for verse. (Even his allegories are painstakingly tailored to a realist origin, a realist frame, and a realist linear progression.) Often Levine seems to me simply a memoir-writer in prose who chops up his reminiscent paragraphs into short lines. Here he is, in his 1981 volume, *One for the Rose,* on the subject of his first suit, a brown double-breasted pin-stripe with wide lapels:

> Three times I wore it formally: first with red suspenders to a high school dance where no one danced except the chaperones, in a style that minimized the fear of gonorrhea . . . Then to a party to which almost no one came and those who did counted the minutes until the birthday cake with its armored frosting was cut and we could flee. And finally to the draft board where I stuffed it in a basket with my shoes, shirt, socks, and underclothes and was herded naked with the others past doctors half asleep and determined to find nothing.

An American Fifties' autobiography — is there any compelling reason why it should be called poetry? Certainly it is not notably improved by being cut into the short lines in which it appears in Levine's verse version:

> And finally to the draft board where
> I stuffed it in a basket with my shoes,
> shirt, socks, and underclothes and was
> herded naked, etc.

Levine's line breaks (unlike Williams's or Ammons's) are not particularly witty or arresting. Levine's notion of a poem is an anecdote with a flush of reflexive emotion gushing up at the end, like "that flush / of warmth that came with knowing / no one could be more ridiculous than I," with which Levine ends the tale of the brown suit. Levine does at times attempt poems of mythical or symbolic status, but he is not happy without his clenched toe-holds of circumstantial evidence. He is entirely aware of the division in himself between "items" on the one hand, and yearnings on the other; and he mocks his own notion (a still ineradicable one in him) that "poems" — *real* "poems" — are about love or the rose or the dew, and are sonnets "in fourteen rhyming lines."

He writes a somewhat petulant account of this affliction in a poem of thirteen adamantly unrhyming lines called "Genius." In it, he first enumerates a characteristic list of his sordidly and surrealistically realistic "items" ("An unpaid water bill, the rear license / of a dog that messed on your lawn,") and then says that with these images "a bright beginner could make a poem / in fourteen rhyming lines about the purity / of first love or the rose's many thorns." This opposition of the squalid and the rhapsodic seems to me, even in jest, a deficient aesthetic. It owes something to Stevens's notion of making poems while sitting on a dump, using language to deny the refuse that you see; but Stevens did not linger long in that crude view.

When Levine shades off into the various forms of his sentimental endings (togetherness, doom, death, the sad brown backs of peonies, what have you) it is easy to lose faith in his good sense. The writer who thinks up these disastrous endings has never, it seems, met the writer who writes the beginnings — or indeed who writes whole poems. We are either on the loading docks at the Mavis Nu-Icy Bottling Company (or at the airport where the porter is mopping up) — or we are at these stagy dénouements.

The airport poem, which has a convincing atmosphere at the beginning, ends with a passenger, now returning home, dreaming

> of tears which must always fall because water and salt
> were given us
> at birth to make what we could of them,
> and being what we are we chose love
> and having found it we lost it over and over.

This is only a step away from Lois Wyse or Rod McKuen. It combines the false lachrymose and the false vatic and the false unctuous all at once, trading on vague echoes of religion ("were given us at birth") and philosophy ("being what we are"). I prefer any day, even when he is disavowing it, the Levine of a vivid America —

the oily floors
of filling stations where our cars
surrendered their lives and we called
it quits and went on foot to phone
an indifferent brother for help.

I am not convinced that Levine's observations and reminiscences belong in lyric poems, since he seems so inept at what he thinks of as the obligatory hearts-and-flowers endings of "poems." Perhaps if he didn't think he was writing "poems" he could leave off his romantic organ tones and be truer to his stubborn earthiness. "All of me," he says with some truth, "[is] huddled in the one letter ["n"] that says / 'nothing' or 'nuts' or 'no one' / or 'nobody gives a shit.' But says it / with style."

Levine's moody shrugs of disavowal mask a dismay at being an intellectual; he seems to find it a disloyalty to his origins. His definition of style, in the poem I have been quoting, betrays the problem of his unintegrated nature (poet and truculent boy) better than I could do:

But says it
with style the way a studious boy learns
to talk while he smokes a cigarette or pick
his nose just when the cantor soars before
him into a heaven of meaningless words.

This — another failed ending — takes the easy way out by *calling* style picking your nose (in an affectation of indifference) while at the same time finding *real* style in the cantor's ascent (meaningless though it may be) into the heaven of words. The chip on Levine's shoulder has become the beam in the eye of his poetry. He believes, as a poet, only in what he can see and touch. That much is believably rendered; the rest — all those portions of the human world that we label philosophical, on phantasmagorical, or playful, or hypothetical, or contrafactual, or lawlessly paradoxical — escape him. They seem to escape Jared Carter and Adrienne Rich too, if we look at them whole. Probably they escape our solemnly sociological culture, for the most part; and a culture gets the poets whom it nurtures. The poets of a different persuasion — Merrill, Ammons, Nemerov, Ashbery, to name only four — are in the minority, and seem likely to remain so.

23

Charles Wright

Lashed to the syllable and noun,
                    the strict Armaggedon of the verb,
I lolled for 17 years
Above this bay with its antimacassars of foam
On the rocks, the white, triangular tears
        sailboats poke through the sea's spun sheet,
Houses like wads of paper dropped in the moss-clumps
        of the trees,
Fog in its dress whites at ease along the horizon,
Trying to get the description right.
                                If nothing else,
I showed me that what you see
                    both is and is not there,
The unseen bulking in from the edges of all things,
Changing the frame with its nothingness.
                    ("A Journal of True Confessions")

Restless and observant senses provide the words for the unseen in
Charles Wright, as they did for the religious poets Henry Vaughan
and Thomas Traherne, both (given that their subject was the unseen)
unnervingly visual writers. All ways of formulating the paradox of
the unseen felt in the seen falsify the experience of that paradox, in
which the reports of the senses are accompanied by some aura (not
felt by most of us, perhaps) of what is not there but makes its presence
felt — eternity, death, transcendence, extension, rhythm: the unseen
can go by many names. Visual reports in poetry rarely go unattended

by such an aura; but the creation of the aura in words puts a bizarre stress on the writer. Fog along the horizon could be described by any number of analogies; here, the aura lies in the complex personification, "Fog in its dress whites at ease," but the relaxed formality of that comparison does not exhaust the aura, since the disturbing note of a sheet of water "torn" by sails participates in it, as does the reassuring and slightly absurd metaphor of foam antimacassars on the rocks, and the disorderliness of the littering houses. If the aura of this landscape is the aura of a long habitation ("17 years"), then a sense of arbitrary military posting, relaxation in a parlor, seamless experience punctuated by painful rips, and a fate careless of its scatterings of habitation all combine in the "seen unseen" of the bay. Valéry draws a similar harbor with an aura of its own in "Le Cimetière Marin," but he takes care to give a logical air to his images, and would not combine antimacassars and dress whites in the same stanza. The freedom to follow the aura without respect to thematic consistency of imagery is a mark of modernist verse (Eliot's ragged claws cohabiting with bats with baby faces and so on). But this freedom is also peculiarly and necessarily the mark of poets whose concerns turn inward to the screen of contemplation, away from the sociopolitical world and the world of narrative. For such poets neither narrative (which confers a clue through the labyrinth of consciousness) nor sociopolitical reality (which confers contemporary "urgency") is an available option. They turn inward, and skyward: "There is no sickness of spirit like home-sickness / When what you are sick for / has never been seen or heard" ("A Journal of English Days").

The title of Wright's recent book, *Zone Journals,* suggests time modified by space. The time is the region around his fiftieth year; the zones traversed in the volume include California, Virginia, England, and Italy. There are other notable modern journal-volumes of the fiftieth year: Lowell's *Notebook,* Ammons's *Snow Poems,* Merrill's *Divine Comedies.* These books, far more quotidian (in the best sense) than Wright's bring into sharp relief the very different nature of Wright's journals — brooding, lyrical, painterly, contemplative. No marches on the Pentagon here, no historical emperors and tyrants, such as figure in Lowell; none of the sanguine dailiness or scientific curiosity of Ammons; none of the domestic comedy of Merrill (Wright mentions his wife and son only glancingly in his

verse). Wright's poetry reproduces the circling and deepening con-
centration that aims at either obliteration or transcendence, blankness
or mysticism. But Wright stops short of either polarity because he
remains bound to the materiality and the temporal rhythm of lan-
guage, whereas both Eastern nothingness and Western transcendence,
at their utmost point, renounce as meaningless both materiality and
time.

The very nature of poetry — a temporal art forever reformulated
— suggests that no object or scene of present contemplation can last
any longer than the moment of attention (a Keatsian point dwelt on
by contemporary poets other than Wright, such as Ashbery in "Self-
Portrait"). Seeking recourse against the evanescence of contempla-
tion, Wright turns to the abiding memory of his predecessors in
contemplation, who compose an aesthetic pantheon including Li Po,
Dante, Petrarch, Leonardo, and Sidney; Keats, Poe, and Dickinson;
Picasso, Rothko, and Pound. The exemplary quality of the life of the
artist, and the question of the function and survival of art, preoccupy
Wright in these journals.

At some moments, nothing seems more alive to Wright (as to
anyone responsive to the headiness of aesthetically formulated lan-
guage) than the voice of the great formulators, no matter how long
dead. Dante appears here and speaks live words to the poet (as he
had appeared to Eliot in the Quartets, as Joyce appears and speaks
to Heaney in *Station Island*). "The voice that cannot be stilled by
death or the passage of time": this is one definition, the most as-
suaging one for the poet, of poetry. There are lesser definitions,
though still powerful. "The presence that haunts the place it dwelt"
might be the definition that for Wright fits Dickinson and Poe, whose
houses in Amherst and Baltimore the poet is seen visiting, hearing
no voices but finding a place where "the spirits come and my skin
sings" ("Journal of the Year of the Ox," 23 May; henceforth quo-
tations from this long poem will be identified by date alone). But
presences themselves fade: Petrarch's full life ("the tapestries and
winter fires, / The long walks and solitude") comes down after a
half-millenium to "the one name and a rhyme scheme" (3 August).
What are artists, in fact, but dust? "Fulke Greville lies in his stone
boat in the church of St. Mary . . . / Hermetically sealed in stone"
("A Journal of English Days"). As if to emphasize equally both the
importance of the artist's birth and his eventual remoteness in time,
Wright keeps note of birthdays in his English journal:

"October 17th, Sir Philip dead / 397 years today."
"Cézanne . . . died there today / 77 years ago."
"Sunday, October 30th, Pound's birthday 98 years ago."

And he includes a "Short Riff for John Keats on his 188th Birthday."
Our ahistoric "eternal voices" are thereby placed firmly in lost time,
where Wright also places, as a past but unobliterable piece of Amer-
ican history, the defeated Cherokees of Virginia, who in 1806 ceded
their sacred burial lands to the invaders. Wright knows that as the
earlier inhabitants of his territory are, so will he be.

At the same time, history itself preserves not only the shame of
massacres and exploitation but also the exemplary lives of saints and
artists who confirm the poets' faith in the extension of imaginative
possibility, not only in themselves but in us. Cézanne "made us see
differently, where the hooks fit, and the eyes go," says Wright's
English journal; and the "Journal of True Confessions" carries even
further the example of what being imaginative means, by way of a
story about Leonardo told by Vasari. Presented with an unusual
lizard, Leonardo, dissatisfied even with the uncommon, proceeded to
embellish it:

> [He] made wings for it out of the skins
> Of other lizards,
>   and filled the wings with mercury
> Which caused them to wave and quiver
> Whenever the lizard moved.
>   He made eyes, a beard and two
>   horns
> In the same way, tamed it, and kept it in a large box
> To terrify his friends.
>   His games were the pure games of
>   children,
> Asking for nothing but artifice, beauty and fear.

Leonardo's coalescing of the biologically real lizard ("The real is only
the base. But it is the base," said Stevens), the scientifically invented
mercury-wings, the anthropomorphic beard, and the mythological
horns becomes a parable of aesthetic energy, delight, and imaginative
intimidation.

Artifice, beauty, and fear, all in the elaborate game of metered language, are the materials of Wright's art as well. Leonardo's humor and wit (the lizard, once unmasked as artifice, must have amused) are not present in Wright, whose liturgical solemnity is corrected only by the ironies of death and futility. But at least these powerful ironies are always present: the ultimate evanescence of everything, the round of the seasons making and breaking natural forms, the inevitable self-replaceability of language.

It is in his evocations of the seasons that Wright displays both the gorgeousness of his descriptive equipment and his gift for the pathetic fallacy. At the same time, these recurrent seasonal tableaux, by their ostentatious substitutiveness, call their own reliability into question. If on one day the clouds are "cloud banks enfrescoed," on another they are "Mannerist clouds," on another "cloud-tufts that print a black alphabet / along the hillsides." An infinite number of adjectival substitutions, one feels, are possible for the clouds; and although in another poet visual accuracy would be uppermost, in Wright the symbolic arbitrariness of the mind's play is at least as visible in such passages as any putative appearance of the clouds. For all Wright's debt to Hopkins and Pound and Stevens, he is less hard-edged in description than any of them, more dreamy. His beautiful landscapes are a symbolic means, rather than a visually specific end.

The landscapes consequently abound in the pathetic fallacy, which aims in Wright not at its classical unobtrusiveness but rather at an overt and unashamed pathos:

> The rain lying like loose bandages over the ground;
>
> ("English Journal")

> The rain, in its white disguise,
>   has nothing to say to the wind
> That carries it, whose shoulders
> It slips from giving no signal, aimlessly, one drop
> At a time, no word
> Or gesture to what has carried it all this way for nothing.
>
> ("Journal of the Year of the Ox")

These passages may be arbitrary when considered as visual descriptions of rain, but no longer seem purely contingent when considered emotionally as resonances of a suffusing inner life.

The realm of meditation which Wright has made his own has been often described in the vocabularies of theological, philosophical, and psychological speculation. Nonetheless, it does not feel, as we inhabit it, like a place called "mortal sin," or "proprioception," or "the superego." It feels by turns soft, or hard, or brilliant, or drifting, or pallid, or violent. In his discipleship to the Italian futurist poet Dino Campana, whose *Orphic Songs* he has translated, Wright learned a sensuous, rich, and seductive vocabulary for inner sensation. Here, for comparison, are some images from Campana, in Wright's translation: "The moon . . . rose up in a new red dress of coppery smoke . . . in solitary and smoky vapor over the barbaric clefts and slices." "The Telluric melody of the Falterona [mountain range]. Telluric waves. The last asterisk of the Falterona's song gets lost in the clouds." "A long veranda . . . has scribbled a many-colored comment with its arches." Like Wright, Campana was a pilgrim homesick for the eternal ("O pilgrim, O pilgrims who go out searching so seriously"), but his violence of color and utterance have been modulated in Wright into something which, while still sensual and ecstatic at once, is more mournful and less hallucinatory.

Journal-poems are for Wright a departure from his earlier crystalline short lyrics and exquisitely finished sequences aiming for inevitability of effect. A journal-poem allows for the chanciness of travel, and the form serves Wright especially well in the long poem "Journal of the Year of the Ox," the centerpiece of *Zone Journals*. The year 1985, covered by the journal, is crowned by some summer months spent in Italy (where Wright did his military service and studied as a Fulbright scholar). The glowing set piece in the center of the sequence describes the opulent Renaissance frescoes in the Schifanoia Palace of the dukes of Este in Ferrara. These frescoes are important to Wright because they so ideally represent the world as he conceives it — an ampler, more beautiful, and more ordered cosmos than that perceived by the senses alone (though including the testimony of the senses, and expressible only in sensuous forms).

The frescoes, covering the upper portion of the large palace hall, are divided into three levels: the highest level displays the triumphs of gods invoked as patrons of Ferrara (Ceres, Apollo, Venus, and so on); the middle level displays the signs of the zodiac and their graceful

attendant wardens or "deans" (so called because each figure is re-
sponsible for ten days of the month); and the lowest level displays
various civic and social activities of the duke of Este. All three levels
are of a striking beauty, but in each case the beauty is of a decorum
to match the subject: the gods move in a radiant anagogical atmos-
phere of light, glory, and throngs of divine attributes; the zodiacal
signs and their deans, by contrast, exist in a fixed and allegorical
emblematic simplicity of outline against a solid-colored background;
while the duke acts in a busy social sphere of Italian civic and
geographical detail. Here is Wright responding to the art that so
perfectly complies with his sense of life, allowing as it does not only
for ideational panoplies and seasonal symbols but also for the realities
of courtiers, horses, peasants, and grapevines:

> Through scenes of everyday life,
> Through the dark allegory of the soul
> > into the white light of eternity,
> The goddess burns in her golden car
> From month to month, season to season
> > high on the walls
> At the south edge of Ferrara: . . .
> Reality, symbol and ideal
> > tripartite and everlasting
> Under the bricked, Emilian sun.
> . . . . .
> Borso d'Este, Duke of Ferrara and Modena, on a spring day
> On horseback off to the hunt:
> > a dog noses a duck up from a pond,
> Peasants are pruning the vines back, and grafting new ones.
> . . . . .
> Such a narrow, meaningful strip
> > of arrows and snakes.
> Circles and purple robes, griffins and questing pilgrims:
> At the tip of the lion's tail, a courtier rips
> A haunch of venison with his teeth;
> At the lion's head,
> > someone sits in a brushed, celestial tree.
> . . . . .
> Up there, in the third realm,
> > light as though under water

Washes and folds and breaks in small waves
Over each month like sunrise:
                                        triumph after triumph
Of pure Abstraction and pure Word, a paradise of white
    cloth
And white reflections of cloth cross-currented over the cars
With golden wheels and gold leads,
                                        all Concept and finery:
Love with her long hair and swans in trace,
Cybele among the Corybants,
Apollo, Medusa's blood and Attis in expiation:
All caught in the tide of light,
                                        all burned in the same air.

                                        (25 July)

A hymn of such passion and distinction justifies both itself and the fresco it celebrates. The lavish iconography of the Renaissance, with its fertile mixture of classical, neo-Platonic, alchemical, astrological, and Christian elements, was after all a human invention:

Is this the progression of our lives
                or merely a comment on them?

Wright's question suggests that the extent to which such a fresco represents our lives, or is an analogy to them, is an earnest of what the fully rich life of consciousness can be, how it can place the "real" (the duke's daily round) in the light of cosmic orderly change (the zodiac) and suffuse it with the light of human motives idealized (Love, Wisdom, Art, Commerce). Here, it is not a political superstructure that gives significance to personal and civic activity; it is rather the superstructure of the sensuous, the affective, and the intellectual that gives meaning to the political.

Summer in Italy releases in Wright a flood of responsive exaltation. At home, in the winter, he is more likely to feel the downward pull of mortality; this is made gentle, in the following quotation, by the song-like mode that Wright allows his meditations to assume from time to time:

One, one and by one we all sift to a difference
And cry out if one of our branches snaps
                              or our bark is cut.
The winter sunlight scours us,
The winter wind is our comfort and consolation.
We settle into our ruin

One, one and by one as we slip from clear rags into feathery
    skin
Or juice-in-the-ground, pooled
And biding its time
                backwashed under the slick peach tree.
One, one and by one thrust up by the creek bank,
Huddled in spongy colonies,
                              longing to be listened to.

Here I am, here I am, we all say,

                                        I'm back,
Rustle and wave, chatter and spring
Up to the air, the sweet air.
Hardened around the woodpecker's hole, under his down,
We all slip into the landscape, one, one and by one.

Folk song and the blues hover here, as elsewhere, behind Wright's
poetry, and distinguish him from his most potent mentor, Pound. He
is the only one of the tribe of Pound not to feel Pound's aversion to
syntax, and Wright's poetry, in its play of syntactic subordination
and dominance, reclaims an elaborate intellectuality for the Poundian
image. In spite of their intellectuality, the poems remain finally sen-
suous objects in a pilgrim shrine. "Our lines," says Wright in "A
Journal of True Confessions," "seem such sad notes for the most
part, / Pinned like reliquaries and stop-gaps / to the cloth effigy of
some saint." Wright's Christian upbringing remains imaginatively
present to him, secreting a nacreous nostalgia for the vocabulary
that, had it only suited his century, would have best suited his sense
of things. Without the ability to assert, at least in any conventional
dogma, the intuitions of faith, he is left with the biological conser-
vation of matter as the only resurrection he can count on, "juice-in-
the-ground, pooled / And biding its time." In his zones of dislocation

— between the Christian and the biological, between Europe and America, and between the allegorical and the visible — Wright finds a scene of writing unique to himself and to his historical moment, and phrases it over and over in his musical and grieving half-lines, themselves the very rhythm of contemplative musing.

24

Amy Clampitt

Amy Clampitt writes in *The Kingfisher* (1983) a beautiful, taxing poetry. In it, thinking uncoils and coils again, embodying its perpetual argument with itself. The mind that composes these poems wants to have things out on the highest premises; refinement is as natural to it as breathing. Like all poetic minds it thinks in images, drawn here from an alluring variety of origins — nature (from Iowa to Greece), religion (from Athena to Christ), science (from geology to entomology), art (from manuscript illumination to Beethoven), and literature (from Homer to Hopkins). Clampitt is unselfconsciously allusive; the poems are rich with geographical and literary texture, a texture that supports and cushions and gives body to the meditation — sometimes eager, sometimes resentful — that forms the main strand of each poem.

Clampitt's poems, the best ones, are long, as complex ruminations have to be. Clampitt is a woman in middle age contemplating, in retrospect, a difficult Iowa childhood and adolescence, a move East and travels in Europe, and, in the present, love and friendship, periods of happiness on the Maine coast, and recently the death of parents. This life is very discreetly presented, in ways almost bare of anecdote; and yet the intensity of response in Clampitt's language suggests a life registered instant by painful (or exalted) instant. If Iowa has not had a poet before, it has one now.

Here is Clampitt's Iowa, its frightful weather (blizzards in winter and tornadoes in summer) vengefully and exactly drawn:

398

                          the air,
that rude nomad, still domineered,
without a shape it chose to keep,
oblivious of section lines, in winter
whisking its wolfish spittle to a froth
that turned whole townships into
one white wallow . . .

                          Against
the involuted tantrums of spring and summer —
sackfuls of ire, the frightful udder
of the dropped mammocumulus
become all mouth, a lamprey
swigging up whole farmsteads, suction
dislodging treetrunks like a rotten tooth —
luck and a cellarhole were all
a prairie dweller had to count on.

Such "description" has in another sense nothing to do with Iowa
weather and everything to do with the barbarism of farm life, unaes-
thetic and uncivilized, presenting itself to the child Clampitt as one
full of male wolfish spittle and female udders of ire, where one hid
out and hoped for the storm to pass without tumultuous dismem-
berment. Against all that inexplicable violence, there occurred, the
poem concedes, occasional moments of sweetness, experienced per-
haps in the undergrowth of a woodlot:

                    Deep in it, under
appletrees like figures in a ritual, violets
are thick, a blue cellarhole
of pure astonishment.
                    It is
the earliest memory. Before it,
I/you, whatever that conundrum may yet
prove to be, amounts to nothing.

That a poem beginning with the barbed-wire fencing in an Iowa
woodlot should end (after its savage weather report in the middle)
with the philosophical conundrum of identity, is surprising, but only
until one sees how typical such a proceeding is in Clampitt, where

one thing is sure to lead to another. I take "The Woodlot" as typical because it, like most Clampitt poems, seems at once unpredictable and conclusive, straying into an expressionist fantasy with the storms, distilling a purity of feeling with the violets, and raising fundamental questions of a metaphysical order in its conclusion.

All of these qualities are displayed in Clampitt's several bravura pieces in *The Kingfisher,* of which the most transfixing is her three-part piece "Triptych": its parts are called "Palm Sunday," "Good Friday," and "Easter Morning." These poems are about the human inclination to cruelty and to victimage, sometimes in the name of love, sometimes in the name of art, sometimes in the name of religion. In the first, Clampitt writes of "the gardener's imperative . . . to maim and hamper in the name of order," and, worse, of "the taste for rendering adorable / the torturer's implements." The art of the garden has its hidden mulch of entrails; ritual ("Sing, / my tongue, the glorious battle") requires the gallows.

There follows the heart of "Triptych," a Good Friday meditation on the mutual relation of victim and predator, phrased as a long, brilliant set piece on the Darwinian survival of the fittest (and death of the unfit), on our descent from vegetarian primates and our adoption of carnivorous habits, on the evolution of sacrificial ritual (the Passover) in order to institutionalize the victim in religion, and on women's peculiar addiction to masochistic piety. What I have said gives only the briefest sketch of what animates this poem: the vivid colors of the writing do justice to the exacerbated sensibility that here considers our evolved, but primitive, behaviors.

"Good Friday" begins with a picture of the chain of predators. Lions in Serengeti have killed a wildebeest; vultures gather to join the lions in their bloody feast; maggots follow the vultures; and they are all so innocent in their instinctive savagery that the restless mind of the poet asks, "How did a notion that killing was *wrong* ever arise in our evolutionary history?"

> Think of the Serengeti lions looking up,
> their bloody faces no more culpable
> than the acacia's claw on the horizon
> of those yellow plains: think with what
> concerted expertise the red-necked,

down-ruffed vultures take their turn,
how after them the feasting maggots
hone the flayed wildebeest's ribcage
clean as a crucifix — a thrift tricked out
in ribboned rags, that looks like waste —
and wonder what barbed whimper, what embryo
of compunction, first unsealed the long
compact with a limb-from-limb outrage.

Clampitt's momentum, once started — "Think . . . think" — takes over the whole poem, until at the end, when we are asked to think of Passover (and its extension in Good Friday), we see the victim convincing itself that it once had the glory of being the killer:

think, whatever
rueful thumbprint first laid the rubric
on the sacerdotal doorpost, whose victim,
knowing, died without a murmur,
how some fragment of what shudders,
lapped into that crumpled karma,
dreams that it was once a tiger.

This meditation on the lion and the lamb (with biblical roots in Isaiah and literary roots in Blake) is given a distinctively modern note not only by Clampitt's evolutionary perspective ("The spearpoint glitters in the gorge . . . at Olduvai") but chiefly by her lashing out at the immemorial appeal of victimage to women: "think how Good Friday / can . . . serve" as

an ampoule of gore, a mithridatic
ounce of horror — sops for the maudlin
tendency of women toward extremes
of stance, from virgin blank to harlot
to sanctimonious official mourner —
myrrh and smelling salts, baroque
placebos, erotic tableaux vivants
dedicated to the household martyr,
underwriting with her own ex votos
the evolving ordonnance of murder.

This shrapnel-burst of language flings out in rapid succession caricatures of the Virgin Mary, Mary Magdalen, and the Marys at the tomb of Jesus, and thence progresses to all the virgin martyrs and sanctimonious female saints, half erotic and half religious, all projections of the complicity of both men and women in the creation of the socially sanctioned "household martyr" who herself worships at these altars, contributing her mite to the sado-masochistic joint rite of marital brutality and submission. Refusing the easier conventional views of both religion and women, Clampitt lays bare the unpleasant satisfactions she perceives.

Finally, we come to "Easter Morning," the last poem of "Triptych": it has finished with those rites of the body, and rises in a bodiless purity. It gives up on all "the travesties that passed as faces" and on the "insistence / on the need for naming": poetry, like sex, is of the body. Instead, all is now "imageless," "grace":

> the unction
> of sheer nonexistence
> upwelling in this
> hyacinthine freshet
> of the unnamed
> the faceless

In its inhuman and disembodied stillness, "Easter Morning" tells us that while we are in the body we cannot escape the bloody ritual of Good Friday. There has not been for a long time a poem that sees us so helplessly in love with the rhythms of victimage and brutality, societal, sexual, and religious.

If Clampitt often leaves us exhausted by her headlong and pitiless investigations into the roots of behavior — which by themselves would be only horror stories if they were not mediated by her exquisite lines — she can also revive us by the way she can lose herself in the *visibilia* of the world. In a one-sentence fifty-line poem on fog, named, as a painting might be, "Marine Surface, Low Overcast," she takes on the specific task of the poet who wants to represent as many lusters and hues and transitions as a painter can. These old rivalries between painting and poetry renew themselves in each generation, and many notable recent poems (Bishop's "Poem," Lowell's poem "Marriage" on the Arnolfini portrait, and Ashbery's "Self-Portrait in a Convex Mirror," among others) have renewed questions about aesthetic illusion in painting and poetry.

Clampitt's debts in her descriptive poems — to Keats's luxurious lingerings, to Hopkins's Ruskinian notebooks and poems, and to Marianne Moore's scientific notations — are joyfully assumed. Among the interesting new things in Clampitt's descriptive vocabulary, visible in her "Marine Surface," is a whole lexicon of the diction of women. This lexicon (which did not particularly interest Dickinson, Moore, Bishop, or Plath) is a natural resource for Clampitt. It appears here in words relating to cloth, thread making, and fashion (herringbone, floss, déshabille, spun, fur, stuff, train, rumpling, suede, texture, nap, sheen, loom, fabric), in other words connected to household activities (churn, stir, solder, whip to a froth) and household objects (buttermilk, velouté, looking-glass, sheets, basin). Clampitt runs words through her fingers like someone spinning with a distaff: she looks at the fog and writes:

> Out of churned aureoles
> this buttermilk, this
> herringbone of albatross,
> floss of mercury,
> déshabille of spun
> aluminum, furred with a velouté
> of looking-glass,
>
> a stuff so single
> it might almost be lifted,
> folded over, crawled underneath
> or slid between . . .

(The two pieces of the quotation are typical of Clampitt's liking for mysteries of texture followed by the plain and simple; a knot of words draws us to the page, and the simplicities of statement then unsnarl the riddle. This is a very satisfying procedure, appeasing in turn the love of conundrum and the love of direct feeling.)

Clampitt's language changes like a change in weather. If a moment before it has been raining fabric and cooking, next it rains anatomy: the fog becomes

> a mane of lustre
> lithe as the slide
> of muscle in its
> sheath of skin,
>
> laminae of living tissue,
> mysteries of flex

The inventions of the natural world are so manifold, Clampitt makes us see, that only by responding to their prompting, in their marvelous changes, can "pure imagining" equal them. Testing the feasibility of invention in language against the changeableness of natural appearance is the tireless work of the writer who values the visual world (and many do not). But it is not just visual "rendering" (by whatever analogies) that makes visual poetry "work." Poetic diction has its own laws that must be satisfied along with the requirements of the eye. Poetic diction demands that words be linked one to the other so that it will seem that they "grew" there by natural affinity. The tried-and-true linkage by sound is most beautiful (as here in "albatross" and "floss") when there is some disproportion — as here in word length and semantic category — between the members, so that alliance does not resemble identity.

The best-known form of linkage is by those semantic alliances I have already mentioned — where "floss" calls up "spun" and "stuff." But there are many other connecting strategies — the flutter of a single vowel repeated, with different sounds, like the *u* in churned, aureoles, buttermilk, mercury, spun, aluminum, furred, velouté — a frequency of *u* far beyond its normal distribution in language. There are also linking patterns of length and shape (here, "buttermilk" and "herringbone" and "looking-glass"); patterns of syntax (*of*, X, *of* Y, *of* Z); and "deceiving" syntactic patterns of the same sort, where "folded over" *looks* like "crawled underneath," but the first is something one does *to* a blanket, while the second is something one does oneself with respect to the blanket; however identical the two phrases look, syntactically they derive from two different kernel sentences

("I folded over the blanket; I crawled underneath the blanket"), where the first verb is transitive, the second intransitive.

I mention all these details to show how, in Clampitt's poems, words, like neurons, put out branches to other words; the synapses thus formed are commands to the reader's processing apparatus to close the gap, to make the fleeting association. All of this linguistic patterning must accompany accurate visual rendition, or the poem will lack the fuel to make itself go. It is literally by such small electrical jumps that a poem refuels itself for the next inch of travel down the page. Clampitt has luxury to spare in this quarter, as she varies her fabric from sheer to thick, extending and diminishing her musical line, damasking her surface with pattern.

All this decorative change of pace is indispensable in poetry, in the sparest as well as in the most ornamented. But poems also, like essays, benefit from interesting thoughts; and like novels, they benefit from interesting incident. Clampitt's intellectuality and her curiosity about life give her the virtues of the essayist and observer of event. The two long elegies in memory of her parents admit us to precincts of deep feeling, intermingled with intense thought. The poem about her mothers's death — a long journey-poem called "A Procession at Candlemas" — traces the daughter's long bus ride back to the death-bed, a passage impelled not only by duty but by an atavistic instinct of mute ritual toward the shriveled mother, which Clampitt traces back to the Greek rites of Athena, the worship of the ancient wooden image on the Acropolis:

> An effigy
> in olive wood or pear wood, dank
> with the sweat of age, walled in the dark
> at Brauron, Argos, Samos . . .
>
> [the] wizened cult object, kept
> out of sight like the incontinent whimperer
> in the backstairs bedroom, where no child
>
> ever goes — to whom, year after year,
> the fair linen of the sacred peplos
> was brought in ceremonial procession.

Clampitt's elegy for her father ("a farmer / hacking at sourdock") is densely interwoven, in almost indescribable ways, with reflections on Beethoven. To enter a Clampitt poem is to enter a distinguished mind that then goes on an unpredictable journey of memory, association, musing, description, judgment, pining, correction, and imagining. Here, the reflections turn around the twin poles of the farmer's engagement with nature and the composer's engagement with art. What connects them is the revolutionary impulse ("*Freiheit!*") to correct the malevolence of the wild, to overturn the prison walls of the conventional, to "disrupt / the givens of existence." The father so rashly trusts his powers that on an ill-fated morning he sets out "to rid the fencerows of poison ivy." He digs up the ivy and burns it, but

> The well-meant holocaust became
> a mist of venom, sowing itself along
> the sculptured hollows of his overalls,
> braceleting wrists and collarbone —
> a mesh of blisters spreading to a shirt
> worn like a curse. For weeks
> he writhed inside it. Awful.

This shirt of Nessus is the retribution of the wild against the rebel. Earlier, the poem had rendered a pianist playing Beethoven's Opus 111 (from which the poem takes its name), "a downward wandering / disrupting every formal symmetry," "Beethoven ventilating, / with a sound he cannot hear, the cave-in / of recurring rage." These are the polemics of the twin arts of the farmer and the composer, the negative effort against the given. Later the poem gives us, for each, the positive effort toward the creation of a new sort of beauty.

First, the composer; he makes

> out of a humdrum squalor the levitations,
> the shakes and triplets, the *Adagio*
> *molto semplice e cantabile*, the Arietta
> a disintegrating surf of blossom
> opening along the keyboard, along the fencerows
> the astonishment of sweetness . . .

Next the farmer: far from home, he

> stopped the car
> to dig up by the roots a flower
> he'd never seen before — a kind
> of prickly poppy most likely, its luminousness
> wounding the blank plains like desire.
> He mentioned in a letter the disappointment
> of his having hoped it might transplant —

The father dies in a torment like the ivy-poisoning prolonged — "that awful dying, months-long, hunkered, / irascible," groaning "for someone / (because he didn't want to look / at anything) to take away the flowers." But a change occurs in the dying; and the last act of the poem speaks for a spirituality that aims at a total mastery of organic nature in the name of inner freedom:

> Beethoven, shut up with the four walls
> of his deafness, rehearsing the unhearable
> *semplice e cantabile*, somehow reconstituting
> the blister shirt of the intolerable
> into these shakes and triplets, a hurrying
> into flowering along the fencerows: dying,
> for my father, came to be like that
> finally — in its messages the levitation
> of serenity, as though the spirit might
> aspire, in its last act,
> to walk on air.

This, then, is the twinned plot of the poem. But Clampitt's own progress toward art makes a third plotline twined with her father's and Beethoven's lines of protest and creation. Clampitt grows up in a place where art seems both dead (in contrast to nature) and seductive (as the road away from the farm toward civilization and spirituality). Art comes from a place far from the plowshare's virgin soil, "a region where the dolorous stars / are fixed in glassy cerements of Art"; worse yet, in Iowa high art is tamed down to the bourgeois parlor and its adornments, an upright piano and suitable reproductions:

> an upright Steinway
> bought in Chicago; a chromo of a Hobbema
> tree-avenue, or of Millet's imagined peasant,
> the lark she listens to invisible, perhaps
> irrelevant: harpstrings and fripperies of air
> congealed into an object nailed against the wall,
> its sole ironic function (if it has any)
> to demonstrate that one, though he may
> grunt and sweat at work, is not a clod.

Thinned out and domesticated in the poverty of Midwestern "culture," Beethoven, no longer a titanic force, is only a name attached to recital pieces:

> here,
> his labor merely shimmers — a deracinated
> album leaf, a bagatelle . . .

But what room had the hard-pressed prairie for the nostalgias of culture? Clampitt remembers grandparents' and parents' tales:

> there's
> no dwelling on the sweet past here,
> there being no past to speak of
> other than the setbacks: typhoid
> in the wells, half the first settlers
> dead of it before a year was out;
> diphtheria and scarlet fever
> every winter; drought; the Depression,
> a mortgage on the mortgage . . .

These are twice-told tales, a child's puzzling through the language of the past: what could it mean "a mortgage on the mortgage," and incomprehensible epics of unheard-of diseases? But the troubles were all instanced as a defense: "What time had we for culture; what use was it to us?" ask the ranks of farmers.

But the impressionable child, taken to hear the pianist on "the Lyceum circuit," hears art as an irresistible counterforce to fatigue, depression, and sullied hands:

                              High art
as a susurrus, the silk and perfume
of unsullied hands. Those hands! —
driving the impressionable wild with anguish
for another life entirely: the Lyceum circuit,
the doomed diving bell of Art.

We see this impressionable child again in the superb poem "Imago":
there she is "the shirker propped / above her book" reading about
Andersen's little mermaid, who pays for disliking *her* original home
"by treading, at every step she takes, / on a parterre of tomahawks."
The child in the farmhouse feels "A thirst for something definite so
dense / it feels like drowning." It is the thirst for outline and form,
though she does not yet know that aesthetic hunger by name. She
tries to write, but her efforts are disapproved of. Finally, "either /
fed up with or starved out of / her native sloughs" she "trundle[s]
her / dismantled sensibility elsewhere." We see her, too, in the poem
called "Meridian," appalled by her mother's daily life: the child feels

apathy at the meridian, the noon
of absolute boredom : flies
crooning black lullabies in the kitchen,
milk-soured crocks, cream separator
still unwashed : what is there to life
but chores and more chores, dishwater,
fatigue, unwanted children . . .

This girl reading in the parlor, watching in the kitchen, preparing for
the writer's immersion in the diving bell of art, becomes the woman
who wonders, in "Imago," what it would have been like to live a
purely biological life, to have succumbed to those hormones that
dictate emerging from one's chrysalis, turning briefly into that sex-
ually alit female to whom males helplessly advance, then copulating
and dropping one's litter before dying. In the most hypnotic piece of
writing in this strenuously written book, Amy Clampitt looks with
a frightening intensity at the sexual evolution of the biological female.
Her symbol for this purpose is the imago of the luna moth emerging
from its chrysalis with all its terrifying lurid sexual apparatus of
specialized evolution. The moth in its timing obeys the inexorable
water clock, the clepsydra, of the biological imperative:

the terrible clepsydra of becoming
distils its drop : a luna moth, the emblem
of the born-again, furred like an orchid
behind the ferned antennae, a totem-
garden of lascivious pheromones,

hangs, its glimmering streamers
pierced by the dripstone burin of the eons
with the predatory stare out of the burrow,
those same eyeholes. Imago
of unfathomable evolvings, living
only to copulate and drop its litter,
does it know what it is, what it has been,
what it may or must become?

There is a relentlessness in this passage that shows Clampitt going
very deep in the diving bell, deeper than ornament, down to the
riddle of biology and consciousness as they contend in human desire.
The eyeholes that "stare out of the burrow" as man evolves out of
the bestial lair are the two masks of consciousness, tragedy and
comedy, that had appeared earlier in the poem:

a pair of masks whose look, at even
this remove, could drill through bone:
the tragic howl, the comic rictus,
eyeholes that stare out of the crypt.

Passages like the one on the luna moth, where every stroke counts,
where a phrase like "the dripstone burin of the eons" pierces before
it is understood, guarantee themselves by their rich suggestiveness
(even without their echoing connections to other parts of the poem).
The brain of the writer, in these moments, is being ransacked: storage
places are thrown open, experiences rummaged through, to find the
word or image that will suit — in meaning, in shape, in sound. The
brain finds "clepsydra" from history, the moth-as-soul from Psyche's
myth; then the zoological and botanical gardens of the mind cast up
rapidly "fur" and "fern," "orchid" and "antennae"; anthropology
throws in the totem, the laboratory contributes the pheromones, the
studio the burin, architecture the dripstone, geology the eons; and
the old vocabulary of sexual allure rises to burnish the lines with

"lascivious," "glimmering," and "predatory." Behind it all hangs the visual picture of the intricately colored patterning of the female luna moth seen in her moment of emergence.

As a poem about the adolescence of the female, "Imago," with its look at the dreamy girl reading fairy tales leading to its violent stare at sexuality, marks a new stage — speculative, brooding, and powerful — in the poetic mirroring of female experience. Women's training and reading have historically been very narrow, and the metaphors that came naturally to male writers — from physical activity, government, theology, the arts — were not so likely to spring to the mind of women who had never assumed an active role in the world and who had never been introduced to the varied disciplines of learning. One knew that in time women's privation, at least in learning, would disappear (it has not yet disappeared in the active life). In Clampitt's poetry we see a mind vigorously reaching for whatever it needs by way of illustrative detail, and finding it easily, in abundance. To join such unimpeded freedom of movement is exhilarating.

In one of her poems about Greece, Clampitt speaks of being "whelmed / into vertigo by gulfs spanned for a moment / by so mere a thread," the gulfs in question being those of space and time, spanned by language and memory. Clampitt's poems, especially those reaching backward in geological, historical, or personal time, and those reaching out in space to Greece, to England, to Italy, cause some of that same vertigo by their far-cast associations. A mere thread of language spanning the gulfs of the mind and the world — it is a definition of poetry that suits many of the fifty poems gathered in *The Kingfisher*. There are of course slighter poems in the volume — occasional poems, minor descriptions, some poems where feeling is in uneasy balance. But for me Clampitt is the poet of the poems where her powers are at full stretch, exerting themselves to be adequate to "the transparent strata / of experience, the increment of years."

Though Clampitt published two small books before *The Kingfisher* (*Multitudes, Multitudes,* 1973; *The Isthmus,* 1981), the advance in this collection over those preceding it is dumbfounding. When we read a book of American poems by a contemporary writer, we often forget that America will be remembered, when we are all dead, by the memorials of its culture; in them others will find out what we felt at what we saw (as Stevens put it). Embodying their century, the minds that produce cultural objects are intellects "engaged in the hazardous / redefinition of structures / no one has yet looked at," as Clampitt says in "Beach Glass." A century from now, this volume will still offer a rare window into a rare mind, it will still offer beautiful objects of delectation; but it will have taken on as well the documentary value of what, in the twentieth century, made up the stuff of culture. And later yet, when (if man still exists) its cultural terminology is obsolescent and its social patterns extinct, it will, I think, still be read for its triumph over the resistance of language, the reason why poetry lasts.

25

Dave Smith

Dave Smith originally seemed to me a regional Southern writer. He grew up in Virginia, graduated from the University of Virginia, and wrote memorable poems about the oystermen of Chesapeake Bay. He was influenced by Faulkner and Robert Penn Warren. But even in his first book, *The Fisherman's Whore* (1974), there were nonregional poems. His second book, *Cumberland Station* (1977) — for which he received an award from the American Academy and Institute of Arts and Letters — though it continued the regional strain and became a family chronicle as well, contained some poems aiming in an allegorical direction, which I judged at the time too bald. As if to show that the poet knows his own direction better than the critic, Smith emerges in his third volume, *Goshawk, Antelope* (1980), as a distinguished allegorist of human experience. The rich local color of the Virginia and Maryland sketches has been joined by local details from Utah and a desolate Wyoming. The family (Smith's wife and three children, and shadowy parents and grandparents) continue to play a large part in the story. But these particularities are now subdued to looming shapes of universal fate and emotion.

Smith is torrential, impatient, exasperated. His language is theatrical, even melodramatic. His earlier masters are Hopkins, Whitman, Crane, and Thomas — poets whose temperatures, rarely temperate, become volcanic or icy at will. The "peaceable and healthy spirit" that Keats hoped to attain eludes such poets. They are outraged in pain or felled by ecstasy; at their most moderate, they are crucified by hope. It might be premature to expect from Smith, at the age of thirty-seven, a calmer eye or a more ironic tone. He is an openhanded spender of language, fixing most characteristically on those moments of horror or excitement or rapture which in life demand no holding back, no irony, no mediating reflection. However, no poem can exist without mediation, and Smith's most estranged moments come in his consciousness of the gap between being and language. In a typical Smith poem (not, perhaps for that reason, necessarily one of the best), an extreme situation plunges us into extremity: a child is bitten in the face by a dog; he is taken to the hospital; eventually, he dies. Before he dies, he relives the terror of the dog's attack:

> Under tubing that hangs and shines like gravity's spillage
> your son opens his mouth to scream off the dog
> suddenly looming at him five floors up, a raw
> hole oozing under his eye.
>   . . . You are murderous
> when you see in his collapsed face the human image, meaty,
> and seeping so when you think of this later it seems
> the instant of no time, a dead-stopped
> frieze that is everything.

To make of any instant "a dead-stopped frieze that is everything" is Smith's Keatsian ambition, phrased here with un-Keatsian brutality. In the crisis of death, the Bible does not help ("you pick up the pebbly Gideon like your father's, finger-reading the words"), the doctor cannot help, and art cannot help, either:

> I must tell you there is no way for clinician or artist
> to draw from that room the awful pus of death.

The fact that art — like religion, like medicine in this case — makes nothing happen sets Smith at teeth-grinding odds with his own vocation. Even the conceiving of a new child by the parents will not change the savaging of this one. Every day, Smith says, we read in the paper of another child killed:

>   Headlines
> in the morning paper are early set in sterile caps
> above home snapshots.

The counters that Smith opposes to "the wreckage of promise" are passion and hope — explicitly named but as explicitly doubted:

"Passion, if you once believe in it, is a way of hope." Whether life is best considered in the agonized terms of its worst events is the question raised, often by Smith himself, throughout this book.

Keats, too, thought in terms of giant agonies, but he also said, less theatrically and more tellingly, that "but to think is to be full of sorrow." In Smith's best moments, the lurid highlighting of storm is abandoned for the light of day, and he, like Keats, thinks of the poet's chief burden as consciousness, face to face with the unconscious earth. As you wake in the morning, Smith says:

> The world is full,
> you are of this fullness, only you are
> what the world cannot remember in first
> raw light and nakedness.

The love of the world which comes "raking you with passion" is not reciprocated:

> Why have you lived
> if not for this love? Only it waits in a cry
> of elementals nothing explains, nothing,
> and does not seem to understand you.

Smith's blank denial of the Wordsworthian faith that "the clouds were touched, / And in their silent faces [I could] read / Unutterable love" stands at the core of his work; wedded to the shapes and sounds of the earth, which he feels reverberate in him, he fears that all this rewording may be futile. When he suspects a final illegibility and illiteracy in nature, he feels rage.

Smith retells again and again a primal deception:

> Lying awake in this moonless room
> I think of stars like a crowd of pinched seeds
> falling into the apples, sending little brass hooks
> shooting through the white pulp.

> By the time the apple's brown ache comes who will know
> the stars have been stolen, who always rose
> like fathers, in dignity, over the globes in the grass?

This is the Smith of the controlled voice, of the confident metaphor. The poem, "Between the Moon and the Sun," ends less well, in a reminiscence of "Dover Beach" and "The Waste Land" combined, as Smith's anger gets the upper hand:

> Come to the window and I will show the world without
> dreams, starless, mouthing itself, and the apples
>
> growing black with nothing to tell us. Nothing.

The obverse of this nullity, Smith would say, is passion and hope. Oddly, poetry is as unaccommodating to positive assertion as it is to positive negation: either will immediately bring a poem to an end. A poem can prolong itself, can continue its existence, only through doubling back, over and over, as Coleridge said, on its own logic. Prolongations in Smith often take the form of slow alterations of consciousness, transformations of memory, unrollings of narrative, histories of grief. Once the speaker (or his surrogate) becomes wordless, after emotion has exhausted itself or has been transmuted into an animal cry or a vegetable motion, the poem ends.

Many of Smith's poems assume the form of a passage from innocence to experience. Innocence is enunciable, but experience falls silent. An implicit paradox emerges: when the last innocence vanishes, there will be no more words. It is as if the poet had a stake in remaining to some degree the boy he was, the adolescent the boy became, the young man the adolescent became; if he does not, he will no longer be able to write. It is a peculiarly Romantic conviction that adulthood is inimical to expression and spontaneity, and no soil has been more fertile for it than a young country like America. Smith, who is all care in expression, can scarcely be said to hold this conviction consciously, yet the poems again and again suggest it.

I will instance one very beautiful poem about adolescent love, "Hawktree." A boy, in spring, falls in love with a girl whose name he will not even whisper in the profane assemblies of youth. He sees her standing under a pine tree: "He watched her burn like a candle in the cathedral of needles." Unable to make the slightest move toward her, he waits, certain of the claim he feels upon her, linked as they are, he is sure, by nature. The girl disregards him, and joins the society of young men whose "trucks rooted along the road of colored pleasures." In an Ovidian metamorphosis, the young man himself becomes a pine tree. The extraordinary ending is read almost literally, as an account of the warping of a life by the first failure in love:

> Slowly he knew his arms furred
> with a fragrant green darkness . . .
> Already
> he felt himself sway a little
> in the desert wind, in the wordless
> emptied gnarling he had become.

With experience, desire turns wordless and emptied; poetry is innocence preserved.

No poet has ever wanted things more violently, even as a child. There is a Christmas when, "with a war raging and a father gone," the child gets from his mother the one thing he has longed for: a white holster for his gun, "the leather stiff and white, the red tears of glass, the black fake fur in tufts making a pony's shape." An almost disordered happiness follows:

> All day I will draw guns,
> deep in a child's joy,
> shaking the cedar like a bomb.
> *Happy,* I will shoot at her, *happy,*
> until at last the words bang
> from her mouth as she holds me,
> saying *yes, yes, yes.*

This is an unnerving poetry, willing to go so far into demand, and equally far into denial. It is, in the literal sense, unbalanced; figuratively, it often loses its balance. Its shameless evoking of its ultimate terms, love and death, dares us to deny our own obsession with them.

The goshawk and antelope of Smith's title move through the book — the hawk predatory, paternal, talons stretched out in desire; the antelope mild, fleet, free. In the title poem, a goshawk plunges, "as shapeless as obsession," while the poet, imagining himself into the antelope, tries to "buck off whatever the air had sent down." The "aching wingless shoulders of the antelope" become linked with a

mother's pain, obliquely caused by the father. The poet, fleeing like
the antelope "from what was unseen and there, like the red print of
a hand about to fall," wants to

> see for once what had died
> out of my life but would never leave or
> come back as it had been —
>
> like the slow growth of an antelope's legs into freedom
> and away from desire's black whirling dream.

Looking for what was where it used to be is the occupation of poets.
At the end of this search, the poet longs for

> the flare
> of absence that came, had fallen into
>
> the accusing goshawk face of my father in that dark room
> where I walked too late, where the glowing fur-tufts
> of candle shadows drift on her face and his
>
> and what was held has become, suddenly, lost like breath.

The poems come to an end breathless or wordless after their
sometimes obscure scenarios of guilt or terror. The obscurity lies not
only in the telling (Smith's Faulknerian convolution of discourse is
not always justified, though it is responsible for some of his most
intense effects) but also in the origin of the events in life, which leaves
so little behind. Smith indentures himself, with an almost disabling
intensity, to the entire past: except for us, as Stevens says, the total
past felt nothing when destroyed, and Smith aims, with his tenacious
memory, at an enormous work of restoration. Not only is his own
past to be restored but also the past of landscape and the past of
history. Yet this multiplicity in Smith is at war with his ethical
strictness. He wishes to mark out life into what Hopkins called black,
white, right, wrong. Relentlessly, he divides the world: this lives, this
dies, as his plum tree ("In the Yard, Late Summer") says. Love and
death are a single message, as "Messenger," the first poem in *Gos-
hawk, Antelope,* tells us. Against these simplicities comes the wing-
beat of Smith's words:

Note by note by note we arrange what's known for song
while trees tower over us, spreading a storied gray-
gold that keeps what must be found, lost, and found.

"Trying to understand" is one force that moves these poems, and
Smith hurls himself repeatedly against recalcitrant mysteries. When
he abandons direct battering, he takes to circuitous and dogged
routes. Manifestation (the morning light, the look of the world) is
what he is given; understanding and emotion are what he demands.
The two possibilities he awaits are revelation (when manifestation
meets understanding) and disgust (when it does not). Revelation,
beautiful in the moments when it comes as pure harmonic notes
("like moments so rare nothing dies"), is not always kindly. As we
watch the plum tree drop "its thousand planets of sweet flesh" in
the late summer wind, we wait for the end:

            Knowing ourselves
    wingless and bestial, we wait
    for the sun to blow out,
    for the return of that first
    morning of pink blossoms
    when we saw the dark stains
    of our feet printing
    what we were on that
    dew-bed of the world.
    The tree, too, waits
    in its old unraveling
    toward a naked silence,
    its language wild and shocked.

Smith asks our complicity in his lending of language to the tree; if
we remember "that dew-bed of the world" — and we have no better
metaphors for youth than those drawn from spring — then we may
offer our language to the tree in reciprocity, as a metaphor for its
unravelling.

Smith remembers Rilke in wishing to name the things of the earth,
and he remembers Wordsworth in wanting to feel the joy and grief
of the earth's seasons. At the close of the poem "Night, Our Hands
Parting the Blue Air," all the elements in Smith ride in balance:

Each sound of the cooling earth wants to become
our speech. We hear, we can hardly bear
not to leap up in joy and tears,
but there is only darkness and no one
sliding out of leaves where the world monstrously

gargles its syllables without meaning until we try,
driven red-eyed beyond sleep, to pray.
Calling the names of parents
who were the future and are,
now, the past, we want to fill
the dark with our hands . . .

We sink into ourselves as we invent
someone who loves us. He climbs the hill
where the gold has trickled deep blue.
Light from our kitchen falls into his eyes.
Night, giver of morning, comes on, swirling over us.

Here desire for speech, emotion, love, and a home meets death, illusion, insomnia, syllables without meaning, deliquescence. Implicit in the closing line is a prayer of hope: "Descend, O Night, Giver of Morning." And an implicit knell of doom lies in the declarative kernel of the same line: "Night comes on, swirling over us."

At his most truthful, Smith undoes his hopes almost as he utters them. When desire and hope overmaster vision, he risks sentimentality; when the hurling and the battering dominate reflection, he risks noisiness; when earnestness impels him, he risks explicitness. In syntactic momentum and surcharge of vocabulary, he risks excess; in ethical uprightness, he risks puritanism. He is Hebraic rather than Hellenic; flexibility and moderation are as foreign to his dour apocalypses as to his impelled communions. There are words that one would like, on first impulse, to forbid him: "love," "huge," "hungry," "joy," "fear," "hard," "memory," "kill," "dream," "longing," "boiling," "blood," "lost," "promise," "hope," "scream," "terror," "black," "naked," "dark," "wordless." He disarms our wish to censor his vocabulary by announcing that he knows his own repetitions — sounding occasionally too much like a Rilke he does not resemble:

We walk and find there are only a few words
we want to say: water, root, light, and love . . .

From time to time, someone calls out but we know
only the words whispered from the wall of leaves:
water, root, light, and love.

Instead of avoiding those worn or too evident words, Smith will
take them up, fling them on the page, force us to digest them anew
in his contexts, trusting that they will take on a fresh meaning, or a
reinforcement of their old meaning. I prefer the poems in which he
least depends on those words, and is least extravagant in noise. As
a final example of Smith at his best, I will take "Rain Forest," where
we find his most explicit account of how it seems that poetry happens
within him. He renders this mysterious process in the first person
plural, as if it happened within all of us, as, by memory and insight
and ancestral provocation, we discovered our identity. In the rain
forest (which is Smith's version of Platonic preexistence):

> We are the dream,
> before we know better, of an old grotesque
> stonecutter . . .
> We have entered the huge inward drift behind
> his eyes and wait to become ourselves. We stare
> through limpid eyes into the vapor-lit past
> where breath, wordlessly, like a near river
> seams up, seams in and out and around darkness . . .
> [A] trunk rises thick and black as a monument
> that rings when struck. Here the hiking path,
> a crease, stops, then spirals around into stumps.

This still, occluded landscape writing shows Smith at his most pow-
erful — brooding, recollected, withdrawn. The demiurge-stonecutter
begins his work on us as, in silence, we recall our origins:

> We stand silent
> in the earliest air remembered, hearing at last
> the distant and precise taps of the mallet
> until our clothes, as if rotted, fall away
> and the feckless light fixes us on the column
> of our spines.

The poem becomes a meditation on Keats's urn and Yeats's dancer as we, under the hands of the stonecutter, become statuary, marble men and maidens in inhuman perpetual motion:

> Without warning, we begin to dance,
> a bird cries, and another. Our feet seem to spark
> on the hard dirt as we go round the black tree
> and for no reason we know we see ourselves
> throwing our heads back to laugh, our gums
> and teeth shiny as cut wood, our eyes marbled,
> straining to see where it comes from, that
> hoarse rasp of joy, that clapping of hands
> before which we may not speak or sing or ever stop.

Smith does not evade the inhuman aspect of art (the marbled eyes, the wooden gums) or its ritual circling around a black fetish. But we seem to require the fertility of the process — that breath seaming up, seaming in and out — and we require as well the product: that hoarse rasp of joy, that clapping of hands, that dance. Before it appeared, we could not speak or sing; like Keats's fair youth, neither can we now stop, or leave our dance.

There are other beauties in "Rain Forest" — our relation to the old stonecutter (one of Smith's angry patriarchs), the soft setting of the scene ("the green mothering of moss knits shadow and light"), the proleptic phrasing ("the afternoon a long glowing stalk of marble"), the theoretical and Rilkean challenge: "there are only a few words we want to say." One can scarcely ask more of a poem than what Smith here offers us. On the plane of life, "Rain Forest" says something about ancestors, identity, and creation; on the plane of imagination, it takes us into the chiaroscuro of its green "elaborate grotto"; on the plane of mythology, it links itself to Plato; on the plane of literature, it looks back to Wordsworth and Keats; on the plane of aesthetics, it announces a theoretical challenge to Keatsian stillness; on the plane of ethics, it allows the coexistence of the ugly and the lovely in its universe. It glitters, to borrow one of Smith's best lines, with the mind's assertive flow.

Smith's weight is unenlivened by humor, or self-mockery, or an easy urbanity; he is solemn, harsh, driven, obdurate, hungry for some guarantees — which he wants to create as much as to experience — of promises kept, love exchanged, hope confirmed. His bitter self-taste (as he names it from Hopkins) sits ill with his domestic yearnings. Since he is an accomplished watcher of inner states, he will write a changing poetry. He has come very far from his first, raw poems published in small chapbooks; the measure of the distance traveled is in part the measure of the talent.

26

Frank Bidart

In the harrowing poems of Frank Bidart's volume *The Sacrifice* (1983), it is difficult to distinguish the cries of the saint from the shrieks of the damned. The forms that Bidart used earlier in *Golden State* (1973) and *The Book of the Body* (1977) — the dramatic monologue, the case history, and an eccentric punctuation — recur here, but they are put to new uses in the six poems that make up the book. In Bidart's strange combination of excruciating confession and clinical detachment, the book considers the war to the death between mental (or spiritual or aesthetic) life and the life of the body (sexual, appetitive, seductive). The desires of the Christian saints to mortify the flesh, to refuse food and sexual experience, and to abjure society, become here only special instances of the universal asceticism demanded, at least to some extent, of everyone who finds himself living the life of the mind. The grim words of St. Paul, that the spirit lusts against the flesh, and the flesh against the spirit, concern the same struggle that appears here centrally placed in a poem by Catullus, *Odi et amo*. Bidart treats the poem as a rebuttal; an opponent says, "Why do you hate the object of desire so much?" and the poet answers,

> I hate *and* love. Ignorant fish, who even
> wants the fly while writhing.

The writhing of this book between desire and disgust reappears in the elegy on a friend who died of cancer. The friend has vacillated in life between grasping at experience and repudiating it:

alive, you abruptly needed
not to answer the phone for days: ballet tickets
unused: awake all night: pacing
the apartment: untouchable: chain smoking.

At death, offered the cup of "Forgetfulness," does the divided soul
reach for it gratefully? The poem decides not: to become pure spirit,
solitary, is not within human capacity. On the contrary, souls at the
general Resurrection, given another chance at life, would choose a
life of the body more social and more human than before: "*The
phone is plugged in, please call, / I will answer it.*" This fantasy is
guaranteed by the final act of the dying friend, who staves off death
in order to see her sister once more and mend the relationship, asking,

DO YOU FORGIVE ME?
Then: WILL YOU MISS ME?

— the voice reduced to the barest of exchanges.
 The soul's need to acknowledge and enter into the social and
domestic world, and the absolute irreconcilability of that world with
the mental world — solitary, estranged, fierce, concentrated — brings
Bidart's chief protagonists toward either suicide or madness. In the
long poem that begins this book (and that won the *Paris Review*
prize in 1982), "The War of Vaslav Nijinsky," Nijinsky's madness
moves within a double guilt, the personal guilt felt by the dancer
toward his family, whom he attempts to kill, and the common or
collective guilt for which the artist is the expressive channel — in the
case of Nijinsky, the collective sin of World War I. In their several
ways, modernist artists felt the necessity of embodying in their work
the change in consciousness produced by the war: when Eliot wrote,
"Jerusalem Athens Alexandria / Vienna London" he included the
contemporary catastrophe in the spectacle of the inevitable collapse
of each culture. Yeats aspired to the lofty unreachableness of Hi-
malayan monks or the gaiety of Chinese sages who watch as "all
things fall and are built again"; but both Eliot in "The Waste Land"
and Bidart in "Nijinsky" suggest that the artist cannot, like monks
or sages, detach himself. Instead he must reenact the cultural crisis
in himself, re-presenting, through the sense-medium of art, the his-
torical moment, known for what it is.

The contorted drama of Bidart's "Nijinsky" is pieced together from factual sources, but it arises from these pages as a play of voices (in this sense, too, it descends from "The Waste Land"). Nijinsky's voice is by turns hysterical, grief-stricken, horrified, elegiac, manic, and sane — but always intense, uninterruptable, compelling, as he holds us with his glittering eye. Nijinsky possesses three type fonts: CAPS for important words and axiomatic truths (chiefly ghastly ones); *italics* for a rise in pitch, an insistence; and roman for a base line. Nijinsky's wife and friends talk and write in prose printed in roman. They use normal punctuation; Nijinsky uses Bidart's full repertoire of notation, including ellipses, dashes (some preceded by a comma or a colon, some not; some followed by a semicolon, some not), exclamation points, quotation marks, and so on. Nijinsky speaks only in verse, in short bursts of one or two lines, some beginning at the left margin, some along different tab-stops (so to speak) across the page. We may conclude from this that "ordinary people," who feel (either by nature or by will) none of the divisions which disturb artists, keep an even and uninterrupted "prose" tenor; divided souls have italic intensities, irregularities of emotional pulse, elliptic reveries, exclamatory excitements, and upper-case insights. The irreconcilability of the two styles — Nijinsky's feverish broken utterance and the world's "sane," reasonable, and offended prose — enacts Bidart's aesthetic dilemma. He avoids the sentimentality attending the stereotype of the *poète maudit* by making Nijinsky both dangerous and unjust toward his wife and children. In his wish to throw pure lyric up against the most ordinary prose, as if to say that lyric had to take stock of its relation to the everyday management of life, Bidart is a descendant of Pound and Williams. The mutually critical relation of solitary lyric and the social world (to put the quarrel in only one set of many possible terms) can no longer, after the modernists, be avoided.

Bidart's sympathies with the lyric side of the quarrel are evident; but in making his poem one about guilt, he also reflects the predicament of the innocent bystanders who suffer from their contact with genius, and asserts the falsity of any claim that the artist, however pure his aesthetic intent, can escape human error, evil, or destructiveness. Like Yeats, Bidart chooses a self-choreographing dancer as the case in which the artist, his art, and the medium of his art are indistinguishable from one another. But Yeats's dancer was probably female, and in any case, though solitary, entirely lyric, and grateful to the eye. Bidart's dancer is male; he dances a dance so horrible that people flinch, and includes the destructive and even psychotic elements of human life in his art, as he dances World War I:

> When the audience was seated, he picked up a chair, sat down on it, and stared at them. Half an hour passed. Then he took a few rolls of black and white velvet and made a big cross the length of the room. He stood at the head of it, his arms opened wide. He said: "Now, I will dance you the War, which you did not prevent and for which you are responsible." His dance reflected battle, horror, catastrophe, apocalypse. An observer wrote: "At the end, we were too much overwhelmed to applaud. We were looking at a corpse, and our silence was the silence that enfolds the dead."
>
> There was a collection for the Red Cross. Tea was served. Nijinsky never again performed in public.

Though the content of Yeats's poetry reflects "battle, horror, catastrophe, apocalypse," that content for the most part is conveyed by a form of exquisite modulation, firm syntax, and lofty stanza-form: Yeats never lost his attachment to *ottava rima,* rime royal, the sonnet. And his dancer stood, among other things, for that harmony of form that could enclose and mediate the disorder of life. When Eliot wrote "The Waste Land" in broken form (though a form haunted by the specter of lyric musicality) he began the process that we can see present in Bidart's broken form. But Bidart's verse has no ghost of the pentameter behind it. It comes out in short, impulsive phrases, those phrases characteristic of the American lyric since Williams.

The rhythm of life that lies behind this book is phrased most baldly in the title poem, "The Sacrifice," which takes the life of Jesus as the paradigm of earthly life, but not in the usual religious fashion. Here, the essential actors are Christ and Judas, the betrayed and the betrayer. Jesus loved the world, underwent betrayal by someone who purported to love him, and sacrificed his life, shouldering the guilt of the world; Judas, shouldering the guilt of his action, killed himself. The modern instance offered by the poem is that of a daughter unable to bear her mother's death agony, yet unable to kill her; feeling she has betrayed her mother, she kills herself. By taking such a banal instance — filial helplessness at the parental deathbed — Bidart forces the issue with each reader, refusing to euphemize one of the commonest causes for "irrational" guilt:

> Christ knew the Secret. Betrayal
> is necessary; as is woe for the betrayer.

One could almost be reading graffiti; the melodrama of the style derives from the modern ripping away of veils.

A far more successful poem, I think, is "The Confessional," a long imitation of a psychiatric session, or series of sessions, in which the analyst speaks in italics and the client in the fantastic "lyric" mode of Nijinsky. The client exposes the relation between himself and his mother — their *folie à deux* casued by her obsessive love for him, her "nervous breakdown," her demands, his obsessive love for her, his success in supplanting both his father and stepfather:

> — I assure you, though I was a *"little boy,"*
> I could be far more charming, sympathetic,
> full of sensibility, *"various,"* far more
> an understanding and feeling
> ear for my mother's emotions, needs, SOUL
>
> than any man, any man she met, —

The result, when the client grew to adulthood, was a stranglehold he felt he had to break:

> TO SURVIVE, I HAD TO KILL HER INSIDE ME.

This relation is contrasted with the relation of Augustine and his mother Monica: they, according to the *Confessions,* succeeded in attaining an idyllic relation, both aspiring, in a joint project, to sainthood. The wretched veiled hostility between the client and his mother, mutually critical in adulthood (*"Forgiveness doesn't exist"*), lasted until death.

In the poem, the idyll between Augustine and his mother takes place in a long lyric flight, with musically sustained sentences generating clause after clause of aspiration and rapture. The poem sees this as a fantasy no longer available to us, and it ends crucified on its twin analytic truths:

> *Man needs a metaphysics;*
> *he cannot have one.*

Against this voice of reason, Bidart's volume places its last idyll, a "translation" of the opening of Genesis, the *ur*-poem. (In the modern manner, this is a re-creation, depending on various previous English translations, with help from commentators about the meaning of the Hebrew.) Here there are no frenzied or analytical italics: God speaks in caps and the narrator speaks in roman, with caps for the large items in the universe (HEAVEN, EARTH, OCEAN, SEASONS, and so on). The punctuation, too, is seemly — commas and periods. But we see (tutored by Bidart's previous practice) that the narrator and God are both composing poetry (with the irregular lines, the varying left margins, the uneven groups of lines, that we know from Nijinsky's speech). Can there be a poetry of this sort, the "translation" asks — a poetry of creation without madness, destruction, "intensity," hysteria, betrayal? Can a measured and rhythmic lyricism be attained in this century?

In reaching back to the moment before guilt and betrayal entered the world, Bidart asks whether there is an imagination as benevolent as it is grim, one that in the midst of conflict can stop to imagine harmony. The Genesis poet lived in a fallen world; he knew the story of Adam and Eve, and Cain and Abel. And yet he was able to write of something idyllic. In recalling the vegetarian prescription for man ("YOUR MEAT SHALL BE / PLANTS, SEEDS, FRUIT . . . / NOT THE CREATURES OF THE EARTH"), Bidart's poem makes the protest against slaughter made earlier by Nijinsky's dance. In ending his volume with the prelapsarian ideal invented by the Genesis poet or by his culture, Bidart allies himself with those artists who say, like Yeats's father, that poetry concerns itself with the creation of paradises — but, Bidart would add, only in the exceptional instance.

The purposes of lyric, as they emerge from Bidart's book, are several. In the first place, lyric serves as a repository for the visonary and the harmonious, as in Augustine's and Monica's joint heavenly flight, or as in God's supreme invention of the cosmos. In the second place, lyric serves as a vehicle for emotions and actions too "intense" for "prose"; lyric is needed for the reproach to the conditions of existence underlying "The Confessional," for the violent incorporative act of the artist in taking the whole activity of his culture into consciousness and re-enacting it in expressive form, for deathbed betrayals and erotic paradox. Thirdly, lyric serves as the genre for literary aria; surrounded by the *recitative* of every day, the voice in lyric elaborates itself into the *bel canto* of words (of which Bidart's inventive notation is itself a symbol). Lastly, lyric is the genre of pressure; it compresses into a few pages, in a montage of cinematic flashes, the strains of a whole life, and it compresses as well, by means of a few symbols, the metaphysical dilemmas of mind and flesh.

27

Michael Blumenthal

Michael Blumenthal's second collection of poems, *Days We Would Rather Know* (1984), adds a buoyant and odd new presence to contemporary American poetry. On the one hand, Blumenthal's characteristic subjects are those normally considered tragic, ranging from tragedies of fate (the Holocaust) to tragedies of consciousness (for example, the dark suspicion that all one's so-called "knowledge" is only socially conditioned opinion). On the other hand, Blumenthal is certain that life exists to be lived, that the senses are to be enjoyed, and that the mind is bound to have some convictions. Like many poets, he lives in two universes at once, and at any moment the weather of his happier sensual poems can be clouded over with doubt, or the storms of his somber poems can shake off their tears. Blumenthal's capacity for inner volatility makes the poems exhilarating to read, full of lifts and turbulence. Social pieties, for instance, fall away like shed garments in an irrepressible poem about flying, "Over Ohio":

> You can say what you want about the evils of technology
> and the mimicry of birds: *I love it*. I love the sheer,
> unexpurgated *hubris* of it, I love the beaten egg whites
> of clouds hovering beneath me, this ephemeral Hamlet
> of believing in man's grandeur. You can have all that
> talk about the holiness of nature and the second Babylon.
> You can stay shocked about the future all you want,
> reminisce about the beauties of midwifery. I'll take this
> anyday, this sweet imitation of Mars and Jupiter, this
> sitting still at 600 mph like a jet-age fetus. I want to
> go on looking at the moon for the rest of my life and seeing

> footsteps. I want to keep flying, even for short distances,
> like here between Columbus and Toledo on Air Wisconsin:
> an Andean condor sailing over Ohio, above the factories,
> above the dust and the highways and the miserable tires.

In its ending, this boyish poem admits the places where most of our time has to be spent — in life's factories and highways. Mostly, at the end, looking at the "miserable tires," Blumenthal is feeling what Hopkins called "the jading and jar of the cart, / Time's tasking." Without the tires and the factories, the poem would buy its elation too easily. As it is, the slide down from the helium of "*I love it*" to the drudgery of the human mileage is typical of Blumenthal.

Even in the grimmest poem here, Blumenthal finds a moment for quizzical humor. His father's siblings are by now all dead; looking at a family photograph, Blumenthal addresses his father:

> How it must make you think, constantly now, of
> your own dying, that last piece in death's long puzzle
> of jigsaw and reunion.

The odd metaphor of the puzzle reanimates the word "jigsaw" as a metaphor for Death's scythe, and enables the end of the poem:

> I hold this piece
> of you in my hand, wanting to hide it from whoever
> is playing, wanting to abort this long puzzle of dyings.

The domestic contest between the gods who want to put the last pieces of the photograph-puzzle in place and the son who tries to retain it alive in his poem is unexpected, in its comic pathos, in a tragic poem. Earlier in the poem, there is an equally unexpected comic view of what life offers the son — "just one more night of / listening to the feathers make love inside the pillow." It is these surprising inner breezes that prevent Blumenthal, when he is writing a sad poem, from becoming portentous; the poems have charm.

Monotony of tone is the first sign of a poet's own boredom with his writing: and so Blumenthal's variety of tone is a good sign. He commands that freshness of collocation that we call imaginativeness. Of God (considered imaginatively) he says:

Had he rescued the nightingales from the floods
and not shrouded the planets in secrecy,
> *Dayenu.*

Had he shrouded the planets in mystery
but not enticed us with the light that shines from them,
> *Dayenu.*

Had he enticed us with the light that shines from the planets
but not created the pasqueflower to console us in winter,
> *Dayenu.*

Though this lovely cascade of language has its origins in the "Passover litany thanking God for the blessings bestowed upon the Jews" (Blumenthal's note for the unaware; *dayenu* means "it would have sufficed for us"), it is handsome in itself, as it connects nightingales and planets, pasqueflower and light, and (later), misers, mist, and dandelions. There is a positive joy in finding an excuse to prepare such a liturgy.

Blumenthal's book improves as it advances. By the end, to my eye at least, Blumenthal is being stricter on himself, both formally and morally, as he arrays the claims of griefs and difficulties against the claims of undeniable appetites. (The appetite to learn, to believe, to create, and to know is as compelling to Blumenthal as the appetite to touch, taste, and see.) Against the appetites stand the angels of death and doubt, casting their shadows. The simplest version of this confrontation appears here in that notoriously difficult genre, the Holocaust poem. A violinist in Buchenwald continues to play, "And the children, as if in answer, burn." Art goes on and evil goes on, parallel planes that never meet. No real interaction between the drive of art and the angel of death can be envisaged in this allegorical portrait. A far better poem, "The Bitter Truth," shows Blumenthal still struggling with eros and thanatos, but the two principles have been internalized, and fight it out on home ground. The poet addresses his wife, and questions the impulse of exclusivity in love or aesthetics: "How can I tell you that you are beautiful? / And that she, too, is beautiful? *And she / And she and she and it and he?*" The view that "wins" is that one may live in, but not finally act by, skepticism:

> To tell the truth is merely
>
> To repeat the words *I do not know* until they

become insufferable: because to tell the truth
is to say hardly anything at all, and nothing

Delights like something said often and with
great conviction; because if I tell the truth
I too must end with *I do not know.*

These are a young man's poems, dizzy with discovering that some-
thing can be affirmed, that the world can be loved. From time to
time, Blumenthal's obedient return to the quotidian — to miserable
tires or the darkness of afternoon — seems merely something mel-
ancholy learned in childhood fighting against the real exuberance of
physical health and spiritual beginnings. He would like to see a great
Mozartian circle of reconciliation in the world, like the one he rep-
resents, comically, as "Jungians & Freudians at the Joseph Campbell
Lecture," where the opposing camps (the fat purple-dressed Jungians
and the gray Freudians "thin / from all their *Lieben und Arbeiten*")
eventually come to a union where "everyone leaves happy" —

The Jungians crying Freudian tears
into their lavender garments,
the Freudians purple with laughter
in their dark gray suits,
everyone delighted and friendly
over Jungian wine and Freudian doughnuts
in the pale, white room.

Such a happy ending may be taken as a propitiatory emblem offered
by a spirit frightened of ill feeling. The more ill feeling Blumenthal
encounters, the greater is the strain on his comedy, and one might
prophesy that down the road the humor will necessarily become
blacker.

There are seventy poems in *Days We Would Rather Know,* some
on classic themes ("The Snowstorm"), some whimsical, some grim.
The grim ones are perhaps the most interesting. Blumenthal writes
of why "we live at odds / with what we need," of "men letting /
their best testimony run like wax down / The thighs of a stranger,
until we betray / the hero that lives inside us." He is not sanguine
about what it means to write poetry:

Very few write back
It's like a long correspondence

with an autistic child: Every cry's
a cause for ecstasy.

From this base of emptiness, the poems ascend in a long yearning.
Many of the poems are about wishing, a theme that Blumenthal takes
up in prolonged and fine-grained investigations, delicate and forceful
at once. The formal inventions in which these inquiries are couched
match the processes of hope and dream that they describe. "Days
We Would Rather Know" is constructed around a convoluted time
scheme of the now, the then, and the wished-for:

There are days we would rather know
than these, as there is always, later
a woman we would rather have married
than whom we did, in that severe nowness
time pushed, imperfectly, to then.

And "Wishful Thinking" is strung on a set of frames each beginning
"I like to think," each more hopeful and evanescent than the one
before, until it all ends in the self-transcendence of the phoenix, a
dream canonized by literary desire. It is these spirals of wish that
are, at this moment, Blumenthal's signature:

I like to think that ours will be more than just another story
of failed love and the penumbras of desire. I like to think
the moon that day was in whatever house the astrologists
would have it in for a kind of quiet, a trellis lust could climb
easily and then subside, resting against the sills and ledges,
giving way like shore to an occasional tenderness, coddling
the cold idiosyncrasies of impulse and weather that pound it
   as it
holds to its shape against the winds and dust storms
of temptation and longing.

The powerful flood of this yearning will have an ebb, perhaps, as
powerful. The *beau mont*, said Stevens, is a hill of stones. At the
moment, however, Blumenthal brings to the current spare and
gloomy scene a rush of spirited and scattering joy, an abrupt sense
of self, and a free-moving syntax. Rilke, Nemerov, O'Hara, and
Berryman (among others) have gone into his making, but at his best

he sounds like nobody else. I cannot think of anyone in America just now who might write as Blumenthal does about looking down on one's house after death:

> Rising from the small, singular cots
> of our celestial villages, we look down
> on this: the mold mimicking grass
> as it devours the ledges, the ivy
> climbing like a pack of young boys
> into the opaque windows, the willows
> weeping and mopping their wet brows
>
> against the shingles. Each year,
> the earth is reclaiming more and more
> of its progeny of sand: the heavens
> reabsorb their tears from between
> the bricks, the termites recycle
> their mute homunculi of wood and ashes.

Though there are lively signs of verbal connection here (the mold, the mimicry, the mopping and the mute: the reclaiming, reabsorbing, recycling: "pack" and "opaque," tears and termites, sand and ashes), the courage of the passage comes from its plain refusal of euphony in moments of stress: "Each year, the earth is reclaiming more and more of its progeny of sand." Around that statement the ivy climbs, the willows weep, and the termites chew their homunculi. Blumenthal's fine sense of where to draw the line in style is his best claim on our attention, and his willingness to attempt all sorts of attitudes and genres is a good augury for the future.

28

Louise Glück, Stephen Dunn, Brad Leithauser, Rita Dove

The catchall nature of the label "lyric poetry" is put into relief by four such different species of the genus as the books I take up in this essay: Louise Glück's *The Triumph of Achilles*, Stephen Dunn's *Local Time*, Brad Leithauser's *Cats of the Temple*, and Rita Dove's *Thomas and Beulah* (all published in 1986). A duckbill platypus, a panda, a whale, and a monkey, gazed at, do not immediately suggest the label "mammal." And what we remember, visually, of these animals is not their uninteresting potential for lactation but their wonderful singularity of appearance. In the zoo of the new (Sylvia Plath's phrase) these four books are arresting forms. Of their authors, two (Dunn and Glück) are in midcareer, while Dove and Leithauser, both in their thirties, are publishing third and second books respectively. In writing briefly about each of these poets, I want to take up the aims of lyric as they become visible in their work.

Louise Glück has tried in her poetry to give experience the permanent form of myth. Hers is the sort of lyric poetry that turns away from specific details and observations (names, places, dates, quotidian details — what Lowell, for instance, made the stuff of poetry) to an abstract plane, sometimes narrative, as in the Greek myths, sometimes archetypal, as in the encounter of Man with Woman. The tendency for lyric to turn mythical is often irritating to readers who yearn for biography (Who was the Fair Youth? Who was the Dark Lady? Who, for that matter, was Shakespeare?) as if facts would resolve meaning. We all began as sophomores in this respect; but we learn as we read more poetry that it is possible for novelistic detail to obscure, rather than reveal, fictive experience — that the lean shape of myth is the nakedness guaranteeing all stories.

437

A better argument for mythical lyric is that the beauty possible for mythical or archetypal poetry — with its own lexicon and thesaurus of images — is different from the beauty of the historical quotidian (which too has a lexicon of its own, a specific museum of images). In the treatment of Christian anecdote, for instance, there have always been what one could call artists of essence (those, for example, who painted hieratic crucifixions showing a monumental and untormented Christ in glory on the cross) and, on the other side, artists of the actual (those who painted crucifixions exhibiting a tortured corpse in a realistic social setting).

The chief obstacle in writing mythical or archetypal poetry is that the story is already known, its conclusion familiar. Interest consequently has to center almost entirely on interpretation and manner. (It is no accident that Milton, who decided to retell archetypal stories that every literate person already knew by heart, became the poet with the most highly developed manner in our history.) Glück retells, in "Mythic Fragment," Ovid's story of the myth of Daphne, saved from Apollo's advances by her father the river god Peneus, who turned her into a laurel tree. The lyric poet, facing a narrative, must choose the point at which the lyric aria will occur: Glück gives us Daphne's postmetamorphic voice. The tree, once a girl, retells the myth with the brevity proper to lyric:

> When the stern god
> approached me with his gift
> my fear enchanted him . . .
> I begged my father in the sea
> to save me. When
> the god arrived, I was nowhere,
> I was in a tree forever. Reader,
> pity Apollo: at the water's edge,
> I turned from him, I summoned
> my invisible father — as
> I stiffened in the god's arms,
> of his encompassing love
> my father made
> no other sign from the water.

This may be the first time that the myth of Daphne has been retold as a Freudian story, the tale of a girl too much in love with her father

to accept a lover. "Reader, pity Apollo," she says; we are to reflect
on the many young men who lose the young women they pursue to
that unacknowledged rival, the father. And pity Glück's Daphne:
begging her father to save her, she imagines that the result will be
Apollo repelled, herself unchanged. Instead, she stiffens into the wood
of the sexually unresponsive. Her last words are, "Of his encompas-
sing love / my father made / no other sign from the water." The
blankness of that vista — as the stiffened bark looks to the silent
shore — is characteristic of Glück's poems of desolation and impos-
sibility. In this Oedipal retelling of the myth there are no compen-
satory moments — no laurels bound about Apollo's brow, no ecstatic,
Straussian joy in leafiness. The manner of the poem has changed the
manner of the myth, turning Ovid's story into a demystifying modern
story of virginity, revealing its roots in incestuous desire.

Glück's poems bend erotic stereotypes into her own forms of
mannerist anguish:

> I have been looking
> steadily at these elms
> and seen the process that creates
> the writhing, stationary tree
> is torment, and have understood
> it will make no forms but twisted forms.

That splendid Yeatsian close states the poetic of Glück's book: writh-
ing, to be stationary; stationary, to be writhing. This is the poetic
of myth — animating what is eternal, freezing what is temporary
and vanishing. As Glück's two adjectives imply, motion does not
cease, but any notion of "progress" or "advance" or "improvement"
ceases. Yeats at one point called himself a marble triton growing old
among the streams; that moment when a poet becomes marble is the
moment of myth. Myth and archetype offer themselves as the only
formally tenable vehicles for a sense of the unchangingness of writh-
ing human experience. The older we get, the more we "progress,"
the more we find our situations anticipated in Ovid, in Homer, in
Genesis.

It is no accident that aphorism suits archetype. Glück shows an
aphoristic talent that harks back to the Greek Anthology:

> You have betrayed me, Eros.
> You have sent me
> my true love.

"Only victims," she says elsewhere, "have a destiny." And she offers these Yeatsian lines:

> Why love what you will lose?
> There is nothing else to love.

This couplet may resemble, in content, Yeats's lines in "Nineteen Hundred and Nineteen": "Man is in love and loves what vanishes, / What more is there to say?" But the chill of Glück's preordained universe is different from the historical turbulence of Yeats's interpenetrating gyres; his manner is tragic rather than fatalistic. Glück's manner suits her matter; the manner is as stationary, as foreseen in its pastness, as her myths.

Glück's nonmythic poems here, chiefly about love, are as ahistorical and nonquotidian as her myths. A long love affair which has come to an end is reviewed in a sequence called "Marathon." Some of it seems to me to topple over the line that separates self-scrutiny from self-dramatization: "We have acted a great drama." On the other hand, Glück's harsh and self-incriminating valedictory to the lover who has made her conscious of her greed in passion sticks powerfully in the mind:

> Sooner or later
> you'll begin to dream of me. I don't envy you
> those dreams. I can imagine how my face looks,
> burning like that, afflicted with desire — lowered
> face of your invention — how the mouth betrays
> the isolated greed of the lover
> as it magnifies and then destroys:
> I don't envy you that visitation.

I don't recall this precise human moment elsewhere in poetry. One aim of lyric poetry is to trace a contour not recorded before; saying the unsaid is a mark of the poet's courage, and Glück is not lacking in it.

The title poem of Stephen Dunn's sixth book, *Local Time*, asserts —
in the greatest possible contrast to Glück's glacial myths — a need
to stay in touch with the local:

> What was foreign never occurred
> until we heard it here,
>
> wasn't that true?
> And didn't enough happen here?
>
> The retarded girl nearby
> swallowed stones.
>
> Schultz stepped off that ledge,
> everyone knew,
>
> because his house wasn't home.

With Schultz and the retarded girl we are far from Ovid. Many poets
who deal with the local, as Dunn does, fall into a gritty naturalism.
Dunn, for all his affirmation of plain speech and plain encounters
(an earlier book was called *Work and Love*), has a delicacy of touch
in treating his plain material. Of his many poems on marriage and
the gulf between male and female experience, I quote "He/She," a
poem about the different ways boys and girls grow up, and the
consequent limitless possibilities for misunderstanding in marriage.
The poem begins with a marital argument and continues the argu-
ment into the next day. This too is a moment rarely treated in poetry
— a moment of tangled accusation and comprehension:

> Brought up never getting punched
>   in the mouth for saying more
>   than the situation can bear,
>
> she argues beyond winning,
>   screams indictments
>   after the final indictment
>
> has skewered him into silence,
>   if not agreement.
>   The words she uses

means she is feeling something large
　which needs words, perhaps
　　the way Pollock needed paint.

Next day the words are unimportant
　to her, while all
　　he's thinking about

are the words she used —
　if recovering from them
　　is possible.

Years ago, the schoolyard taught him
　one word too many meant
　　broken fingers, missing teeth;

you chose carefully, or you chose war.
　You were the last word
　　you let live.

She was in the elsewhere girls were,
　learning other lessons,
　　the ones men learn

too late or not at all; you took in,
　cared for, without keeping score
　　you shaped a living space

into a kind of seriousness.
　Retract those words, he says.
　　But she is only

sensing his reserve, his inability
　to perceive that her wrong words
　　meant so much hurt and love.

Because Dunn's poems explore contrary theses (emotional, intellectual, aesthetic), he needs to be quoted whole. He navigates slowly through shoals, peers into shallows, marks buoys, and makes port in uncertainty. He is, in his later books, a careful poet, balancing his stern bare passages with delightful flurries of visually and phonetically pleasing language. We wake, he says of the married, to the pleasure of being alone, but

> Soon the equally mysterious world of women
>   and men, of momentary
> common agreement and wild misunderstanding,
>
> will impose itself naturally on the simplest event.
>   Anatomy will send
> its differing messages to syntax and sense.

The language here has many charms, from the simplest (a host of
double letters) to the more complex affinities of "equally" and "nat-
urally," of "mysterious" and "misunderstanding," of "wild" and
"will," "simplest" and "syntax," "send" and "sense." The "matter"
— how the mysteriousness of the sexes to each other imposes itself
on the simplest domestic event — generates the inner paradoxes
joining mystery and simplicity, imposition and naturalness, agree-
ment and misunderstanding, syntax and the senses. At his best, Dunn
encodes mystery in speech that remains plain in vocabulary, while
doing syntactic and structural justice to psychological complexity.

Dunn is an autobiographical poet. We learn of a father and grand-
father attached to drink, a father intermittently out of work, the
grandfather a storyteller, a mother "insisting with Carlyle on an
Everlasting Yea," while the son is the one in the Roman Catholic
family "needing to debunk, destroy." Dunn leaves Catholicism, mar-
ries, has children. His idea of a poem is a room (the old pun on
stanza) in which everything has been "grooved and tongued . . .
wedged, fitted, nailed." He is proud of "the miter work and joists, /
the fluted molding above the door." The image of the poet as artisan
suits Dunn's reflective poems, but I find something sentimental and
willed about the working-class anecdotes in which he attempts a
language simpler than his own — one, for instance, in which a
cocktail waitress (presumably attending Dunn's creative writing class)
says, "On my night off I try to write," and continues:

> That poem I gave you about the girl
> who disappears in her own room,
>
> did you know, Steve, who she was,
> that it wasn't creative writing at all?

The waitress's predicament is not made the poet's own, and the poem
remains a form of aesthetic slumming. The problems faced by a lyric

poet writing about an inarticulate milieu from which he has distanced himself by education and cultivation are not easily solved.

Dunn, to his credit, is far bleaker, less "lyrical" than the creative-writing waitress in her self-annihilating fictions. Because he is a solitary trying, against his nature, for domesticity, there is an attractive tension to his work, testified to by the grind of withdrawn reflective language against plot and incident. Poems written by men about the difficulties of domestic life have been fairly rare before this century. Dunn is adding honest poems to this recent genre; and watching a genre evolve can have, for literary people, the interest that watching a new volcano has for geologists.

The two younger poets here, Brad Leithauser and Rita Dove, are as different from each other as Glück and Dunn. Brad Leithauser seems to be trying to see what can be made in our time from the poetics of Marianne Moore, with a leavening of Elizabeth Bishop. *Cats of the Temple* is more openly self-conscious even than his first book, *Hundreds of Fireflies*, which attracted notice for its meticulous art. Here one sees again his capacity for taking pains, visible chiefly in the elaborate rhyming of his stanzas and in the minuteness of his descriptions. He writes here, for instance, a poem in five five-line stanzas (similar to the symmetrical art George Herbert sometimes used, in which the number of lines per stanza matches the number of stanzas). In this poem, where a stuffed tortoise stands for the reflexive consciousness mated to a heavy, material body, fifteen lines (the first three of each stanza) rhyme in the sound "oh" (though one slant rhyme creeps in). This device, like other, similar ones throughout the book, serves to insist on the artifice of the poems: no one could mistake these poems for artless "speech." Leithauser forms part of the (no doubt salutary) backlash against the unadorned, apparently "artless" poetry that has been around since William Carlos Williams made it attractive.

If Leithauser did not adopt Marianne Moore's manner so strenuously one would read him in a less distracted way. One is often made so conscious of the perfectly mimicked model that the poem begins to seem a form of ventriloquism. Moore's characteristic practice in many poems, for instance, was to describe an unusual animal in syntactically prolonged sentences with moral asides, and then to end with an ethical reflection. This is how Leithauser proceeds in the poem on the stuffed tortoise: a description (the alive-looking tortoise with its neck lunging forward); a contrast (with its companion stuffed animals who look very dead); a moral aside (on the Aesopian fable of the tortoise and the hare); and then a return to description, this time invoking the pathetic fallacy ("as if that tough, undersized head / yearned to outstrip its ponderous cargo"). Here is the Moorelike close:

> — The time's not ripe for that? If so, the true
> burden on his back may be years which offer no
> movement casual or quick enough to escape
> a painstaking, on-the-spot review.

Leithauser has had, like Moore, the misfortune of having his putative subjects mistaken for his real ones. A promotional statement from *Publisher's Weekly*, sent out by Knopf with *Cats of the Temple*, says of his work, "Nothing is too trivial to be noticed — the encounter of a toad and a damselfly, for example, or an ostrich in the Kyoto zoo being offered a pretzel by a frightened child." Well, the poem about the toad and the damselfly is (as Leithauser says), "for the fabulist" about an instant in which the poet would like to see the "resolution of mind and mass," and in which each — soul and body, to use the old terms — "had felt the other's opposed appeals." And the poem in the zoo uses the ostrich's hestitation to accept the pretzel as a thirteen-line illustration in a sixty-line poem about our wish to believe in free will. It would be more accurate to present Leithauser as a poet interested in matter and spirit, determinism and free will, who uses fine-grained description to bring these matters to sensuous apprehension.

This promotional statement does poetry a disservice in implying that one need only be "a wizard of description" (its phrase for Leithauser) to make a poem. Description can be, and often is, one of the liveliest achievements of lyric (Stevens called poetry "description without place") — but description can never be divorced, in any poem worth the name, from evaluation and interpretation. The statement goes on to claim that Leithauser is "modest about the extraordinary refractory powers of his own painterly mind." I hope *Publisher's Weekly* means "refractive"; and I hope that in the future Leithauser will write his own promotional descriptions of his work, if only to ensure their accuracy and literacy.

Leithauser has reacted against the confessional poetry that was the mainstay of the Sixties and Seventies. He aims at "memory turned selfless," for which his image is a spider web turned, by a trick of light, invisible, yielding to the eye only "what incidence had blown there: / some seeds, needles, threadbare / leaves, a curled gray feather." This is an admirable aim, one which may well enable Leithauser eventually to write poems in which the web is genuinely invisible — as it cannot be, I think, in Leithauser's adopting of Moore's voice. One can ask whether the web can ever be invisible in the formal, stanzaic verse that Leithauser writes. Of course; the web becomes "invisible" not only through formal repetition (till the measure seems "natural," as in Shakespeare's sonnets) but also through melodiousness (as the sentences seem "inevitable" in their rightness of rhythm). Leithauser's rhythms, however, often call attention to themselves by their irregularity, their noncoincidence with syntax and line endings. In four-syllable lines, we see

> a young man perched
> commandingly
> on a boulder
> whose barnacle-
> gripped, weed-strung base
> the sea rinses.

"A young man, perched commandingly on a boulder, whose barnacle-gripped, weed-strung base the sea rinses." It is hard to know just why Leithauser has written this description four syllables at a time. The connection between prosody and matter here is not self-evident, not even pleasing, not even quizzically amusing.

What I find most interesting in Leithauser's work is not his concern with spirit and body, a topic worthy enough but often rehearsed, but rather his investigation into his own kind of maleness, into the sort of man he is and would like to be. He often uses one of his symbolic animals as a way to write on both maleness and the enterprise of being an artist. The seahorse, "a mild, compromising / Creature," winged like Pegasus, "glides / With a forking, oblique / Efficiency, the winglike / Fins behind his ears aflutter." This beautiful and closely observed passage on the alert and eccentric motions of the seahorse leads to a consideration of the seahorse's quasi-androgynous powers:

> this mailed male
> . . . bears in his own brood pouch
>   A female's transferred conceptions
> And seems to move (those fins
> By turns transparent) through
>   Telekinetic promptings, while his
> Turreted, nonsynchronous
> Eyes are taking in two
>   Views at once.

This male is double- rather than single-minded, delicately intuitive, armored and maternal, receptive to inner promptings, and mild rather than warlike; it is a convincing self-portrait of a new maleness precisely because of its oddity.

Leithauser's search for perfection has, I think, been insufficiently noticed. He wants an "unsullied original"; he looks for "miraculous pristine passages." (Those who want the perfect, if deprived of God, turn oddly often to the world of animals, who, since they cannot be other than they are, are therefore helplessly perfect.) For Leithauser, those pristine passages

>   wait beside you
>   always, if only it were known *which*
> floorboard to take the crowbar to,
> *which* stone uproot on the hillside, if only
>
> you dared to; this tunnel, here, into a breath-
> taking incandescence so intense the
> body is as nothing in the path
> of its streaming, weightless and homeless and
>
> helpless, hopeful and afraid.

This is Leithauser's furthest reach in *Cats of the Temple*, and it is encouraging for the future. The Lawrentian "streaming" in incandescence, afraid and helpless and hopeful, is at the furthest remove, however, from the dead objects in the invisible web. The latter are visible in Leithauser's admiration of a Japanese house with all the paraphernalia of living invisibly tucked away; the former is visible, in the same poem, in the noises penetrating the house from the street outside. I do not mean that Lawrentian "streaming" is preferable to

Japanese containment; it is just that either is poor without the other. Leithauser has used many contained forms with great ingenuity; he has not yet, I think, found the syntax and prosody for the momentum of "streaming" and helplessness. It is not clear what he will become when he sheds his dependency on Moore; he will still, I assume, have a self-effacing poetic, and it will be interesting to see how he embodies it next.

I conclude with a remarkable book composed of two sequences, *Thomas and Beulah*, by Rita Dove. Thomas (born in 1900 in Wartrace, Tennessee) and Beulah (born in 1904 in Rockmart, Georgia) are husband and wife; they are modeled, one guesses, on Rita Dove's grandparents (the cover photo, a snapshot of a middle-aged black couple standing in front of their car, is credited to Ray A. Dove and dated 1952, the year of Rita Dove's birth). Though the photograph, and the chronology of the lives of Thomas and Beulah appended to the sequence, might lead one to suspect that Dove is a poet of simple realism, this is far from the case. Dove has learned (perhaps from Charles Wright's "Tattoos") how to make a biographical fact the buried base of an imagined edifice. But unlike Wright, who writes meditations almost Chinese in their stillness, Dove is principally a poet of dramatic force — a quality found relatively rarely in lyric, a genre by its nature reflective, circling, and static.

Before I come to Dove's management of dramatic power, I should sketch the story behind the sequence. When Thomas and Beulah marry, he is twenty-four, she twenty. Thomas has already lost his best friend, who, after a drunken dare from Thomas, drowned in the Mississippi leaving only his mandolin behind. Thomas carries the mandolin north with him to Akron, plays it halfheartedly, and eventually hangs it from a nail on the parlor wall. Thomas works in Akron for Goodyear, at the Zeppelin factory; after the Depression puts him out of work, he sweeps offices part time. Over the years, he and Beulah have four daughters. Thomas becomes domesticated enough to sing in the church choir. When the war comes, he works again for Goodyear; Beulah works in a dress shop, then makes hats. At sixty-three, Thomas dies of his second heart attack; Beulah dies six years later, at sixty-five. Their lives span the first sixty-nine years of this century; they represent, among other things, the migration of rural southern blacks to the industrial cities of the north. This great social movement — one of the most important for American history

in the twentieth century — finds here its first extended poem. But
the sequence of poems is also the history of a marriage.

Dove's epigraph reads, "These poems tell two sides of a story and
are meant to be read in sequence." We have Thomas's side ("Man-
dolin," twenty-three poems) and Beulah's side ("Canary in Bloom,"
twenty-one poems): together they make up Thomas and Beulah's
story. The poems make up a true sequence: that is, most are richer
for, and in fact only intelligible in, the context of the rest. The first
poem of "Mandolin" is called, simply, "The Event": in it we see
Thomas and Lem, Lem's drowning, and the mute mandolin left
behind. I came across this poem a few years ago in the *Ontario
Review*; it was the first poem I had ever read by Dove, and it sent
me out looking for her first two books, *The Yellow House on the
Corner* and *Museum*; I was not disappointed. This is what I read:

> Ever since they'd left the Tennessee ridge
> with nothing to boast of
> but good looks and a mandolin,
>
> the two Negroes leaning
> on the rail of a riverboat
> were inseparable. Lem plucked
>
> to Thomas's silver falsetto.
> But the night was hot and they were drunk.
> They sat where the wheel
>
> churned mud and moonlight,
> they called to the tarantulas
> down among the bananas
>
> to come out and dance.
> *You're so fine and mighty; let's see
> what you can do*, said Thomas, pointing
>
> to a tree-capped island.
> Lem stripped, spoke easy: *Them's chestnuts,
> I believe.* Dove
>
> quick as a gasp. Thomas, dry
> on deck, saw the green crown shake
> as the island slipped

under, dissolved
in the thickening stream.
At his feet

a stinking circle of rags,
the half-shell mandolin.
Where the wheel turned the water

gently shirred.

When I first read this poem and some of its companions from
"Mandolin," I experienced the best of all poetic delights — feeling
that something was very beautiful and not knowing why. New forms
of beauty declare themselves only gradually. It seems to me now that
a rapid succession of dramatic "takes" is Dove's perfected form; she
almost always refuses editorializing, musing, and "leading" the
reader. Her brilliance lies in her arrangement of content; as the
elements of meaning find their one inevitable form, juxtaposition
alone takes on the work of explanation. Here, in a later poem, is
Thomas (who had hoped for a son) after domestic life has worn him
down. He has had four daughters, his wife prefers her canary to him,
Lem's mandolin is nailed for good to the parlor wall, and the yellow
silk scarf Thomas wore while courting Beulah hangs discarded on
the silent mandolin. The diminution of man by marriage is summed
up in this "Compendium":

He gave up fine cordials and
his hounds-tooth vest.

He became a sweet tenor
in the gospel choir.

Canary, usurper
of his wife's affections.

Girl girl
girl girl.

In the parlor, with streamers,
a bug on a nail.

The canary courting its effigy.
The girls fragrant in their beds.

Thomas, the syntactic ruler of the first two stanzas, survives only as a pronominal adjective in the canary's stanza, and vanishes after that. The biting fourth stanza enumerates the successive disappointments of the childbirths. The mandolin is "a bug on a nail" in Thomas's reductive gesture to the lost Lem. Finally, Thomas is obliterated within the female domain of the narcissistic (if poetic) canary and the fragrant daughters. The poem is no less strict than sympathetic. The *frisson* one feels when form matches fact is present here, never more so than in

> Girl girl
> girl girl.

This is perfectly simple, perfectly mimetic ("It's a girl"), and perfectly expressive (since by its fourth appearance the word "girl" has been turned into something faintly grotesque).

For the Depression year of 1934, when Thomas is unemployed, Dove finds a poetry of what could be called the disarticulated. When the work that holds a day together is gone, the day falls apart into its separate scraps. Dove updates 1934 unemployment with images from contemporary unemployment. Thomas doesn't even have a coal furnace to occupy himself with; the house has a gas heater. It is hard to stay indoors idle. He won't drink (because drink caused the death of his friend), but drink is the temptation of the unemployed. So is infidelity. Dove doesn't say any of this outright, but it is all deducible from her elegant shorthand:

> What to do with a day.
> Leaf through *Jet*. Watch T.V.
> Freezing on the porch
> but he goes anyhow, snow too high
> for a walk, the ice treacherous.
> Inside, the gas heater takes care of itself;
> he doesn't even notice being warm.
>
> Everyone says he looks great.
> Across the street a drunk stands smiling
> at something carved in a tree.

> The new neighbor with the floating hips
> scoots out to get the mail
> and waves once, brightly
> storm door clipping her heel on the way in.

Detail has drama in Dove. The Beulah poems have their own details — a dustcloth, stained wallpaper, hats. The domestic confinement offers less to Dove's imagination than the more varied life in the Thomas poems, but the closing picture of Beulah's deathbed as the sun enters the room is one that remains tenacious in the mind. Stevens said in his elegy for Santayana that it is poverty's speech that seeks us out the most, and "the afflatus of ruin," as Stevens called it, is present in Dove's elegy for Beulah. The poem is called "The Oriental Ballerina," after the small figurine of a Chinese ballerina that dances on Beulah's jewel box. Dove's principle of composition here is a cinematic crosscutting between the exotic claim on Beulah of the beautiful (expressed in clothes, hats, jewel boxes, idealized female grace in the paltry ballerina) and the poverty of her death. Dove's severity of touch — her most commanding strength — is present here in the austere inventory of the sickroom. As "the radio scratches out a morning hymn" — "The Old Rugged Cross" — we see the "over-sized gardenias" on the wallpaper; this is an America

> where the bedrooms of the poor
> are papered in vulgar flowers
> on a background the color of grease, of
> teabags, of cracked imitation walnut veneer.

In the room, signs of age and sickness:

> a straw nods over
> the lip of its glass and a hand
> reaches for a tissue, crumpling it to a flower.

The sun hesitates at

> a knotted handkerchief that has slid
>
> on its string and has lodged beneath
> the right ear which discerns
> the most fragile music
>
> where there is none.

These sickbed details, as I have said, play in counterpoint with the description of the dancing ballerina. A seamless art stitches together the passages of Beulah's decline and the ballerina's tireless pirouette. The Bishop-like fantasy that the Oriental ballerina has risen straight from China, where life is aesthetically conducted, is perhaps not entirely successful. It is needed, though, for the end of the elegy, the final faded and cheated moments of Beulah's life:

> The head on the pillow sees nothing
> else, though it feels the sun warming
>
> its cheeks. *There is no China,*
> no cross, just the paper kiss
> of a kleenex above the stink of camphor,
>
> the walls exploding with shabby tutus . . .

In the ellipsis, Beulah dies, the dismayed outcry *"There is no China"* in her heart. Dove's bleak sense of the limits of art saves her, here and elsewhere, from making the absolute claims for art's powers that are sometimes found in lyric poets.

Thomas and Beulah manages to keep intact the intensity of the drama and inexplicability of life and marriage. The mutual criticism of Dove's Akron couple, their enterprise and defeat, while specified to a degree that is satisfying as fiction, will remind readers of analogous episodes in the years 1900–1969 undergone by their own parents or grandparents. Dove does not suggest that black experience is identical with white experience, but neither does she suggest that it is always different. Beulah's experience of motherhood — her terror of doing it wrong, her exhaustion and lack of privacy, her irritation at the grown girls — is universal. But Beulah's anger when her daughters take her to the Goodyear company picnic after Thomas's death will be personally familiar only to black readers:

> Now this act of mercy: four daughters
> dragging her to their husbands' company picnic,
> white families on one side and them
> on the other, unpacking the same
> squeeze bottles of Heinz, the same
> waxy beef patties and Salem potato chip bags.

Over the segregated picnickers floats the Goodyear company symbol
— "a white foot / sprouting two small wings." Beulah's interior
monologue, here as elsewhere, has the naturalness and accuracy of
art concealing art. Dove has planed away unnecessary matter: pure
shapes, her poems exhibit the thrift that Yeats called the sign of a
perfected manner.

I would not want to do without Dove's modernist spareness, Dunn's
stubborn argumentation, Glück's mythic exaltation, or Leithauser's
fastidious moralities. Each of these writers has found an idiosyncratic
way to stylize temperament in language, to turn over a furrow of
unplowed ground in diction, and to sketch a contour of contempo-
rary American living and thinking. For each poet, I would wish gifts
complementary to those already possessed: for Dove, a relaxation of
her tense drama into an occasional digressiveness; for Dunn, a fan-
ciful rhetoric to ornament his plain speaking; for Glück, an ironic
humor turned on her theatricality; for Leithauser, a Whitmanian
generosity and carelessness added to his sedulous art. Most writers,
having found themselves, repeat themselves. The best one can wish
for these gifted poets, all of them working at the margin of the
unformulable, is that they find in the future additional possibilities
of style beyond those they already know how to manage. As Auden
said, however, new styles of architecture entail a change of heart,
and that cannot be willed into being.

29

Jorie Graham

Jorie Graham's second book, *Erosion* (1983), brings the presence of poetry into the largest question of life, the relation of body and spirit, a relation more often considered by theologians and philosophers these days than by poets. Graham's subject is the depth to which the human gaze can penetrate, the opening in reality into which the poet can enter. Under the clothed she seeks out the naked; over the soil, the air; inside the integument, a kernel; through the cover of the grass, the snake; from the bowels of the earth, the disinterred saint. Against writers who press against the opacity and resistance of the material world, she suggests its profundity and penetrability — though there seems to be no stopping place for that penetration.

This is a poetry of delicate and steady transgression in which the spirit searches the flesh and the flesh the spirit, melting and dissolving the boundaries thought to separate them. The nature of the spiritual, as Graham sees it, is to be entirely rooted in the physical, and in consequence her poems have a strong visual and sensuous presence leading to a lofty inner vision — "a puzzle unsolvable till the edges give a bit and soften." It is that softening that allows us to enter these "syllables becoming thought" where "blossoming sustains the linear."

I have been quoting from Graham's excellent first book, "Hybrids of Plants and of Ghosts" (Nietzsche's definition of man). Though the second book is recognizably descended from the first, it takes up far more hazardous subjects, including autopsy, extermination camps, murder, and blindness. The serene depth ultimately attained by these poems has been taught to Graham (who grew up in Italy) by the contained tragedy of painting: There are poems here about Masaccio, Signorelli, Piero della Francesca, and Klimt. Because paintings station

figures around a central tragedy or moment of crisis and yet find a
way to exhibit them in form, they can be a guide to the poet. One
painting that Graham writes about is Piero della Francesca's *Ma-
donna del Parto,* which shows the pregnant Virgin standing in a blue
dress buttoned down the front; she is ready to give birth, and two
angels are beginning to let down the curtains that will shield her
from our sight. The painting itself presents a single moment held in
suspension, but the poet retemporalizes the crisis, freeing the event
once more into history:

> Inside, at the heart,
> is tragedy, the present moment
> forever stillborn,
>
> but going in, each breath
> is a button
>
> coming undone, something terribly
> nimble-fingered
> finding all of the stops.

At the heart of these poems, some "contained damage" rests,
enclosed by a damasked surface. The evenness of Graham's line and
the gravity of her gaze suggest the length of time that the damage
has been considered. "In / the finished painting / the argument / has
something to do / with pleasure," says a poem that takes up both
sexual and moral anguish. Over the rent in creation, the artist con-
structs a fabric; "the fabric defines the surface, / the story, / so we
are drawn to it."

Graham's pictorial surface is sometimes alive with movement, at
other times contemplative and still. In "Salmon," for instance, the
visual offering is first an unstoppable salmon run, "tearing and leap-
ing, a gold river / and a blue river traveling / in opposite directions."
The energy of the spawning salmon is replaced by the energy of an
embracing couple, watched by a child:

> I watched, at noon, through slatted wooden blinds,
> a man and a woman, naked, eyes closed,
> climb onto each other,
> on the terrace floor,
> and ride — two gold currents

wrapping round and round each other, fastening,
unfastening.

Finally the leaping gold river of the salmon run and the entwined
gold currents of the human couple are absorbed, in their mutual
oblique relation, into a wide visual atmosphere — a golden sunset
light, deeply absorbed by the stone of walls, rendered in the adjectives
of contemplation:

> the light
> at the end of the day, deep, reddish-gold, bathing the walls,
> the corridors, light that is no longer light, no longer clarifies,
> illuminates, antique, freed from the body of
> the air that carries it.

The reader moves on the textured visual surface from the gold of
instinctive spawning to the gold of willed pleasure to the golden
uselessness of atmosphere when it is no longer useful for seeing things
in a practical sense. "What is it / for the space of time / where it is
useless, merely / beautiful?" Graham asks about light. We are led by
this question to the work of the artist, driven by an impulse linked
by goldenness to that of sex, but we would not make the metaphysical
link unless the visual gold made it for us. The libidinal gold, here as
elsewhere, encircles a terrified center, including

> mother attempting
> suicide, the white night-flying moth
> the ants dismantled bit by bit and carried in
> right through the crack
> in my wall . . .

The powerful magnetism of the golden surface of the artwork remains
the mystery that draws us again and again to its tragic origins.

The attempt to find all the stops, to range through the gamut of
possibility, makes Graham a poet of landscape and memory as well
as a poet of art. She is expert in finding in the natural world, in her
own life, and in history correspondences for those spiritual motions,
impulses, currents, apprehensions, and emergings that intangibly
make up our inner life. Her poetry, though so fully at home in the
mental, the imagined, and the speculative, grounds itself nevertheless

in that desire that is, as she says, the engine, the wind of the body: "Passion is work / that retrieves us / lost stitches. It makes a pattern of us."

Graham does not avert her glance from the relentlessness of the search of art. In a poem on Signorelli's *Resurrection of the Body,* she reminds us of the painter's use of autopsy to ensure anatomical accuracy, extending even to the autopsy of his dead son:

> But the wall
> of the flesh
>   opens endlessly,
> its vanishing point so deep
>   and receding
>
> we have yet to find it,
>   to have it
> stop us. So he cut
>   deeper
> graduating slowly
>   from the symbolic
>
> to the beautiful. How far
>   is true?

The believable motion in these poems — farther and farther inward, then upward and outward — is carried on intensely, slowly, and often painfully. In elaborating her intricate surfaces over damage and grief, Graham continues, with her haunting indwelling musicality, to make a pattern that constructs us as we read it.

Credits

The chapters in this book originally appeared in the following publications:

1. *Bulletin of the American Academy of Arts and Sciences* 36, no. 2 (November 1982): 15–29.
2. *New York Review of Books*, November 7, 1985.
3. *New Yorker*, May 3, 1982.
4. *Times Literary Supplement*, June 25, 1976, p. 775.
5. *New York Review of Books*, May 8, 1976.
6. *New York Review of Books*, November 20, 1986.
7. *Salmagundi*, no. 41 (Spring 1978): 66–68.
8. *What Is a Poet*, ed. Hank Lazer (Tuscaloosa: University of Alabama Press, 1987).
9. *Textual Analysis: Some Readers Reading*, ed. Mary Ann Caws (New York: Modern Language Association, 1986).
10. Two essays on Heaney, *New Yorker*, September 28, 1981, and September 23, 1985.
11. *New Yorker*, November 10, 1986.
13. *New Yorker*, December 31, 1984.
14. *New Yorker*, March 19, 1984.
15. Three essays on Ashbery (one also on Glück): *New Yorker*, March 16, 1981; *New York Review of Books*, July 16, 1981; *New York Review of Books*, June 14, 1984.
16. *New Yorker*, January 13, 1986.
17. *New Yorker*, February 15, 1982.
18. *Critical Inquiry* (13, no. 4 (Summer 1987).
19. *New Republic*, November 11, 1981.
20. Three essays on Ammons: one delivered at Salem College in May 1986, and published by the North Carolina State Council on the Humanities in a pamphlet celebrating Ammons' sixtieth birthday; *New Republic*, April 25, 1981; *Poetry* 141, no. 1 (October 1982).

21. Two essays on Merrill: *New Yorker*, May 21, 1984; *New Republic*, August 5, 1985.
22. Two essays on Rich (one also on Carter and Levine): *New Republic*, January 7 and 14, 1985; *New York Review of Books*, December 17, 1981.
24. *New York Review of Books*, March 3, 1983.
25. *New Yorker*, June 30, 1980.
26. *New Republic*, October 10, 1983.
27. *New Republic*, April 16, 1984.
28. *New York Review of Books*, October 23, 1986.
29. *New York Times Book Review*, July 17, 1983.

The following complete poems are reprinted by permission:

Ammons, "Two Possibilities" and "The Eternal City," from *Collected Poems, 1951–1971*, by A. R. Ammons. W. W. Norton and Company, Inc. Copyright © 1972 by A. R. Ammons.

Ashbery, "Songs without Words" from *Shadow Train* (New York: Viking, 1981) and "At North Farm" from *A Wave* (New York: Viking, 1984).

Berryman, "So Long — Stevens" from *The Dream Songs* by John Berryman. Copyright © 1965, 1966, 1967, 1968, 1969 by John Berryman. Reprinted by permission of Farrar, Straus and Giroux, Inc., and Faber and Faber Ltd.

Blumenthal, "Over Ohio" from *Days We Would Rather Know* (New York: Viking, 1984).

Davie, #2 from "Two from Ireland," "Advent," "July, 1964," "The Nonconformist," "Life Encompassed," all from *Selected Poems* (New York: Carcenet, 1985).

Dove, "The Event" and "Compendium" from *Thomas and Beulah* (Pittsburgh: Carnegie-Mellon University Press, 1985).

Dunn, "He/She," from *Local Time* by Stephen Dunn. Copyright © 1986 by Stephen Dunn. Reprinted by permission of William Morrow and Company, Inc.

Glück, "Night Piece" and "The Sick Child" (part 2 of the poem "Descending Figure"), copyright © 1976, 1977, 1978, 1979, 1980 by Louise Glück. From *Descending Figure* by Louise Glück, published by The Ecco Press in 1980. Reprinted by permission.

Heaney, "Chekhov on Sakhalin" from *Station Island*. Copyright © 1985 by Seamus Heaney. Reprinted by permission of Farrar, Straus and Giroux, Inc., and Faber and Faber Ltd.

Lowell, "Hell" from *History*. Copyright © 1967, 1968, 1969, 1970, 1973 by Robert Lowell. Reprinted by permission of Farrar, Straus and Giroux, Inc.

Merrill, "Grass" and "Palm Beach with Portuguese Man-of-War" from *Late Settings*. Copyright © 1985 James Merrill. Reprinted with the permission of Atheneum Publishers, a division of Macmillan, Inc.

Milosz, "The Poor Poet." Copyright © 1973 by Czeslaw Milosz. From *Selected Poems* by Czeslaw Milosz, published by The Ecco Press in 1980. Reprinted by permission.

Index

Addams, Jane, 369
Adorno, Theodor, 5, 46; *Aesthetic Theory*, 1
Amichai, Yehuda, 38
Ammons, A. R., 33, 51, 306, 310–342, 368, 385, 387; "On Being," 324; "Cascadilla Falls," 319, 320; *A Coast of Trees*, 329, 334, 341; "Coming Round," 324; "Concerning the Exclusion of the Object," 320; "Corsons Inlet," 315; "Easter Morning," 323, 326, 327, 330, 332, 341; Essay on Poetics, 311; "The Eternal City," 322; "Extremes and Moderations," 317; "First Caroling Said-Song," 314; "Four Motions for the Pea Vines," 317–318; "Grace Abounding," 336–337; "Hardweed Path Going," 312; "Hibernaculum," 316, 323, 325; "An Improvisation for the Stately Dwelling," 332; "I Want Back," 340; "Meeting Place," 337–338; "Poverty," 331; "Providence," 339, 340; "Second Carolina Said-Song," 314; "Singling and Doubling Together," 338; *Snow Poems*, 324, 389; "Sphere," 315, 316, 324, 325; "Swells," 331, 333; "Tape for the Turn of the Year," 330; "This Black Rich Country," 318; "Two Possibilities," 321; "Uplands," 330; *Worldly Hopes*, 339–341
Andersen, Hans Christian, 302, 409
Anthony, Susan B., 369
Arcimboldo, Giuseppe, 68
Arensberg, Walter, 88
Aristotle, 22, 51, 96
Arnold, Matthew, 46, 83, 93, 95, 229,

260, 347; criticism of, 11–12, 25, 28, 43; "Dover Beach," 416; on Wordsworth, 106
Ashbery, John, 10, 16, 78, 90, 224–261, 335, 387; on Bishop, 292; "Corky's Car Keys," 245; "Description of a Masque," 259; "Destiny Waltz," 257; *Evening in the Country*, 53; "Fear of Death," 226; "Fragment," 231; "Haibun," 259; "Haunted Landscape," 238; *Houseboat Days*, 225, 227–228, 233; "Landscapeople," 240; "At North Farm," 252–253; and pathetic fallacy, 335; *Rivers and Mountains*, 225; *Self-Portrait in a Convex Mirror*, 224, 225, 226, 227, 390; *Shadow Train*, 242, 244, 247; "The Skater," 231; "The Songs We Know Best," 259; "Songs without Words," 245; sonnets of, 244; *The Tennis Court Oath*, 225; *Three Poems*, 225, 247; *A Wave*, 252–257, 259–261; *As We Know*, 225, 232, 237
Auden, W. H., 73, 167, 168, 169, 171, 368, 454; and Merrill, 350, 353; and Plath, 277; and Spender, 171–172, 173

Babel, Isaac, 114
Bach, Johann Sebastian, 382
Balzac, Honoré de, 62
Baranczak, Stanislaw, 210, 214
Barthes, Roland, 19, 26, 58–74; *Camera Lucida*, 68; *Critique et vérité*, 65; *A Lover's Discourse*, 64; *The Pleasure of the Text*, 15–16, 18, 58, 69; "Reflections on a Manual," 61; *The Responsibility of Forms*, 58, 68, 70, 73; *Roland Barthes* (autobiography), 59–60, 64,

465